CHINESE FICTION

OF THE

NINETEENTH

AND

EARLY TWENTIETH
CENTURIES

MASTERS OF CHINESE STUDIES

CHINESE FICTION

OF THE

NINETEENTH

AND

EARLY TWENTIETH

CENTURIES

Essays by
Patrick Hanan

MASTERS OF CHINESE STUDIES
VOLUME 2

Columbia University Press / New York

Columbia University Press wishes to express its appreciation for assistance given by the Chiang Ching-kuo Foundation for International Scholarly Exchange in the publication of this book.

COLUMBIA UNIVERSITY PRESS
Publishers Since 1893
New York   Chichester, West Sussex
Copyright © 2004 Columbia University Press
Library of Congress Cataloging-in-Publication Data
Hanan, Patrick.
Chinese fiction of the nineteenth and early twentieth centuries /
Patrick Hanan.
p.   cm. — (Masters of Chinese studies ; vol. 2)
ISBN 0–231–13324–3 (cloth)
1. Chinese fiction—Qing dynasty, 1644–1912—History and criticism.
2. Chinese fiction—20th century—History and criticism.   I. Title:
Chinese fiction of the nineteenth and early twentieth centuries.
II. Title.   III. Series.
PL2437.H36   2004   2004041338

Columbia University Press books are printed on permanent
and durable acid-free paper.
Printed in the United States of America
Designed by Lisa Hamm
c 10 9 8 7 6 5 4 3 2 1

Contents

CHINESE FICTION

OF THE

NINETEENTH

AND

EARLY TWENTIETH

CENTURIES

Introduction

THE ELEVEN RESEARCH ESSAYS in this volume, although written as independent pieces, share a common subject, Chinese fiction of the nineteenth and early twentieth centuries,[1] particularly its relationship to the Chinese and western traditions. (The western tradition gradually became accessible to Chinese writers during the period.) This approach embraces influence as well as intertextuality, imitation as well as originality, and also intercultural transmission—a cluster of notions for which I would like to borrow the old term "literary relations," but with a new meaning. My purpose is to describe, so far as I can, some of the movements in Chinese fiction during this period, especially in terms of creativity.

The first essay affirms the fact of artistic experimentation in the nineteenth-century novel. Literary historians have never considered the nineteenth century a creative period for Chinese fiction, unlike the seventeenth century with its brilliantly innovative short fiction or the eighteenth century with its great and remarkably inventive novels. One gets the impression from histories of fiction that fresh creativity and experimentation disappeared until 1902, when Liang Qichao issued his famous call for a new fiction and launched a journal under that title. But we have only to examine the major novels of the nineteenth century, such as *Hua yue hen* (Traces of flower and moon), *Ernü yingxiong zhuan* (Moral heroes and heroines), *Haishang hua liezhuan* (Flowers of Shanghai)— and, I would add, *Fengyue meng* (Illusion of romance)—to find not only that creativity flourished but also that some of the innovations foreshadowed those of the twentieth century.

To substantiate this claim, I found it necessary to examine at least one significant element of fiction. The most suitable for my purpose was the narrator, because the narrator is generally considered the most static element in traditional Chinese fiction. The first essay discusses a single aspect, "voice," by which is meant the narrator's identity as well as his relationship to author, reader, and text, rather than "perspective," which is the aspect that western literary criticism has always stressed. When the finest nineteenth-century Chinese novels are considered in terms of the narrator's voice, they are found to differ in numerous ways from previous fiction as well as from one another; the century was, in fact, a time of constant experimentation. In this essay the voices that the novelists created are roughly categorized. First is the Personalized Storyteller, in which the narrator presents himself as an individual; he is the antithesis of the generic storyteller of Chinese fiction. *Ernü yingxiong zhuan* and *Hua yue hen* are prime examples. Second is the Virtual Author, in which the narrator first equates himself with the author, then backs away from that claim and names someone else as author, someone closely resembling him—his double, in fact. *Fengyue meng* and *Pin hua baojian* (Precious mirror for judging flowers) are the prime examples. Third is the Minimal Narrator, in which the narrator's usual functions of explanation, evaluation, and commentary are reduced to a bare minimum. *Haishang hua liezhuan* is the great example. Finally is the Involved Author, in which the author-narrator becomes a secondary character in the novel and the situation of his writing it is dramatized. *Hualiu shenqing zhuan* (Love among the courtesans), *Haishang chentian ying* (Shadows of the mundane world of Shanghai), *Haishang mingji sida jingang qishu* (A strange tale of the four guardian gods, courtesans of Shanghai), and *Nanchao jinfenlu* (Fleshpots of Nanjing) are all examples. These last four works were written in the aftermath of the treaty that concluded the Sino-Japanese war, a conflict—more particularly, a treaty—that created a ferment of reformist thinking among younger intellectuals. None of the four is particularly notable in itself, but taken together they can be seen as a modest advance wave preceding the great wave that resulted from Liang Qichao's call for a new fiction.

The second essay, "*Illusion of Romance* and the Courtesan Novel," reinforces these conclusions by examining one novel comprehensively, not merely in terms of a single feature. *Hua yue hen, Ernü yingxiong zhuan,* or *Haishang hua liezhuan* would have served the purpose well, but instead I chose *Illusion of Romance* (*Fengyue meng*), an equally remarkable work, mainly because it has never received its due. (One reason may be that Lu Xun somehow overlooked it in his pioneering history of Chinese fiction.) *Illusion of Romance* traces the liaisons of five prostitutes with their favorite patrons from the initial meeting to the bitter parting or the tragic end. The relationships form a complex, symmetrical structure unprecedented in the Chinese novel. Even more significantly, *Illusion of Romance* is the first true city novel in Chinese, not just because it is set entirely in a single city (Yangzhou) but because it focuses obsessively on the life of that place, with the result that the city becomes itself a theme. *Illusion of Romance* is a Yangzhou novel not only in its descriptions but also in its conscious connection to Yangzhou history and culture. The first and greatest of the Shanghai city novels, the *Haishang hua liezhuan* of 1892, another courtesan novel, followed *Illusion*'s example in offering a strong sense of a particular locality as well as a realistic treatment of the world of prostitution.

A second major theme of this volume concerns the principal interventions by westerners in the course of the Chinese novel during the century. I have devoted a disproportionate number of essays to this subject, mainly because it has rarely, if ever, been treated by scholars. At first, it may seem strange that a foreign resident of China would choose to dabble in Chinese fiction, but a number of westerners were so impressed by the persuasive power (and the educational and entertainment value) of fiction in their own countries—as well as by the fact that Chinese fiction seemed to cross class and regional boundaries— that they sought to promote their various purposes by composing and translating fiction in Chinese.

By "interventions" I mean fiction composed or translated by westerners and their Chinese assistants for the Chinese public—and also a fiction contest for Chinese writers promoted by a westerner. It was through such interventions, which began quite early in the century, that Chinese readers gradually gained a little knowledge of western fiction and its methods. By contrast, the earliest translations initiated by Chinese writers alone were of a few Sherlock Holmes stories in 1896 and *La dame aux camélias* in 1899.

In separate essays I attempt to describe the motives and situations of the composers, translators, or promoters, as well as the nature of the novels they produced. Although westerners were the initiators, virtually all of the novels were the work of at least two people, a western "speaker" who gave an oral rendering in Chinese and a Chinese "writer" who took this down and worked it into a form acceptable to Chinese readers. Some such arrangement was the norm for translations into Chinese during the nineteenth century.

Christian missionaries, hoping to use novels to spread their doctrines, were responsible for the first intervention. Their fiction has no claim to literary merit, but it is significant in terms of relations between the cultures. The earliest "missionary novel" dates from 1819, and throughout the rest of the century missionaries and their assistants were active in composing and translating novels with strong religious content. The most prolific author was Karl Gützlaff, who composed seven or eight novels during the 1830s, one of them narrated by a Chinese persona of Gützlaff himself. However, by far the most influential of the missionary novels was Timothy Richard's summary account of Edward Bellamy's *Looking Backward, 2000–1887*. Bellamy's work, which is not specifically Christian, suited Richard's stated purpose of "general enlightenment."

Two trends can be seen in the course of the missionary novel during the century. Beginning in the 1850s, there was an increasing tendency to address missionary fiction to children rather than adults. In addition, the missionaries and their assistants ceased to use the form of the traditional Chinese novel and reverted more and more to that of the foreign novel.

The second and third interventions were made by men associated with the Shanghai newspaper *Shen bao* and its journal *Yinghuan suoji* (Trifling notes on the world at large), the first literary journal published in China. In 1872 three works of English-language fiction by well-known authors were excerpted and published in the newspaper, and from 1873 to 1875 the translation of a long English novel was published in installments in the journal. In an essay about the latter, entitled "On the First Novel Translated Into Chinese," I establish the identity of the original English novel and argue that the translation was probably the work of a certain *Shen bao* editor with the collaboration of the newspaper's English owner. Most of the essay, however, is devoted to an attempt to describe the translation *as* a translation. A huge gulf existed between the expectations of Victorian readers and those of readers in imperial China. I adopt the perspective of so-called "descriptive translation studies" in order to examine the novel in terms of its position between the extremes of "preservation"—the attempt to replicate the features of the original text (and the original culture) in the reader's language, so far as that is possible, and assimilation—adapting the features of the original text as necessary in order to make them seem familiar, and hence acceptable, to readers of the translation. Since any single feature of a text can be considered this way, it is necessary to examine a number of significant ones before generalizing about the translation as a whole.

The (vernacular) translation of the novel, entitled *Xinxi xiantan* (Idle tales from morning to evening), can be described as moderately assimilative, adapting the English novel *Night and Morning* by Edward Bulwer Lytton in countless ways in order to meet the expectations of Chinese readers. At the same time, for their own didactic purposes the translators took care to explain elements of western culture ranging from trivial customs to governmental institutions.

The three works excerpted in the *Shen bao* were published a little before *Xinxi xiantan*, but I have placed the essay that deals with them, "The Translated Fiction in the Early *Shen Bao*," after "On the First Novel Translated Into Chinese," because it is more convenient to discuss translation theory as well as the translators' identities in connection with the longer work. The three works of fiction, which are translated into literary Chinese, illustrate different degrees of assimilation. In all of them the setting is transferred to a place in or near China, and superficially there is little about them that would indicate an exotic origin. In the most extreme case, that of a Chinese version of Washington Irving's "Rip Van Winkle," the story is fundamentally altered to fit a familiar Chinese theme. In another, a version of "A Voyage to Lilliput," Swift's satire is omitted and only Gulliver's adventures retained. The third translation, based on a novel by Frederick Marryat, represents its original much more closely. Presumably, all three works were chosen because they fit the broad Chinese fiction category of *zhiguai* (records of the strange).

In order to characterize these translations more distinctly, I have compared them briefly with three novels translated by Lin Shu, the famous turn-of-the-century translator. Although Lin Shu has been much criticized for his omissions and alterations, he proves to be more of a "preservationist" than his predecessors.

The fourth kind of intervention was the fiction contest, which took place in 1895, in the immediate aftermath of the humiliating treaty that terminated the war with Japan. It was staged by John Fryer, an Englishman who had spent thirty years in China translating scientific and engineering texts for the Jiangnan Arsenal in Shanghai. He had also created a scientific journal, helped found the Polytechnic Institution in Shanghai, and established a science bookstore. From his position at the Polytechnic, he had conducted prize essay contests on subjects of practical importance, but in May 1895, he saw his chance amid the clamor for reform to attack what he called the "three evils" plaguing Chinese society—opium, the examination essay, and foot-binding. From his bookstore he advertised a prize contest for the best novels and stories that both attacked and suggested remedies for these evils. He also laid down certain prescriptions: the fiction should deal with ordinary life in a realistic fashion, and its reformist message should be fully dramatized, not merely presented in long speeches. Altogether 162 entries for the contest were received, but none was ever published; all have presumably been lost.

Nevertheless, the contest was not without effects. First, it promoted the use of the novel as a means of attacking social ills. Second, Fryer's prescriptions, published in the *Shen bao* and missionary journals, as well as the criticism he offered in his report on the submissions, may well have influenced people's thinking. Finally, two novels *have* survived that were written to his requirements even if they were not submitted to his contest. They can reasonably be regarded as the first modern Chinese novels, if the word "modern" is taken as requiring two conditions: a concern on the part of the writer with the national crisis and an attempt to express that concern by nontraditional methods.

The seventh essay takes up two of the first translations—that is to say, translations initiated by Chinese—into the vernacular. Both were by single individuals, rather than the usual pair—an indication of the rapidly spreading knowledge of foreign languages at the turn of the century. One is of a Jules Verne novel, the first half of which was translated by Liang Qichao in 1902; the other is of a sensational French detective novel translated by Zhou Guisheng in 1903. The often tortuous relationship between the original and the translation in this period is well illustrated by the two works. Liang's, for example, is a Chinese version of a Japanese version of an English version of the French original. (Although much has been added and much lost in the course of the multiple translation, the versions represent their originals passably well.) Both translations appeared in journals founded and edited by Liang Qichao, and both, in different ways, carried an ideological burden. The translators also found themselves torn between western and Chinese forms of narration, and they explain to the reader their technical problems in presenting western fiction in Chinese.

The eighth essay returns to the theme of creative experimentation, but at a later date, after Liang Qichao's call for a new novel, and discusses it again with regard to the narrator, this time in terms of perspective as well as voice in the fiction of Wu Jianren.

There are two reasons Wu is the most suitable subject for such a study. Some of his fiction survives from before Liang Qichao's call, and of all the major late-Qing novelists, he is the one most inclined to technical experimentation, particularly with regard to the narrator. Knowing no foreign language, he must have acquired his knowledge of western techniques from either translations or hearsay. We know that he profited from the French novel translated by his friend Zhou Guisheng. A comparison of two remarkable stories by Wu shows the extremes of his methods, ranging from minimal narration to a complex use of author-narrator and informant. At the same time, when the situation seemed to call for it, he was quite capable of reverting to the most traditional methods.

The body of the essay examines the three novels by Wu that largely restrict narration to a single character, the first one a first-person narrator, the others third-person centers of consciousness. All three are concerned with his critique of Chinese society. Rejecting the old authoritative narrator, he has left the interpretation to a naïve or ignorant subject who gradually matures under instruction from other people as well as through his own experience—an effective method for presenting what Wu Jianren saw as the central problems of his time. Each novel focuses on the cultural crisis facing China, rather than on the individual interests and desires of its narrator.

The use of a first-person narrator in *Ershinian mudu zhi guai xianzhuang* (Strange things observed over the past twenty years) was a breakthrough in Chinese fiction. Although the experiment was successful enough, a good deal of contrivance was required to present a panoramic social critique through the mind and voice of a single person. The word "*mudu*" in the title, meaning observed by the narrator, applies to the narrator's own experience but not to the many experiences related by others, and some of the narrator's adventures are mere pretexts for recounting interesting stories.

Xin shitouji (New story of the stone) takes Baoyu, hero of the eighteenth-century *Shitouji* (Story of the stone, better known as *Honglou meng*, Dream of the red chamber), as its single center of consciousness. The novel can be described as consisting of two processes of discovery by Baoyu: his growing disillusionment with western civilization in the first half, and his entrancement with the utopian vision of the Civilized Zone in the second. (The zone outdoes the West in scientific progress while retaining the traditional Chinese morality.) *Shanghai youcanlu* (Adventures in Shanghai), the third novel, continues Wu's critique of contemporary society with a satirical exposé of the self-styled revolutionaries of Shanghai, who are depicted as poseurs and hypocrites.

The ninth essay is concerned with the romantic novel in the early twentieth century. A great amount of attention has been paid to the satirical fiction of the period, such as Wu Jianren's *Ershinian mudu zhi guai xianzhuang*, but very little to the romance. The most famous so-called romantic novel of the first decade was Wu's own *Hen hai* (Sea of regret), but although the author himself gave it this label, he actually wrote it in *opposition* to the contemporary romance. "Specific Literary Relations of *Sea of Regret*" argues that the novel was a tacit response to two slightly earlier works, a personal account in diary form supposedly written by a leading courtesan and, more significantly, a genuinely romantic novel by an unknown author. While accepting certain ideas and situations from the personal account, *Sea of Regret* takes a different approach toward the narrator, and also deliberately rejects the other work's explicit description of violence. The novel Wu Jianren reacted against is a romance, in the sense that it focuses on the autonomy of the individual in the matter of romantic love. *Sea of Regret* rejects that notion utterly, and instead defines the function of *qing* (love or passion) as an emotional stimulus to perform our family and societal obligations. Romantic love, by contrast, is mere infatuation. The essay claims that by examining *Sea of Regret* in relation to the personal account and the novel we can arrive at a more precise appreciation of its meaning.

The tenth essay, "The Autobiographical Romance of Chen Diexian," studies a series of romances of the following decade, the 1910s. They share some features of the typical romances of that period, but they also differ markedly, ending in stalemate and frustration rather than tragedy. The most notable, *Huangjin sui* (The money demon), is a *bildungsroman* as well as a candid autobiography that traces the author's romantic history from his boyhood up to his early twenties—a dominant theme, almost an obsession, in Chen Diexian's writing. It is also the culmination of an autobiographical trend in the Chinese novel that goes back at least to the *Story of the Stone.*

The final essay, "The Technique of Lu Xun's Fiction," echoes several topics raised in the other essays, particularly that of the narrator's voice and perspective, which Lu Xun used with unparalleled subtlety. Whereas the earlier writers acquired their knowledge of foreign literature haphazardly, Lu Xun made a thorough search through the contemporary literature of countries whose situations resembled China's in order to find suitable models of technique. His dominant method is irony, of several kinds—presentational, situational, juxtapositional, and the irony of character.

NOTES

1. All but one of the essays were written within the last six years. Chapters 1, 7, and 9 have not been previously published. Chapter 2 appeared in the *Harvard Journal of Asiatic Studies* 58.2 (Dec. 1998): 345–72, under the title "*Fengyue meng* and the Courtesan Novel," and chapter 3 appeared in the same journal, 60.2 (Dec. 2000): 413–43. Most of chapters 4 and 5 was combined into an article that appeared in *Chinese Literature: Essays, Articles, Reviews* 23 (2001): 55–80 under the title "A Study in Acculturation: The First Novels Translated into Chinese." Chapter 6 was published anonymously in Judith T. Zeitlin and Lydia H. Liu, eds., *Writing and Materiality in China* (Cambridge: Harvard University Asia Center, 2003), 317–40. Chapter 8 appeared in Hu Xiaozhen, ed., *Shibian yu weixin* (Taipei: Institute of Literature and Philosophy, Academia Sinica, 2001), 550–88. Chapter 10 appeared in the *Lingnan Journal of Chinese Studies*, n.s. 2 (Oct. 2000): 261–81. Chapter 11, the only early essay, appeared in the *Harvard Journal of Asiatic Studies* 34 (1974): 53–96. The romanization has been changed to pinyin, references to Lu Xun's stories have been switched to a later edition of his collected works, and some excisions and other changes have been made in the text.

CHAPTER 1

The Narrator's Voice
Before the "Fiction Revolution"

N INETEENTH-CENTURY FICTION is very far from the stagnant genre it is sometimes said to be.[1] The finest nineteenth-century authors were both creative and experimental; their novels show significant changes well before the date (1902) at which Liang Qichao issued his call for a "New Fiction."[2] In this chapter I propose to examine these authors' artistic experimentation in terms of one key element, the narrator.

The narrator in fiction is usually defined in terms of his degree of knowledge (omniscient, restricted, external, etc.) and his reliability. Viewed from that angle alone, the pre-modern Chinese novel is bound to appear somewhat static. Not until Wu Jianren's *Ershinian mudu zhi guai xianzhuang* (Strange things observed over the past twenty years, 1903–10) or, by a more stringent definition, *Qin hai shi* (Stones in the sea, 1906), does one find the consistent, restricted narration that is a virtual signature of the modern sensibility in fiction. But there are other aspects of the narrator—his identity; his nature; his relationship to text, author, and editor; the situation in which he narrates and the audience whom he addresses; as well as his attitude toward and judgment of the events narrated—that show constant, significant change throughout the nineteenth century.

The clearest distinction between the two meanings of "narrator" is that given by Gérard Genette, who considers the latter under the heading of "voice" and the other under "perspective," summing up his distinction with the aid of two questions, "Who speaks?" (voice) and "Who sees?" (perspective).[3] Perhaps because of the residual power of the storyteller simulation in China, the concept of voice has particular relevance for pre-modern—and even for modern—Chinese fiction.

The narrator is responsible for delivering the whole of the work to the reader or listener and, strictly speaking, the work should be considered as a whole. However, for my present purpose I shall take advantage of the traditional novel's tendency to mark the narrator's various functions with formulaic phrases and confine myself to those functions as marked. One purpose of the phrases was to sectionalize the text, since the traditional format did not allow for paragraphing, but they do much more—they call attention to the narrator's discourse, i.e., to the various other functions he performs in addition to that of narrating events. These are inevitably intertwined, but it is still helpful to try to separate them. Genette divides them into directing, communicative, testimonial, and ideological. Let me group them somewhat differently, to suit the Chinese case: management (of time, focus, etc.); formal description, especially in set pieces; explanation; metanarrative, i.e., commentary in the text on the novel's composition and progress; interaction with narratees, simulating dialogue with an audience; evaluation, reflecting ideology; and personal revelation. The last two functions will largely determine the reader's image of the narrator.

I present the various developments of the narrator in roughly chronological order.[4]

The Personalized Storyteller

One important nineteenth-century trend is backward, toward the simulation of oral storytelling—an odd development, considering that even in the seventeenth century novelists frequently mixed up the terms that properly belong to either oral or written narration. The new kind of storyteller, however, is far removed from the old anonymous practitioner dispensing his received wisdom in unspecified circumstances—he is now a sharply personalized figure with his own individual opinions. In theory there are two narrators in each of these novels: the simulated oral narrator who delivers them, and the narrator in the text that the "oral narrator" is purportedly using; but in practice, as we shall see, the functions of interaction, explanation, evaluation, and personal revelation are all presented as the contribution of the "oral narrator."

The outstanding example of the personalized storyteller is Wen Kang's *Ernü yingxiong zhuan*, whose title should be translated as either "moral heroism" or "moral heroes and heroines."[5] Surely no previous Chinese novel has ever had so lively, exuberant, and loquacious a narrator![6] Its forty chapters contain hundreds of significant utterances by the narrator, some of which run on for pages, explaining and giving background information, as well as analyzing and evaluating the progress and quality of the narrative. Most of the interventions—the word is amply justified in this case, for the narrator uses it himself (*da cha*)—are specifically addressed to his listeners, whom he calls "gentlemen," referring to himself as either "your storyteller" or "I, your storyteller."

In the prologue chapter we are told by the author, Yanbei Xianren (The Idler of Yanbei), how he came to write the book. One day he was suddenly transported from the classroom in which he was studying the classics to the tribunal of a god who was on the point of sending down a new batch of souls to earth. The Idler watched as the souls lived out their earthly existence; then he awoke and wrote down as much as he could remember. His book was revised by someone else and evidently published, because in the next chapter we find a storyteller at work with this novel as his material. (The storyteller does not have exclusive use of it, however, for he mentions having heard the tale told somewhere else.)

The storyteller-narrator interacts constantly with his audience, keeping us aware of both his and their presence. At one point he worries that latecomers may not be up to date with the story (chapter 23, p. 401). He stresses that he is merely relating a text and explains that his knowledge is limited (23.405, 31.592). He plays with his audience's expectations, as in the following example from chapter 6. Someone has fallen down. Is it An Ji, the young hero? The narrator at first teases his listeners with the thought that An Ji might be dead, then says he is afraid that his audience has not been paying attention:

> "Now calm down, will you. It wasn't young An at all. How do I know that? Well, he was tied up to a pillar, so just think for a moment—how could he possibly slump to the ground? Well then, since it wasn't him, who do you suppose it was?" (6.87)

He also counsels patience when he (or rather the text) is delaying the action, as frequently happens. On at least one occasion, something reminds him of a lengthy joke, which he proceeds to tell. At the same time he keeps up a running commentary on the text, defending and explaining, but also criticizing its progress, technique, and structure. His remarks amount to an internal critical commentary, the most striking case in Chinese fiction, even more striking than Li Yu's in the seventeenth century. Generally he defends the author, sometimes by referring to the example of other fiction and even of classical prose, but he also criticizes him for his deviousness, for playing games with the reader (13.200). He inveighs against the use of a narrative cliché like *yisu wuhua* ("there's nothing further to be said about the events of that night," 37.771), but then proceeds to use it himself (38.773).

He also makes frequent reference to the author, inferring the man's nature from the text. After complaining of the novel's prolixity, a pointed criticism in the case of this work, he remarks:

> I wonder if the author suffered a lawsuit like this himself and just wrote it all down. Or perhaps he was simply idle, with too much time on his hands. (22.391)

A few chapters later he speculates again about the connection between author and event, this time as if from personal knowledge:

> What did it have to do with him? Just think of all the waste of ink, the wear and tear on brushes, the loss of his heart's blood, the ruined eyesight. . . . The fellow really ought to find regular employment and try to make something of himself. (28.529)

These comments are significant as fiction criticism,[7] but they also play a part in the novel itself. They claim to lay bare its workings, its composition and structure, just as the narrator's constant interaction with his audience has laid bare the narrating situation. In addition, the transparent device of having one persona of the author relate a text by another persona offers numerous opportunities for humor, which the novel takes up with gusto.

Most of the narrator's interventions, however, are devoted not to criticism but to seemingly endless explanations and analyses, particularly of the reactions and motives of the characters. In this respect the behavior of the narrator accords with the novel's general discursiveness—its innumerable arguments, disquisitions, and recountings. There is no great difference between the narrator's voice and, say, An Xuehai's, except that the narrator's is more lively.

It is scarcely possible to take the novel as a heroic tale. Nominally it is about filial revenge—a son and a daughter set out to avenge their fathers, both of whom have been framed by higher-ups—but without the girl's help the boy would have failed, and she never even attempts vengeance, because her father's enemy has already been executed. Only a few chapters—from chapter 4, when the daughter, Shisan Mei (Thirteenth Sister), first appears, until chapter 10, when we leave her—consist of heroic action directly narrated, and even in these a good deal of the action is verbal. The single flurry of fighting is confined to chapters 5 to 7, which is the section we remember, perhaps because we have seen it played out on stage. This section is certainly graphic enough, but immediately after the mayhem Thirteenth Sister sits down—*and proceeds to talk about it!* As the narrator says, she "spent the evening slaughtering people and then delivered herself of a long screed" (8.118). There is clearly a farcical element here, a trace of parody combined with a crude humor that we rarely find in the rest of the novel. For example, An Ji is too embarrassed to get down from the bed where he has been tied up because he has wet his pants; then Shisan Mei and Zhang Jinfeng both go and relieve themselves in the wash basin, there being no privy, but they neglect to empty the basin, with predictable results when the next person comes to use it. In fiction this kind of comedy is usually designed to undercut the dignity of the people involved.

Little of the text is dramatized, most of the serious action being recounted by the characters. The story of how Sister's father was driven to his death by an official because he, the father, would not allow the official's odious son to marry her—all this is *told* to the audience by An Xuehai! What dramatized action there is is elaborated endlessly with speeches, plans, analyses, passages of thought. There is even an element of teasing lightheartedness in this process. Facts such as the cryptic origin of Sister's name are withheld for an unconscionably long time. The whole carefully planned and executed charade by which An Xuehai dissuades Sister from seeking revenge is, strictly speaking, unnecessary, because her enemy is already dead. In sum, the novel's topic may be the moral heroic, but its mode is primarily discursive. The narrator's comments are both a clue to and a major part of that mode.

It is possible to link the novel's extraordinary discursiveness to its equally extraordinary foregrounding of fictional composition and oral delivery. "Parody" is too strong a word for what this work does, but "playful subversion" is certainly justified. It playfully subverts the norms of theme and genre, toying with the medium as well as with our expectations, displacing action with discourse.

The other well-known novel with a personalized oral narrator is Wei Xiuren's *Hua yue hen* (Traces of flower and moon).[8] Its narrator is characterized at greater length and even more specifically than the narrator of *Ernü yingxiong zhuan*, but he plays a very different role.

Hua yue hen's opening is unprecedented in Chinese fiction. The novel establishes its simulated oral context right at the beginning, as the narrator, addressing an audience, launches into a disquisition on *qing* (feeling, especially love or passion). He explains that this disquisition arose from an argument he had with a schoolmaster in his hometown, a man of orthodox views who, while admitting the existence of *qing*, insisted in the characteristic moralist's way that the only proper use of it was as an emotional stimulus for the practice of the societal virtues. Against this view, the narrator argues that in the present age the true man of feeling has no choice but to find an outlet for his *qing* in natural beauty, literature, and relations with courtesans. He goes on to distinguish people who wear masks to hide their feelings from those who show their true faces. The former do so to conform with the social proprieties, their masks being undeniably useful for success in public life. The man of feeling, however, who does show his true face or faces, is seen by others as nonconforming and difficult, and he generally ends up as a failure, although occasionally his worth will be discerned by a sympathetic courtesan. The argument amounts to an apologia for the man of feeling frustrated in his career. Its relevance becomes apparent when the narrator's audience praises his heroes and heroines for showing their "true faces." (This they certainly do; the courtesan Liu Qiuhen even has an "attitude"—to use a current colloquialism.) The contrast in *Shitouji* (Story of the stone) between Lin Daiyu, who tends to show her true face at any given moment, and Xue Baochai, who wears a social mask, will inevitably occur to the reader, and may well have been at the back of the author's mind.

After arguing for these values, the narrator goes on to tell how he began work as a storyteller in Taiyuan in Shanxi with this book as his material. He then invites the people he is addressing to come to a certain teahouse to hear him perform. After the performance, at the end of the second-to-last chapter, he urges his audience not to disperse yet, because there is a fascinating episode still to come. In the final chapter, a friend of the hero Wei Chizhu, someone who has appeared at several key points in the novel, pays a visit to Taiyuan twenty years after the deaths of Wei and Liu. The friend takes part in a spirit-writing séance held at the site of the brothel to which Liu belonged, and then manages to locate an old man who has been charged with looking after Wei's shrine.

That night the old man dreams of a play about a chrysanthemum-viewing party arranged at the brothel by Liu for Wei, and also for their friends Han Hesheng and Du Caiqiu. (The play dramatizes an incident told in chapter 23, at the height of the love affair between Wei and Liu.) When the old man awakens, he finds beside his pillow a book called *Hua yue hen*, of which we are left to conclude that Wei was the author. Although he is unable to read the book, the old man is convinced it must be valuable, so he buries it. Eventually the poverty-stricken narrator, digging in his garden, unearths it and tries to make a living as a storyteller, using the book as his material.

A play entitled *Hua yue hen* has already been mentioned (51.411). Han Hesheng, after a dream about Wei and Liu, writes a play, of which scene 2 is entitled "The Chrysanthemum Party"; we are presumably meant to conclude that this scene is the one played out in the old man's dream. In any case, the latter functions as a haunting reminder, after the novel is over, of the heights attained by the ill-fated romance.[9]

The narrator's comments are frequent and prominently marked, but their functions are very different from those of *Ernü yingxiong zhuan*. Some are little more than phatic, designed merely to keep the channels of communication open, but the greater number explain some event, fill in the details of someone's background, or identify a person or a place. A few are evidently there simply to introduce a topic or highlight an issue. Some of the lengthiest concern Taiping history, especially the infighting among the Taiping leaders. Others are of critical interest, pointing out coincidences between events or the importance of this or that character, but there is no attempt at literary theorizing, nor is there any comparison with other novels. A few comments are of thematic import, notably the expositions on talent and destiny in chapters 22 and 36. But unlike *Ernü yingxiong zhuan*, there is no running commentary on the author, and little evaluative comment. Exposition is left mainly to the characters themselves, to Wei, Du, and the priest Xinyin (the last in chapters 28 and 34).

What is the virtue of this particular narratorial method? At first sight it seems an odd feature in a novel that is literary in three senses, namely, the prime aesthetic importance given to poetry and literary criticism by the participants; the high social value placed on writing and, more generally, on culture by the narrator; and the idealized treatment accorded *mingshi*, men of letters. The narrator's discussion of *qing* and authentic expression ("true faces") in chapter 1 is surely a key to the artistic and moral values of the work, since true faces signal the value of individual expression. This is a novel of romantic identification; hence the expression of feeling conveyed in poems, letters, and speech is perfectly appropriate. But the comments in the rest of the book, so clearly marked as to form a separate stratum, are not so easy to explain.

With one exception, the background piece on Wei in 8.51–52, all of the major explanatory and background information comes in marked comments by the narrator. If we ignore them, the rest of the novel, despite many lacunae, moves in roughly chronological fashion. (Incidentally, this novel is meticulous in its time-keeping, and also in its nearly contemporary dating, particularly as it approaches the moment of writing.) It seems as if, by relegating all explanation to a different stratum, the author has chosen to emphasize the remaining text's linearity. He has made a virtue, an aesthetic virtue apparently, of separating the discursive functions from the narrative.

There may also be a practical reason for doing so. The novel covers a broad range of people and events in different places—it has multiple story lines—and it delights in juxtaposing events that occur in different places, rather like the Southern drama, which derives extra meaning from the artful juxtaposition of scenes. Like the scenes of the drama, too, many of the novel's chapters are self-contained, so that a new chapter represents a break in the story line, often introduced by some general reflection. A strong, obtrusive narrator is needed to manage time, place, and focus.

Let me introduce a third novel whose use of the storyteller simulation is even more complex—*Yuchanji* (Jade toads), a novel in 53 chapters by Cui Xiangchuan that carries a preface dated 1837.[10] Its most remarkable feature is that the author is dramatized under his own pseudonym as a sort of *deus ex machina* who punishes the malefactors in a notorious case of historical injustice. He then makes friends with a man who goes on to edit and publish the manuscript that he (the author) has written about his adventures. Both are fully dramatized characters, the author appearing throughout, the editor at the beginning and end. However, neither is represented as *narrating* the book. That task is performed by an individualized storyteller working from his memory of other tellings of the story as well as from a performance script that he has bought.

The actual author, Cui Xiangchuan, appears in the novel as Tongyuanzi, the Master Who Apprehends the Primal Mystery, which is the sobriquet of a Han dynasty figure, Huang Shigong, whose identity he has evidently appropriated. The editor goes by the name of Tiandanren (Serenus), and he is indeed serene except for one thing: his reading of history has convinced him that many gross historical injustices have gone unpunished, and so he has compiled a work called *Du shi wen tian* (Questions for heaven drawn from a study of history). He shows the work to the author, who includes some of it at the beginning of his text.

We know most of this from the storyteller's discourse in the first, middle, and last chapters. He introduces himself as an elderly gardener in a village outside Yangzhou, who makes a living by growing chrysanthemums. A man of some education, he is patronized by the local literati, who persuade him to write a poem. His poem describes his favorite pursuits and ends with a couplet about going to the city market to sell his flowers and then, in the afternoon, visiting the Jiaochang (Parade) to listen to the storytellers.

When the literati press him about the stories he has heard there lately, he praises one called *Shi'er yuan Yuchanji* (Jade toads, twelve destinies), which he says was written by Tongyuanzi and published by Tiandanren. (He gives us some information about both men, particularly the latter and his historical studies.) He can remember about three quarters of what he has heard, but in any case he has a script that he can always turn to. After offering to tell the story the following day, he tidies up the room, fills some vases with chrysanthemums, and composes a verse prologue to stick on the wall. Here is his welcoming spiel:

> Greetings, gentlemen! You're here nice and early, I must say. The boy will be along in a moment to offer you some tea. I'm now going to relate that new story I told you about yesterday, in the first place to express Tiandanren's feelings, secondly to open your eyes for Tongyuanzi's sake, and thirdly, to enhance, as best I can, the beauty of this autumn scene for your enjoyment.

Chapter 27, the middle chapter, is a sort of interlude in which the narrator, not the author, discourses on the novel's moral message and its meaning in people's lives. He warns against the familiar sins of excess, quoting a poem by Tongyuanzi, and categorizes various career types and their karmic fates before returning to the story proper. Chapter 53, the last chapter, relates the meeting of Tongyuanzi and Tiandanren.

The novel has some odd features. At the beginning of certain chapters, characters speak directly, identifying themselves, something that suggests a prosimetric form. This brings up the question of the novel's origins. It is not, as scholars have assumed, adapted from the lost *tanci Yu chanchu* (Jade toads),[11] but it does develop the central motif of that work, dramatizing the author and editor-publisher and specifying the narrative situation. It seems that Cui Xiangchuan has acknowledged his debt to a certain *tanci* by presenting his own novel as a simulated performance of it.[12]

The Virtual Author

The term "virtual author" applies to novels, professedly based on personal experience or observation, that first imply they are by the narrator and then back off and attribute the writing to someone else. In theory two narrators are at work, as in the case of the personalized storyteller. The most notable examples are *Fengyue meng* (Illusion of romance), which has a pseudonymous author's preface of 1848, and *Pin hua baojian* (Precious mirror for judging flowers) by Chen Sen, of which there is an 1849 edition. They happen to be the two earliest courtesan novels, but they belong to very different types of the subgenre, *Fengyue meng* leading the way to *Haishang hua liezhuan* (Flowers of Shanghai) and *Pin hua baojian* leading to such romantic works as *Hua yue hen* and *Qinglou meng* (Dream of green bowers).[13]

The first chapter of *Fengyue meng* consists of a prologue in which the narrator tells of his own disastrous experience in the brothels of Yangzhou and then explains how he obtained the manuscript of this book. Except for a few sentences at the end, the whole of this chapter is represented as spoken by him. The rest of the book, except for the closing section, is said to be a manuscript that he has been given.

In the prologue chapter he refers to himself in the first person, using the storyteller's term of self-reference, *zaixia* (your humble servant), as he gives us his views on the origins and prevalence of brothels and the dangers they represent for young men. It is a lively disquisition, in which he claims to have observed the youth of Yangzhou in the process of becoming obsessed with prostitutes and also addicted to opium (regularly available in the brothels). Having spent upwards of thirty years in the brothels and been double-crossed on countless occasions by courtesans, he is now utterly disillusioned. While walking outside the city, he loses his way and finds himself on Mount Self-Delusion, where he comes upon two old men. One is the heavenly matchmaker, The Old Man Beneath the Moon, who has been rusticated for letting his compassion overrule his sense of duty. His companion is a certain Guo Lairen (a pun on the word for "veteran" or, in this case, "roué"), who wasted his life on the Yangzhou courtesans until he saw the light; he has now written down his observations in a manuscript entitled *Fengyue meng*. When the narrator asks about the book's contents, Guo defends it in a disquisition that resembles, in somewhat amplified form, the Stone's defense of the novel *Story of the Stone*. He ends by asking the narrator to publish the book so as to "open people's eyes."[14]

In the final chapter, while the people in the street are arguing over the meaning of a courtesan's suicide, they notice an old man, white-haired and toothless, clapping his hands and singing as he goes along. His song, patterned on the Daoist's poem in chapter 1 of *Story of the Stone*, is a condemnation of the brothel and all its works. Someone in the crowd identifies him as Guo Lairen, a man obsessed with courtesans, and speculates that he may have gone out of his mind after being tricked one more time by a courtesan. A short intervention by the narrator follows in which he explains that it was only after Guo climbed Mount Self-Delusion that he became a hermit and later an immortal. The narrator closes the book with four poems of his own.

I call this virtual authorship because the narrator's admitted experiences parallel those of the fictional Guo. Why did he need to invent a double to take on the author-narrator's role? Hardly for discretion's sake—he is writing under a pseudonym, and in any case he freely admits his libertine past. To have written in the first person, besides being too revolutionary to contemplate, would no doubt have placed intolerable restrictions on his knowledge at any given moment. Perhaps an element of convention is at work here; as in the case of *Yuchanji*, the novel has to be written by someone such an immortal who has attained enlightenment.

The novel itself, apart from its beginning and end, is relatively lacking in narratorial comment or even explanation; it has to be interpreted largely on the basis of the characters' words and actions, which must be taken ironically. This is city life, particularly brothel life, that is being observed, often with painful accuracy—material objects, manners, customs, vices, bureaucracy, the law. Evaluative comment, especially moralizing comment, would only have diluted the effect of what amounts to an indictment of a particular time, place, and social class.

The other novel, *Pin hua baojian* by Chen Sen, is generally considered a courtesan novel, although its "courtesans" are young actors who take the *jeune fille* (*xiao dan*) role in the drama. The love affairs between the young actors and their patrons are never consummated, at least in the case of the main characters. The principal affair is between Mei Ziyu and the actor Du Qinyan, who are sixteen and fourteen, respectively, as the novel opens. The other is between Tian Chunhang, twenty-two, and the actor Su Huifang, sixteen, but Tian's age is misleading, because he is a bohemian intellectual down on his luck and it is the actor who is the patron, initially at least. By contrast, nothing but loathing is reserved for the older men who seek sexual favors from Du and Su. The approved romantic relationship seems to be a kind of sublime adolescent passion, aesthetic rather than sensual, sentimental yet platonic, that matures into a close friendship between kindred spirits. It is worth noting that Du Qinyan, the main character of the novel, finally escapes actor status and becomes a "gentleman."

The reason for including this novel under the "virtual author" rubric is that, after seeming to assert a claim of authorship, the narrator backs away from it. He talks first of the glories of the Beijing theater and of the "play-loving people" he is going to describe with his "playful brush."[15] The most remarkable of these are the gentlemen who keep their feelings (*qing*) within the bounds of propriety, and also the actors who preserve their chastity. But after asserting that the book is based on things he has seen and heard, the narrator blandly informs us that he doesn't know the author's identity or even when the book was written. This is curious, because the author's preface happens to be the most circumstantial account of a Chinese novel's composition yet written. The pose must be a convention—claiming authorship without finally admitting it. The narrator is very free with his management of time, his summary recounting, his comments on the novel's progress, and his evaluation, including scathing attacks on the sexual predators, but exposition is left entirely to his characters. Talk is the stuff of this novel, talk in the sense of gossip. There are whole chapters of talk, particularly about plays, as well as a good deal of expressed thought and analysis of feeling, none of which is attributed to the narrator.

With *Qinglou meng* (Dream of green bowers),[16] of which the first edition was published in 1878, we go beyond the "virtual author" to the avowed author, although still not without some equivocation. The novel is ascribed to Muzhen Shanren, which happens to be the pen name of the actual author, Yu Da. In imitation of *Story of the Stone*,[17] it begins with the words "Muzhen Shanren says. . . ." The first part of chapter 1 tells Muzhen's dream of being transported to heaven and reincarnated as Jin Yixiang, the hero of the novel. Then one day he meets the Daoist who gave him a magic mirror and, on awakening from his dream, recalls the events depicted in the mirror and writes them down. At the end of the book, after achieving immortality, Jin returns to find in a bookshop a novel called *Qinglou meng* that recounts his own life. The author of the novel is a friend named Yu, and the events are partly those of Jin's life and partly those of Yu's (64.541). This is as close as one can get to avowed authorship without quite reaching it.

The Minimal Narrator

Haishang hua liezhuan (Flowers of Shanghai)[18] by Han Bangqing, serialized partially in 1892 and published in full in 1894, marks a reversion to the minimal narrator of the eighteenth-century *Rulin waishi* (The scholars) by Wu Jingzi. The author says he based his intersecting technique (*chuancha*) on *Rulin waishi*,[19] but he evidently also took his minimal narrator from that source. In fact, the narrator's role is even more restricted than in *Rulin waishi*; whenever possible the author lets all background information, even the names of people, emerge in the course of conversation. Ostensibly, the narrator is there just to narrate and present action and speech; even description is generally omitted except when given by characters. The novel is a tour de force of minimal narrative, and its peculiar power derives from that fact.

The prologue in the first part of chapter 1, however, is entirely different. There another kind of narrator, an effusive narrator in the mock storyteller style, interacts archly with an imaginary audience as he presents the origins of the novel in mythical terms. The author, having described his mission (to offer his own experience to his readers as a negative example), tumbles out of the sky and, in a brilliant authorial stroke, bumps right into his lead-off character, Zhao Puzhai, on a busy Shanghai street. The ensuing fracas is broken up by a foreign policeman, after which the narrative follows Zhao. Similar switches of focus after chance encounters occur with sometimes bewildering frequency throughout the novel, but the effusive narrator's voice is never heard again, not even at the novel's end.[20]

Haishang hua liezhuan influenced many novels in the late Qing, but more with its intersecting technique than with its minimal narrator.

The Involved Author

The first direct stimulus to create a specifically new fiction came from a contest sponsored by John Fryer, the Shanghai translator and bookshop owner, in May 1895, in the immediate aftermath of the Treaty of Shimonoseki.[21] In his newspaper and journal advertisements, Fryer called for a *shixin xiaoshuo* (new fiction) that would attack the three great evils of Chinese society—opium, the examination essay, and foot-binding—and offered prizes for the best entries.

The prizes were duly awarded, but none of the 162 or more entries was ever published; presumably all have been lost. However, two novels have survived that were written to Fryer's prescription but apparently never submitted to him. *Xichao kuaishi* (Delightful history of a glorious age), published in Hong Kong in December 1895,[22] deserves to be regarded as the earliest extant modern novel. Its narrator, who sees China as a sick society and the age as one of decline, opens with a symbolic vision of the sun emerging after an eclipse. The novel is devoted primarily to eradicating the three evils, to which the author has in effect added another: official corruption. Its hero, surnamed Kang (after Kang Youwei), is a brilliant man, disdainful of the examination essay, who presents the emperor with twelve recommendations for reform. Following signal achievements in suppressing a Muslim rebellion in Gansu, he is made President of the Board of War and proceeds to reform military recruitment and training along western lines. At the height of his power, Kang heeds supernatural advice and leaves his post to go off and become an immortal.

The narrator's function is minimal, especially at the beginning of the novel. The character who observes the sun emerging is not even named; he is simply "the provincial graduate," who is later reincarnated as the hero. There are no poems or set pieces of description, and evaluative comment is sparse, except on the subject of official corruption. The novel's modernity appears elsewhere than in its narrator's voice.[23]

It is the second of the two novels, *Hualiu shenqing zhuan* (Love among the courtesans),[24] that opens up a distinctive new use for the narrator. By "involved author," I mean not merely that the narrator openly professes to be the author, but that the writing situation itself is dramatized. According to the author's preface, the novel was written in 1895 in response to Fryer's advertisement and published in 1897 in revised form. It faithfully, indeed skillfully, carries out the aims of the contest, despite reading at times like a 1950s novel of social reform. It is set in present time, with the Taiping rebellion anachronistically inserted. Much of the action is local, near the author's hometown of Quxian in Zhejiang, and some use is made of family history. More importantly for my purpose, the novel is placed in a narratorial context more elaborate than any we have seen before.

The author, Zhan Xi (1850–1927) was an ardent reformer who served as staff adviser and tutor in various parts of China.[25] His novel follows the fortunes of the Weis, a prosperous Quxian family, particularly one generation, roughly contemporaneous with him. There are four sons and one daughter, and the three older boys are either addicted to opium or obsessed with the examination essay (in order to make enough money to be able to patronize courtesans), while the daughter, of course, has to endure having her feet bound.

The causes of the family's downfall are dissipation and fecklessness on their part, compounded by the ravages of the Taiping rebellion. Forced to flee in different directions, they eventually succeed in reforming themselves and building a modern community. Although the novel is set in the recent past, it has a satisfying, indeed idyllic ending, not unlike the endings of the visionary or utopian novels of the next decade.

There are two important figures outside the family itself. One is the Weis' family tutor, whose advanced skills in writing examination essays fail to qualify him for any work whatsoever, even as a journalist or army clerk. The other is Zheng Zhixin, a reform-minded local figure, who is completely cynical about the examination system. He seems to be an alter ego of the author's; his age and his examination status tally, and it is he who tells the author the story of the Wei family.

The narratorial context is elaborate. The author himself appears at the beginning, providing some of the same information he has given in his preface.

He does not use the first-person pronoun, however, referring to himself as Lüyixuan Zhuren, Master of the Studio of the Green Impression, or simply as Master. He argues that China can achieve wealth and power only through scientific and industrial education, but that before such education can take effect the three evils must be eradicated. He had wanted for decades to write a book opening people's eyes but was never in a position to do so. Then in the summer of 1895 he noticed an advertisement for Fryer's contest in a Shanghai newspaper. The advertisement claimed that the novel was the most effective means of changing people's hearts and minds and pinpointed these three as China's principal evils. Impressed by the idea, the Master thought over what he had seen and heard and decided to focus his novel on just a few people and events. For his subject he chose his neighbors, the Wei family, and the story of their decline and eventual triumph.

The subject is taken up once more in the second-to-last chapter, when the Weis, having painfully reformed themselves, are energetically practicing their new principles and growing rich. To serve as an example to others, they seek some way of publicizing their achievements. Zheng Zhixin, the alter ego of the author, comments that he has a friend, the Master, who might well be able to turn their experience into a novel.

At the time the Master is not interested, but six or seven years later, on seeing Fryer's advertisement, he has a revelation about the power of fiction and calls to mind the Weis' achievement. Within a few days he has finished the novel, which he shows to his employer (he is working as a tutor). The employer encourages him to publish it, and even to go to Shanghai and show the manuscript to Fryer. Before he can do so, the Master has a nightmare in which he is confronted by the various interest groups his book has offended. They protest that opium is the mainstay of the tax system and doubly indispensable now that a huge indemnity has to be paid to Japan; that officials throughout the country have obtained their jobs by means of the very essay he proposes to abolish; and that small feet are the working capital of the courtesan. The courtesans' protest includes the following:

"If bound feet are so bad, why is it that you men swoon away at the mere sight of them? To hear you talk, if women would only unbind their feet, they'd be able to go and work in the fields. But don't you realize? It would take us a whole year in the fields to make as much money as our bound feet will make for us in a single night!"

The preface explains that Zhan Xi did not submit his entry to Fryer but kept it with him while he traveled about the country on various tasks. Then in

1897, back in Shanghai, he thought of it again and, after obtaining the blessing of the influential Wang Tao (1818–97), revised it and had it published.

The novel is laced with personal and contemporary references. At one point the tutor Kong and his patron meet the famous courtesan Su Yunlan, and the narrator tells us what will become of her: she will marry, and her former lover, known as Shouhe Ciren, will write the novel *Duanchang bei* (Heartbreak stele) in despair over losing her (14.57). Shouhe Ciren is the pen name of Zou Tao, whose novel, originally known as *Haishang chentian ying* (Shadows of the mundane world of Shanghai), is my next example of the involved author.

No novel before *Haishang chentian ying* had ever appeared with such copious and explicit connections to the author's life.[26] The narrative proper is preceded by a selection of Su Yunlan's letters to the author, all of them dated, tracing the course of their affair from 1893 until the end of 1895, at which point she decided to marry someone else.[27] In one letter she refers to a draft of part of the novel that Zou has sent her, and criticizes it for its lack of unitary structure as well as its use of people's real names. She also suggests—a trifle heartlessly, one is inclined to think—that her decision to marry another man will provide Zou Tao with the ending for his novel that he has long been seeking. Her letters and poems are followed by the author's half-realistic, half-mythical account of the novel's composition in which he claims that he is using this love affair as a pretext for venting his lifelong frustration.

At the end of chapter 60, when the heroine has been restored to the position in heaven from which she had been banished, the author appears before her tribunal and admits that he is writing a novel about her. The book closes with his last, undelivered letter to Su Yunlan.

The author, Zou Tao (1850–1931), was an ardent reformer.[28] According to Wang Tao, his mentor, who wrote a long and revealing preface to the novel, Zou compiled a number of "useful" works, several of which are listed. Even without this information, his reformist views are easily deduced from the novel itself.

Zou also followed another interest of Wang Tao's—his sentimental attachment to courtesans. As early as 1878, he wrote a preface under his own name to Yu Da's *Qinglou meng*, and he actually appears in that novel as the character Zou Bailin (*Bailin* means "worshiper of Lin Daiyu," the heroine of *Story of the Stone*). His two interests come together in *Haishang chentian ying*. The principal characters are Su Yunlan (her name is retained) and Han Qiuhe, both of whom are sent down from heaven. Han acquires a prodigious amount of new learning, while some of the courtesans in the novel cultivate scientific interests of their own. One of them is actually an American from Massachusetts who happens to be both a chemist and engineer and also to have a good command of Chinese.

Wang Tao speaks in his preface of the novel as being complete, following revision, by 1896. After Su Yunlan's marriage, according to Wang, Zou revised the fifty-two chapters he had written, added several more, and changed the name of his book from *Haishang chentian ying* to *Duanchang bei*. As we have seen, Zhan Xi refers to the latter title in his own novel published in 1897. Although the earliest known edition is dated 1904, we can assume that *Duanchang bei* was first published about 1897.

The novel has a special prologue in which the author-narrator gives his personal view of *qing*, one that "doesn't seem to quite fit the principles laid down by the sages."[29] Turning to the question of why the novel was written, he tells of falling in love with Su Yunlan but being too poor to buy her out. Much of his book was written as wish fulfillment, to relieve his fits of depression. Its events are mostly true, unlike those of *Story of the Stone*. He regrets that he has lost contact with Su Yunlan, and only wishes he could have kept her as a friend. He also wonders how she will feel on reading his novel.

Chapter 1 gives the mythical origins of the text as inscribed on Heartbreak Stele, which had mysteriously descended from heaven. Chapter 2 tells how, after the text had been copied out, it was criticized as imitating *Story of the Stone*, and the author decided not to publish it. Then the manuscript was stolen, but fortunately a friend had retained a copy that was complete except for a few chapters. The author finished it off and had it printed.

He then offers a self-portrait together with an alternative version of the origins of the text. His life has been dogged by ill fortune. A Shanghai courtesan urged him to write something and his friends suggested a novel, but he demurred. Then he had to leave Shanghai and go elsewhere as a staff adviser, and he began to warm to the courtesan's advice. A friend recommended that he first draw up a plan for the novel, listing the characters with their various ages, natures, etc., and urged him also to pay attention to structure and language. Zou bridled at this well-meant advice—after all, he protested, he did know something about composition—but he remained blocked in his writing until he had a dream in which he was permitted to read this manuscript. He then copied down what he could remember, filled out the narrative as necessary, and worked on it over the next three years.

At the end of the novel, as I have said, Su Yunlan, now installed in heaven, receives a report that a writer is working on a novel about her and summons him to her court. Unaware of her identity, he declares that he will refrain from criticizing his beloved in this novel, but that if she goes on refusing to see him, he will write another novel of a very different kind.

These are by no means the only self-references. A courtesan says that she has heard that he—using his pen name—is writing a novel called *Chentian ying* of which the alternative title is *Duanchang bei*, and worries that he may make courtesans look ridiculous (5.72). He intervenes under the same pen name to describe a structural problem (10.136). There is also much byplay by the author-narrator (*zuoshude*). To one of his mock questions, a "reader" retorts, "If I knew the answer to that, I wouldn't be reading the book" (15.221). The same chapter ends with one of the characters saying, "Wait a moment while the author gives his brush a rest." At least one long discussion expresses his concerns; it is on the misuse by officials of funds intended for modernization (19.299–302).

The narrative is slowed down by frequent long explanations of the characters' backgrounds, but most of the book's copious information is conveyed by the characters themselves. One woman even argues the case against marriage (16.244–45).[30] Han Qiuhe discourses on a wide variety of subjects, including weaponry, ballistics, mining, the newspaper business, astronomy, ballooning, military strategy, history, geography, Buddhism, Judaism, Christianity,[31] heaven and hell, western drama (complete with a detailed account of one performance), and the western circus. The interest shown in foreign culture, particularly religion (see chapters 36–37), stands in sharp contrast to the more practical concerns of *Hualiu shenqing zhuan*.

Not every novel took so enthusiastic an attitude toward reform. *Haishang mingji sida jingang qishu* (The strange tale of the four guardian gods, courtesans of Shanghai) is a 100-chapter novel that the scholar Wei Shaochang has shown to be by Wu Jianren.[32] It is Wu's first known novel, published a good five years before his celebrated *Ershinian mudu zhi guai xianzhuang*. In it we have a unique opportunity to see the kind of fiction a prominent late-Qing novelist wrote before the time at which late-Qing literature is supposed to have begun. The first fifty chapters were published in the fifth month of 1898 and the second fifty in the following month, not long before the crackdown on reform movement. Something of Wu's skeptical attitude toward foreign ideas is already apparent in this novel, which contains a decidedly satirical portrait of Kang Youwei as a pundit.[33]

It is a courtesan novel about the Big Four of the contemporary Shanghai scene, including Lin Daiyu and Sai Jinhua. (This may well be the first fictional treatment of either woman.) When the novel appeared in 1898, Wu was editing a tabloid called *Caifeng bao*, while Li Boyuan, later to become a famous novelist himself, was editing another one called *Youxi bao*. Such tabloids existed partly to provide news, or rather gossip, about the demimonde, and Wu's novel was heavily advertised in both.

In chapter 1, the author-narrator opens with a criticism of current fiction's delight in fantasy and stress on mere entertainment. He says he expressed this opinion to his friends, who urged him to write a novel himself to awaken people from their slumber, and he decided to create one distinctively his own. In the belief that the characters of a novel should reflect real people, he surveyed the Shanghai scene and asked himself what kind of karma could possibly have produced the Big Four courtesans. He concluded that they must have been demons in heaven who felt the desire to experience human life. Then, lest anyone be harmed by their ferocious natures, they were forced to undergo a sex change before arriving on earth.

In chapter 50, at the end of the separately published first half of the novel, there is a comment to the effect that the foregoing is mere prologue. The comment is taken up at the beginning of chapter 51, where the author-narrator expresses his view that fiction has no definite form of its own. People have speculated as to why he stopped at chapter 50: had he run out of things to say, or was he merely tantalizing the reader? Neither, he claims; he simply needed time to organize. He proceeds to comment on the current social scene. The brilliance of the former Shanghai literati is now much dimmed. Customs have become more and more decadent; hearts have changed for the worse. The brothels are full of wantons who prefer the company of actors and carriage drivers to that of writers (a familiar complaint among writers). Of course there are still plenty of poetasters willing to write doggerel in praise of the current mediocre crop of courtesans. The second half of the novel shows a distinct shift in mood; the courtesans, relatively benign before, have now become vicious.

There are two notable self-references that justify placing this novel in the "involved author" category. In chapter 39, a character named Kang Junmo (a satirical representation of Kang Youwei)[34] remarks that there is a certain Chousi Zhuren (Master of the Silk-Reeling Studio) in Shanghai who wants to write a book called *Renjian wangliang zhuan* (A tale of monsters among men) satirizing the city's philistines and phony literati (103). Since Chousi Zhuren is this author's pseudonym, the remark might refer to this novel, but it might also refer to another project Wu Jianren had in mind, which eventually bore fruit in *Ershinian mudu zhi guai xianzhuang* (Strange things observed over the past twenty years, published from 1903 to 1910).[35]

Again, in chapter 99 the narrator says, "Let us tell how at that time there lived in Shanghai a certain Chousi Zhuren . . ." (257). A short biography follows that resembles Wu's own, except that his home province has been changed from Guangdong to Guangxi. One day our author is sitting at home reading the *Shiwu congshu,* a title that suggests a compendium drawn from Liang Qichao's journal *Shiwu bao,* when a friend remarks on the tedium of all these reformist discussions and invites the author to go and listen to a story-teller. In the teahouse the author is astonished to find that the *tanci* being per-formed is on exactly the same subject as his unfinished novel. He falls asleep at the table, then awakens in the last chapter of his novel and decides to write his conclusion to it in the form of a scene from a play. At the end of the scene, af-ter the Big Four have been exorcised, a god comes on stage and asks, "Where can I find a literary man to write a book called *Haishang qishu* (Strange tale of Shanghai) that will awaken the world from its slumber?" (262).

Nanchao jinfenlu is yet another attempt to dramatize the narrating situa-tion.[36] It was published in the tenth month of 1899, after the crackdown on the reform movement, a fact that may explain why it has so little to say of re-form except for the examination system. "*Nanchao*" means Nanjing, and "*jin-fen*" means something like fleshpots, but *Nanchao jinfenlu* cannot be regarded as a courtesan novel.

After a routine discussion of predestined partings and reunions, the narra-tor addresses his readers directly and explains how he came to write the novel. He had a boyhood friend who left home at the age of twenty and traveled as far away as Nanjing. Not until two decades later did he meet the friend again, only to find him frustrated and bitter, railing against women and officials and condemning the ingrates who spurn the friends who have helped them climb the ladder of success. The narrator tries to switch the conversation to a more pleasant subject, that of courtesans, but the friend is as disillusioned as ever. The famous Shanghai courtesans have eyes only for actors, not writers, and the gilded youth of the city simply indulge the courtesans' whims. Nanjing is ad-mittedly a little better; it has more culture, and he did find one courtesan there who showed him sympathy. The narrator is skeptical, suggesting she must have had some ulterior motive, but the friend protests that he saw it with his own eyes. "If you don't believe me, here's my notebook to prove it" (1.6). The notebook so impresses the narrator that he agrees to turn it into a novel.

At the end of the second-to-last chapter, he speaks personally again. He has worked the notes into a novel, but there are still one or two points he needs to check on. In the final chapter, he tells us what these points are, then reverts to his own sad story. While serving as an official in the capital, he was falsely accused of some misdeed and now has to eke out a living as a tutor. At this point the friend returns, clears up the uncertain points, and shows the narrator a second notebook, which he would also like to see made into a novel. The narrator agrees, but explains that if he starts now, he will lose his job; he will need to wait until the year's teaching is done.

A similar example is provided by *Ping Jinchuan quanzhuan* (The complete tale of the pacification of Kokonor), of which an 1899 edition exists.[37] The novel tells of Nian Gengyao's campaign against the Mongol insurgents in Kokonor in 1723 and, like other novels of warfare, especially those set in remote regions, it is full of magic. Perhaps the most striking case is the episode in chapter 13 in which, after Daoist and Buddhist magic have failed against Islam, Christianity is called in. The pope is induced to fly out (literally) from Rome to Kokonor, where he routs the insurgents simply by pointing his crucifix at them.

In both prologue and epilogue, the author, Zhang Xiaoshan, claims that one of his ancestors served on General Nian's staff and left behind a diary describing the campaign in great detail. Because the diary was in a style accessible only to literary men and scholars, Zhang has rewritten it in the vernacular for a wider audience.

The First Wave

These last five novels, a considerable portion of the known fiction written between 1896 and 1900, distinguish themselves from earlier fiction by identifying the author with the narrator and by dramatizing the writing situation. If we add to them *Xichao kuaishi*, written in 1895, the six novels can without much exaggeration be regarded as a first wave of innovation, preceding the far greater wave of the late Qing (1902–11).

In varying degrees all of these works were written in response to the modern crisis, which came to a head in 1895 with widespread protests over the Treaty of Shimonoseki. (The 1895 protests were eclipsed only by those over the Treaty of Versailles twenty-odd years later.) But attitudes toward the crisis differed widely from this decade to the next. For all their alarm, Zhan Xi, Zou Tao, and the anonymous author of *Xichao kuaishi* were dedicated to the cause of reform and resolutely optimistic about China's future. Wu Jianren may have mocked Kang Youwei and other political pundits, but he was relatively mild. By comparison, the novelists of the following decade, including the later Wu Jianren, were profoundly pessimistic about the fate of China. The contrast is clearest in the symbolic visions at the beginning of *Xichao kuaishi* and Liu E's *Lao Can youji* (Travels of Lao Can), the former of the sun re-emerging after an eclipse, the latter of an impending shipwreck.

But can the novels' use of the "involved author" technique, as distinct from their themes and subject matter, also be seen as a response to the crisis? To some extent, perhaps. In such a time a novelist might well tend to discard the old impersonal narrator associated with the fiction of entertainment and speak "in his own voice," in effect adopting the form of self-reference characteristic of some nonfictional genres. (It is significant that the prologues and epilogues of two of the novels contain material similar to that found in their prefaces, uniting the genres of preface and novel.) Such a novelist would also tend to make clear just how and why he, as an individual, came to write. But my survey of the previous fifty years, sketchy as it is, shows that fiction had begun to anticipate both developments. The narrator had been particularized in the "personalized storyteller" novels, while the narrator and author had been practically identified with each other in the "virtual author" novels. The first wave may have arisen partly in response to the military and political crisis, but, much more significantly, it was a natural development in the history of Chinese fiction.

NOTES

1. Notable exceptions include David Der-wei Wang's *Fin-de-Siècle Splendor* (Stanford: Stanford University Press, 1997), the most comprehensive study of thematic modernities.

2. See his "Lun xiaoshuo yu qunzhi zhi guanxi" (On the connection between fiction and the governing of the people), *Xin xiaoshuo* (New fiction) 1 (tenth month, 1902): 105–108. He calls for a "revolution among novelists" and for "renovating the nation's fiction."

3. See *Narrative Discourse, An Essay in Method,* trans. Jane E . Lewin (Ithaca: Cornell University Press, 1980), 212–62, and *Narrative Discourse Revisited* (Ithaca: Cornell University Press, 1988), 79–83; and *Fiction and Diction,* trans. Catherine Porter (Ithaca: Cornell University Press, 1993), 68–79. Although the concept of voice has long been recognized, it has not been given its full importance because it has been conflated with perspective under "point of view."

4. Note that my first two categories are more or less contemporaneous. I have chosen not to include *Haiyouji* (Ocean adventure), because its date is uncertain—one (inaccessible) edition, it is claimed, was published in the eighteenth century. It is a remarkable work with four serial narrators, two of whom are participants in their own narratives: an anonymous narrator A at beginning and end; a second narrator B in chapters 1 and 3–7; a third (oral) narrator C in chapters 1–3; and a text by C as revised by B that we read at the same time as character D reads it in chapters 8–29. Only when C tells his story orally to B is the narrative in the first person. See the Shenyang: Liaoshen shushe, 1990 edition. *Jinzhong zhuan* (Tale of the golden bells), written at some time between 1871 (internal reference) and 1896 (date of preface),

also purports to have been written by one of its participants, a man who, needless to say, did not write in the first person. See the Leshantang edition. *Xiyi meng* (Chen Tuan's dream), of which there is an 1809 edition, represents itself as written in part by the Yuan dynasty Confucian philosopher Xu Heng, who appears as a character in the novel. See the Shenyang: Liaoshen shushe, 1992 edition.

5. The edition of reference is that by the Renmin wenxue chubanshe (Beijing, 1983). The title is usually understood to mean "lovers and heroes," but the hero's two weddings both take place under duress, and there is precious little love in the book. If we follow the god's definition as given in the prologue (4–5) and echoed elsewhere in the novel, the terms *ernü* and *yingxiong* refer to our motives for virtuous conduct in our social relations, the former denoting the emotional basis (love for parents, etc.) and the latter the will to act.

6. Novels that derive from actual oral narrative usually display far less exuberance on the part of the narrator.

7. For an analysis of the criticism, see David Rolston, *Traditional Chinese Fiction and Fiction Commentary* (Stanford: Stanford University Press, 1997), 304–11.

8. The edition of reference is that by Renmin wenxue chubanshe (Beijing, 1982).

9. David Der-wei Wang points out the implications of the word "traces" in the novel's title. See *Fin-de-Siècle Splendor*, 75.

10. See the edition in the Guben xiaoshuo jicheng series (Shanghai: Shanghai guji chubanshe, 1990).

11. *Tanci* were narratives, mostly in verse; some were performed, others were intended mainly for reading. For an account of *Yu chanchu*, see Jiang Ruizao, *Xiaoshuo kaozheng xubian* (reprint, Shanghai: Gudian wenxue chubanshe, 1957), 371. It is concerned with the injustice done to the early Ming statesman Yu Qian, while *Yuchan-ji* is set in the Jiajing period (1522–66).

12. Prosimetric forms like the *tanci* may well have influenced fiction in respect of the personalized narrator and the "virtual author" (see the next section). *Tanci* and *guci* that were intended mainly for reading flourished at this time, and some of them contain material describing their composition and particularizing their author-narrators. It is possible that the narratorial self-consciousness in the nineteenth-century novel had its parallel, and even to some degree its source, in these forms.

13. See chapter 2.

14. *Fengyue meng* (Beijing: Beijing daxue chubanshe, 1990), 6.

15. See *Pin hua baojian* (Taipei: Sanmin shuju, 1998), 1–2.

16. See the edition by San Qin chubanshe (Xian, 1988).

17. It is generally believed that the remarks attributed to the author at the beginning of *Story of the Stone* were originally not part of the text proper, but a prefatory note mistakenly copied into the text. However, until the middle of the twentieth century they were universally accepted as part of the text, and as such they exerted a considerable influence on fiction.

18. See the edition in the Zhongguo jindai xiaoshuo daxi series (Nanchang: Baihuazhou wenyi chubanshe, 1993).

19. See the remarks (*liyan*) that the author attached to the early installments of his novel. They are reprinted in the edition of reference, 3–5.

20. A rare example of the narrator's comment is his analysis of Zhao Erbao's thinking in chapter 55.

21. For the background of the contest, see chapter 6 of this book.

22. See the modern edition in the Zhongguo jindai xiaoshuo jingpin daxi series (Hohhot: Nei Menggu renmin chubanshe, 1998). The novel does not mention Fryer, but it does deal explicitly with his "three evils."

23. Several other novels might be mentioned here, including two that depict the anti-Japanese resistance in Taiwan, *Tai zhan shiji* (True account of the war in Taiwan) and *Taiwan jinguo yingxiong zhuan* (Tale of female heroes in Taiwan), both published in the middle of 1895 while the fighting was still going on. Note the convergence between fiction and journalism. For the former, see the reprint, Taipei: Guangwen shuju, 1976. There is also *Tongshang yuanwei* (The reason behind the opening of our ports), first published in the journal *Baihua yanyibao* in 1897; see Chen Bohai and Yuan Jin, *Shanghai jindai wenxueshi* (Shanghai: Shanghai renmin chubanshe, 1993), 244. On the *Taiwan jinguo yingxiong zhuan*, see Qin Shou'ou, "Wan-Qing xiaoshuo souyi—*Taiwan jinguo yingxiong zhuan* de faxian," *Shu lin* 1 (1980): 48–49.

24. Reprint, Beijing: Beijing shifan daxue chubanshe, 1992.

25. Poems by him appear as early as 1875, in journals such as the *Siming suoji* published by the Shenbaoguan. For other information, see chapter 6.

26. See the reprint in the Zhongguo jindai xiaoshuo daxi series (Nanchang: Baihuazhou wenyi chubanshe, 1993).

27. See chapter 1, 4–8. In chapter 43 she is represented as reading poems from her own collection.

28. For biographical information, see *Wuxi xianzhi* (Shanghai: Shanghai shehui kexueyuan chubanshe, 1994), 1036–37, as well as Chen Ruheng, *Shuoyuan zhenwen* (Shanghai: Shanghai guji chubanshe, 1981), 86–89, 105–107.

29. See 13.

30. Cf. the author-narrator's remark about the inequality of the sexes in the prologue, 11.

31. Zou Tao evidently knew a good deal about religion, particularly Catholicism. He later taught in Shanghai at the Qiming Girls' School, which was founded by a French Catholic order; see *Wuxi xianzhi*, 1036–37.

32. See his "*Haishang mingji sida jingang qishu* shunei youguan zuozhe wenti de ziliao," *Wan-Qing sida xiaoshuojia* (Taibei: Shangwu yinshuguan, 1993), 143–50. A reprint of the novel is available in the Zhongguo jindai xiaoshuo daxi series (Nanchang: Baihuazhou wenyi chubanshe, 1996).

33. See 102–103 and 133–34. Yan Fu and Wang Tao may also be targets of satire.

34. Strangely enough, one of the names of the Kang in this novel is very similar to one of the names of the Kang of *Xichao kuaishi*.

35. Cf. the demons, goblins, and monsters, denizens of Shanghai, that are excoriated in chapter 2 of Wu Jianren's *Ershinian mudu zhi guai xianzhuang*, reprint in Zhongguo jindai xiaoshuo daxi series (Nanchang: Jiangxi renmin chubanshe, 1988), 6.

36. Reprint, Beijing: Zhongyang minzu xueyuan chubanshe, 1994.

37. There is a reprint in the Zhongguo shenguai xiaoshuo daxi series (Chengdu: Bashu shushe, 1989).

CHAPTER 2

Illusion of Romance *and the Courtesan Novel*

·

I N HIS ACCOUNT of the Chinese courtesan or brothel novels, for which he employed the term *xiaxie xiaoshuo*,[1] Lu Xun distinguished three types, based on the level at which the novels' main characters, particularly their courtesans, were depicted:[2] idealized representation, in *Pin hua baojian, Hua yue hen*, and *Qinglou meng*; realistic representation, in *Haishang hua liezhuan*; and demeaning or derogatory representation, in Zhang Chunfan's *Jiuwei gui* (Nine-tailed tortoise) and other works. He described the three types as succeeding one another in time, as different stages in the fiction writers' perception of the courtesan.

Although the courtesan novels share other characteristics besides their setting—an unprecedented degree of explicit contemporary reference, for one thing, plus a highly self-conscious authorial stance—Lu Xun's distinction, at least between his first two types, is surely valid, for they prove to be associated with fundamentally different kinds of fiction. The idealized type, as he explains, is associated with the romance of brilliant and beautiful heroes and heroines (*caizi jiaren*), and the realistic type is associated, to some degree, with the cautionary novel. His notion of historical stages, however, is hardly tenable. At the time he wrote, he was unaware of the courtesan novel *Fengyue meng* (Illusion of romance), which carries an author's preface of 1848 and clearly belongs to the realistic type. To judge from patterns of intertextual reference among the courtesan novels, the first two types at least must have formed separate streams during the nineteenth century.[3]

My aim in this essay is twofold. First, I shall show that *Illusion of Romance* is rooted in a specific locality, the city of Yangzhou, and that, as the first Chinese "city novel" in any meaningful sense of that term, it constitutes the main literary context within which the first of the Shanghai city novels, *Haishang hua liezhuan*, was written and should be read. Second, I shall introduce *Illusion of Romance*, on which little has been written, by discussing some of its key qualities as well as the chief problem it presents to the critic.

The earliest known edition of *Illusion of Romance* was published in Shanghai in 1883 by Shenbaoguan, the publishing house of the *Shen bao* newspaper.[4] Quite possibly it was the first printed edition, for several of the novels published by that house had previously existed in manuscript for a considerable time. The preface, written in Hongmei guan (Red plum hall) and dated the winter solstice of 1848, is by an author who gives his pseudonym as Hanshang Mengren, The Fool of Hanshang, i.e., of Yangzhou. The name Red Plum Hall may tell us a little about him. It appears in the novel as the site of a riddle competition put on for the public by a society of local literati (10.66–68). Prizes are offered for guessing quotations from texts ranging from the classics and *The West Chamber* (*Xixiangji*) to books of divination. (Contestants are supplied with a seven-character clue to the quotation together with the name of the text.) Thirty-two riddles are actually printed in the novel, although only two are solved; presumably the others were put there for the reader to solve on his own. Since the riddle society is presented as one of the features of Yangzhou, it seems likely that Red Plum Hall represents the Zhuxi Chunshe,[5] the famous Yangzhou riddle society of the day, and that the author was a member of it. This, plus the extensive knowledge he shows of local artists and calligraphers as well as of local song and oral narrative, suggests that he was a Yangzhou literatus working the lighter side of literature.

The author claims in his preface that the novel is based on his own observations during some misspent years in the Yangzhou brothels. In the prologue chapter, chapter 1, the narrator describes a similar experience of his own:

In the ignorant folly of his youth your narrator was himself much drawn to idle pleasures and spent upwards of thirty years addicted to the brothel scene. I don't know how many prostitutes fell in love with me and swore vows of eternal fidelity. Some were going to marry me, others were just going to live with me, but without exception they all made off with my money. Some became wives to other men, while others cleaned me out and then took off for home, often to start up again in some other port. When the love they had professed for me was over, they scattered in all directions. As a result I have come to regard the house of joy with a cold and critical eye, as a place too dangerous to visit. (1.4–5)

Chapter 1 goes on to ascribe the actual narrative to someone else, a certain Guo Lairen, an obvious pun on a word that means a veteran or old hand, in this case a roué. Guo, a veteran of the Yangzhou brothels, has seen the error of his ways and now, as a Daoist immortal in training, has written this novel as a warning to others. He hands the manuscript to the narrator and asks him to get it published. This account of the origin and transmission of the text is clearly indebted to *Story of the Stone*, which influenced other novels of the period in similar fashion.

Han Bangqing's *Haishang hua liezhuan* (Flowers of Shanghai), which was published in a few installments in 1892 and then in full as a book in 1894, differs sharply from *Illusion of Romance* in technique; yet at the beginning it seems tacitly to acknowledge the influence of the earlier novel. It, too, has a confessional prologue and purports to be based on the personal observation of the author, a veteran of the brothel scene.[6] He now conceives of his experience as a dream and is writing this novel to warn others. On awakening from his dream, he literally bumps into Zhao Puzhai, one of his chief protagonists, who has just arrived in Shanghai to stay with an uncle. As a young man eager to sample the fleshpots, Zhao is the approximate equivalent of Lu Shu, one of the chief protagonists of *Illusion of Romance*, who has arrived in Yangzhou to stay with an aunt and uncle. There are other similarities between the two novels, for example, between Lu Shu's euphoric dream that turns into nightmare and the similar experience of Zhao Puzhai's sister. *Illusion of Romance*'s concentration on a single city and a few sites within it—something not found in the "idealized" courtesan novels—may also have influenced Han Bangqing. Both novels give precise itineraries within the central city, listing streets and lanes, a feature that sets them off from previous works. Finally, *Illusion of Romance*'s use of some Yangzhou dialect may have encouraged the later author to use Shanghai dialect in his novel, though he confined it to the dialogue. For these reasons, and also because of its realistic level of representation, it seems likely that *Illusion of Romance* formed an important part of the literary context within which *Haishang hua liezhuan* was written.

Despite this relationship, Shanghai is still an important element in *Illusion of Romance*. The city is referred to twice, once as the only place where a certain kind of intricate workmanship can be found, and once when we are told that someone from a Shanghai brothel has come to Yangzhou to recruit courtesans (3.17 and 25.178). The novel also suggests that the great days of Yangzhou are already past, now that its monuments and gardens have been allowed to fall into disrepair (5.30). Eventually, of course, in the last third of the nineteenth century, Shanghai did surpass Yangzhou as a brothel scene. A striking symbol of this is the fact that, by 1900, a mere six years after the appearance of the first Shanghai novel, a Shanghai version of *Illusion of Romance* was published.[7] All of its place names were changed to Shanghai locations, and its principal courtesans were transmogrified into the most famous prostitutes of the contemporary Shanghai scene.

The First City Novel

Certain Chinese novels are known for their concentration on the family compound as a separate milieu—they might be called milieu novels. In both the sixteenth-century *Jin Ping Mei* and the *Story of the Stone* the scene inside the compound is presented more insistently and coherently than the world outside and makes a far greater impression. But if we think of milieu in a broader sense, for example, as the public or semipublic areas of a city, *Illusion of Romance* seems to be the earliest such novel and Yangzhou the first city to be so treated. By comparison, the accounts in *Rulin waishi* of the pleasure quarter of Nanjing or the West Lake at Hangzhou are confined to only a few chapters.

A novelist, as distinct from a geographer, tends to describe a city in terms of his characters' observation and movement—a city of the eye and the foot, so to speak. Beyond that, he may give people's perception of a city, of its culture and traditions, in a word, of its ethos. In both respects *Illusion of Romance* is substantially a new development in Chinese fiction.

The novel is set entirely within the city of Yangzhou, which in the Qing dynasty meant the twin counties of Jiangdu and Ganquan. Yangzhou is announced as the setting (and to some degree the subject) in the prologue chapter. After giving a brief account of the founding of brothels during the Warring States period, the narrator continues:

> Brothels were originally designed to enrich the state and facilitate commerce, but the evil practice spread throughout the land and, as age followed age, it has even in recent times extended beyond our borders. In the city of Yangzhou, which has always tended to favor an ostentatious luxury, the pleasure quarter is equal to that of any city, even Suzhou, Hangzhou, or Nanjing, and untold numbers of men, addicted to the brothel scene, have met financial ruin and sometimes death there.

He goes on to underline his presence as a witness to the corruption of the city's youth:

I have personally observed such youths as these, who, while still dependent on the earnings of their fathers and elder brothers, like nothing better at the age of fourteen or fifteen than to dress up in gorgeous clothes of the latest fashion. At first it's just a matter of gathering in groups of three or four along Commerce Street (Maimaijie) off the Parade (Jiaochang) and drinking tea and throwing dice for prizes such as porcelain, fruit, and trinkets. But then they may chance to see a pleasure boat emerging from the water barrier at Tianning Gate and perhaps there will be prostitutes on board whom someone has brought along on an excursion—prostitutes dressed up either as girls or as boys, all of them in vivid colors, their faces powdered and rouged. They will be singing operatic arias or popular songs, and their soft, melodious voices will be accompanied by the haunting notes of a flute. At this sight the youths will positively ache with desire and, after a hurried consultation, will hire a boat and go off in pursuit. Yet even this is just a matter of gazing at girls; it may cost a little money for the boat and the refreshments, but no great harm has been done. The real danger comes when someone in the group knows the house the girls come from and takes his friends along. After an introductory tea party or two, they gradually become well acquainted with the prostitutes and go on to hold parties there and stay overnight. (1.2)

After establishing the Yangzhou setting, the narrator takes us to a vantage point on Commerce Street from which the tea drinkers can observe the passing pleasure boats. The same scene is played out later in the novel when the main characters and their courtesan paramours are themselves the objects of attention (5.30).

Much of the rest of chapter 1 is spent on the narrator's vigorous argument about the dangers of the brothels and a staple item to be found there—opium. Chapter 2, the opening of the novel's action, is set wholly in the Fanglai teahouse, which is on the Parade, the heart of the Yangzhou entertainment quarter. Three of the five principal male characters are having tea there when they are joined by two younger men. One of them, Lu Shu, has just arrived from Changshu and, on dropping in for a cup of tea, he recognizes his sworn brother Yuan You. (The two men had met while Yuan was living in forced exile in Changshu.) Lu is introduced to the others, Wu Zhen and Jia Ming,[8] and these four are then joined by Wei Bi, son of a wealthy attendant official, who takes a keen interest in male bonding; two chapters later, he will propose that the five, all confirmed or aspiring rakes, swear an oath of brotherhood.

After Lu Shu's entrance, we are told in an aside about not only his background but also the route he took to the teahouse. He reached the Parade, looked at the various sideshows, sampled some storytelling, watched a "foreign" peep show, and finally visited the teahouse. This information, though structurally unnecessary, is obviously important to the author, not merely to tell us a little about Lu Shu's nature but also to give us a sense of the center of Yangzhou.

In chapter 3 we follow Lu Shu's progress in present narrative time as he goes from his uncle's house, where he is staying, to Yuan You's. But when he reaches Paper Money Checkpoint (Baochaoguan or Chaoguan) beside the water barrier and bridge at Tianning Gate, the author launches into a full set piece of description, the only one in the novel (3.14–15). This is the hub of the city, with its crowded pedestrian traffic, government offices (of Ganquan County), inns, and shops. The set piece itself is situated at a key point in the novel. It focuses first on the checkpoint as a junction for both water and land transportation, a hub of commerce not only for the city and its environs but also for vast areas of China. It is the place's centrality with regard to travel and transport that is being emphasized, rather than any intrinsic importance it might have. A contrast is then drawn between the dread, awe-inspiring organs of government and the bright lanterns of the inns and the shop signs advertising the latest prices.

The piece goes on to describe the crowds. No novel is better than *Illusion of Romance* at giving a sense of urban crowding. Masses of people flow over the bridge, entering or leaving the city; bearers of vegetables, fish, water, and firewood—in fact, bearers of everything from orchids to night soil—jostle their way forward. There are also the swift sedan chairs of the salt merchants, as well as supplicants pleading with passersby: women offering to mend or patch clothes, friars beating their wooden fish, boys dressed up as girls.

We follow Lu Shu until he reaches Gengzi Street, where he sees the famous perfumeries, some of them besieged by customers buying perfume, creams, and powders, others deserted. He continues past Taiping Dock as far as Little East Gate, where he has to ask directions of a shopkeeper. He proceeds along some other streets until he arrives at North Willow Lane, where once more he has to ask directions. The purpose of the itinerary is partly to show the effect Yangzhou has on Lu Shu, but mainly to give an impression of the center of the city.

The novel names two dozen streets and lanes, some of them many times, as well as gates, bridges, and docks. Routes are frequently given, although never again in such detail as in Lu Shu's itinerary. It is noteworthy that the novel actually ends in the street, as crowds jostle to see the courtesan Shuanglin's tablet taken to the archway constructed in her honor (32.227–230). We see this event through the eyes of Mu Zhu, a naïve cousin of Yuan You's who has just come up from the country. A debate arises among the spectators as to the morality of Shuanglin's actions. Suddenly the crowd catches sight of a madman clapping his hands and singing as he makes his way along the street. His song is a condemnation of the brothel and all its works, of which he portrays himself as the victim. He crosses Taiping Bridge and goes as far as the crossroads, where he vanishes in a puff of wind. He is Guo Lairen, the former roué, now enlightened, who is on his way up the mountain to write this book.

The greater part of the novel is set in the Fanglai teahouse and in two brothels, the Jinyulou and Qiang Da's Place. The teahouse is where the five friends routinely gather for breakfast. Their courtesan paramours are distributed between the two brothels: Yuexiang in the Jinyulou; Guilin, Fenglin, Shuanglin, and Qiaoyun at Qiang Da's Place. However, most of chapter 3 is spent in Yuan You's parents' house, of which an elaborate description is given, most of chapter 4 is set in the Jinyuan noodle house, and other scenes occur in restaurants and a prison.

Yangzhou is further described in the course of some notable excursions by boat, which occupy much of chapters 5, 13, and 16. Chapter 13 takes place at the Duanyang Festival, allowing the reader to experience through the eyes of Lu Shu and Yuexiang some peculiar local customs (boys diving for ducks in Slender West Lake, for example). The other two excursions are to temples, one so that the five friends can take the oath of brotherhood, the other so that they can celebrate Yuexiang's recovery from an illness. Each occasion provides views of crowds of spectators, entertainers, and beggars.

As we have seen, the novel displays its local consciousness from the very beginning, concerning itself with the city's ethos and people's perception of it. Some of the Yangzhou legend is simply taken for granted. No reader would fail to connect the courtesans of Yangzhou with the Tang poet Du Mu's famous line about "awakening from a ten-year Yangzhou dream."[9] It lies behind the title of this book, which means the dream or illusion of love, from which the author has just awakened. Another commonplace is the fact that Yangzhou was famous for producing concubines (and frequently prostitutes). Some of the women characters give harrowing accounts of their childhood training.

Two Yangzhou works are actually quoted in the *Illusion of Romance*. One is *Yangzhou huafanglu* (The pleasure boats of Yangzhou) by Li Dou,[10] which Lu Shu mentions in chapter 5. Lu Shu has read about the famous gardens and ancient buildings of Yangzhou and expresses his disappointment that some of them have fallen into ruin.[11] The *Huafanglu*, one of the most elaborate accounts of a Chinese city and its inhabitants ever written, was, according to Li Dou's preface, the product of thirty years of observation (1764–95)—a point that recalls the *Illusion of Romance* author's own thirty years in the Yangzhou brothels. It may not be too fanciful to suggest that the novelist's decision to write a Yangzhou city novel was to some degree prompted by Li Dou's work.

The other work quoted is one entitled *Yangzhou yanhua zhuzhici* (Bamboo branch songs on the pleasure houses of Yangzhou) that seems not to have survived. The bamboo branch song is a four-line poem that typically describes some local scene, custom, or peculiarity, often with satirical intent. It seems highly likely that this collection of songs did exist. The poems quoted are close in subject matter and spirit to some existing bamboo branch songs, particularly those by anonymous authors.

Four of the songs are given in the novel. The first is quoted by Yuan You in chapter 5 to explain a Yangzhou slang term for a woman with "large"—i.e., natural—feet (5.26). The Yangzhou brothels were noted for employing women with unbound feet at a level below that of the courtesan proper; such feet had an erotic appeal for certain clients. Yuan You says the collection of songs was composed by a friend of his and contained ninety-nine poems, the same number as in the best-known Yangzhou collection, the *Yangzhou zhuzhici* of Dong Weiye,[12] the preface to which is dated 1740. *Yangzhou yanhua zhuzhici* is quoted once by the narrator to illustrate a point, once by Yuan You, once by the courtesan Shuanglin, and once by Lu Shu, the visitor to Yangzhou, who, while speaking to his paramour Yuexiang, prefaces his quotation with the words "I've seen a poem in that *Yangzhou yanhua zhuzhici* of yours that sums it up nicely" (18.128). Several poems are quoted to make a satirical point about the brothels. One or two match their narrative context closely, and the text may well have been arranged to accommodate them.

In less obvious ways, other features of the *Fengyue meng* also convey something of Yangzhou's peculiar ethos. The riddle society in chapter 10, for example, is explained as a Yangzhou peculiarity, even though Lu Shu claims that Changshu has something similar. Eight of the nine artists whose work hangs in Yuan You's parents' house (3.16) are identifiable, and all prove to be Yangzhou contemporaries or near contemporaries, some of them not very well known. The Lizhentang, referred to in chapters 2 and 20, is a Yangzhou institution, a refuge, in the words of the local history, "for girls who have lost their chastity and have nowhere else to turn."[13] One prostitute flees to the refuge, presumably to be married off, and another plans to use it as a threat, to force her uncle to give up legal control of her (2.12 and 20.142). The Lizhentang in Yangzhou was constructed in 1840, only a few years before the novel was written, as the gift of a rich salt merchant. When Shuanglin contemplates her future in chapter 20, she notes two distinctive features of the Yangzhou brothels: the bully-boy protectors (*bashi*), who batten on prostitutes, and the gangs of extortionists. But the novel contains numerous other examples of things distinctively Yangzhou—to do with language, customs, food, music, and entertainment.

Yangzhou Origins

Illusion of Romance is also associated to some degree with the tradition of Yangzhou vernacular and oral narrative, even though it represents a new development. The most obvious comparison is with a sixteen-chapter novel entitled *Yaguanlou* (Bella Vista Hall),[14] of which only the author's pseudonym is known. There is a Yangzhou edition of 1821, two or three decades before *Illusion of Romance* was written, and the writer of the preface, who is presumably the author, identifies himself as from the city. All of the action, with the exception of one trip up north and one to Guangzhou, is set in Yangzhou—well over 90 percent of the narrative. Furthermore, the novel contains Yangzhou place names, customs, and entertainments, as well as a sprinkling of Yangzhou dialect. But unlike *Illusion of Romance*, it makes no attempt to present the city in terms of human experience. It describes various amusements around the Parade, including the peep show, several excursions by boat, and some Yangzhou customs, including one or two of those described in *Illusion of Romance*, but gives little actual sense of the city.

The settings of *Yaguanlou* are similar to those of *Illusion*—one teahouse and two brothels—but most of the action takes place in the hero's own house. Only to a limited degree can it be described as a courtesan novel. The hero, Guanbao, a rich young man thoroughly spoiled by his mother, takes a series of mistresses who are largely, but not exclusively, courtesans. He is led astray by two sworn brothers who depend on him for money—a very different relationship from that of the sworn brothers in *Illusion*. This is the old theme of the wastrel son squandering the family fortune on gambling and prostitutes. However, *Yaguanlou* has an extra level—karmic causation. Guanbao is the reincarnation of an out-of-town merchant whom his father has cheated, and the son's debauchery is the merchant's posthumous revenge.

Despite these complications, *Yaguanlou* does help us understand the provenance of *Illusion*. It has some important common elements—opium smoking, loan sharking, and whoremongering. It tells of moneylending at exorbitant rates of interest (known as *fang huozhai*), far higher than the maximum three percent per month allowed by law.[15] At one point the hero's mother recommends this kind of moneylending to her son as a more secure livelihood than that of a salt merchant. The way the youthful hero first falls for the courtesans resembles the general account given in the prologue chapter of *Illusion of Romance*; in fact, the latter could have been based on *Yaguanlou*, just as Guanbao could have been a model for Lu Shu. Other points in common are the sworn brothers and the way they pair off with prostitutes and cheat one another when the opportunity arises. At the same time, the two novels differ in their description of the brothel; in *Yaguanlou*, for example, there are no bully-boy protectors or gangs of extortionists.

A more important difference between the two works is the level of representation of the courtesans. If we apply Lu Xun's distinction, by which the courtesans of his second type are "realistic," that is to say, in possession of some sympathetic—or at least human—qualities, and those of his third type are ruthless schemers, all the courtesans of *Yaguanlou* belong to the third type. Nor can the men be said to have any redeeming qualities—the satire is unrelieved. It seems likely, therefore, that *Illusion*, a "realistic" novel of Lu Xun's second type, developed, to some degree at least, from a novel of his third type.

Yaguanlou was based on an actual incident that took place in Yangzhou.[16] There is no evidence that the incident ever gave rise to oral narrative, but some of the novel's characteristics can be observed in Yangzhou fiction that appears to be closely related to oral literature. An example is the novel *Qingfeng zha* (Qingfeng Lock),[17] of which an 1819 edition exists. Its material was created by an eighteenth-century Yangzhou storyteller named Pu Lin, who included himself in his own story in the person of a notorious rascal and ne'er-do-well who eventually mends his ways.[18] Pu Lin's subject matter was established in Yangzhou storytelling in the eighteenth century and remained in the repertory well into the twentieth. The novel as we have it bears signs of hasty adaptation, perhaps from memories of oral performance, and it shows a distinct lack of proportion by focusing on a few big scenes to the detriment of the whole. Although not set in Yangzhou, it contains several features found in both *Yaguanlou* and *Illusion*. Some of the action is set in teahouses and a brothel, and the courtesans are on the same low level as those of *Yaguanlou*. Both loan sharking and gambling are dwelled upon, and some use is made of Yangzhou dialect. It would seem that *Yaguanlou*, a written novel, is related to a strain of Yangzhou oral narrative that dealt with low life in a satirical manner.

At first sight the structure of *Illusion* seems derivative of *Story of the Stone*, but the influence is slight, confined to sections of the beginning and end. The account of the text's origin with its two immortals is clearly drawn from chapter 1 of *Story of the Stone*, while the song sung by the madman in the last chapter is an imitation of the *haoliao* poem chanted by the lame Daoist. The confessional tone of the preface sounds like the remarks attributed to Cao Xueqin at the beginning of the novel, and the *Illusion* prologue's defense of its fiction on grounds of actuality was probably suggested by the similar defense in *Story of the Stone*.

The actuality that the prologue speaks of, particularly the specificity of description, is one of the most remarkable features of *Illusion*. Clothes, jewelry, and accessories, notably those of the dandy Lu Shu and the glamorous courtesan Yuexiang, are described with a degree of precision that one associates more with a museum catalogue than a novel.[19] The specificity of dress and other trappings is no doubt intended to emphasize the characters' shallowness, but specificity seems also to be regarded as a literary value in itself. For example, a beauty's tiny foot size, if it is noted specifically at all in fiction, is usually described as a traditional three inches, but in *Illusion* there are no three-inch feet; those of the courtesans range from under four inches (Fenglin, Yuexiang) to just four inches (Guilin), four and a half inches (Shuanglin), over five inches (Qiaoyun), and six inches in the case of the chanteuse Wenlan. Another example is the author's precise location of his novel in contemporary Yangzhou. His concern for exact description, which presumably springs from a desire to record a particular milieu at a particular time, helps to account for this novel's peculiar impact on the reader.

Structural and Other Features

Illusion is concerned with the fortunes of five couples, the five men who meet in the teahouse in chapter 2 and their courtesan paramours. Remarkably, no one character, nor any one pair of characters, can be considered primary. On the surface, Lu Shu's affair with Yuexiang is the main element; he is infatuated with her, as the novel reminds us in a kind of refrain, and he squanders money on her, only to be rejected in the end. He is the classic wastrel son and she the classic schemer. Had he not been a rake before he came to Yangzhou, he would precisely match the young men described in the prologue. But Lu's story is over by chapter 22; his own lack of money combined with pressure from his uncle and friends have forced him to return home. The pivotal role in the novel belongs to Yuan You; he is the one who brings all of the others together. Moreover, his affair with Shuanglin culminates at the end of the book in his death and her suicide, and it is the morality of her actions that the bystanders are arguing about when Guo Lairen appears. Yet although Yuan You and Shuanglin's story is certainly a major element, it seems no more significant than Jia Ming's long and ambivalent relationship with Fenglin or Wu Zhen's suffering at the hands of the lower bureaucracy or, for that matter, Lu Shu's affair with Yuexiang. Wei Bi and Qiaoyun may command less of our time and interest, but the other four pairs of lovers seem of roughly equal importance.

The stories of the couples are interwoven with considerable finesse. The men are continually meeting at the teahouse for breakfast and at one or the other brothel for dinner parties. One liaison, that of Wu Zhen and Guilin, is already in existence before the novel opens; it is at Wu's invitation that they go to Qiang Da's Place, where Guilin works, and it is there that Yuan You meets Shuanglin and Jia Ming meets Fenglin. The novel is one long series of breakfasts, dinners, parties, and excursions attended by many of the same people— the seemingly idle but actually quite busy life of the flâneur and the courtesan.

All five men are introduced to the reader in chapter 2 in the Fanglai teahouse. Yuexiang appears in chapter 5—she is a new courtesan in town, and the men decide to invite her to join them on their excursion. The other courtesans are introduced in chapter 6, and by chapter 10 the liaisons have been established. Chapter 16 is spent on the excursion to a temple to give thanks for Yuexiang's recovery from an illness. This is the exact midpoint of the novel, and it resembles the miniclimax in the middle of a Southern drama, the so-called *xiao tuanyuan*. Immediately afterward, in chapter 17, Yuexiang catches Lu Shu *in flagrante delicto* with a maid (the one with the natural feet) and becomes even more outrageous in her demands for jewelry. Within a few chapters, Lu Shu's money has run out, and he is driven from the brothel and eventually from Yangzhou. Wu Zhen's catastrophe follows soon after.

Even in the early chapters, the dangers that threaten the brothel, particularly its owners and courtesans, are not ignored. Gangs pretend to have been treated with disrespect and retaliate by breaking up the furniture and stealing anything of value; after mediation by the brothel's adviser, they are bought off with dinners and apologies. Dangers also come from rapacious precinct heads, self-appointed protectors, and disgruntled former customers. The gang's raid occupies much of chapters 7 through 9, while former customers try to assert their old rights in chapters 14 and 17, and in chapter 22 the protector Wu Gengyu, rebuffed by Wu Zhen when he requests a loan, informs on him as an opium smoker and hands him over to the authorities.

The prefect's crackdown on opium and his subsequent closing of the brothels are the main public events that occur. The crackdown spells disaster for Wu Zhen, an addict, and the closing of the brothels pushes Yuan You and Jia Ming into making decisions about their paramours that they would otherwise have deferred. Since Qiang Da's Place is closed, Yuan and Jia have to find somewhere else for Shuanglin and Fenglin to live. Eventually Yuan You takes Shuanglin as his concubine, infuriating his wife, but pleasing his parents, who are desperate for a grandson. Jia Ming hesitates, then hesitates again, about marrying Fenglin—perhaps he really hasn't enough money—and eventually she decides to accept an offer from a visiting official and depart for Beijing.

Illusion has its share of well-established structural devices—characters who serve as foils to other characters, events and references that foreshadow and echo other events, and dreams with prophetic as well as psychological significance. One device that the novel uses to particular effect is the illustrative episode. At the end of chapter 2, as the friends discuss the merits of the local courtesans over breakfast, they are interrupted by a man who joins them uninvited from another table (2.12). He asks if they have heard the latest news, then proceeds to tell them of two recent incidents. A courtesan abused by the jealous wife of her paramour has hanged herself, and a young girl forced into prostitution by her father has escaped from the brothel and taken refuge in the Lizhentang. In the latter case, after mediation by a secretary of the local magistrate, the brothel paid off the precinct head and the constables and so avoided prosecution. In the former case the dead courtesan's family are expected to demand heavy compensation.

These items are delivered with relish by a man who clearly enjoys the thought of the payoffs. After he has returned to his table, Yuan You identifies him as Wu Gengyu and explains how he spends his time: freeloading at the brothels and making money from a variety of rackets. He then adds:

> "I've known him a long time, but whenever we happen to meet I just give a nod in his direction. We've never been what you could call friends. I can't imagine what made him descend on us like this and give us this load of rubbish. Wasn't it absurd?"
>
> "It's best to steer clear of that type of person and treat whatever he says as if you'd never heard it," said Jia Ming. (2.13)

Wu Gengyu is our introduction to the bully-boy protectors. He turns out to be the protector of Guilin, with whom Wu Zhen has established a liaison, and later in the novel he will ask Wu Zhen for a loan to pay off a gambling debt. But the episode also has another significance. It comes just as the five are discussing courtesans from a connoisseur's point of view, and the two news items convey a very different perception, that of the courtesan as victim. We never hear of these two cases again; they are of no further importance to the novel. Clearly, they are included here only because they contradict the romantic visions of the courtesan that the five men have been conjuring up.

Two other such illustrative episodes occupy chapter 4. Both occur in the Jinyuan noodle house, where the five friends meet for breakfast before going on their first excursion. Yuan You, the loan shark, runs into a borrower who has been delinquent in repaying a loan. After a furious argument that has to be mediated by Jia Ming, the borrower agrees to an extension of the loan at a much higher interest rate. The whole scene is designed to show the loan shark in action—it has no other significance. The second part of the chapter deals with Wei Bi's reserving a boat for the excursion that will be described in chapter 5. His servant returns from the dock to say that the boatmen are insisting on double the usual fee. Wei Bi immediately sends the servant off to the local authorities with one of his father's name cards and a request that they seize and hold the best boat for him. The episode is designed to show Wei Bi using his father's clout to his own advantage.

Brothel Realities

In Chinese literature the brothel is generally seen from the outside. If its inner workings are mentioned at all, it is usually to stress the greed of the owner or madam in insisting on too high a price for a courtesan's redemption. From *Illusion*, however, we can piece together a comprehensive account of how a girl of poor family was forcibly trained in the arts and graces of the courtesan, then leased to a brothel by the head of the family in return for either a flat fee or a percentage of her earnings, which came largely from the subtle pressure she exerted on customers for jewelry, clothes, parties, and entertainment. She was likely to have a self-appointed protector, someone who would expect to enjoy her favors from time to time as well as to receive presents from her, but despite his so-called protection, she still faced dangers from jealous former clients and gangs of hooligans. Continually offering opium to her clients, she also ran the risk of becoming addicted herself. *Illusion of Romance* may well be the first Chinese novel to give a convincing picture of brothel life. Here is Fenglin, the courtesan who forms a liaison with Jia Ming, describing her background:

"Tell me about your family," he said. At first she said nothing, but when he persisted, she heaved a sigh and began: "You mustn't laugh at me, though. I lost my mother as a child, and my father was a drunk and a gambler, and he went and promised me to Lan Siniang, a hairdresser in a brothel, as a child wife for her young son. When I was six they took me to Qingjiang to learn music and singing, but I resisted—and suffered more abuse than I care to re- member, physical as well as verbal. My mother-in-law set up a house of her own in Qingjiang with a dozen or so girls in it, and when I was twelve she forced me into the same filthy business. I don't know *how* much money I made for them! But my husband and brother-in-law whored and gambled and smoked opium, and they also slept around with the other girls—up to all sorts of shenanigans. They got involved in several nasty lawsuits and ran up debts of over a thousand taels. We couldn't remain in business there, so we did a flit back to Yangzhou, where the three of them, my mother-in-law, my husband, and his brother, have rented a single tiny room and need four or five hundred cash a day just for living expenses. I'm nominally on a per- centage basis here, and I had to take out an installment loan even to buy my bedding. All the jewelry and dresses I had in Qingjiang disappeared into the pawnshop, and every day now I have to meet my payments and also buy food, flowers, cosmetics, and other odds and ends, as well as a little of that damnable stuff.[20] Meanwhile, not a day goes by that they aren't after me for more money. I haven't been here very long and so far I don't have a single steady client. How am I going to cope?" (7.50–51)

The novel does not neglect the management either, especially in the case of Qiang Da's Place. Qiang himself is a former servant in a brothel who has man- aged to become an owner. In addition to negotiating with the families, who sometimes seize the girls back once they have received payment, and trying to attract and keep customers, he has occasional problems with the calculated vi- olence of gangs, who claim to have good connections with the lower bureau- cracy, and also with attempted shakedowns by precinct heads. He needs an ad- viser with diplomatic skills as well as political knowhow, such as a doorman or a runner in the county offices, to mediate any disputes that may arise. This ad- viser, besides his monthly retainer, will also receive brothel privileges and sea- sonal presents. All of these problems are aired in chapters 7 to 9, not long af- ter the last of the principal courtesans has been introduced to the reader. In chapter 9, Qiang holds forth at length to his adviser, a doorman in the coun- ty offices who, though illiterate, has considerable savvy, on the subject of his financial and management difficulties.

Illusion is also the first novel to give convincing pictures of opium addicts.[21] One is the courtesan Fenglin, whom I have just quoted; the other is Wu Zhen, one of the five friends, whose paramour is Guilin. His story, in fact his downfall, is told in detail in chapters 22 to 25. It is as powerful an exposé of the lower bureaucracy as anything found in the satirical novels of the late Qing.

That Wu Zhen is an addict is made clear early in the novel. In chapter 3, during a visit with his friends to Yuan You's parents' house, he insists on smoking both before and after lunch, and also tries to introduce Lu Shu to the practice. But although he is arrested for smoking opium and is ultimately sent into exile, it is not the addiction that gets him arrested, for some of his jailers are also users, if not addicts; it is the fact that he has fallen foul of Guilin's protector, Wu Gengyu.

Wu Gengyu has gambling debts and sees Wu Zhen as a promising source of a "loan." He puts his request to Wu Zhen, who says he will get back to him in a couple of days, at which point Wu Gengyu goes off to another courtesan's room (22.157–158). To appease him, Guilin secretly sends him a packet of opium.

Wu Zhen tells her he is not going to agree to the loan. He is offended to be taken for a neophyte, and anyway, he fancies himself a fairly tough character.

"You have to bear in mind that those people are none too bright, making their living as protectors," said Guilin. "But since he's brought up this matter, I really think you ought to give him *something*, no matter how little, just to stop a trivial matter from developing into a real nuisance."

"If I did that, I'd *never* be able to go out and have any fun. A loan here, a loan there—I simply don't *have* that kind of money! I've come across plenty of toughs and hooligans like him in my time, and even if I don't give him a thing, he'll never be able to lay a finger on me! If you're thinking he might bear me a grudge, well, those people who caused all that ruckus here, You Deshou, Yan Xiang, and the rest of them—they were accused by some house or other,[22] and a few days ago they were all arrested by order of the prefect and given a hundred strokes with the light bamboo. Right now they're on public display in the Parade, locked in the big cangue. I'd cool down a bit, if I were him, or he may be in for a nasty surprise."

"If you don't have any money for him, why didn't you tell him so to his face?"

"I was afraid he mightn't take it too well, so I fudged the issue, but he's bound to come and ask you about it tomorrow. Just give him my apologies

and tell him I said that I don't have any money right now and that I can't lay
my hands on any, either."

"How *very* clever of you! Leaving your dirty work to me."

"But you're not the one he's trying to get the loan out of! All you have to
do is tell him what I just told you."

When Wu Gengyu visits her, Guilin, evidently trying to be even-handed, tells
him everything Wu Zhen has said, not merely the message she has been asked
to deliver, and Wu Gengyu is predictably furious.

The prefect's crackdown on opium smoking gives him his chance to get
even. (The cyclical date given a little later in the novel corresponds to 1839, a
year of drastic government measures against opium use.) With the aid of a couple of constables, Wu Gengyu plans to catch Wu Zhen as he satisfies his daily
habit in Guilin's room. The intention is not to send him to jail, merely to ex-
tract a hefty bribe. To arouse the constables' interest, Gengyu has told them
that Wu Zhen not only works at the customs, which is a lucrative job, but also
comes from a rich family. (In fact, he holds only a minor job and is alienated
from his family.) Wu Zhen is encouraged to light his pipe and is then arrested, after which negotiations are carried on in the brothel with Wu Gengyu as
mediator. To apply extra pressure, the constables have also arrested Guilin and
Qiang, the brothel's owner. Their adviser comes rushing up and, after promising the constables a large sum of money, manages to get both Guilin and
Qiang off. Wu Zhen, however, cannot, or rather will not, offer a large enough
sum. He is clapped in jail and held in irons. Worse still, he has no chance to
appease his craving for opium.

When Yuan You hears what has happened, he is appalled at Wu Zhen's
naïveté: "That sort of thing should *never* be allowed to go to court!" (23.164).
Gradually he succeeds in getting his friend's irons removed and some opium
brought into the jail. His first step is to see the jailer, who allows him to visit
Wu Zhen in prison. Wu tells him it is no use approaching his relatives, but his
wife has money she will contribute. Yuan invites the jailer to a teahouse to discuss the cost of removing the irons, which are gradually killing Wu Zhen, but
the jailer cannot take the responsibility himself; he will have to get the approval
of his superior, whom he now fetches. More tea is poured, and the question is
put again. It turns out that everyone in the prison will have to benefit, to the
tune of at least 300 silver dollars in all. Yuan insists that they are grossly over-
estimating Wu's resources; if he'd had just one hundred on him at the time of
the arrest, he wouldn't even be in prison. The jailer replies that Yuan must be
joking; it isn't often they catch a big fish from the customs, and they are going

to make the most of the opportunity. Yuan quotes the saying: "Your troubles are only as large as the amount of money you happen to possess" (24.167).

The two men settle for 100 dollars, subject to confirmation by their colleagues. As they part, Yuan brings up another matter: how to get some opium into the jail to satisfy Wu Zhen's habit. The jailer takes Yuan to a nearby opium den, where he smokes a pipe himself while Yuan buys some prepared opium to take to Wu.

When Yuan next meets the jailers, their demands have risen, but after much haggling, he gets them to agree to 120, to be handed over in front of the county offices that evening. He goes immediately to see Wu Zhen's wife and tells her that the total cost will come to 180. (Although he doesn't say so, he intends to take a cut, as a sort of broker's fee.) By pawning all of her valuables she manages to raise 100, and says she will borrow the remainder from her relatives. Yuan hands 70 to the jailers that evening and promises to pay the other 50 the next day.

All of this effort has succeeded only in getting the irons off Wu Zhen and maintaining his opium habit. Next comes the attempt to free him, or at least to get him a light sentence. Yuan realizes that it would be useless to accuse the constables of a frame-up, so he offers money to the county clerk, who recommends a limited confession: Wu Zhen should say that he took opium for health reasons and was trying to cut down when he was arrested. Under present conditions, a period of exile is the best that can be hoped for. The clerk drafts the confession for Wu Zhen to sign, and Yuan quietly takes another cut.

I have given only the most general outline of a practice of extortion that is worked out in agonizing detail. The narrative is a cynical but credible commentary on the workings of the lower bureaucracy in a case in which the authorities are trying to overcome a well-entrenched practice by fiat.

Thematic Contradictions

The modern reader's main problem with *Illusion of Romance* is a familiar one with Chinese cautionary fiction: how to relate the body of the novel to the explicit moral theme enunciated in its prologue and epilogue. We cannot necessarily regard the prologue as a proposition that the rest of the work is going to substantiate; it is just as likely, perhaps more likely, to be a mere lead-in to the novel, proceeding from a well-worn theme into fresh, nuanced, sometimes ambivalent material. *Illusion*, however, resists even this kind of explanation. Its prologue is argued vigorously in distinctly individual terms, and in the case of two pairs of lovers in the novel, Yuan You and Shuanglin, Jia Ming and Fenglin, it seems as if the author is deliberately flouting—or at least testing to the breaking point—the very strictures he himself has delivered.

Other cases fit the strictures well enough. Lu Shu is the sort of infatuated young man who ruins himself on account of a rapacious courtesan. Wu Zhen suffers a disaster he would not have had to face except in a brothel; we do not know where he acquired his addiction, but we do know that his arrest and exile are caused by the greed and spite of his paramour's protector. Nothing much happens to Wei Bi, except that he is cheated of a hundred taels, a sum he can easily afford. But Yuan You and Jia Ming and their paramours, whose stories are the last to come to a head, are exceptions. Let me deal with Yuan You and Shuanglin first, as the less problematical case.

Shuanglin is the character to whose thoughts we have the most direct access. She is better educated than any of the other courtesans; in fact, she is fully capable of competing with her clients at their literary games. At one point her lover, Yuan You, the ill-educated descendant of a family of office holders, asks her to teach him how to write poetry. As she prepares to commit suicide—Yuan You is on his deathbed—she puts her talents to use in composing a prose testament and a long valedictory poem. She is also the one character who is given an extended interior monologue (in chapter 20), as she reviews her life and considers her probable future if she fails to leave the brothel.

Shuanglin is also the character who most clearly contradicts the portrait of the courtesan given in the prologue. She marries Yuan You instead of eloping with someone else; she hands him her own money to invest; she tends him faithfully during the worst of his illness; she wins the approval of his parents, and she at least tries to do the same with his wife, a classic termagant. Finally, she poisons herself just as her husband dies. The morality of her actions is the subject of the street debate I have mentioned.

However, hers is hardly the simple story of a virtuous prostitute. After sleeping with Yuan You, she has an ominous dream and goes to a temple to draw a divination slip, which she misinterprets to mean she is destined to marry him. To test his commitment, she disingenuously urges him to go back to his wife, with whom he has quarreled. Yuan You buys Shuanglin from her uncle, using the balance of the money he has gathered on behalf of his friend Wu Zhen, but their happiness is not fated to last very long.

On his deathbed Yuan You offers Shuanglin his outstanding loans, some of them made with her money, and urges her to find a young husband. Instead she dresses in her finest clothes, writes her testament and valedictory poem, then mixes raw opium with wine and lies down beside him. Discovered in a comatose state, she revives sufficiently to spit out the antidote she has been given. His parents are deeply moved by her actions, a contemporary poet writes a long poem in her praise, and she is duly honored by the state.

As her funeral procession winds its way along the street, a debate springs up among the bystanders (32.228). In effect, the author is handing over the moral interpretation of her actions to the people in the street. One of them pities her for her martyrdom and her poetic talent. A second agrees, reserving a special condemnation for Yuan You's wife, who in her fury has dishonored Shuanglin's corpse. A third blames the brothel (and by implication Shuanglin) for breaking up Yuan You's marriage, as a result of which he has died without an heir. A fourth acknowledges the danger of the brothels, but still suggests that Shuanglin has behaved nobly. A fifth will not accept even this formulation; if Yuan You had not set up house with her, he would not have worn himself out and died.

The story of Jia Ming and Fenglin does not end as nobly. Their relationship is too complex to describe here, but it repeats, over and over again, this general pattern: she seeks to become his concubine, putting the question to him more and more directly in different ways, while he continually ducks the issue. He lacks the money, apparently, to buy her from her husband, but he also seems unwilling to commit himself, particularly to a woman with a swarm of relatives. When the brothels close, however, he does take her as his mistress. She nurses him faithfully when he is ill, performing, like Shuanglin, the duties that his wife shrinks from. (Unlike Shuanglin, she has succeeded in ingratiating herself with the wife.) But whenever she suggests marriage, he demurs.

After one illness, Jia Ming is so grateful for Fenglin's nursing that he writes her some poems, one of which speaks of marriage in the next life. She asks him to have the poems framed so that she can hang them on her wall, but he is so embarrassed people might see them that he downplays their seriousness.

When the brothel has to close, she tells Jia Ming that, if she had only known about the closing, she would have accepted an offer she received a few days before (25.178). Someone had invited her to move to Shanghai and mentioned a loan of forty silver dollars. Jia asks her why she didn't take it. She could have given twenty to her relatives and spent the other twenty on clothes and travel. Business in Shanghai would probably have been better than in Yangzhou, and she could have made some money there before coming back. She gives several reasons for not doing so. First, she couldn't bear to leave him. Second, she might not have succeeded and, were she unable to repay the loan, she would have found herself "sold to Shanghai." Anyway, her creditors probably wouldn't have let her leave.

Jia Ming will not accept the first reason, dismissing it as mere flattery. But in the end he rather grudgingly agrees to make her his mistress. We are told that he is glad at the thought that she wants to marry him, but he never tells her so. He provides an expensive antidote for her opium addiction, but she only pretends to take it, while surreptitiously continuing to smoke. Anyway, the crackdown soon ends, and she is able to smoke freely again. Once established in her own house, Fenglin is visited by a series of relatives, and Jia Ming silently but reproachfully endures the additional expenditure. When her sister-in-law, a prostitute, flirts with him, he is not above responding to her overtures.

Compare the episode of the Shanghai offer with that of their breakup. In chapter 29, Fenglin, who has not performed as a courtesan since becoming Jia Ming's mistress, suddenly receives an invitation to sing for a visiting official from Beijing. At first she declines, but Jia intervenes and urges her to accept. It will provide them with money for opium, he says, and more or less pushes her into going. She returns with a ten-ounce ingot of silver, and they smoke together.

"There's something funny I want to tell you," she says, after describing the evening. "He simply adores my feet and wants to marry me!" Jia assumes she is not serious, but the next day a second invitation arrives, and this time she returns even later at night and tells him: "This Mr. Lu really does want to marry me and is prepared to pay whatever it costs to buy me out. So I'm here to talk it over with you. What do you think, should I go or not?"

Jia Ming was silent for some time while he thought about it.

"Suppose I tried to talk you out of it," he said at last. "You don't have too many clients in Yangzhou these days; in fact I'm the only one. I'm a good ten years older than you are, and I have a wife and children and can't afford to marry you. I'm not a rich man by any means—all this is superficial, just for show. If I persuaded you to stay and you did well here, there wouldn't be any problem, but if you didn't succeed and ended up worse off than you are now, you'd be sure to blame me and say, 'Oh, I had this marvelous opportunity, but that Jia fellow stood in my way and wouldn't let me go, and that's what got me into this wretched state.' On the other hand, let's suppose I encouraged you to accept. Well, in the first place the man comes from Shandong and serves in the capital, where living conditions are nowhere near as good as they are here in the south. You've lived on West Bank in Qingjiang, so you know what I mean. Moreover, you're a smoker and he's not. He has this sudden urge to take you back with him, but there's no knowing whether he'll let you go on smoking. And there's one other thing. You told me yesterday that he married off a concubine of his to a tailor, even after the woman had borne him a son who got appointed to the Academy. That shows the sort of man *he* is! Look, I'm greatly obliged to you for bringing this problem to me, but I really can't settle it for you. You'll just have to work it out for yourself. If you can't, you can always go off to a temple, burn a little incense, get a divination slip, and ask the Bodhisattva what's best for you." (29.203–204)

Without further discussion, Fenglin arranges to marry the official.

Jia now regrets urging her to sing. Under his breath he condemns her for her heartlessness:

When I first met her, she was wearing *bronze* earrings! Just think what I did for that woman! And when opium was banned and the brothels closed and she had nowhere to go, think how pitifully she pleaded with me! And how I found her a house and furnished it for her, taking care of everything down to the last detail! But now that she has a home of her own and doesn't need to worry about the daily necessities, she's constantly hounding me about marriage. My trouble is that just now I can't come up with the full sum for her husband. I really regret encouraging her to accept that invitation the other day. She's only just met this fellow Lu, and already she's after his money, completely forgetting the two or three years we've spent together and all the vows we've taken. How close we've been! And now she wants to go and marry *him*! I never imagined, when I wrote those poems for her the other day, that the lines "And if our hearts are truly loving now, \ Let's hope that in the next life we'll be wed" would turn out to be so prophetic! But now I understand—as a general rule, *all* courtesans are hypocrites, no matter how sweet their words are. But if I utter the slightest criticism of her and the news gets out, people will only say that I'm sore because she's marrying someone else after I've spent a lot of money on her. (29.205)

At a private farewell dinner Jia Ming and Fenglin exchange songs. Hers is a pledge to join him in the next life, his a bitter reproach. She tells him she is using her new husband's money to release her from her family obligations, and that she hopes eventually to return to Yangzhou and take up with him again. He scoffs at the idea; she should plan to spend the rest of her life with her new husband. But he can't help worrying about her opium habit. How will she cope on the way to Beijing? He advises her to prepare some opium in advance. They smoke a final pipe together and then go to bed, where neither sleeps.

Next morning she simply says good-bye to her mother-in-law and steps into the sedan chair without a glance at anyone else. At this point Jia Ming's bitterness overflows, and he turns to the others present, who all have tears in their eyes. "*She* isn't crying, so why should you? Just think of her as if she'd dropped dead" (29.207). Fenglin pretends she hasn't heard.

We hear no more of her, but we do learn of his reactions, especially his self-pity—while steadily denying that she means anything to him. At the Mid-Autumn Festival, he writes a traditional poem about her that Yuan You, who is no critic, praises as "fresh and new in its diction, revealing your idealistic love and her treachery. Marvelous! But brother, since she's acted in such bad faith, you really don't need to go on pining for her" (30.212). Unconvincingly, Jia Ming now downplays his feelings; he doesn't normally think of her, he says, but the other evening she just happened to pop into his mind and he wrote this poem as a *jeu d'esprit*.

The case of Jia Ming and Fenglin almost fits one of the warnings of the prologue chapter: that the courtesan, after promising to marry one client, will wait until he has bought her out and then elope with someone else. But it does not quite fit, because Jia has not bought Fenglin from her husband; he has merely set her up in a house that he has borrowed from relatives. He has furnished it and provided a couple of maids, and has remained patient while her relatives visited and were given presents. He tolerates, then appreciates, her decision to buy a little girl who will one day, presumably, be put to work as a courtesan herself. But Jia still falls short of the prologue's stereotype. Furthermore, although he tells Yuan You that he is only waiting until he has enough money to marry Fenglin, he has never told her this, but remained noncommittal in the face of her suggestions. The reader is entitled to believe that, if he had once declared his firm intention to marry her or even expressed the wish that she stay with him, she would not have left.

In considering the relationship of prologue and epilogue to the rest of the novel, we should note that the moral stance the author takes in the prologue was virtually the only one he *could* take. (*Haishang hua liezhuan* adopts the same position in its prologue, but so briefly that most readers probably fail to notice it.) The author cannot call for the closing of the brothels—he doubts they can ever be eliminated. Nor can he appeal to the courtesans, who are not free agents, or their families, who are beyond redemption. But with perfect plausibility he can lecture the young men of the city and shower them with warnings—even if the rest of the novel complicates, conditions, and even belies his message.

The relationship between prologue and fictional narrative can best be looked at from the aspect of genre. The Chinese cautionary novel is a complex form that may incorporate a polemical essay (the prologue) along with the narrative, and both tend to obey their own generic imperatives. In this case the essay does so to the full, making its points vividly and uncompromisingly while striving for the maximum rhetorical effect. Such an essay has no place for the ambiguity of moral judgment, the subtle interplay of desire, ethic, and action that we recognize as constituting a major strain of fiction, one of which the rest of *Illusion of Romance* is an outstanding example.

NOTES

1. Literally, fiction about prostitution.
2. See "Zhongguo xiaoshuo de lishi de bianqian." It was first published in 1925; see the annotated version appended to Lu Xun, *Zhongguo xiaoshuo shilüe* (reprint, Beijing: Renmin wenxue chubanshe, 1979), 452–53. The *Zhongguo xiaoshuo shilüe* itself makes the same distinctions, but less explicitly.
3. For example, Zou Tao's *Haishang chentian ying* (Wang Tao's preface dated 1896), which undoubtedly belongs to Lu Xun's first type, contains several references to *Pin hua baojian* and *Hua yue hen*, but none to either *Fengyue meng* or *Haishang hua liezhuan*. Zou also wrote the preface to the first (1878) edition of *Qinglou meng*, in which he appears as one of the characters.
4. In addition to the 1883 movable-type Shenbaoguan edition, there are two early block print editions: an 1884 Shanghai edition and an 1886 edition, both of which appear to derive, directly or indirectly, from the Shenbaoguan. References here are to the edition by Beijing daxue chubanshe (Beijing, 1990). The only annotated edition is the one edited by Wang Junnian in *Xiaoshuo erjuan*, Zhongguo jindai wenxue zuopin xilie series (Fuzhou: Haixia wenyi chubanshe, 1990). It has a short but excellent introduction, which points out that Lu Xun's notion of historical stages is invalid. The same point is made independently by Tao Muning in his *Qinglou wenxue yu Zhongguo wenhua* (Beijing: Dongfang chubanshe, 1993), 216–17.
5. See *Guanglingqu zhi*, Zhongguo renmin gongheguo difangzhi congshu reprint (Beijing: Zhonghua shuju, 1993), 569. One of the society's anthologies is reprinted in Gao Boyu et al., eds., *Zhonghua mishu jicheng* (Beijing: Renmin ribao chubanshe, 1991), 1:367–423. The formula used in the novel known as "Zhaoyangge" was a specialty of the Yangzhou riddle society.
6. Some of these same features would also apply to Sun Jiazhen's *Haishang fanhua meng* (Dream of the fleshpots of Shanghai), which suggests that *Illusion of Romance* may also have influenced that novel. The point is made by Wang Junnian, *Xiaoshuo sanjuan*, Zhongguo jindai wenxue zuopin xilie series (Fuzhou: Haixia wenyi chubanshe, 1991), 157.
7. The 1900 lithographic edition, entitled *Mengyou Shanghai mingji zheng feng zhuan*, is still in existence. It has been reprinted under a number of different titles, e.g.,

Shanghai mingji zhuan, Zhongguo lidai jinshu xuancong series (Hefei: Huangshan chubanshe, 1993).

8. Obvious puns lie behind some of the names in the book; for example, Wu Zhen is "without truth," Jia Ming is "false name."

9. From his poem entitled "Qian huai." See Feng Jiwu, ed., *Fanchuan shiji* (Beijing: Zhonghua shuju, 1962), 369.

10. References are to the edition edited by Zhou Guangpei (Yangzhou: Jiangsu Guangling guji keyinshe, 1984).

11. Chap. 5, page 30. The ruin is attested to by Ruan Yuan; see his (1839) colophon to Li Dou, *Yangzhou huafanglu*, 7–8.

12. See the edition in Xia Youlan et al., ed., *Yangzhou zhuzhici* (Yangzhou: privately published, 1992). A fifth bamboo branch song, described as from a collection entitled *Yangzhou hushang zhuzhici* (Bamboo branch songs on the lake at Yangzhou), is also quoted (5.30).

13. See Yan Duanshu et al., ed., *Xuzuan Yangzhoufu zhi* (1874), 3.7b.

14. For a photographic copy of an 1867 manuscript similar to the 1821 edition, see the Guben xiaoshuo jicheng series (Shanghai: Shanghai guji chubanshe, 1990).

15. On loan sharking in China in the early nineteenth century, see Li Longqian, *Ming Qing jingjishi* (Guangzhou: Guangdong gaodeng jiaoyu chubanshe, 1988), 519–21.

16. See Caiyu Daoren (pseud.), *Jigua canzhui* 6.17a–18a. The author's preface is dated 1872.

17. Li Daoying et al., eds., *Qingfeng zha* (Beijing: Beijing shifan daxue chubanshe, 1992). Based on an 1874 edition, it has been collated with the 1819 edition.

18. See Wei Ren and Wei Minghua, *Yangzhou quyi shihua* (Beijing: Zhongguo quyi chubanshe, 1985), 49–53.

19. The elaborate description of clothing is noted by Wang Junnian, *Xiaoshuo erjuan*, 9.

20. I.e., opium.

21. On the subject of opium in the fiction of the nineteenth and early twentieth centuries, including much reference to this novel, see Keith McMahon, *The Fall of the God of Money* (Lanham, Md.: Rowan and Littlefield, 2002), 139–73.

22. The prologue notes that if a courtesan has formed a liaison with an official or staff adviser, she can lodge a "pillow accusation" against the people who are oppressing her. That is presumably what has happened in this case.

CHAPTER 3

The Missionary Novels of Nineteenth-Century China

"In the form of a novel," "after the style of a Chinese novel"
—Alexander Wylie, commenting on two works
by Karl Gützlaff published in 1834

B
Y "MISSIONARY NOVELS" I mean narratives (in the form of novels) that were written in Chinese by Christian missionaries and their assistants. A score of such works, either composed or translated by missionaries, exist; they outnumber the few works of secular fiction that were translated into Chinese in the course of the nineteenth century. Scholarly attention has deservedly been paid to the latter in terms of their influence on the modern Chinese novel, but the missionary novels have been entirely overlooked. In this essay I shall introduce the missionary novel, trace the course of its development, and speculate about what effect it may have had on the Chinese novel.

My account is limited to works by Protestant missionaries simply because the sources are readily available; I do not mean to imply that no such works were written by Catholic missionaries.[1] At least four comprehensive bibliographies of Protestant writings in Chinese were issued during the nineteenth century, and three more in the early years of the twentieth. The earlier bibliographies are: Alexander Wylie's *Memorials of Protestant Missionaries to the Chinese, Giving a List of Their Publications, and Obituary Notices of the Deceased, with Copious Indexes* of 1867; two catalogues of the Chinese books, mainly Christian literature, that were displayed at the international exhibitions held in Philadelphia in 1876 and in London in 1884;[2] and John Murdoch's *Report on Christian Literature in China, with a Catalogue of Publications* of 1882.[3] The later bibliographies include two by Donald MacGillivray published in 1902 and 1907,[4] and George A. Clayton's *Jidu shengjiao chuban geshu shumu huizuan* of 1918.[5]

It should be kept in mind that the authors or translators of these novels—the missionaries themselves or their family members—were in most cases helped by Chinese assistants, variously described as assistant pastors, teachers, pundits, or senior evangelists. The work of composition or translation was normally a tandem process, with the author or translator giving an oral version of the text and the assistant writing it down. The latter was no mere scribe, however, but more of a collaborator, correcting mistakes and rendering the oral version into acceptable literary form. A frequent complaint among the missionaries was that their assistants, men schooled in the difficult prose of the examination essay, could not bring themselves to write a simple enough Chinese.

The missionary Griffith John, in describing the varied work expected of the assistant, or pundit, as he called him, explained that most missionaries left the actual writing to their pundits.

> When they [the missionaries] want to publish, they convey to the pundit the substance *viva voce*, which he puts into good, idiomatic Chinese. Though the missionary may not be able to *compose* himself, he ought to be able to form a critical judgment, on the composition of his pundit. This power is acquired in course of time in connection with extensive reading, and it is all that is necessary in order to turn out productions of incomparably greater value than the missionary can ever hope to turn out by his own unaided ability.[6]

Two general questions need to be answered before the missionary novel can be considered in the context of nineteenth-century literature. First, can this kind of text, which might equally well be described as a narrative tract, really be taken as either a traditional Chinese novel or a Chinese version of a western novel? I believe it can. The novels I shall describe are generally in the vernacular (Mandarin or a regional dialect) in hopes of reaching a wider readership; they are divided into chapters, often called *hui*; and they employ the narrative methods of either the traditional novel or pre-modern western fiction. Some of the missionary authors, for example Karl Gützlaff and James Legge, affirm that they are writing in the form of the traditional novel, even as they make clear—like many a Chinese novelist before them—that the content of their work is to be sharply distinguished from that of the typical novel. In his *Memorials* Alexander Wylie describes two of Gützlaff's works as novels. Of *Shu zui zhi dao zhuan* (The doctrine of redemption), published in 1834, he remarks: "In this the author has aimed at a narrative illustration of the great leading doctrine of the gospel; the work being written in the form of a novel, in 21 chapters, with a preface and an appendix" (56). Of *Chang huo zhi dao zhuan*

(The doctrine of eternal life), published in the same year, Wylie writes: "This is also written after the style of a Chinese novel, in which the author endeavors to inculcate Christian principles by a personal narrative, in 6 chapters, with a short preface" (56). Finally, the earliest of the missionary novels, William Milne's *Zhang Yuan liang you xiang lun* (Dialogues between the two friends Zhang and Yuan), has been included in two recent bibliographies of Chinese fiction.[7]

The second question concerns the circulation of the missionary novel. Was it confined to the relatively small circles of Christian converts and hence of no significance in the general context of Chinese literature? No. Tracts, at first given away free and later sold cheaply through an elaborate network of colporteurs as well as through bookstores, were the main proselytizing instrument in the nineteenth century, and missionaries, particularly in the early period, compiled scores of works in Chinese; in Wylie's *Memorials*, Gützlaff is credited with no fewer than 61 titles, many of them substantial works, and Walter Henry Medhurst with 59. A good indicator of wide circulation is the pioneer novel by Milne that I have just mentioned; it was probably the most frequently reprinted Chinese novel *of any kind* during the century. After initial publication in Malacca in 1819, it went through as many as thirty editions, admittedly by Christian presses, through 1886, a period that is well documented.[8] And it remained popular thereafter; the *Jidu shengjiao chuban geshu shumu huizuan* cites no fewer than seven separate editions of the book within the previous seven years.[9] There were surely enough copies of such works circulating in China, particularly in the cities, to satisfy the curiosity of any literate person.

It makes sense to treat the course of the missionary novel in terms of its major authors or translators—Milne, Gützlaff, and Legge; then Ferdinand Genähr, William C. Burns, and the other translators; and finally Griffith John—before turning to the question of its significance for Chinese fiction. In this account I shall omit the countless pieces of short fiction and focus instead on the more substantial kind written in chapters.

William Milne (1785–1822)

This onetime shepherd boy from Scotland spent only nine years in Asia before his death, but he was responsible for several innovations. He established the first magazine, *Cha shisu meiyue tongji zhuan* (The Chinese monthly magazine), which ran from 1815 to 1821 in Malacca and was distributed by merchant ship along the Chinese coast. And he wrote the first missionary novel, *Zhang*

Yuan liang you xiang lun (1819), in twelve chapters, creating a fictional framework that allowed his argument to be communicated more effectively.[10] The book recounts twelve meetings between a Christian believer and one of his neighbors, at which the two men discuss the major themes of Christian doctrine. Milne places the dialogues firmly within a narrative context but makes few concessions to the form of the vernacular novel, far fewer than do Gützlaff and Legge. The emphasis is mainly on the neighbor, on his questions, doubts, and emotional reactions to discussions and events.

Although Milne's is the first and most famous of the missionary novels, a fictional framework was also employed by Robert Morrison (1782–1834), the earliest Protestant missionary in China. His *Xiyou diqiu wenjian lüezhuan* (Tour of the world), a geographical primer, appeared in 1819.[11] Told in the first person by a Chinese from Sichuan, it is an account of his travels through Tibet and India to Europe, incorporating essays on astronomy, geography (complete with a map of the world), the calendar, the British court with its limited monarchy, and British customs (no segregation of the sexes, etc.). After several years, the traveler returns via America, is wrecked on the Ryukyus, but manages to reach Guangzhou on a Chinese merchant ship. Morrison's *Gushi Rudiyaguo lidai lüezhuan* (An outline history of Judea), published in 1815, is written in a level vernacular and betrays some features of vernacular fiction, for example, in its addresses to the reader (*kanguan*).[12] These books illustrate the closeness of the early missionaries to the Chinese fictional tradition, a closeness that is most pronounced in the case of Karl Gützlaff.

Karl Gützlaff (1803–1851)

Before Gützlaff began to write his novels, Walter Henry Medhurst (1796–1857) had composed a short work entitled *Xiongdi xutan* (Fraternal dialogues), which he published in 1828 in his *Chi xuan cuo yao* (Monthly magazine). I have not seen it, but Wylie in his *Memorials* describes it as "a series of conversations between two brothers, regarding idolatry and other Chinese practices."[13] Medhurst also translated two short narrative tracts by the British and Foreign Bible Society and published the translations in his magazine.

Karl Gützlaff, or Charles Gutzlaff, as he called himself when writing in English, was born in Prussia and came to Asia under the auspices of the Netherlands Missionary Society, of which he soon declared himself independent.[14] Thereafter he supported himself from the estate of his first wife, an English missionary whom he had met and married in Malacca, and also by occasional grants from the missionary societies. Beginning in 1835 he held a series of appointments with the British government, from 1843 on as Chinese Secretary to the governor of Hong Kong. During all this time he maintained a hectic pace of writing and preaching.

Gützlaff was by far the most colorful and controversial of the nineteenth-century missionaries, the sort of person who attracts strong epithets, not all of which one associates with missionaries. He has been described as opportunistic, ebullient, flamboyant, hyperactive, indestructible, and as having his ambitions fueled by egotism. He has been called an inveterate optimist, a man of fanatical zeal, a visionary, a missionary adventurer, an astute publicist, and, in the most sweeping generalization of all, by Arthur Waley, "a cross between a parson and a pirate, charlatan and genius, philanthropist and crook."[15] Even his physical qualities impressed people. A fellow missionary describes him as "personally short, stout, gross in his tastes and manners, active in his movements, rapid in speech, and cheerful and engrossing in conversation,"[16] while another acquaintance refers to his "great face" and "sinister eye."[17]

Of these characterizations I shall choose two that have some bearing on his fiction writing: his soaring ambition and his talent for publicizing both his work and himself. In 1830, while translating the scriptures in Thailand, he determined to visit China—an illegal and dangerous act at the time.[18] He had become close to the Chinese residents of Bangkok, and claimed to have been adopted into the Guo clan from Tong'an in Fujian. Shortly after his wife died in childbirth, Gützlaff's long-sought opportunity came—the offer of passage on a Chinese merchant ship up the coast of China. Although seriously ill himself, he seized the chance. As his ship waited to clear the harbor, he heard the news of his infant daughter's death.

On the voyage, during which he endeavored to pass himself off as Chinese, he met surprisingly little opposition to his distribution of tracts. News of his exploit created a sensation around the world. In Medhurst's words, it "struck most of our English readers with amazement. It had long been supposed that China was hermetically sealed." But it also aroused controversy. Medhurst continues, "Some people said that Gützlaff was a man of such an ardent temperament, enterprising spirit, and inventive genius, that he might safely venture where others dared not go." Others, however, were more skeptical: "There were not a few, also, who insinuated that his lively imagination, and confident expectation, had led him to give too high a coloring to things."[19] So great was the furor that Elijah Coleman Bridgman, editor of the *Chinese Repository*, in which the account of Gützlaff's voyage was first published, felt obliged both to verify the account and to soothe the feelings of those who could not or would not emulate him: "We may not extol one course of conduct because it is novel and striking, nor undervalue a different one because it is humble."[20]

For his part, Gützlaff exploited the voyage with gusto. After writing a graphic account for the *Chinese Repository,* he published it separately, then combined it with an account of his second voyage, and finally combined it with accounts of both his second and third voyages. In Europe and America he quickly became famous. He followed up his first success with a second voyage on board the *Lord Amherst* at the request of the East India Company. Then he made a third journey on the opium trader *Sylph,* owned by William Jardine, who needed him as an interpreter and shrewdly overcame Gützlaff's scruples by dwelling on the opportunity to further his "grand object" of distributing Christian literature in China.[21] This and subsequent voyages on opium ships occasioned some criticism from his fellow missionaries, but one cannot help feeling that his critics were in much the same position as the soldiers in *Mencius* who, having retreated fifty paces, sneered at those who had retreated one hundred paces.[22] The activities of the Canton missionaries at the time were heavily supported by opium merchants Lancelot Dent and William Jardine.

Gützlaff's self-promotion and his insistence that the Chinese coast was open to Christian proselytizers created a good deal of animosity among the other missionaries, which, being Gützlaff, he did nothing to mitigate. In 1838 he published his *China Opened* in London in two substantial volumes, with the subtitle "A Display of the Topography, History, Customs, Manners, Arts, Jurisprudence, Etc., of the Chinese Empire."[23] In it he said, "Protestant missionaries have been anxious to occupy the outposts, rather than to enter the Chinese empire" (2:238) and also, even more cuttingly, "China is open to Christian heroes and martyrs, but shut against a weak faith and wavering mind" (2:237). The ambiguous title itself seems a trifle brazen; if China was open, there could be little doubt as to who had opened it.

The review of Gützlaff's book in the *Chinese Repository* was written by the young Samuel Wells Williams.[24] He began by noting the celebrity of the author and the *éclat* surrounding him, then proceeded to analyze the title:

The title of the book too, is calculated to attract notice and excite expectation. Mr. Gutzlaff, some time ago published, as a discovery, that China was open; and this he repeated, until many people in western lands believed it; but China still obstinately remaining shut as close as ever to all permanent general intercourse, he has occupied the leisure from the duties of his office by endeavoring so to describe the society and its inhabitants, that they shall be open to the minds of his readers in all their multiform phases.

He went on to criticize the materials as thrown together in a "vague, rambling, helter-skelter style," and also referred darkly to "unblushing plagiarisms." After fifteen pages of unremitting condemnation, he wound up his review as follows: "With this brief notice we dismiss *China Opened.*"

Gützlaff's book was certainly slapdash; it could hardly have been otherwise. From 1834 to 1839, under difficult conditions, he published at least 34 works in Chinese, many of them substantial, including a universal history, a history of Britain, half a dozen novels, a monthly magazine, a universal geography, and a history of Judea, as well as explications of the scriptures. During the same years, he wrote in English a *Sketch of Chinese History* in 900 pages and *China Opened* in 1,080 pages, as well as numerous accounts of his voyages, to say nothing of shorter pieces. Yet, despite its obvious faults, there is much new material in *China Opened,* material that his reviewer was not disposed to see.

What is interesting about Gützlaff's account of his first voyage is his own flamboyant soul-searching. Of his decision to travel to China, he writes:

> I am fully aware that I shall be stigmatized as a head-long enthusiast, an unprincipled rambler, who rashly sallies forth, without waiting for any indications of divine providence, without first seeing the door opened by the hand of the Lord;—as one fond of novelty, anxious to have a name, fickle in his purposes, who leaves a promising field, and restless hurries away to another,—all of whose endeavors will not only prove useless, but will actually impede the progress of the Savior's cause.[25]

He talks vaguely of unnamed accusers and ultimate vindication and then returns to his soul-searching: "Egotism, obtrusive monster!—lurks through these pages."[26] The same theme is echoed in his sermon "Pride and Humility" in the *Chinese Repository* of December 1833: "The fuel of ambition is in our hearts; Satan throws in the spark, and the fire becomes unquenchable."[27] By contrast, of his decision to serve as interpreter on the opium trader *Sylph*, he writes only: "After much consultation with others, and a conflict in my own mind, I embarked in the *Sylph.*"[28]

Gützlaff's self-aggrandizement and furious zeal to spread the gospel are inseparable from his novel writing. In a burst of activity, he published eight works that can be classified as novels, six of them from 1834 through 1838, the other two undated. His interest in fictional settings and techniques is also found in other works. *Cheng chong bai lei han* (Faithful letters), published early in 1834, consists of a series of letters by the eldest son of a Fuzhou family who travels as far as England and writes back to his relatives.[29] Gützlaff was presumably influenced by Morrison's *Tour of the World*, but the letters contain more of moral reflection and exhortation than of geography. An extra flourish is lent by quotations from poems by Li Bai. There is some discussion of Christianity, but it does not dominate the book. His *Sheng shu zhu shu* (Explanation of the scriptures), published in 1839 in five chapters (*hui*), consists of a dialogue between a Chinese father and his sons.[30] It is written in the vernacular and uses various fictional devices. In his work Gützlaff is careful to give all dates in terms of Chinese chronology. His history of Britain, *Da Yingguo tongzhi* (1834), and his history of the world, *Gujin wanguo gangjian* (1838), are hybrid forms, combining fiction with history. The *History of Britain*, in particular, is written in the vernacular and makes some use of the features of traditional fiction. Its central narrative is the story of a man named Ye who travels to London and teaches Chinese there for over twenty years before returning. His adventures are quickly disposed of, and the bulk of the book is devoted to his explanations to neighbors and friends about conditions in Britain. The author-narrator imposes his own comments in the form of a prologue at the head of each chapter. In works such as these Gützlaff sprinkled quotations from the Chinese philosophers, especially the *Mencius* and the *Guan Zi*, as well as from poets like Su Shi. Similar references are found in his *Dong xi yang kao meiyue tongji zhuan* (Eastern western monthly magazine), begun in the middle of 1833, in which he includes numerous short vernacular items written in anecdotal form.

Gützlaff obviously learned from Morrison's use of fictional contexts but also, more significantly, from Milne's *Zhang Yuan liangyou xiang lun*. In March 1829, while in Bangkok, he was visited by a man who "had got hold of Milne's dialogue of chang and yuen, which he had read to some profit."[31] In his account of his third voyage, he discusses the Chinese reception of the Christian literature he distributed:

> The treatise which pleased them most, was a dialogue between *Chang* and *Yuen*, the one a Christian and the other an ignorant heathen. This work of the late much-lamented Dr. Milne, contains very pointed and just remarks, and has always been a favorite book among the Chinese readers.[32]

We do not know when Gützlaff began to read Chinese fiction, possibly as early as 1828 during his first visit to Thailand. *China Opened* has a short section entitled "Works of Fiction" that is concerned mainly with historical fiction.[33] Gützlaff names five historical novels and explains that this is a mere fraction of the total number: "Every great man has his biography, every catastrophe its romancer." He goes on to say, "Though there is much trash among them, there are various excellent productions, which every foreigner, who wishes to write a good Chinese history, ought to read."

As to other kinds of novel, he mentions only the "*Shi-tsae-tsze*," i.e., the *Shi caizi*, which he calls "the lucubrations of the ten talented men, a collection of choice novels." One of the ten, however, "cannot be read without shuddering." I am not sure which novel might have induced the shudder, but perhaps he was referring—inaccurately—to *Jin Ping Mei*, which was generally known at the time as *Diyi qishu* (First of the extraordinary works).

Elsewhere in *China Opened*, which reveals a certain sensitivity to Chinese style, Gützlaff makes clear his preference for simple language: "Amongst the literati of the present day, there exists a strong bias in favor of a phraseology which the vulgar cannot understand."[34] The novel form appealed to Gützlaff as fiction and also because it was written in the vernacular. In an 1834 essay he wrote that Chinese must be written in "an easy, idiomatic and pleasing style, so that while [compositions] afford instruction they may be read with delight."[35]

As early as 1833, while on his third voyage up the coast, Gützlaff was handed what was evidently a text of the *Xiangshan baojuan* by the monks of the Putuo monastery.[36] He describes it as a "Buddhistic novel," commenting that it was written in "an intelligible and even a low style." He saw "The Story of Fragrant Hill," as he calls it, as an example of the use of fiction for religious propaganda.

In September 1838, he began publishing in the *Chinese Repository* a series of detailed accounts of Chinese works, principally historical fiction. He describes seven novels, beginning with *Sanguo zhi tongsu yanyi*, which he praises as "one of the best productions of the Chinese."[37] He also wrote accounts of *Shenxian tongjian* (A general history of the gods and genii), *Da Qing huangdi sheng xun* (Sacred instructions of the emperors of the great Qing dynasty), *Zhinang bu* (A supplementary sack of wisdom), *Liaozhai zhiyi* (Extraordinary legends from Liaozhai), and the complete works of Su Shi. His accounts of the historical novels have a certain value: most of them had never been noted before by foreigners, who focused on romances of the *caizi jiaren* (brilliant and beautiful) type. His account of *Story of the Stone* might also have been quite valuable if he had not grown impatient after struggling through the first few chapters. Being Gützlaff, he did not lay the book aside, but charged ahead—only to bring eternal ridicule upon himself by mistaking the hero's gender ("the lady Pauyu").[38]

As early as 1835, and particularly in his accounts of these works, Gützlaff continually hurls barbs at unnamed "sinologues." In effect, he is distinguishing himself from others as someone who knows the language well and, more important, is familiar with the kinds of literature that people actually read.

There are "whole libraries in Chinese houses, in which no book is ever touched except novels."[39] The *Shenxian tongjian* consists of "a variety of works of fiction, which contain much about the popular creed, and throw more light upon these mysteries, than the most elaborate treatises."[40] The *Nan Song zhizhuan* is "one of the most interesting books we have read," and "the best sinologues may learn from it."[41]

Gützlaff's earliest novel was probably *Shu zui zhi dao* (The doctrine of redemption), in three *juan* and twenty-one *hui*, published in 1834 with preface and postface by the author. He rewrote it in condensed form in two *juan* and eighteen *hui* and published it under the title *Shu zui zhi dao zhuan* in 1836. The two versions are so different they deserve consideration as separate works. The condensed version is preserved in several libraries, but the original version survives only in the British Library, and even that copy is incomplete, consisting of the last two *juan* only. The original has some features of the traditional novel, for example, the poems at the head of each chapter, that are trimmed in the condensed version.

Here, as elsewhere in his novels, Gützlaff writes in an exuberant but awkward style, with an overuse—sometimes a misuse—of traditional narrative devices. For this reason, and because of his occasional mistakes, I am inclined to think that Gützlaff did not rely on a Chinese assistant as the other missionaries did, or at least not to the same extent.

The novel is set wholly in a Chinese context in the Ming dynasty. The characters are at a high social and intellectual level; the hero is a Hanlin scholar who happens to be a Christian. (Later in the nineteenth century, we find heroes of missionary fiction who are at a lower social level.) Much of the content consists of sermons, and there are also translated prayers, hymns, and parts of the Gospels.

Changhuo zhi dao zhuan (The doctrine of eternal life) was probably Gützlaff's second novel. It was published in 1834 in six *hui*, with a preface by Gützlaff dated the summer of that year.[42] Set in the Qing dynasty, it tells of a high official named Li Rui who is greedy, arrogant, and ambitious. A spendthrift abroad, he is a skinflint at home. Unlike those who are content with what God (Shangdi) has provided for them, and who confess their sins and seek salvation through Jesus, he seeks fame and riches—and indulges, moreover, in sexual license. But happiness eludes him, and he is plagued by a constant, uneasy feeling that he has offended God's commandments. Under the instruction of an old man who shows him a book (i.e., *Genesis*) about the creation of Heaven and Earth, he turns from his evil ways, but is still at a loss as to what to do. To relieve his depression, he starts taking opium.

Later, when he finds that prayer has no effect, he becomes afraid. A Buddhist priest visits him, but Li Rui, a staunch Confucian, is unimpressed. At this point, his libertine cronies, disgusted with this new and reformed version of their old friend, turn against him. He is accused of a crime, stripped of his rank, and sentenced to exile. A Christian who is a Hanlin scholar visits him before he leaves.

On the way into exile, he thinks of the statement in *Mencius*—there is no mention in the novel of the source—about Heaven's testing a man before conferring on him great responsibility,[43] and he begins to preach about Jesus to his fellow exiles, to little or no effect. Beaten up, he is comforted by a Christian doctor, who speaks to him of Jesus as the redeemer of sins. He dies in exile.

Li Rui's only son Tianci (Gift of Heaven) was too sick to accompany his father, but the Christian doctor now tells him of his father's conversion and death. Tianci visits his father's grave and, persuaded by the doctor, accepts the faith. Later, in the capital, he joins a group of Christians and is baptized. On his death he goes to Heaven.

Like the other missionaries, Gützlaff tried hard to inculcate in the Chinese the same acute consciousness of sin that he felt in himself. Chinese themes such as filial piety and *baoying* (reward and punishment) are interwoven with Christian doctrines of original sin and eternal life.

In his preface Gützlaff explains why he has written the book in conversational style (*xutan*)—because people are unable to understand the principles of the faith just by reading the Bible. He also strikes a personal note by referring to his first wife Mary Newell, who had died in Bangkok in 1831. She has attained eternal life in Heaven, he writes, and he hopes that his readers will study his book and eventually join her there.

The one novel of Gützlaff's that is not primarily concerned with religious matters is *Shifei lüelun* (A general discussion of right and wrong), published in 1835 in six *hui* without preface or postface.[44] The "right and wrong" of the title refers not to moral issues but to factual truth with regard to the foreign countries' relations with China, particularly those of Great Britain. It is probably no coincidence that this was the year Gützlaff began his service for the British government. The novel is one long plea for China to enter into reciprocal trade relations with other countries. It asserts that foreigners, in particular the British, are neither "red-haired foreign devils" nor barbarians, but that they represent an advanced culture. (One proof that Gützlaff offers: no fewer than ten thousand books are published in Great Britain every year.) Britain does not deserve to be regarded as a tribute country, in terms of either culture or military power. The book's refrain is "Within the four seas, all men are brothers." The aim is to impress the reader with the reasonableness of the foreign merchants' case, and also with the wealth and power, the good government and wholesome mores of the foreign countries. Christianity in Britain is brought up only in the final chapter, along with an account of such matters as education (for girls as well as for boys), language and script, and marriage customs (young people can meet and decide for themselves whether they want to marry). Some emphasis is given to the position of British women; they are able to become authors, and "husbands don't treat their wives as maids."[45]

In addition to the plea for reciprocal trade relations, other matters affecting the foreign merchants are aired in *A General Discussion of Right and Wrong*. It is grossly unfair to exclude from Canton the wives and families of the men who work in the factories there—it offends against the bond between husband and wife that is recognized by Confucianism. The foreigners are also defended against the familiar charge of spying. Since they already have the most elaborate maps imaginable, why would they need to spy?

In imitation of Milne's novel, this one consists mainly of a series of meetings between two men. Chen Zeshan from Guangzhou, who was orphaned as a youth, made his way to London and set up a shop and prospered there. After twenty-five years in London he returns home and engages in a series of arguments with a friend named Li who holds a full set of xenophobic prejudices. Li throws up argument after argument, only to find each one knocked down by Chen's explanations.

Zheng xie bijiao (Orthodoxy and heresy compared) is a short novel in three *hui* that was published in 1838 with a preface by Gützlaff.[46] It concerns three companions and their attempts to understand Christianity. One of them, a Christian, leads a second to the faith through a series of arguments, but fails to convince the third. (The work bears some resemblance to Milne's.) The main question is whether Christianity is to be judged as orthodox (*zheng*) or heretical (*xie*).

Huimo xundao (Persuasion and instruction) is another short novel of three *hui* that was published in 1838.[47] Set in the Qing, it concerns a Suzhou merchant who moves to Shanghai for business reasons. He is self-centered, avaricious, and litigious, and cannot change his ways despite counseling from a Christian friend. After his death his ample property is divided among his three sons, who proceed to debauch themselves in various ways. The friend urges them to reform, and he succeeds with the eldest, who dies at peace with himself, hoping for eternal life. By contrast, the second son dies of syphilis. With the third son the friend is again successful; the young man repents his sins and eventually becomes a Christian.

Xiaoxin xiaofu (Little faith, little happiness) is a short novel that I have not seen.[48] Wylie describes it as: "A narrative tract in three books, chiefly dialogue, illustrative of the doctrine of faith. The scene is laid in Soo-chow and Hang-chow, and the time is the Yuen dynasty. It has a short preface."[49]

Hui zui zhi dalüe (A treatise on repentance) is an undated novel in four *juan* with a preface explaining the author's motivation: he wrote it because he found that most biographies do not give due importance to the subject of repentance.[50] The work qualifies as the earliest novel in Chinese with a first-person narrator. (Scholars usually accord that distinction to Wu Jianren's *Ershinian mudu zhi guai xianzhuang* [Strange things observed over the past twenty years], which began publication in 1903.) This novel opens with an "I" who falls asleep and dreams, which suggests the influence of *Pilgrim's Progress,* but the dreamer turns out to be both the hero and the narrator of the book. In his dream a shepherd explains to him the meaning of the bridge before his eyes; it symbolizes human life, and the dreamer has to cross it before entering paradise.

The narrator's surname is Guo, and he comes from Quanzhou prefecture. Guo was Gützlaff's Chinese surname, and his adoptive family came from Tong'an in Quanzhou prefecture. It seems clear that the dreamer-narrator is a Chinese persona of Gützlaff.

Guo has a number of encounters, one with a man who, in his desire to get into Heaven, has put his faith in Buddhism. The narrator explains that entry into Heaven cannot be bought, and that in any case Buddhism is of no help. There is also a gifted student and writer who has committed murder for gain. No one suspects him of the crime, but God sees all, and the student suffers constant pangs of guilt, the image of his victim always present before his eyes. Curiously, he is also surnamed Guo. He may represent the young Gützlaff, burdened with a consciousness of sin that could only be expiated through Christianity.

Gützlaff turned to fiction writing more often than any of the other missionaries,[51] but it cannot be said that he reached the widest audience. I have not heard of any second editions of his novels, and by the end of the century, all of his writings were out of print. The general reasons are obvious enough: he wrote at too great a speed and with too little care, risking incoherence.[52] His own abilities in Chinese, though extraordinary, were simply not equal to the task of appealing to the highly literate readers he sought.

James Legge (1815–1897)

Legge translated a Chinese novel before he ever attempted to write one. He arrived in Malacca in 1840 and before long was appointed principal of the Anglo-Chinese College. By the middle of 1842 he had formulated his grand design of bringing out an edition of the Four Books and Five Classics ("the Gospels, as they have been called, and the Pentateuch of China"), equipped with translation and notes "which might serve as a standard work to the foreign student of Chinese literature, and lay open to the general reader the philosophy, religion and morals of that singular people." He asked his most capable student, He Jinshan (variously transcribed as Tkin Shen, Ho-tsun-sheen, and Ho Tsun Shin) to start translating, of all things, the *Shu jing* (Classic of documents). It soon appeared that a work

> so obscure and elliptical demanded a greater mastery of the English language than he (the translator) was possessed of. As a preliminary exercise, therefore, I put "Ching Tih's Rambles" into his hands, and, finding, as the translation proceeded, that the work increased in interest, I resolved, as I could find leisure, to revise his version, as well for my own improvement in the Chinese language as in the hope that it would prove both acceptable and useful in the public.

This passage (and the previous passages quoted) come from Legge's preface to his translation of the novel *Da Ming Zhengde Huang you Jiangnan zhuan* (A tale of the travels through Jiangnan of the Zhengde Emperor of the great Ming dynasty), a work in forty-five chapters by He Mengmei of Guangdong that carries an author's preface of 1832.[53] The novel tells of the young emperor's traveling incognito to the Jiangnan area, particularly Suzhou, in the course of which he discovers the true state of corruption and sedition among his closest advisers and also meets two beautiful women, whom he proceeds to add to his harem. Legge goes on in his preface to defend the novel as "founded on fact as much as most European historical novels," and claims that the translation will convey "a more accurate idea of the Court of China, and the position of its Emperor, than it is possible to obtain from works of more pretension and greater merit."

He describes the translation as faithful, although "Chinese scholars may differ perhaps in their reading of two or three of the stanzas to the several chapters,—as indeed the translator differed from himself at different times; but Chinese poetry is confessedly obscure, and several teachers have been consulted in every case of doubt."

This may well be the most faithful and complete translation of a Chinese novel up to that time, but Legge's remark about the poems is a trifle disingenuous. The poem before chapter 26 echoes Robert Burns, while that before chapter 21 reveals in the sober-sided missionary a schoolboyish streak of humor. It begins:

Learning how pleasant 'twas for one through Keäng Nan's fields to jog,
The gamesome prince his servant begs, and follows him incog.

The translation was published in London in 1843 under the title *The Rambles of the Emperor Ching Tih in Keäng Nan, a Chinese Tale.* Legge's preface is dated June 16 of that year, at Malacca. In his choice of a novel he was clearly influenced by Gützlaff, who in the *Chinese Repository* of June 1840 had published a full account of the work, translating the title in just this way.

Legge put his knowledge of the traditional novel to use in writing lives of two biblical figures. Previously, such lives had been told in a simple literary Chinese with no suggestion of fiction; usually they were given the title *yanxinglu* (record of words and deeds), an established biographical form. Gützlaff, for example, had written *yanxinglu* of Moses (1836), Daniel (1837), Paul (1837), John (1837), Peter (1838), and Joseph (n.d.). Perhaps he thought the form more suitable for the lives of such venerable figures. Legge, however, composed novel-style lives of Joseph in six chapters (*Yuese jilüe*, preface dated 1852) and Abraham in four chapters (*Yabolahan jilüe*, preface dated 1857).[54] Except for the dates, both works share the same Chinese preface, which expresses concern that readers may regard the content of the narratives as mere fiction (*xiaoshuo*): "This narrative, although it resembles fiction in form, is really not to be classed as fiction." The content is from the Bible, he explains, and he is using the form of fiction only because the Bible is so complex that it puts people to sleep.

In both narratives he is careful to use Chinese chronology, putting Joseph in the Shang dynasty and Abraham in the Xia. His chapters end on the familiar anticipatory note: for example, "If you are wondering where Joseph was, you must turn to the next chapter to find out." There are also critiques (*ping*) at the end of each chapter; one comment at the end of chapter 2 of *Joseph* explains that "in olden times men took precedence over women, but Joseph was an exception."

In obvious imitation of Legge, George Piercy, an English missionary stationed in Guangzhou, composed a life of Elijah (*Yiliya jilüe*) in six chapters.[55] His preface borrows heavily from Legge's.

Ferdinand Genähr (d. 1864), William C. Burns (1815–1868), and Other Translators

The first translated novel in Chinese[56] was, it seems, the *Jinwu xingyi* (A model of a golden house), either from Hermann Ball's *Thirza, oder die Anziehungs-*

kraft des Kreuzes or Elizabeth Maria Lloyd's English translation, *Thirza; or, the Attractive Power of the Cross*, published in 1842.[57] The novel tells of the conversion of a Jewish girl to Christianity. It divides the text into three unnumbered chapters and supplies a full array of traditional Chinese narrative devices. The translation was done by Ferdinand Genähr, a protégé of Gützlaff's who was working in Guangdong province, and published in 1852.

The most notable translation was William Burns's version of *Pilgrim's Progress, Tianlu licheng*. He translated part 1 into a simple literary style and published it in 1853 and then, while in Beijing, turned it into Mandarin and published that translation in 1865. He followed with part 2 in 1866. This was not the first translation of *Pilgrim's Progress* into Chinese, but it was the first complete one, and by common consent the best. Burns's journal tells of finishing part 1:

> I was enabled to complete the last revised copy of Bunyan's *Pilgrim* (first part) in Chinese, which has occupied us from June 1, 1852, until now, with the exception of a month at the end of last summer, when through feverish sickness I was obliged to lay it aside. The whole has been looked over by Messrs. Doty and A. Stronach [fellow missionaries in Xiamen] with their teachers, and the work has been benefited by a number of their suggestions. One hour after finishing the last sheet in the form in which it will be printed, I received from Shanghai a copy of the *Pilgrim* in Chinese, printed two years ago by Mr. Muirhead of the London Society, chiefly for the use of pupils. It is not, however, a continuous translation of the whole.[58]

One can almost hear the sigh of relief in the last sentence.

Unlike Genähr, Burns uses few features of traditional fiction, the chief exception being the occasional poem emphasizing a point. At times he departs quite far from Bunyan's text, and in part 2 he expressly makes additions designed to "increase the usefulness of the work to native women by showing the principles that should rule in a Christian marriage."[59]

Other translations of novel-length narratives from the 1850s through the 1880s are generally of well-known fiction and published by the various tract societies. Some works were translated several times. There was also much secondary translation among literary, Mandarin, and dialect versions. The typical translator was a missionary's wife serving as principal of the mission school.

Significant changes are apparent between the early works of Milne and Gützlaff and these later ones. The former were aimed at adults, even highly educated adults, and they are full of argument and persuasion. The latter are generally about children, and instead of offering argument and persuasion they tell of children's noble suffering, bravery, and piety.

Narrative methods also changed. The earlier novelists tended to imitate the form of the traditional novel and even to use Chinese chronology, but from the 1850s, their successors made less and less attempt to simulate the Chinese novel—their translations, in short, become "straight" rather than genre translations. Perhaps by this time the translators thought their readership was familiar enough with foreign methods of narration.

The earliest translation of a narrative tract was probably that by Samuel Kidd in 1829 of *Le Pauvre Horloger de Genève* by César Malan (1787–1864).[60] A revision by Justus Doolittle was published in 1855 in six chapters plus prologue.[61] The most famous narrative tract translated into Chinese was undoubtedly *Little Henry and His Bearer,* by the prolific author of moral tales suffused with evangelical fervor, Mary Martha Sherwood (1775–1851). First published in 1814, it is said to have gone through one hundred editions in the next seventy years. In China, Caroline P. Keith began translating it into Shanghai dialect in November 1852, according to one of her letters: "I have just commenced, with one of the oldest pupils, the translation of 'Henry and His Bearer.'"[62] Her translation was published in 1856 under the title *Hengli shilu,* and it was followed by a Mandarin version by Henry Blodget in 1865 under the same title.[63] Later it was translated into several dialects.

The tract *Seppili the Swiss Boy* was translated into Ningpo dialect in 1861, into Shanghai dialect (both character and romanized versions) in 1868, and then into Mandarin in 1873 (translated by Helen Nevius as *Haitong gushi*).[64] *Jessica's First Prayer* (1867), the best known story by Hesba Stretton (pseudonym of Sarah Smith, 1832–1911) was translated by Adelia M. Payson in 1878 into Fuzhou dialect as *Pin nü Leshijia.*[65]

Mary Harriet Porter, sister of Henry Dwight Porter, translated at least four works. In 1875 she published a translation of *Parley the Porter,* an 1810 allegory by Hannah More (1745–1833), under the title *Liang ke yu yan.*[66] She also published another allegory called *Chu ba zhuan,*[67] probably a translation of Charlotte Maria Tucker's *The Giant Killer; or the Battle which All must Fight* (1856). In 1882 she published a translation of the famous *Christie's Old Organ, or "Home Sweet Home"* by Catherine Augusta Walton under the title *Anle jia,*[68] a work that was first published only in 1875.

Also in 1882, Porter published a more interesting translation, that of *The Cottage on the Shore, or Little Gwen's Story,* in thirteen chapters under the title *Guinuo zhuan.*[69] It is interesting partly because the original novel is somewhat removed from the extreme piety of the other works, but chiefly because it is told in the heroine's (the orphan Gwen's) own words. Only at the end of the novel do we realize that she has been dictating her story to a mentor, who has been writing it down. The original work begins: "I live, when I am at home, in a little turf cottage built on the seashore." The Chinese follows this faithfully, but feels compelled to prefix it with the equivalent of the words "Gwen Evans says."

Griffith John (1831–1912)

Few original works were written after the time of Gützlaff and Legge. Martha Crawford wrote *Sange guinü* (Three maidens), a simple story about three Chinese schoolgirls, and published it first in a romanized form of the Shanghai dialect in 1856, then in Mandarin in 1872.[70] The only considerable new novel I have seen is Griffith John's *Yin jia dang dao* (Leading the family in the right way), which was published by the Hankou Christian Tract Society in 1882. It has a preface by Shen Zixing of Nanjing, who was evidently John's assistant. (His name is coupled with John's in other publications.)[71]

In a letter of October 1882 from Hankou, John refers to what I assume is this book:

> Besides other work, in the shape of daily preaching, teaching, and looking after the Church, I have written six tracts since my return. The last, finished today, is quite a long one, and I believe will make one of the *two* best I have ever composed. In it I describe my ideal Christian in his own life, and efforts to save his own family, relations and friends. It is a sort of a novel, specially adapted to the Chinese.[72]

Yin jia dang dao is a novel in sixteen chapters that shows no allegiance to the traditional form. It concerns a certain Mr. Li, well educated although no literatus, who is married to a literate wife, and they have two sons and a daughter. Li has to go elsewhere to find work, and once there he begins to frequent gambling dens and brothels. With no money left, he cannot bring himself to return to his family. One day he strays into a church, where he hears the pastor talk of God the Creator and of how man cannot redeem his sins alone. He feels a constant sense of unease and starts to regret his follies. He becomes a Christian, works hard, and makes money, then returns home and helps his family to join the church. Along the way the novel makes points against concubinage, foot-binding, gambling, cursing, opium smoking, and the worship of the god Guan Yu, while advocating education for girls and honest dealing in business, as well as the importance of a good death. It does contain some doctrine, but its focus is on practical advice as to how life should be lived.[73]

Timothy Richard

Easily the most influential novel translated by a missionary in the nineteenth century was Edward Bellamy's *Looking Backward, 2000–1887* (1888), which Richard and an unnamed Chinese assistant began translating into literary Chinese in 1891. The translation appeared anonymously in installments in the *Wanguo gongbao* (Review of the times) under the title *Hui tou kan jilüe* (Looking backward, a summary account) and was then published as a booklet in 1894 with the new title of *Bainian yijiao* (Asleep for a hundred years).[74] A vernacular version began appearing in 1898.[75] The translation circulated widely in the aftermath of the Sino-Japanese war when, in a ferment of reformist thinking, some of the secular missionary publications became so popular that they were pirated. The Bellamy novel's projection into the year 2000 influenced Liang Qichao in his first novel, *Xin Zhongguo weilai ji* (The future of new China, from 1902), which in turn helped establish the subgenre of utopian fiction.

In truth, Richard's work can scarcely be called a translation. Its initial title correctly describes it as a summary account, and it consists of a series of chapter synopses that together amount to only a fraction of the original's length. Considered as exposition, however, it is quite effective, because Bellamy's novel consisted almost entirely of ideas that could be easily summarized. But since the original contained nothing specifically Christian, why did Richard choose to translate it? The explanation lies in his conviction that the primary need in China was to enlist the intellectuals in the cause of social reform rather than to try to evangelize the populace, a conviction that put him at odds with most of the other missionaries. When Li Hongzhang invited him in 1890 to become editor of the *Shi bao*, a Chinese-language daily newspaper in Tianjin, Richard leaped at the chance, and proceeded to use the paper (and also a weekly he founded in conjunction with it) as a means of expressing his views on reform.[76] After a full year as editor, he was invited to Shanghai to become Secretary of the Society for the Diffusion of Christian and General Knowledge among the Chinese, and it was there, in the journal that the society directed at the Chinese intelligentsia, that his translation of *Looking Backward* first appeared. Like his and Cai Erkang's translation of Robert Mackenzie's *The 19th Century, A History* (1880), which appeared as a society publication in 1895 under the title

Taixi xinshi lanyao, his version of Bellamy's work formed part of his project of "general enlightenment."[77]

John Fryer and Liang Qichao

The first call for a "new novel" came, oddly enough, from John Fryer, who had spent his entire career translating scientific and engineering textbooks into Chinese. In May 1895 he announced a prize contest for novels that attacked what he saw as the three prevailing ills of Chinese society: opium, the examination essay, and foot-binding. Two novels survive that were inspired by his contest, and they may well be described as the first modern Chinese novels.[78] Liang Qichao's earliest advocacy of fiction was in February 1897, in the course of recommending a reformed curriculum for schools. I believe that the missionary novel had some influence on both Fryer's and Liang's thinking, but in different ways.

Although not a missionary himself, Fryer was closely associated with the Protestant missionaries, serving, for example, as General Editor and Chairman of the Executive Committee of the Educational Association, which was essentially a missionary organization. When he announced the contest, he did so in both the *Shen bao* newspaper and the *Chinese Recorder,* the English-language Protestant missionary organ.[79] In the *Recorder* the Chinese announcement was accompanied by a somewhat different one in English, encouraging "students, teachers and pastors connected with the various missionary establishments in China" to take part, "so that some really interesting and valuable stories, in the easiest *Wen li,* may be produced, of a Christian rather than of a merely ethical tone, which will supply a long felt want and serve as popular reading books all over the Empire." In the following month's issue, he cites as justification for his contest the example of *Uncle Tom's Cabin* in awakening opposition to slavery.[80] *Uncle Tom's Cabin* was, of course, a deeply Christian novel. In addition to Fryer's other motives, we may assume that behind his venture lay the history of the missionary novel as Milne, Gützlaff, and John had practiced it.

The influence of missionary fiction on Liang Qichao is clear in works for children. Magazines like the *Child's Paper* (*Yue bao*), published by a missionary organization in Shanghai from 1875, provided the model for secular publications encouraged by Liang such as the *Mengxue bao* (subtitled "The Children's Educator") of 1897–98.[81] Christian children's fiction also influenced him as he began to develop his ideas on the function of the novel in society.

His first recommendation of fiction came in the new school curriculum that he was advocating in late 1896 and early 1897, particularly in a series of articles on primary education in *Shiwu bao* entitled "Lun youxue." (He was referring to the education of boys from the ages of eight to fifteen.)[82] *Shiwu bao* 17 and 18 are devoted to the kinds of texts to be used in schools, and *Shiwu bao* 19 to the class schedule. In no. 18, for example, published on February 22, 1897, he recommends *wendashu* (question-and-answer texts), noting their use in the study of the Chinese classics as well as in western elementary education. (Catechisms were in use in mission schools for secular as well as religious purposes.) Under "fiction" (*shuobushu*), he lists three kinds of approved subject matter, beginning with the teachings of the sages and the facts of history. The third kind is concerned with social conditions, among which he includes the condemnation of opium, foot-binding, and the examination essay, a trio that surely derives from Fryer's fiction contest.

The schedule outlined in *Shiwu bao* 18 divides the school day into eight one-hour periods preceded by songs of praise for the teachings of Confucius. For the final hour of the day, when the pupils are tired, fiction is recommended.[83] However, by "fiction" Liang did not mean any existing fiction, but a new and improved kind that had yet to be written. We can gain some idea of what he had in mind from two journals intended for schoolboys that began publication later that same year: *Mengxue bao*, which was founded by colleagues of his from the journal *Shiwu bao*, and *Yanyi bao*, edited by Zhang Zhonghe, one of his protégés. Liang wrote a glowing announcement of the two journals in *Shiwu bao*, recommending songs and fiction as the best instruments for education and reform.[84] He based his curriculum, at least in part, on that of the mission schools, which were the most accessible models of educational reform. The second phase of missionary fiction, concerned with children's literature, had evidently influenced his early thinking about the value of fiction.[85]

※

My aim has been to document the existence of the missionary novel as a factor in the introduction of foreign fiction into China. Literary historians have described the translations of the 1870s (see chapter 4) as giving the Chinese literary public its first taste of foreign fiction, but the much larger number of missionary novels composed or translated from 1819 onward also needs to be taken into account. Bellamy's *Looking Backward*, as translated by Timothy Richard and his Chinese assistant, had a direct impact on Chinese fiction. The same cannot be said of the other novels written or translated by missionaries, although they did play some part in the initiatives of John Fryer and Liang Qichao. However, even if we cannot document their influence, these works must surely have helped familiarize at least some of the public with foreign fiction and made it easier for authors to develop their own new forms and methods.

NOTES

1. In the twentieth century numerous works of fiction were published by Catholic presses. See *General Catalogue of Chinese Catholic Books* (Hong Kong: Catholic Truth Society, 1941), 192–98.

2. The 1867 catalogue was published by the American Presbyterian Press and reprinted by Ch'eng Wen Publishing Company, Taipei, 1967. The 1876 catalogue was printed as an appendix to the *Catalogue of the Chinese Imperial Maritime Customs Collection at the International Exhibition, Philadelphia, 1876*, published by the Inspectorate General of Customs (Shanghai, 1876). It was prepared by Alexander Wylie, and the entries are mostly, if not completely, of his own books, which are now in the Bodleian Library; see David Helliwell, "Two Collections of Nineteenth-Century Protestant Missionary Publications in Chinese," *Chinese Culture* 31.4 (1990): 22. The 1884 catalogue appeared as part of the *Illustrated Catalogue of the Chinese Collection of Exhibits for the International Health Exhibition, London, 1884*, China Maritime Customs Miscellaneous Series no. 12 (London: William Clowes and Sons, 1884), 86–117 ("Translations Issued from the Press of the Various Protestant Missions"); there is a copy in the New York Public Library. The major collections of nineteenth-century Protestant Chinese literature are those of the Bodleian Library, the British Library, the National Library of Australia, and the Harvard-Yenching Library. On the National Library collection, see Ching Sun and Wan Wong, eds., *Catalogue of the London Missionary Society Collection Held by the National Library of Australia* (Canberra: National Library of Australia, Asian Collection, 2001). In general I note the location of a book when it is held by only a single collection.

3. Shanghai: Hoi-Lee Press, 1882.

4. *New Classified and Descriptive Catalogue of Current Christian Literature, 1901* (Shanghai: Society for the Diffusion of Christian and General Knowledge among the Chinese, 1902). There is a copy in the British Library. There is also an amplified and updated work of the same title (Shanghai: Christian Literature Society, 1907).

5. Hankou: Shengjiao shuju, 1918.

6. Quoted in Robert Wardlaw Thompson, *Griffith John, The Story of Fifty Years in China* (New York: A. C. Armstrong, 1906), 228. John was one of the few missionary translators to list his assistants at the beginning of his works. In the translations of science textbooks by John Fryer and others beginning in the 1870s, the Chinese partner, that is to say, the writer, is regularly listed. I know of only one case in which the

writer is given the major credit: the translation of Aesop's *Fables* (*Yishi yuyan*) published in Canton by the Canton Press Office in 1840; there is a copy in the Houghton Library, Harvard University. (The work had been previously issued in Canton in four parts in 1837–38.) It is described on the title page as "Written by the Learned Mun Mooy Seen-shang, and Compiled in the Present Form (with a free and literal translation) by his Pupil Sloth." Sloth was Robert Thom, five years a student of Chinese in Canton, whose translation of the late-Ming vernacular story "Wang Jiaoluan bainian changhen" was published in Canton by the Canton Press Office in 1839. (In it he gives Sloth as the only translator, and even complains mildly about his teacher Mun Mooy's habit of giving different interpretations at different times of the same • poetic expression.)

7. Jiangsusheng shehui kexueyuan, *Zhongguo tongsu xiaoshuo zongmu tiyao* (Beijing: Zhongguo wenlian chuban gongsi, 1990), and Wang Jiquan and Xia Shengyuan, eds., *Zhongguo jindai xiaoshuo mulu* (Nanchang: Baihuazhou wenyi chubanshe, 1998). The latter includes two editions of Milne's work, under different titles.

8. I arrived at this number by counting the titles in the 1876 and 1884 catalogues, then adding any editions published in other years in the British Library, the Harvard-Yenching Library, the Phillips Library of the Peabody Essex Museum, and the two catalogues given in the previous note. Since more than one edition may have been published in the same year, the true total is probably higher. It was printed in considerable numbers. Daniel H. Bays, based on a knowledge of seventeen editions between 1819 and 1906, estimated that at least several hundred thousand and probably well over a million copies were printed. See "Christian Tracts: The Two Friends," in Suzanne Wilson Barnett and John King Fairbank, eds., *Christianity in China: Early Protestant Missionary Writings* (Cambridge: Harvard University Press, 1985), 23.

9. See Clayton, *Jidu shengjiao chuban geshu shumu huizuan*, 52–53.

10. See Wylie, *Memorials*, 16–17. For Milne's own account, see *A Retrospect of the First Ten Years of the Protestant Mission in China* (Malacca: Anglo-Chinese Press, 1820), 281–82. An analysis of the theology is given in Bays, "Christian Tracts: The Two Friends," 19–34. The dialogue form was in common use by missionaries in India. The early Jesuits in China, notably Matteo Ricci and Julio Aleni, also used dialogues, but between a foreigner and a local dignitary and with minimal contextualization.

11. There is a copy in the British Library.

12. There is a copy in the Harvard-Yenching Library.

13. P. 29. There may have been another, lost novel in dialogue form, not necessarily by Milne or Medhurst. William Jones, in *The Jubilee Memorial of the Religious Tract Society* (London: Religious Tract Society, 1850), quotes a recent letter from James Legge that mentions Milne's *Dialogues* and also a work consisting of "Discourses principally on the Worship of Parents and Ancestors, between Ho and Woo"; see 698.

14. On Gützlaff, see Jessie G. Lutz, "Karl F.A. Gützlaff: Missionary Entrepreneur," in Barnett and Fairbank, eds., *Christianity in China*, 61–87.

15. *The Opium War Through Chinese Eyes* (London: George Allen and Unwin, 1958), 233.

16. William Dean, *The China Mission* (New York: Sheldon, 1859), 284.

17. Harry Parkes, as quoted in Waley, *The Opium War Through Chinese Eyes*, 233.

18. For these events, see "The Journal of a Residence in Siam and of a Voyage along the Coast of China to Mantchou Tartary" as serialized in *Chinese Repository* from 1.1 (May 16, 1832).

19. *China: Its State and Prospects* (London: J. Snow, 1838), 364–65.

20. *Chinese Repository* 1.5 (1832): 197.

21. See Jardine's letter as quoted in Hsin-pao Chang, *Commissioner Lin and the Opium War* (Cambridge: Harvard University Press, 1964), 95.

22. See *Mencius*, trans. D. C. Lau (London: Penguin, 1970), 51.

23. Published by Smith, Elder in London in two volumes.

24. The review was published anonymously in *Chinese Repository* 8.2 (1839): 84–98. Williams is identified as the author in the *General Index of Subjects Contained in the Twenty Volumes of the Chinese Repository,* which appeared in 1851. There is an undated Maruzen, Tokyo reprint.

25. "Journal of a Residence in Siam and of a Voyage along the Coast of China to Mantchou Tartary," *Chinese Repository* 1.4 (Aug. 1832): 139–40.

26. Ibid., 140.

27. *Chinese Repository* 2.8 (Dec. 1833): 377.

28. See "Journal of a Voyage along the Coast of China from the Province of Canton to Leautung in Mantchou Tartary, 1832–33," *Chinese Repository* 2.1 (May 1833): 20.

29. There is a copy in the British Library.

30. There is a copy in the Harvard-Yenching Library.

31. See Jacob Tomlin, *Journal of a Nine Months' Residence in Siam* (London: Frederick Westley and A. H. Davis, 1831), 105. Tomlin was Gützlaff's companion during most of his first stay in Thailand.

32. *Chinese Repository* 2.2 (June 1833): 54.

33. Pp. 467–68.

34. P. 409.

35. "Christian Missions in China," *Chinese Repository* 3.12 (1835): 566.

36. "Remarks on Buddhism; together with brief notices of the island of Poo-to, and of the numerous priests who inhabit it," *Chinese Repository* 2.5 (1833): 223. Gützlaff's visit took place in February of that year, on his return from his third voyage.

37. See *Chinese Repository* from 7.5 (1838) to 11.5 (1842). The *Ping nan hou zhuan*, "a monument of Chinese genius," is reviewed in 7.6: 281–89; *Shenxian tongjian* in 7.10 (1839); *Da Ming Zhengde Huang you Jiangnan zhuan* in 9.2 (1840); *Zhinang bu* in 10.10 (1841); and the *Sacred Instructions* in 10.11 (1841). Su Shi's works are reviewed in 11.3 (1842), *Liaozhai zhiyi* in 11.4 (1842), and *Honglou meng* (*Story of the Stone*) in 11.5 (1842): 266–74.

38. *Chinese Repository* 11.5 (1842): 268. Westerners were slow to appreciate *Story of the Stone.* John Francis Davis, *The Chinese: A General Description of the Empire and Its Inhabitants* (New York: Harper and Sons, 1836), has a section on fiction that discusses only the popular romances and does not mention it. Alexander Wylie in his *Notes on Chinese Literature* (Shanghai: American Presbyterian Press, 1867) seems mystified by the novel and gives only a qualified assessment; see 205.

39. *Chinese Repository* 10.10 (1841): 554.

40. *Chinese Repository* 7.10 (1939): 567–68.

41. *Chinese Repository* 11.10 (1842): 540.

42. There is a copy in the British Library.

43. *Mencius*, trans. D. C. Lau, 181.

44. There is a copy in the library of the American Philosophical Society.

45. *Shifei lüelun*, 6.36a.

46. There is a copy in the Harvard-Yenching Library.

47. There is a copy in the Harvard-Yenching Library.

48. Samuel Couling, *Encyclopedia Sinica* (London: Oxford University Press, 1917), 221, refers to a complete set of Gützlaff's Chinese works preserved in Munich. The present whereabouts of the collection are unknown.

49. *Memorials*, 61.

50. There is a copy in the British Library.

51. Gützlaff was remarkable among the China missionaries in the extent to which he made use of fiction, and even among the missionaries in India there was apparently no one to equal him. In terms of originality, however, he is not to be compared with the Jesuit priest Joseph Beschi, who in 1740 wrote a novel in Tamil entitled *Paramartha Guruvin Katai* (The story of a guru). In the "free paraphrase" of B. G. Babington's translation, *Strange Surpassing Adventures of the Venerable Gooroo Simple, and His Five Disciples, Noodle, Doodle, Wiseacre, Zany and Foozle* (Boston: Ticknor and Fields, 1861), it is a wildly humorous satire of the Brahmans.

52. Gützlaff's manuscripts were an editor's nightmare. See the letter from Elijah Coleman Bridgman quoted in Suzanne Wilson Barnett, "Practical Evangelism: Protestant Missions and the Introduction of Western Civilization Into China, 1820–1850" (Ph.D. diss., Harvard University, 1973), 100.

53. The 1832 edition is reproduced in the *Guben xiaoshuo jicheng*, third series (Shanghai: Shanghai guji chubanshe, 1990).

54. There are copies of both in the British Library, the former in a Hong Kong edition of 1870, the latter in a Hong Kong edition of 1862.

55. There is a copy in the British Library.

56. The first translation of a novel of general interest was *Xinxi xiantan*, published in installments from 1873 to 1875. See chapter 4.

57. The British Library has a copy of the Chinese translation. It also has the English translation, published by B. Wertheim in London in 1842.

58. Quoted by Islay Burns, *Memoir of the Rev. Wm. C. Burns, M.A.* (New York: Robert Carter and Brothers, 1870), 397–98.

59. Ibid., 516. A second full translation by Thomas Hall Hudson entitled *Shenglü jingcheng* was published in Ningbo in two parts in 1870. (There is a copy in the British Library.) It is divided into chapters (*hui*), and is a more colloquial translation than Burns's.

60. See Wylie, *Memorials*, 49. I have not seen it.

61. *Zhongbiaojiang lun* (Fuzhou, 1855). There is a copy in the Harvard-Yenching Library.

62. See William C. Tenney, *The Conflict and the Victory of Life, Memoir of Mrs. Caroline*

P. Keith (New York: D. Appleton, 1864), 176. The 1856 publication date is noted in Wylie, *Memorials*, 212.

63. See *Chinese Recorder* (May–June 1878): 218.

64. See Irwin T. Hyatt Jr., *Our Ordered Lives Confess* (Cambridge: Harvard University Press, 1976), 477–78, on the original story and the Nevius translation. The 1884 *Illustrated Catalogue of the Chinese Collection for the International Health Exhibition* lists both the 1861 and 1868 editions.

65. There is a copy in the Harvard-Yenching Library.

66. There is a copy in the Harvard-Yenching Library.

67. See MacGillivray, 1907 *New and Descriptive Catalogue*, 67.

68. The British Library has a copy.

69. The British Library has a copy of *Guinuo zhuan*, and there is a copy of *Cottage on the Shore* (New York: T. Whittaker, n.d.) in the New York Public Library. Not until the turn of the century did missionaries expand the scope of the children's fiction that they translated. Laura M. White translated several works, including Frances Hodgson Burnett's *Little Lord Fauntleroy* and Xavier Saintine's *Picciola* (hardly a children's novel), according to MacGillivray's 1907 catalogue. *Picciola* was published in 1901 under the title *Yuzhong hua*; White is credited with the oral translation and Chen Chunsheng with the writing. See Zhou Yueran, *Yanyanyanzhai shuhua* (Shaanxi shifan daxue chubanshe, 1998), 271. White and Chen also collaborated on a Christian novel about contemporary Chinese life, *Wugeng zhuan*, which was published in 1907; see *Zhongguo tongsu xiaoshuo zongmu tiyao*, 1008.

70. There is a copy of the 1872 edition in the Bodleian Library. For the 1856 edition in Shanghai dialect, see *Chinese Recorder* 8.4 (1877): 323.

71. See, for example, *Hong zhuru* (Hankou: Hankou Mission Press, 1882). On Shen Zixing, see Patrick Hanan, "Chinese Christian Literature: The Writing Process," in Hanan, ed., *Treasures of the Yenching* (Cambridge: Harvard-Yenching Library, 2003), 283.

72. Thompson, *Griffith John*, 334–35.

73. Some material has been omitted from the original article on missionaries' discussions from the 1880s and 1890s on the value of fiction. See "The Missionary Novels of Nineteenth-Century China," *Harvard Journal of Asiatic Studies* 60.2 (Dec. 2000): 413–43.

74. It ran in *Wanguo gongbao* from December 1891 through April 1892. The 1894 edition was published by the Guangxuehui (Society for the Diffusion of Christian and General Knowledge among the Chinese).

75. It appeared in the *Zhongguo guanyin baihua bao* 7–8 (June 29, 1898). The translation, by Qiu Wei'e, was never completed.

76. See Richard, *Forty-five Years in China* (New York: Frederick A. Stokes, 1919), 215.

77. See his "Scheme for the General Enlightenment of China," *Chinese Recorder* 23 (March 1892): 131–32.

78. *Xichao kuaishi* and *Hualiu shenqing zhuan*. On Fryer's contest and these two novels, see chapter 6.

79. It appeared in the *Shen bao* of May 25, 1895 as well as in the June 1895 number of *The Chinese Recorder*, among the advertisements at the back of the journal.

80. See *Chinese Recorder* (July 1895): 330–31.

81. The first issue was dated November 1, 1897.

82. *Shiwu bao* 17 to 19 (twelfth month of 1896 to second month of 1897).

83. See *Shiwubao* 18, 1b.

84. "*Mengxue bao* yu *Yanyi bao* hexu," *Shiwu bao* 44 (tenth month, 1897), 5ab. I have seen only nos. 9–11 of the former and none of the latter. The *Mengxue bao* has an account of ancient Chinese history in the form of a novel; presumably the *Yanyi bao* was largely narrative fiction. In his announcement Liang also refers to Japanese education and its use of fiction. On Liang's relations with the missionaries, see Chi-yun Chen, "Liang Ch'i-ch'ao's 'Missionary Education': A Case Study of Missionary Influence on the Reformers," *Papers on China* (East Asian Research Center, Harvard University) 16 (1962): 66–125. Liang served for a short period, from October 1895 to February 1896, as Timothy Richard's secretary, but although he admired missionary organization, he soon came to regard the missionaries as ideological adversaries.

85. On the juvenile fiction that Liang Qichao went on to translate, see Hu Congjing, *Wan Qing ertong wenxue gouchen* (Shanghai: Shaonian ertong chubanshe, 1982), 53–63. See also chapter 7 of this book.

CHAPTER 4

The First Novel Translated Into Chinese

S TRICTLY SPEAKING, *Xinxi xiantan* (Idle talk morning to evening), which appeared in 26 installments in the Shanghai monthly journal *Yinghuan suoji* (Trifling notes on the world at large) from 1873 to 1875, was not the first novel in Chinese translation—religious novels translated by foreign missionaries and their Chinese assistants date from as early as 1852—but it does seem to have been the earliest translation of a novel of general interest.[1] The name of the original "English novel" is not given, and the translator is identified only by a pseudonym, as Lishao Jushi (Layman of the ladle). My aim in this essay is not merely to identify the original work and its translator but also to characterize *Xinxi xiantan* as a work of translation. To do this, it will be necessary to see the original novel in terms of its English cultural context and *Xinxi xiantan* in terms of its Chinese cultural context. (By "cultural context," I mean the intended reader's expectations with regard to genre in its widest meaning, as well as his universe of reference.) Only then, by means of a general comparison of the two works, and with confirmation in this case from the translator's own commentary, can we deduce the governing principles behind his translation.[2]

The Original Novel and Its Author

The translation, which is in vernacular Chinese, proves to be the first half of a long novel entitled *Night and Morning* by the English writer Edward Bulwer

Lytton (1803–73), first published in 1841.[3] It combines two subgenres that Lytton favored: the *bildungsroman* as seen in his novel *Ernest Maltravers* (which, as Lytton himself noted,[4] was indebted to Goethe's *Wilhelm Meister*, the classic of the subgenre); and the "Newgate novel" with its sympathetic criminal hero, a type that Lytton had pioneered in *Paul Clifford* (first published in 1830) and *Eugene Aram* (1832) and for which he had been bitterly attacked. Although Philip Morton (later Philip Beaufort), the hero of *Night and Morning*, is not an intellectual like Ernest Maltravers, the novel is centrally concerned with his moral education in the school of experience. The "night" and "morning" of the title represent the two contrasting phases of his life, loss and misery in the first half of the book, restoration and joy in the second. (In his rendering of the title, the translator has ignored this symbolism.) The criminal character is William Gawtrey, a confidence man, cardsharp, and forger who is shot and killed by the Paris police halfway through the book. A romantic figure, he has been described by a modern critic as "possibly the most psychologically compelling and artistically successful of all [Lytton's] 'Newgate' characters."[5]

In his preface to the 1845 edition of *Night and Morning*, Lytton described the novel as concerned with the law's unreasonable treatment of vice as compared with crime. Although children who committed petty crimes were savagely punished, people who indulged in vice, even though it was far more harmful to society, went free. The prime example of the latter in this novel is the cynical, amoral, and Machiavellian Lord Lilburne. (Lytton, an aristocrat himself, was a harsh critic of the aristocracy, in his novels as well as in his pioneering sociological study, *England and the English* [1833].) Another concern of this novel, according to Lytton, was the quality of so-called respectability, which often obscured a great deal of mean-spiritedness. In *England and the English*, he writes that "the undue regard for wealth produces a false moral standard. . . . A man may be respectable, without being entitled from his virtues to respect."[6] The example here is Robert Beaufort, a character that, Lytton implies, influenced Charles Dickens in his creation of Pecksniff in *Martin Chuzzlewit* (1844).[7] Romance also plays a part in *Night and Morning*—Philip falls in love with two women before he eventually marries Fanny—but a much smaller part than in *Ernest Maltravers*.

The Translators

The only known identification of the translator was made in the Shanghai newspaper *Xinwen bao* in 1905, in an advertisement for a "retranslation" of the original English novel.[8] The advertisement identifies the previous translator as County Magistrate Jiang Zirang. Although the attribution appeared thirty years after the translation, it is so specific that it has to be given some weight. But the question arises: Who *was* this Jiang Zirang? So far no one has been able to say, let alone associate him with either the *Shen bao* or the *Yinghuan suoji.*

We can tell something about the pseudonymous translator from his other writings in both publications. As Yan Tingliang has pointed out, since Lishao Jushi's preface to the translated novel was written in the Xiao Jiluoan studio of his Shanghai residence, he must have been the Xiao Jiluoan Zhu (Master of the Xiao Jiluoan) whose essays are found in both the early *Shen bao* and the *Yinghuan suoji.* Further, Xiao Jiluoan Zhu and Hengmengan Zhu (Master of the Hengmengan), whose writings, particularly his poems, are also found in the newspaper and the journal, must have been one and the same person.[9] Like many contemporary *littérateurs*, the translator evidently had several pseudonyms. As Lishao Jushi, he wrote the introductory preface to the *Yinghuan suoji*, and from its content and tone we can infer that he was the journal's editor. As Xiao Jiluoan Zhu, he wrote the critical commentary to his own translation of *Night and Morning*, as well as several important essays. As Hengmengan Zhu, he is described in the preamble to a friend's poem written late in 1873 as "a noted provincial graduate from Hangzhou."[10] Hengmengan Zhu is also credited with the first poem printed in the *Shen bao*, describing the behavior of westerners at the racetrack.[11] He was evidently a senior editor of the newspaper. In the seventh month of *renshen* (1872), a Japanese visitor called at the newspaper's offices to see the proprietor, Ernest Major, and composed a poem. Four of the people present responded with matching poems; the first was Hengmengan Zhu.[12] This writer evidently tended to use the name Xiao Jiluoan Zhu when writing prose, Hengmengan Zhu or Xiao Jiluoan Zhu when writing poetry, and Lishao Jushi when writing vernacular fiction. On one occasion, in his account of a crime committed in Hangzhou, he playfully employed all three pseudonyms together—as well as a fourth, Xiling Xiashi. Lishao Jushi gave the oral rendering that Xiling Xiashi copied down, Hengmengan Zhu recorded, and Xiao Jiluoan Zhu commented on.[13]

I suggest that the translator was one of the earliest chief editors of the *Shen bao*, a man known by his courtesy name as Jiang Zhixiang. In histories of the *Shen bao* organization it is said that at the time of his appointment as chief editor he was already a provincial graduate from Zhejiang, and that he left the paper on becoming a metropolitan graduate (*jinshi*).[14] Jiang's personal name was, I believe, Qizhang. The first book published by the *Shen bao* was a collection of 500 examination essays entitled *Wenyuan jinghua* (Anthology of literature), which appeared in the seventh month of *guiyou* (1873). In the news-paper's advertisement the book was described merely as prepared by the editorial staff, but there is reason to think that the editor was Jiang Qizhang.[15]

Born in 1842, Jiang Qizhang came from Qiantang county in Hangzhou prefecture and was a stipendiary licentiate of the prefecture before succeeding in the 1870 provincial examinations. In 1877 he succeeded in the metropolitan examinations, after which he was appointed magistrate of Dunhuang county.[16] In the years between 1876 and 1889 the only person surnamed Jiang from Zhejiang who succeeded in the metropolitan examinations was Jiang Qizhang, so if our information about Jiang Zhixiang is correct, there can be little doubt that his personal name was Qizhang.

The writings by Xiao Jiluoan Zhu in the *Yinghuan suoji* and the *Shen bao* tell us something about Jiang Qizhang. He has several essays on western developments, written in a wry, sometimes whimsical tone, such as one on the new aquarium built at Brighton in England, another that shows familiarity—on the writer's part as well as on his readers'—with Benjamin Hobson's *Quanti xinlun* (Treatise on physiology), and a third on the vicissitudes of the steamship *Great Eastern*.[17] There is also an account of a brief visit in the tenth month of 1872 to Nagasaki that shows a keen interest in Japanese customs.[18]

How then do we explain the name Jiang Zirang in the 1905 advertisement? Was Zirang simply another courtesy name of Jiang Qizhang's? A possible explanation is that the writer of the advertisement mistakenly combined Jiang's surname with the courtesy name of the *other* of the two original chief editors, Wu Zirang of Jiangxi.[19]

It is highly likely that Ernest Major, proprietor of the *Shen bao*, worked closely with the translator (presumably Jiang Qizhang) on *Yinghuan suoji*. Major had a good command of Chinese and was actively engaged in the management of the newspaper and its enterprises. The idea of a literary journal of international scope presumably originated with him, and he must surely have involved himself in its operation. Lishao Jushi's introductory preface to the journal refers to advice given by Zunwenge Zhu, Major's studio name. In Qian Zheng's 1878 preface to his anthology *Xieyu congtan chuji* (Powered jade anthology, first series), a work that he edited and published with Major's encouragement, he recalls the time four years earlier, in the summer of 1874, when he visited Shanghai and found Major himself collecting material for the journal. Even if we allow for some exaggeration in Qian's account, it is clear that Major played a large part in the journal's operation.

Including a novel with poetry and essays was probably Major's idea; it was one that would occur far more readily to a westerner than to a Chinese at this time. Presumably it was also his decision to serialize the work; British novelists commonly serialized their works before publishing them in book form. We may go further and suggest that he probably recommended *Night and Morning* to Jiang Qizhang in the first place, and even supplied him with the text. The novelists represented in the early *Shen bao* and in the *Yinghuan suoji* were all standard authors whose works were quite likely to be found in the private library of any well-to-do Englishman.[20] Major must also have helped with problems of interpretation, but we do not know just how much. For example, did he give an oral rendering that Jiang put into writing? Such a two-person method of translation into Chinese was practically universal in the nineteenth century until close to its end, and it would be surprising to find someone translating a novel on his own in the 1870s, particularly one that required special knowledge in a number of fields. True, *Xinxi xiantan* makes significant changes in the order of *Night and Morning*, but these can be accounted for by assuming that the writer revised and adapted his initial draft.

We can easily imagine the different forms that two-person translation might take, depending on how well each person knows the other's language. But if *Xinxi xiantan* was indeed the product of such a collaboration, one possibility can be ruled out: the speaker cannot have checked the writer's work thoroughly, for had he done so, he would surely have noticed some of its mistakes.

If we assume a two-person process in this case, as I think we must, we can assign certain features of the text (for example, some of its omissions and explanations) to the speaker, many more features to the writer, and a few others (for example, its tone) to both speaker and writer. For simplicity's sake, however, I shall not attempt to draw such distinctions here. Depending on the context, the word "translator" will refer to the speaker, to the writer, or to both.

It is easy to understand why Major might have chosen a Lytton novel for this first extended translation into Chinese. Although Lytton's reputation declined drastically in the twentieth century, in the 1870s he was still one of the most famous English novelists—on a par with Charles Dickens. He was known, above all, for his ability to tell a gripping, if sensational, story, and he also had other qualifications to recommend him. In addition to his many novels, plays, and poems, he had written works such as *England and the English*, and he had played a prominent role in British politics. It is not at all surprising that the first notable translation of a novel into Japanese—in 1879—was also of a Lytton novel.[21]

But how does one explain the choice of *Night and Morning* from among Lytton's many works? It was probably chosen because it deals with modern life and with different levels of English society, and also because it is set in France and Italy as well as in England. In Xiao Jiluoan's preface to his translation, he says that the book will extend people's horizons by giving them a knowledge of "Western customs," and the same point is made even more strongly in the "General Colophon to Book One," which declares that reading fiction can change one's attitudes toward foreign customs, that is to say, to foreign culture. The years after the first publication of the translation saw a number of essays and books explaining foreign customs to the Chinese reader, and it seems that Major may have anticipated that trend.

For the sake of convenience, I shall defer the question of the translation's actual reception until after I have characterized its method and purpose.

Describing Translation

All translation mediates between two cultural contexts, both of which need to be taken into account if a specific translation is to be satisfactorily described. The nature of the mediation varies greatly, as indicated by adjectives in common use such as "literal" and "free." (The trouble with these words is that they give the impression that some kind of absolute standard exists.) The variation among translations can be described in general terms as ranging between two poles, preservation in all respects and assimilation in all respects. By preservation, I mean the attempt of the translator to replicate—or at least represent, so far as possible—all of the discernible features of the original work. Typically, he does so out of a belief that these are essential to a true appreciation. By assimilation, I mean the translator's modification of the original into a form with which the general reader is familiar. These are extremes, of course, and the vast majority of translations fall somewhere in the middle.[22] And translators of fiction are seldom, if ever, entirely consistent throughout the course of their work; for example, they generally take a more assimilative attitude when translating dialogue where, in order to obtain a semblance of natural speech, they have to pay attention to the situation rather than the words.

The above distinctions merely provide a conceptual framework for describing translation; they do not amount to a procedure. The number of features in a translated text that can be analyzed in terms of their relative preservation or assimilation of the features of an original text is theoretically limitless. Acumen is needed to select the most significant characteristics, whose treatment will indicate the governing principles behind the translation.

Broadly speaking, the Chinese translation of *Night and Morning* is a work of moderate assimilation, in its narrative and exposition as well as in its dialogue. (Let me make it clear that I am not condemning the translator as "unfaithful";

his is a creditable attempt at translating a difficult work. In any case, my purpose is to describe rather than to evaluate.) His translation modifies or eliminates features, just as it supplements, reduces, or reorders text. So numerous are his changes, most of which are small, that it is not easy to match the translation closely with the English for more than a few sentences at a stretch. However, it is definitely not précis, for the amount it adds to the original probably equals what it omits. Nor does it seriously distort the meaning.

The rest of this essay will be devoted mainly to studying the nature of the *Xinxi xiantan* as translation, which means, in effect, examining its techniques of assimilation. Before I begin, however, let me raise the question of cultural reference.

Novelists can usually explain unfamiliar material by implicit means, but translators have more limited powers, and any translation between cultures as isolated from each other as those of England and China in the 1870s faces a multitude of problems in treating references specific to one culture or the other. The assimilative translator can handle such references in a variety of ways, deleting them when they are peripheral, explaining them when they are essential, but most often seeking out some kind of approximation. All of these methods, but particularly the last two, are likely to provide broad clues to the translator's ideological position and purpose in translating.

Furthermore, all translations, particularly the more assimilative kind, tend to introduce elements specific to the reader's culture, from proverbs and quotations to allusions to people and events. (The introduction may be unconscious.) At a higher level of analysis, translations almost inevitably tend to assimilate the themes and character types of the original work to those of the reader's own culture. The diffusion of such elements in the translated text is another gauge of its assimilative tendencies.

Format, Order, Continuity

Like most of Lytton's novels, *Night and Morning* is furnished—overfurnished, the modern reader will probably think—with epigraphs at the head of each of its five books as well as at the head of each chapter. The epigraphs before the books are taken from a single German poem, "Der Pilgrim," by Friedrich Schiller,[23] while those before the chapters come from English, French, and Latin sources, some quite obscure. The epigraphs were obviously intended to display Lytton's erudition and also, like his frequently heightened style, to raise the literary level of his novel.

The translator deletes all of the epigraphs (except one poem by George Crabbe that he weaves into the narrative)[24] and replaces those before the chapters with the familiar paired headings found in virtually all traditional Chinese novels. Like his lowering of the heightened style, which I shall discuss in the next section, this has the effect of bringing the novel down to the level of ordinary fiction.

It is significant that the translation's chapters rarely match those of the original work. The Chinese chapters are of uniform length, in response to the demands of serial publishing and limited space, but like the typical chapters of Chinese fiction, they always end on a note of formal suspense and then run directly on to the next chapter.

Certain changes were inevitable, whatever translation method was used. For example, the management of time and focus is handled by verbal rather than spatial means, because Chinese punctuation did not offer as many sectionalizing devices as the English. The function of comment is usually signaled with the words *kanguan,* "Readers," or *yuanlai,* "The fact was." The author's comments, which are unmarked in the original, are introduced in this manner in the translation, as are those inserted by the translator, which leads to some confusion since, without consulting the original, the reader cannot always guess whether it is the author or the translator who is commenting.[25]

The translator's identification of characters differs frequently from that of the original in manner and timing. Postponed identification was a favorite device of the eighteenth- and nineteenth-century English novelist. Lytton sometimes withholds identities for a considerable time. For example, Philip Beaufort, father of the Philip who is the hero of the novel (the latter's name is changed to Kangji in the translation for the sake of clarity) appears in the original novel in chapter 1 but is not identified until chapter 2, whereas the translation identifies him early in the first chapter (although it continues to refer to him as "the visitor"). There are also differences in the cases of Catherine (Aige in the Chinese), her son Sidney, Lord Lilburne, and others. This practice did not suit Chinese conventions, and in each case the text has been reordered so as to identify the character first.

Similarly, background information, often withheld in the English, is regularly brought forward in the Chinese. Thus when Philip and Catherine are identified early in the translation, their families are also described and their situations explained. Motivation, often left to the imagination in the original, is regularly explained in the translation. In one or two cases, a mystery is unraveled early at the cost of some of the novel's carefully engineered suspense. For example, Birnie's mysterious hold over Gawtrey—both men are currency forgers in Paris, and Birnie can earn a pardon and a reward if he informs on Gawtrey—is explained early in the Chinese, and the translator tells us why: lest his readers be perplexed.[26] In another instance, he explains the veiled threat issued to Gawtrey by Inspector Favart of the Paris police.[27] While these changes are partly dictated by the reader's need to understand what is happening, they also conform to general tendencies in Chinese fiction.[28]

What of the order in which events are narrated? The translator greatly prefers the chronological order. The one big exception occurs in chapter 4 of book 2, where he turns back in time for the length of a whole English chapter. He does so, presumably, because he is faced with two events occurring simultaneously. Rather than shuttle back and forth between them, he chooses to follow one, involving Philip (Kangji), and then go back and pick up the other, involving his brother Sidney. In this case continuity—continuing the narrative as far as possible with the same focus—is more important than chronological order.

In general, a smooth continuity is vital to the translator. Lytton, like other English novelists of his time, took delight in leaping from one event to another without first setting the scene, evidently hoping for a dramatic effect. He does so frequently at the opening of a chapter; many start out with dialogue before the readers know what the situation is, and sometimes even before they know who is speaking. But such leaps do not suit the Chinese translator. (In general, traditional Chinese narrative may take a leap in either time or focus, but not in both at once.) In the translation, a linking narrative between the events is briefly given, the scene is set, and the participants are identified. The one great exception comes at the beginning of book 3, which in the English opens with an elaborate satirical description of an upper-class marriage salon in Paris run by a mysterious Monsieur Love. In this case the Chinese does follow the arrangement without any linking narrative—but then immediately identifies Monsieur Love as William Gawtrey.[29]

How does the translator break the novel off at midpoint? In the last issue of the journal, he arranges a kind of semiclosure, as Gawtrey dies in a hail of police bullets. But what, then, of Philip (Kangji), he asks his readers, before undertaking to give them a sequel under a different title: "Did he survive? Readers, kindly close this book and think about it for a moment. Kangji is the main figure in this novel. How could he possibly be killed by those bullets?"[30]

Style, Tone, Language Level

The elimination of the epigraphs and their replacement with mundane chapter headings are symptomatic of the most radical kind of change made by the translator: his rejection of Lytton's portentous style.

This subject presents something of a puzzle. When writing nonfiction such as *England and the English*, his biography of Schiller, or his autobiography, Lytton wrote clearly and well; a modern historian has even praised the first work for its graceful style.[31] Lytton's fictional style, however, was criticized even in his own time, and in recent decades it has been roundly ridiculed. I believe that the answer to the puzzle can be found in his unfinished autobiography, which was written probably between 1852 and 1855.[32] Writing of the criticism his novels received, Lytton notes the influence on his early work of Shakespeare and Euripides. From Shakespeare he drew "a desire to investigate the springs of passion and analyze the human heart," but from Euripides "a tendency to arrest narrative, often to the injury of its narrative progress, by moralizing deductions and sententious aphorisms."[33] At first he wrote his fiction slowly, then with more ease:

> But it was not until years afterwards that I attained to rapid facility, and in doing so, forced myself to resign much that would better please the taste, in order not to lose that dash and rapidity of diction by which alone (at least in the works of imagination) we can hurry the reader into passion. For art in fiction is somewhat like art in oratory, the language it uses must often, with purpose, be rough, loose and slovenly. The evidence of impulse must preponderate over that of preparation.

He uses the same analogy with oratory in his remarks on style in *England and the English*: "Fiction, with its graphic delineation and appeals to the familiar emotions, is adapted to the crowd—for it is the oratory of literature."[34] He evidently thought of his heightened style as akin to the language of dramatic soliloquy or oratorical speech. It was something he deliberately turned to in order to "hurry the reader into passion."

Even among Lytton's novels, *Night and Morning* is noted for the "extravagance of its style."[35] The following passage, which comes just after the funeral of Catherine Morton, may serve as an example:

> The funeral was over, the dead shoveled away. What a strange thing it does seem, that that very form which we prized so charily, for which we prayed the winds to be gentle, which we lapped from the cold in our arms, from whose footsteps we would have removed a stone, should be suddenly thrust out of sight—an abomination that the earth must not look upon—a despicable loathsomeness, to be concealed and to be forgotten! And this same composition of bone and muscle that was yesterday so strong—which men respected, and women loved, and children clung to—today so lamentably powerless, unable to defend or protect those who lay nearest to its heart; its riches wrest-

ed from it, its wishes spat upon, its influence expiring with its last sigh! A breath from its lips making that mighty difference between what it was and what it is. (1.5.72–73)

The relations between narrator and reader in the Chinese tradition scarcely allow for this kind of effusion. (He might have expressed some of these sentiments in verse, in the Chinese fashion, but this translator never resorts to verse.) He omits the entire passage, not for any lack of concern over Catherine's death—in fact, the pathos of the episode is considerably strengthened in his translation—but because this kind of portentous meditation had no place in his conception of the novel. He frequently translates Lytton's pronouncements on men and affairs, but he regularly omits the orations with their apostrophized abstractions.

Lytton's heightened style was not confined to passages of grandiloquent reflection. In referring to some young men who showed compassion to an old man struck by a horse, he remarks that they were young and "not yet grinded down into stone by the world's wheels." The Chinese simply says that they "were still young and had a conscience."[36] At more dramatic moments Lytton reached for his heightened style even in dialogue. As Gawtrey prepares to shoot Birnie, who has betrayed him to the Paris police, he shouts: "Thus die my slavery and all secrets!" And when Philip at last realizes the true nature of Gawtrey's criminality, he exclaims: "Frown not on me, man of blood!"[37] Both ejaculations are omitted in the Chinese. Also omitted are portentous expressions like "The Accursed" or "The Outcast" in reference to Philip.

Lytton had another heightened style, shared with many novelists of his time: playful or ironic euphuism. Fishing is described as "the excellent sport of the brethren of the angle" and fishermen as "the Waltons of the neighborhood,"[38] expressions that the Chinese reduces to plain language. When Tom Morton is tempted to eat his father's breakfast muffin, the text runs: "Never did Pythian sibyl, seated above the bubbling spring, utter more oracular eloquence to her priest, than did that muffin—at least the part of it still extant—utter to the fascinated senses of Master Tom."[39] The Chinese simply says that Tom's mouth watered.[40] If there is any irony in the dialogue, the Chinese translates the text without it and conveys the tone by simply inserting an adverbial phrase to modify the verb of saying.[41]

Narrative Technique

Several tendencies can be observed in what may be described as the narrative technique of the translation, notably the tendency to strengthen scenes with additional detail and occasionally to shift the mode from summary to scene, and also the tendency to view a scene through the eyes of a character rather than impersonally. Both are characteristic of the traditional Chinese novel.

Scenes, particularly strongly emotional scenes, are frequently enhanced in the translation, sometimes with extra visualized detail, sometimes with extra dialogue.[42] Long speeches or accounts, in particular, are regularly broken up into dialogue by inserting interjections and questions. Passages of thought, of which there are many in this novel, a good number either supplied or enhanced by the translator, naturally shift from summary to scene, since Chinese narrative tends to treat thought like direct speech.

Whereas the English novel often describes a scene or a person from an Olympian angle or viewpoint, the Chinese describes it from the angle of a character. For example, the scene in which Lord Lilburne joins the MacGregors' party in Milan is conveyed in the original from an impersonal, Olympian perspective, but in the Chinese it is described as Philip Morton (Kangji) observes it.[43] At one point in the novel the English opens in this manner: "One morning, three men were seen entering Paris on foot through the Porte St. Denis. It was a fine day in spring."[44] The translator could not accept the impersonal "were seen," characteristic though it is of traditional English narrative. He changes the order and the angle of view, beginning with the date and the weather, and only then remarks that "the soldiers guarding the wall saw three men entering the Tianni gate."[45]

There is one case in which the translation has been forced to adopt a different solution. The original has told how Philip Morton hid and watched as his cousin Arthur Beaufort came on the scene. The narrator proceeds to compare their looks and physique: "There was no comparison in the natural personal advantages of the two men; for Philip Morton, despite all the hardships of his rough career, had now grown up and ripened into a rare perfection of form and feature. His broad chest, his erect air. . . ."[46] No character was available to make the comparison for the translator, but the passage was too important to omit, so he enlisted his readers for the task: "Readers, please compare the two men."[47] The angle of view may not be a character's, but at least it is not impersonal.

The Reception of Foreign Cultural References

I am using the word "foreign" to mean those references in the original that would presumably have been unfamiliar to the intended Chinese reader of the

1870s. As I have mentioned, in assimilative translation such features may be deleted, adapted, or explained. If they are not important enough to be worth the trouble of explaining, they are deleted. Take, for example, the word "banns," which a dictionary defines as "spoken or published announcements in a church of an intended marriage." The translation already has to explain that marriages were solemnized in church by a pastor and that the fact was recorded in the parish registry, and since it would have meant a good deal of extra trouble to explain the meaning of "banns," the word is conveniently omitted.[48] Again, when Mr. Plaskwith, a Dickensian character who fancies himself a Napoleonic look-alike, says to Philip Morton, "Now fancy me at St. Helena,"[49] the translation, having already inserted a brief account of Napoleon's career, simply omits the reference. There are numerous other examples.

Adaptation usually amounts to replacing a term that would have required explanation with a more general, less distinctive term requiring none. For example, "a postman . . . on his rounds" becomes "a man in ordinary clothes with a pack on his back,"[50] a "steeplechase" becomes a "hunt,"[51] a "horse-trough" becomes a "pond,"[52] "the guillotine" becomes "the execution ground,"[53] "algebra" becomes "arithmetic,"[54] and so forth. A few adaptations are idiomatically apt, even if they bring with them inappropriate connotations; for example, "lynx-eyed" becomes "Qianliyan Shunfenger" (Thousand-*li* Eyes and Downwind Ears), and "Good Heavens!" becomes "Emitofo!" (invocation of Buddha).[55]

Instances of explanation proliferate in this novel, as the translator lives up to his promise to broaden the reader's knowledge and give an account of European customs in simple terms. Sometimes he manages to explain things implicitly, by including the definition with the name, e.g., for Eton, Christ Church, Oxford, the Houses of Parliament, and Napoleon. And instead of explaining a point of British law, he simply slips the phrase "according to British law" into the text.[56]

Explicit explanations, normally signaled by "*kanguan*" or "*yuanlai*," are the majority. Here is a partial list of those that make use of Chinese analogues: public coaches are compared to the passenger boats of Jiangnan;[57] the public parks in London are compared to one recently opened in Hong Kong (note that the English doesn't actually mention parks, it merely says "have a nice walk," which the translator interprets to mean a walk in the park);[58] the color black at western funerals is compared to white in China; Parisian detectives are likened to those of Shanghai and Beijing;[59] the ease with which foreign women can inherit property is compared to the legal wrangling that occurs in China;[60] cardsharps' tricks are likened to those in China;[61] dueling, although set in the past, is favorably contrasted (because it involves only two people) with the general melees that often erupt from disputes in Fujian and Guangdong;[62] passports are compared to internal passes and licenses in China;[63] the title of "lord" in England is compared to titles conferred on Li Hongzhang and Zuo Zongtang;[64] toasting is compared to the drinking of wine forfeits in China.[65]

Of the explanations without a specific Chinese analogue, let me note first the references to the practice of kissing, a subject that for decades was the bane of Chinese and Japanese translators. Kissing is first mentioned when Philip (Kangji) asks his mother, Catherine Morton, for a kiss;[66] the Chinese simply omits any mention of it. On the second occasion, when Philip Beaufort is hugged by his wife Catherine, the English merely says that he "was locked in her arms,"[67] but the Chinese chooses this occasion, that of a wife kissing her husband, to explain the custom to the reader: "According to foreign protocol, women, on meeting relatives, whether they be brothers, nephews, or husbands, join their lips with them in greeting. This is done in front of other people without any qualms at all."[68]

The following is a mere sampling of other items: the liberal courting practices of the West; the fact that clergymen can take wives; wills and testaments; a six-barred gate (important because Philip Beaufort dies trying to get his horse to jump over one); conservatories; Napoleon; the poverty of lawyer's clerks; cemeteries; muffins (because of the importance of the stolen muffin); cracker bonbons; the party games Hunt the Slipper and Blind Man's Buff; Brutus; the Patent Office; the French Revolution from Rousseau to Napoleon; the gesture of tapping one's forehead to signify someone's craziness; country dancing; Jews; the Grand Tour (not named, but correctly inferred from the context); western penal codes; bath-houses; German spas; the Champs Elysées; trouser pockets; policemen's whistles; beards and moustaches (they add dignity, and are not considered strange).

Only rarely does the translator attempt to render one of Lytton's long metaphors directly. When Gawtrey is speaking to Philip Morton about the dangerous condition of France after the revolution, he denies that Napoleonism is finished; its effects have just begun to be felt. "Society is shattered from one end to the other, and I laugh at the little rivets by which they think to keep it together." He goes on: "The vast masses of energy and life, broken up by the great thaw of the Imperial system, floating along the tide, are terrible icebergs for the vessel of the state."[69] The Chinese does not mention the ship of state, which would not have been a common image in Chinese anyway, but it does refer to the dangers facing government as "rather like an iceberg," and says that "little nails aren't able to repair the gaping holes."[70] The references to icebergs and rivets would surely have puzzled the reader, so a little later, at the end of the chapter, the translator returns to "the image of an iceberg that I mentioned before," and explains how icebergs break loose from the icepack at the Pole and float south, presenting a grave danger to ships traveling at night. "That is why I borrowed the image for comparison."[71]

If there were any clear ideological motives behind the translation, this is where one would expect them to appear, in the translator's choice of which foreign cultural references to explain. The explanations would provide him with a splendid opportunity for invidious comparisons between China and Europe. At a later date, from 1900, for example, the translation of a novel that dealt with modern Europe would no doubt be full of comparisons favorable to one culture or the other, probably the European, but that is not the case here. There are a number of comparisons that favor the West, particularly with regard to customs (e.g., courtship and marriage), laws (e.g., the law of inheritance) and institutions (e.g., the Patent Office), but there are also a few that favor China. For example, the inheritance of a title was automatic in England, allowing the vicious Lilburne to succeed to the peerage, whereas in China the succession would have been subject to official approval.[72] But the comparisons, favorable or not, are outnumbered by explanations that simply supply information, from trivial items of mainly ethnographic interest to important facts. The translator rarely allows himself a personal statement, but after describing the party games Hunt the Slipper and Blind Man's Buff, he comments indulgently, "Crude as these games are, [the foreigners] love to play them."[73]

However, if he doesn't reveal any clear political motives, he certainly reveals some personal interests. He gives specifics about things that are treated generally in the original, for example, certain commodities, particularly children's toys. He updates the list of occupations Gawtrey admits to, including "relaying secret market data for the telegraph companies."[74] More significantly, he adds two admiring comments on Napoleon.[75] In general, he offers far fewer moral judgments than one would expect from a novelist of his time.

The Diffusion of Chinese Cultural References

The translation's use of distinctively Chinese cultural references is not confined to its explanations of foreign references. In any case of assimilative translation, in which the overriding need is to be idiomatic, other references are bound to occur. They can be examined on at least two levels, language and theme.

On a basic level of linguistic analysis, the translation contains numerous proverbs and sayings, some distinctively Chinese, which occur not as renderings of western proverbs but simply as elements of the language. It also contains some of the staple images of Chinese fiction. Finally, there are references—probably included inadvertently, simply because they are embedded in the language—to phenomena such as matchmakers, bound feet, and concubines that are not appropriate in the English context.

On a higher level, there are specific references to Chinese culture. For example, Robert Beaufort's vapid wife, completely under her husband's sway, is likened to Xing Furen (Madam Xing) in *Story of the Stone*, and Lord Lilburne, crippled in a duel with William Gawtrey, is compared to depictions of the Daoist immortal Li Tieguai.[76] A cliché about Zhou Fang and Du Fu is inserted in a letter that the translator has largely rewritten.[77] Two lines from one of Li Shangyin's "Untitled" poems are quoted as from "an ancient poet,"[78] but the lines are so famous that they can perhaps be regarded as proverbial. The poems found inside the cracker bonbons are turned into characteristically Chinese poems full of specifically Chinese references.[79]

There are several occasions on which the translation can be seen to have moved in the direction of a familiar Chinese theme. In the original novel, the Welsh village of the early chapters lies in a remote valley rarely visited by tourists. It has nothing to "allure the more sturdy enthusiast from the beaten tracks." Its few attractions certainly do not appeal to the unfortunate clergyman, Caleb Price, who, after a misspent youth at Cambridge, finds himself a virtual prisoner in an out-of-the-way place. The Chinese translation, however, ignores the novel's ironic portrayal and turns the village into an idyllic spot, with the theme of Peach Blossom Spring in the background. With a little more justice, Fernside Cottage outside London, where Philip Beaufort installs Catherine Morton, also becomes a rural refuge in the translation and is actually renamed Peach Blossom Paradise.[80]

A second theme is that of the impoverished scholar. Price, the frustrated clergyman who is coolly satirized by Lytton's narrator, becomes in the Chinese a classic object of sympathy, the penniless intellectual. The translation stresses the pathos of his situation, enlarging the text for the purpose of telling in detail of his unsuccessful marriage suit, his illness, despair, and death.[81] This is in accord with the translator's general stress on scenes of pathos, particularly those involving Catherine, except that in this case the pathos is of Price's own making.

There are other cases in which the English text has been fitted into an existing Chinese theme, for example, the hen-pecked husband theme in the case of Roger Morton.[82] Other themes concern fraternity, filial piety, and karmic destiny. But the most interesting example is the heroic theme embodied by William Gawtrey. As I have explained, he is one of Lytton's sympathetic criminals. His development into a criminal is explained by Lytton partly as a matter of innate temperament but mostly as the product of his environment (he was misled or betrayed by his father, an uncle, and his treacherous friend Lilburne). Lytton sees him as a low-level version of the revolutionary type:

> [Gawtrey] was the incarnation of that great spirit which the laws of the world raise up against the world, or by which the world's injustice, on a large scale, is awfully chastised; on a small scale, nibbled at and harassed, as the rat that gnaws the hoof of the elephant:—The spirit which, on a vast theatre, rises up, gigantic and sublime, in the heroes of war and revolution—in Mirabeaus, Marats, Napoleons: on a minor stage, it shows itself in demagogues, fanatical philosophers, and mob-writers; and on the forbidden boards, before whose reeking lamps outcasts sit, at once audience and actors, it never produced a knave more consummate in his part, or carrying it off with more buskined dignity, than William Gawtrey. (3.4.322)

In the Chinese version of this passage, the law is described as the projection of the court's power. If people are bold enough, some of them will resist that power and declare themselves heroes (*yingxiong haojie*).[83] Earlier, the translation has inserted a passage in which Philip (Kangji) sees Gawtrey as a hero, someone who if successful becomes a king, if unsuccessful a brigand.[84] And in Philip's eyes, Gawtrey remains heroic; later, he sees him as a *haohan*, that unruly but magnanimous physical hero of Chinese fiction, and at the end, after reflecting on Gawtrey's capacity for moving people's hearts and forging strong friendships, he says to himself, "What a hero! Even if he did take a wrong turn and lead the life of a criminal, I still had hopes that he might see the error of his ways. But it's all over now."[85]

In the English context, Lytton's Gawtrey is a somewhat unusual conception. The Chinese translator understandably discards the idea of the "great spirit" behind revolution, demagoguery, and crime, and chooses to fit his Gawtrey within the familiar category of the *haohan* and also within a closely related category, that of the rebel who either topples the dynasty or stands condemned as a brigand. Needless to say, any assimilative translation will tend to take a course like this, fitting unfamiliar themes into similar but far from identical themes in the reader's culture.

The Translator's Commentary

The translator's assimilative purpose is strongly reinforced by his critical commentary, which never points to unfamiliar features, but first defends the novel in Chinese terms and then praises it for its allegedly Chinese techniques. Furthermore, those it chooses to praise are, in some cases, those the translator has either introduced or enhanced himself.

The commentary consists of a short preface, critiques at the end of each of the first four chapters, a colophon at the end of the first book, and some remarks at the end of the translation, as well as a notice in the *Shen bao* of January 4, 1873 announcing the publication of "A Newly Translated English Novel." Although the preface shows a certain influence from Lytton's preface to his 1845 edition,[86] its main concern is to justify the English novel according to traditional Chinese criteria. After a brief history of fiction in familiar terms, it declares that any novelist must abide by the principal moral and social prescriptions of the culture. This novel's positive value lies in its demonstration that fame accrues to the virtuous rather than to the rich. True gentlemen are vividly portrayed and false ones exposed. (The references are to Philip Morton and Robert Beaufort, respectively.) The novel also conveys much information on western customs. Readers should not put it in the same category as "run-of-the-mill novels or useless fiction."

The critiques constantly point out that the techniques used in the novel are those of traditional Chinese criticism, particularly fiction criticism. They argue, for example, that the secret wedding with which the work opens is its nub, "the root of the tree, the source of the stream," and that the church is its symbol. They argue, too, that the novel's oblique approach of focusing on the peripheral figure of Caleb Price is superior to any straightforward account of Philip Beaufort's courtship of Catherine. Philip and Catherine's happiness is far more effectively implied by Price's inability to find a wife and his consequent misery; the technique is that of *hong yun tuo yue*, "painting the clouds to set off the moon," a common critical term. We have already seen how the translator, for his own purposes, tries to show Price as pathetic. The value of contrast is again noted with regard to two letters in chapter 2, an ecstatically happy one from Philip and a pathetic one from Price. As it happens, the translator was himself responsible for rewriting the first letter and for composing the second.

After invoking much of the technical apparatus of criticism in his first critique, he tips off the reader to what he is doing. In praising the novel for its use of distinctively Chinese techniques, he remarks playfully: "I wonder if the author hasn't benefited from the *Works of Genius* of the Mustard Seed Garden."[87] The reference is to the *Six Works of Genius* (*Liu caizi shu*) selected and annotated by Jin Shengtan (1610–61), the most influential fiction critic, and the remark is a humorous acknowledgment of the translator's assimilative attitude.

We have seen how far the translator goes in his attempt to make his work acceptable to the general reader. What can we deduce of the work's actual reception?

Serial publication became the norm for novels at the turn of the century, but except for some marginal cases,[88] it had never been tried before *Xinxi xiantan*. It is likely, as I have said, that the idea came from England, where many novelists, not including Lytton, routinely serialized their novels before publishing them in book form. The initial printing of *Yinghuan suoji* was 2,000 copies, a considerable number for the first literary journal published in China. The notice announcing the translation stresses the heavy commitment made by the publishing company and predicts, inaccurately, that with three or four chapters (*zhang*) appearing each month, the translation will be complete in a year. It shows an understandable concern that Chinese readers might not take kindly to this new way of reading a novel, for the next sentence runs, "Readers must buy and read the journal every month if they are not to lose the thread." The same concern is evident in a notice in the *Shen bao* of October 27, 1873 announcing the completion of book 1; a "General Colophon to Book 1" will be included in the first installment of book 2 summarizing the contents up to this point so that readers can catch up with anything they may have missed. (Book 1 was also separately published as a book; see the notice in the *Shen bao* of January 15, 1874.) The notice of the translation also emphasizes that the work is so clearly written that it will "appeal to both refined and popular taste."

In September 1875, six months after the last installment had appeared in *Yinghuan suoji*, the "complete work" was advertised in the *Shen bao*. In fact, the published book is a hasty rounding-off of the novel by marrying Philip to Eugénie de Merville, a woman with whom, in Lytton's novel, he has a brief love affair before, after many more adventures, he marries Fanny. The advertisement describes the novel as if it were a standard romance of the "brilliant and beautiful" type.

The dropping of the novel at midpoint surely means that it had not found great favor with readers. Not only was the translation never properly completed, it failed to spawn any imitations. The contrast with the Japanese case is striking. In Japan the translations of Lytton's *Ernest Maltravers* and its sequel, *Alice*, in 1879 were so successful that the translator quickly followed them up with more translations from the same author. To most tastes, *Night and Morning* is at least as interesting a novel as *Ernest Maltravers*, and the Chinese translator was, on the whole, more assimilative than his Japanese counterpart despite providing a fuller treatment of the text. One reason for the relative failure of the translation in China may have been its serial mode of publication, to which Chinese readers were not accustomed. Qian Zheng, in his preface to the *Xieyu congtan chuji* from which I have quoted, went on to criticize *Yinghuan suoji* and its successor journals for their limitations on space. Each issue consisted of thirty—actually twenty-four—double pages, which had to be divided among four different kinds of material. This resulted in publication in installments, which led to complaints from readers. I think he must have been referring to *Xinxi xiantan*, which was serialized over a longer period than any other work in *Yinghuan suoji*. In any case, the experiment was not the start of a new trend. Although the Chinese novel *Yesou puyan* by Xia Jingqu was serialized in a newspaper in 1882–83,[89] it was not until 1892 that another Chinese novel, *Haishang hua liezhuan* (Flowers of Shanghai), was published in a journal.

But installment publication can hardly have been the main reason for the novel's reception. The so-called "complete work" appeared as a book in 1875, but no other editions are reported until 1904, a fact that would not indicate any great success.[90] A more likely reason for the apparent failure is that there was not yet a sufficiently large audience for foreign fiction in China. One indication of this is the narrowing of the original focus of *Yinghuan suoji*, which was at first quite cosmopolitan; its successor journals became collections of rather conventional literary pieces. It would be another twenty years before a new generation of Chinese readers, under changed political and cultural circumstances, began to take a keen interest in foreign fiction.[91]

NOTES

1. It ran from the third number of the journal, published in January 1973, to the twenty-eighth, published in March 1975. Two chapters appeared in each number, for a total of 52. After 28 numbers, the journal's name and format were changed and the translation dropped. Later in 1875 it was published in book form by the Shen-baoguan, with three added chapters. The first novel translated (as distinct from composed) by a missionary was probably a short work entitled *Jinwu xingyi* (The model of a golden house), which was published in Hong Kong in 1852; see chapter 3. Note that the *Shen bao* itself published brief versions of three works of western fiction between May 21 and June 15, 1872; see chapter 5.

2. This approach is broadly similar to that of "descriptive translation studies" as presented by Gideon Toury, *Descriptive Translation Studies and Beyond* (Amsterdam: John Benjamins, 1995).

3. The Chinese translation ends after chapter 10 of book 3 of Lytton's novel (there are five books in all) and accounts for only 33 of its 68 chapters. *Night and Morning* was

first published in three volumes, then in two, and finally in one. The translator must have used an edition of 1851 or later, because he has incorporated a footnote that Lytton evidently wrote for the 1851 edition. (The footnote refers to Louis Napoleon's rise to power; see book 3, chapter 3, page 316 of the Lippincott 1865 edition and 3.5.12ab of the Chinese translation in *Yinghuan suoji*.) So many virtually identical editions were published between 1851 and 1873 that it is impossible to say precisely which one the translator used. (He could not, however, have used the Harper edition, which omits the author's 1845 preface, of which the commentator made some use; see below.) My references are to the Lippincott edition published in Philadelphia in 1865, but because no single edition is widely available, I give the book and chapter numbers as well as the page numbers. For convenience, my references to the translation are to the book published by the Shenbaoguan in 1875. (There is a copy in the Shanghai Library.) It consists of a reprint of the chapters appearing in the *Yinghuan suoji*, with no changes except in the fishtail, where the title of the journal has been replaced by "Yingguo xiaoshuo" (The English novel), and the page numbers of the chapter have been replaced by those of the book. Three chapters have been added in the book, 22–24 in *juan* 3. They are based on the next three chapters of *Night and Morning*, chapters 11–13 of book 3. The added chapters are designed to provide a truncated ending, leaving Philip betrothed to the first of his three loves, Eugénie de Merville.

4. See his preface to the 1840 edition of *Ernest Maltravers* (1837).

5. See Juliet John, ed., *Cult Criminals, The Newgate Novels, 1830–1847* (London: Routledge, 1998), introduction, xlv. She goes on to affirm that *Night and Morning* has taken Lytton "beyond the range of conventional morality," echoing a claim that Lytton himself made in his 1845 preface.

6. See Standish Meacham, ed., *England and the English* (Chicago: University of Chicago Press, 1970), 45.

7. See Lytton's 1845 preface.

8. It was first noted by Guo Changhai, "Lishao Jushi he Lichuang Wodusheng," *Ming-Qing xiaoshuo yanjiu* 3–4 (1992): 457–61. The advertisement appeared weekly from May 11 to June 1, 1905. Note that the "retranslation" was really just a reissue. Zou Zhenhuan describes the contents as identical to those of the 1875 edition; see his *Yingxiang Zhongguo jindai shehui de yibaizhong yizuo* (Shanghai: Zhongguo duiwai fanyi chuban gongsi, 1994), 70.

9. For these identifications, see Yan Tingliang, "Guanyu Lishao jushi qiren de diandi yice," *Gansu shehui kexue* 5 (1992): 106–10. In addition to the evidence cited for the identification of Hengmengan Zhu with Xiao Jiluoan Zhu, two other items can be adduced: the introduction to the poem by Hechashan Nong (i.e., Jiang Mei) in the *Shen bao* for the eleventh of the twelfth month of 1872, and the preface to a poem by Zhuanxiang Laoren (i.e., Gu Jingxiu) in the *Shen bao* of the sixth of the eleventh month of 1873.

10. See the *Shen bao* of the sixth of the eleventh month of 1873 (December 25).

11. See the *Shen bao* of the twenty-fifth of the third month of 1872 (May 2).

12. See the *Shen bao* of the eighteenth of the seventh month of 1872 (August 21).

13. See the *Shen bao* of the fourteenth of the first month of 1873 (February 11).

14. See Hu Daojing, "Shanghai de ribao," *Shanghai tongzhiguan qikan* 2.1 (1934): 220, 245.

15. The announcement of impending publication appeared first on the seventh of the sixth month (July 30), describing the book as an anthology of examination essays made by the *Shen bao*. The notice of actual publication appeared on the first of the seventh month (August 23) and ran for a month and a half. No editor is named on the first page of text, and in the preface the editor is given only the pseudonym Yishengge Zhuren. However, the editing is attributed to Jiang Qizhang in *Zhongguo congshu zonglu* (Beijing: Zhonghua shuju, 1961), 2:1563, and there must have been a reason behind the attribution. Six of Jiang's own essays appear in the collection, more than anyone else's, and he is the only contributor whose courtesy name is given, as Zixiang. Essays by several people who exchange poems with Hengmengan Zhu in the *Shen bao* are also included.

16. These facts are derived from the *Zhejiang xiangshilu* of 1870 and the 1922–26 *Hangzhou fuzhi*. No doubt there is more to be discovered about Jiang. The newspaper and the journal provide us with some information. In the title to a poem by his friend Ge Qilong, who under the pseudonym Longqiu Jiuyin (and other pseudonyms) was the most prolific contributor of poetry to both the *Shen bao* and *Yinghuan suoji*, he is given the courtesy title Zixiang. See Ge Qilong, *Ji'an shichao*, 1878, 1, 18b–19b. Poems on a painting referred to here appear also in Huang Duo's *Quyuji*, 4.7ab. Under the pseudonym Luzhou Shiyin, Huang exchanged poems with Hengmengan Zhu in the *Shen bao*. A little more information about the translator can be gleaned from the newspaper and the journal. In the *Shen bao*, Xiao Jiluoan Zhu was responsible for some rather conventional pieces, such as stories of women of humble origin who martyr themselves to the code of widows' chastity. Hengmengan Zhu also possessed a rare copy of a work by Qian Qianyi (1582–1664); see the *Shen bao* for the thirteenth of the twelfth month of 1872.

17. See "Yuleguo ji" (in 1), "Renshen shengji lingji lun" (in 2), and "Ji Yingguo 'Tatong' ju lunchuan dianmo" (also in 2), respectively. The aquarium was officially opened on August 10, 1872. One might have expected the writer to learn of it from the Hongkong newspapers, but he says that his interest was sparked by hearing a western friend (or friends) talking about it, which suggests that at least one of his sources was oral. The second essay also mentions two cases of brain death reported in the West. The fact that in the third essay the name of the steamship *Great Eastern* is transcribed in Chinese characters pronounced "tatong" and explained as meaning merely immense indicates that the writer was dependent on a Chinese-speaking informant.

18. See no. 2.

19. For information about the other editor, see Hu Daojing, "Shanghai de ribao," 244. Wu was engaged as editor at the planning stage, Jiang as the paper was about to be published. In studies of the *Shen bao*, Jiang Zhixiang is described as continuing as a chief editor until 1884, at which point he succeeded in the metropolitan examinations and left the newspaper, but that date must be wrong; no metropolitan examinations were held that year.

20. See chapter 5. By about this time there was also a foreign-language library in Shang-hai, Yangwen shuguan; see *The China Directory for 1874* (reprint, Taipei: Ch'eng Wen Publishing Company, 1971), 8J.

21. *Ernest Maltravers* (1837) and its sequel, *Alice* (1838), were translated by Niwa (Oda) Jun'ichiro as *Karyū shunwa* and its supplement. See *Meiji hon'yaku bungaku shū* (1972) in the *Meiji bungaku zenshū* series.

22. See chapter 5. The *Shen bao* versions of Swift's and Irving's fiction are excellent ex-amples of outright assimilation, because they transform the content into a familiar Chinese form with wholly Chinese cultural references.

23. Lytton published a volume of translations of Schiller's poetry with a biography, *The Poems and Ballads of Schiller* (London: William Blackwood and Sons, 1844).

24. See 103a. It places a paraphrase of the poem in Gawtrey's mouth.

25. Sometimes the translator merely added to the author's, or rather the narrator's, com-ments, thereby compounding the confusion.

26. P. 117b.

27. P. 124a.

28. Some of them may simply be due to a translator's—any translator's—tendency to clarify motivation and add detail. Ria Vanderauwera in her *Dutch Novels Translated Into English* (Amsterdam: Rodopi, 1985) has noticed similar characteristics.

29. P. 94a.

30. P. 156a. When the translation was published in book form with three added chap-ters, this ending was kept intact. The following chapter explains the ending as a nov-elist's attempt to add suspense.

31. John Clive, preface to Lytton, *England and the English*.

32. See Robert Bulwer Lytton, *The Life and Letters and Literary Remains of Edward Bul-wer, Lord Lytton* (London: Kegan, Paul, Trench, 1883), 1:5.

33. Contained in Earl of Lytton, *The Life of Edward Bulwer, First Lord Lytton* (London: MacMillan, 1913). These quotations are from 1:88–89.

34. P. 298.

35. Earl of Lytton, *The Life of Edward Bulwer*, 2:31. The remark is the author's. He de-scribes the novel as "a melodramatic story of adventures in [Lytton's] most flamboy-ant style."

36. Cf. 1.9.145 (English) with 46a (Chinese).

37. See 3.9.90.

38. 1.1.2.

39. 2.3.197.

40. P. 66b.

41. He also smoothes out the jerky dialogue that Lytton favored.

42. For example, in the Chinese version Philip Beaufort asks about Caleb Price's situa-tion (3ab). This is natural—Philip has just explained his own situation to Price—and it also suits the translator's purpose of making Price a pathetic figure. The emotion-al scenes mostly involve Catherine, Fanny's mother, and Fanny herself.

43. Cf. 3.6.351 (English) and 130a (Chinese).

44. 3.7.357.

45. P. 134a.
46. 3.8.370–371.
47. P. 142a.
48. Cf. the English at 1.1.24.
49. Cf. the English at 1.6.104.
50. 1.1.33 (English) and 11a (Chinese).
51. 1.4.55 and 16a.
52. 2.9.248 and 80a.
53. 3.10.6 and 153a.
54. 1.6.102 and 29b.
55. See 3.4.326 and 116b, 2.6.216 and 68b, respectively.
56. P. 24a.
57. P. 31a.
58. P. 45a.
59. Pp. 77a and 122a, respectively.
60. P. 103b.
61. P. 106a.
62. P. 107a.
63. P. 123b.
64. P. 129b.
65. P. 148a.
66. 1.2.42.
67. 1.3.52.
68. P. 13b.
69. 3.3.315.
70. P. 108a.
71. P. 108b. Another case occurs on 130a, where he tries to translate Lilburne's word play at the cost of having to explain to the reader the meaning of "sow one's wild oats" and "ace of spades." (See the English at 3.5.151.)
72. P. 130a.
73. P. 99b.
74. P. 111b.
75. Pp. 29b and 108a. On the other hand, the references to the partition of Poland, a subject that a later generation of writers would surely have emphasized, add little, if anything, to Lytton's text. In the advertisement for the 1905 edition, by contrast, much is made of the partition of Poland and of Napoleon's career.
76. See 44a and 130a, respectively.
77. P. 11b.
78. P. 6a.
79. See 3.1.188 and 3.1.290 in the English and 95b–96a in the Chinese.
80. P. 13a.
81. See chapter 3 in book 1.
82. P. 40b.
83. P. 125b.

84. P. 112b.
85. Pp. 139b and 151ab, respectively.
86. The preface's listing of the functions of fiction seems to be derived from the open-
    ing of Lytton's preface, although none of the functions actually conflicts with Chi-
    nese ideas. Lytton says, "Certainly, in fiction, to interest, to please, and sportively to
    elevate—to take man from the low passions, and the miserable troubles of life, into
    a higher region, to beguile weary and selfish pain, to excite a generous sorrow at vi-
    cissitudes not his own, to raise the passions into sympathy with heroic struggles—
    and to admit the soul into that serener atmosphere . . .". Compare that with this part
    of the Chinese preface: "I hold that a novel should bring calm and delight to the spir-
    it, causing all those under stress and strain to cast aside their cares and gradually
    reach a state of serenity. A novel also inspires readers to heroic ardor when they hear
    of gallant deeds and moves them to sorrow when they hear of harrowing events." At
    this point both Lytton and the translator go on to talk about the moral influence of
    fiction. That the translator had read Lytton's preface is shown by the notice in the
    Shen bao of January 4, 1873, which says, "The westerner declares that his novel is ful-
    ly capable of calming and delighting people's minds and admonishing them about
    their current practices." In his preface Lytton is elaborating upon the general ques-
    tion of "whether to please or to instruct should be the end of Fiction."
87. So far I know, the *Six Works* were never published by the Mustard Seed Garden, a
    seventeenth- and eighteenth-century publishing house, although it did republish the
    two novels among the six. I take the comment as a general reference to traditional
    Chinese fiction criticism.
88. I.e., the versions of "A Voyage to Lilliput" and *The Pacha of Many Tales* in *Shen
    bao*—see chapter 5 below—and one or two works published in missionary journals.
89. In the newspaper *Hu bao* and its successor, *Zilin Hubao*. It had previously been pub-
    lished in book form.
90. For the 1904 date, see Aying, *Wan-Qing xiqu xiaoshuo mu* (Shanghai: Gudian wen-
    xue chubanshe, 1957), 128. In 1904 also, Chen Jinghan began publishing his transla-
    tion of Lytton's *Eugene Aram* from a Japanese version. It appeared in the journal
    Xinxin xiaoshuo under the title *Shengren yu daozei yu*; see Tarumoto Terao, (*Xinbian
    zengbu*) *Qingmo Minchu xiaoshuo mulu* (Jinan: Qilu shushe, 2002), 635.
91. In 1896 Liang Qichao included *Xinxi xiantan* in his "Xixue shumu biao" (List of
    books on the new learning) and praised it for the information it provided on for-
    eign customs; see the edition in *Zhixue congshu chuji* (Wuchang: Xhixuehui, 1897).
    From that point on there was an increasing interest in foreign things, including
    foreign novels.

CHAPTER 5

The Translated Fiction in the Early Shen Bao

IN THE PERIOD from May 21 to June 15, 1872, the Shanghai newspaper *Shen bao*, which had been in existence only a few months at the time, published Chinese versions of three English-language works of fiction. These were not set out in the newspaper under the heading of fiction, let alone of translated fiction; they were simply included among other items of interest.

A Chinese version of a "A Voyage to Lilliput" from Jonathan Swift's *Gulliver's Travels* appeared in four installments under the title of "Tan ying xiaolu" (Notes on countries overseas) from the fifteenth to the eighteenth of the fourth month (May 21–24); a version of the "Rip Van Winkle" story from Washington Irving's collection, *The Sketchbook of Geoffrey Crayon, Gent*, appeared under the title of "Yishui qishinian" (Asleep for seventy years) in a single installment on the twenty-second of the fourth month (May 28); and a Chinese version of "Story of the Greek Slave" (plus a little of the introductory chapter) from Frederick Marryat's *The Pacha of Many Tales* appeared in six installments under the title of "Naisuguo qiwen" (A strange tale of the country of Naisu) on the twenty-fifth of the fourth month, and on the first, second, sixth, ninth, and tenth of the fifth month (May 31, June 6, 7, 11, 14 and 15).[1]

All of the translated works were well known, and two were already regarded as classics. Swift's *Gulliver's Travels* was first published in 1726; "Rip Van Winkle" in 1820; and *The Pacha of Many Tales* in 1835. In the *Shen bao* they are all translated into literary Chinese, unlike *Xinxi xiantan*, the rendering of Edward Bulwer Lytton's *Night and Morning*, which is in the vernacular.[2] Again unlike *Xinxi xiantan*, they belong to the world of strange adventures; all can be placed in the well-established category of *zhiguai* (records of the strange). Both "A Voyage to Lilliput" and "Rip Van Winkle," although very different, are fantastic tales, while *The Pacha of Many Tales* is a humorous parody of *Thousand and One Nights*, and the title of its Chinese version even uses the word "strange." Moreover, the ending of the Chinese version of "Story of the Greek Slave" introduces a familiar fantastic element.

In terms of the range of translation methods (from extreme preservation to extreme assimilation) that I discussed in the last chapter, these literary Chinese translations can all be considered assimilative, but to varying degrees.

"Asleep for Seventy Years" is an extreme case; perhaps it deserves to be called adaptation rather than assimilation. It contains scarcely any element, either of language or content, that would identify it as a translation, let alone one from a very different culture. (If the "Rip Van Winkle" story were not so famous, the Chinese version might never have been recognized as a translation.) The one element from the original that strikes the reader as odd in the Chinese context is Rip Van Winkle's rifle. In the original story, Rip has taken the rifle up the mountain with him, and when he awakens after his strange experience, he finds it still there beside him, but now completely rusty and rotten. This is the first inkling he has that anything strange has happened. The text runs, "in place of the well-oiled fowling piece, he found an old firelock by him, the barrel encrusted with rust, the lock falling off, and the stock worm-eaten." Mr. Wei, his counterpart in the Chinese version, also takes a rifle (*huoqiang*) with him into the mountains, and when he awakens and looks for it, it too is described as rusty and rotten.

Apart from the rifle, very little of the rest of the original is preserved in the Chinese version. It begins by mentioning two examples, the famous case of Chen Tuan, who is said to have been able to sleep for "hundreds and thousands of years," and that of Wang Zhi of the Jin dynasty, whose story exists in a number of slightly different variations.[3] The Chinese version in the *Shen bao* is much closer to the Wang Zhi story than to its English source. For example, in some versions of the former, after finding no one in his village who remembers him, Wang returns to the mountain to seek immortality. It was presumably this kind of text that the translator was thinking of, since he describes both Chen Tuan's and Wang Zhi's stories as dealing with immortality. Under similar circumstances, Mr. Wei also returns to the mountains. We are not actually told that he seeks immortality, but we can assume that that is the reason, since the point has been made earlier that he is attracted only to Daoist teachings. Rip Van Winkle, by contrast, spends the rest of his life in the village, where he regales everyone who will listen to him with the tale of his strange adventure.

After the two examples from Chinese legend, the translator introduces his own version of the Rip Van Winkle story by remarking that a friend had mentioned to him a story similar to these two. He does not know whether it is true or not, nor does he know when it took place, "but according to the story, there was a man named Wei. . . ."

Here is a faint suggestion of the vernacular narrator's characteristic method, strengthened by a proverbial saying added later as a narrator's comment (it is introduced by *suowei,* "this is what is called," which usually introduces a cliché or proverb). The story proper begins with *xiang chuan,* "according to the story," which corresponds roughly to the *hua shuo,* "The story goes," of vernacular fiction. The friend, however, who in the Chinese version is described as giving an oral rendering of the Rip Van Winkle story, is not a feature of vernacular fiction but a common element of the literary tale. We can assume that this friend was a westerner, possibly Ernest Major.

For the most part, as I have said, the Chinese version is closer to the Wang Zhi tale than to "Rip Van Winkle." Key elements of the original story are omitted: the setting, Rip's background and youth; his nature; his shrewish wife, who makes Rip's life and that of his dog miserable (the Chinese mentions neither wife nor dog); Rip's delight in playing with the village children; and his laziness (he neglects his farm to spend his time fishing, shooting squirrels, and hobnobbing with the villagers at the local tavern). It is to avoid his wife's carping that he goes up the mountain with his dog to hunt squirrels. By contrast, Mr. Wei has given up his academic studies for the martial arts, and has then given those up for Daoist teachings and a desire to escape from the world. After he has married and fathered a son and a daughter, there is nothing to prevent him from continuing his studies of Daoism, and he fixes his thoughts on otherworldly things. Observing the ceaseless flux of nature, he has an epiphany that sends him off to the mountains.

In the mountains, the adventures of the two men are again largely different. Rip hears a voice calling his name, then sees a man carrying a keg of liquor who leads him to a hollow "like a small amphitheatre," where various people are playing ninepins. Together they drink the liquor, and Rip falls asleep. By contrast, Mr. Wei sees a rabbit and chases it, then comes upon three old men playing chess. (In the Wang Zhi story, it is several boys playing chess.) One of the men tells Wei that his visit was foreordained. He is led to a cave with a stone door, where a whole new scene opens up before his eyes. The Chinese comments: "It was what is known as another world, not the world of men." Wei then realizes that the old man is no ordinary mortal. The wine they drink has a curious fragrance, and as Wei starts to leave, it takes effect. "You're drunk," says the old man. "Why not sleep here on this bed?"

There are even more differences at the end of the story. On returning to his village, Rip finds no one he knows. His own house is empty and in ruins. The tavern where he used to spend his time has vanished. While he has been away, the American Revolution has occurred, and Rip, a suspicious stranger, narrowly escapes arrest. Eventually he finds his daughter and realizes that twenty years have elapsed since he went up the mountain. He spends the rest of his life telling his story to others. The narrator now raises the question of credibility, something that the Chinese version brings up at the beginning. Wei also finds no one in the village whom he recognizes, but one of his descendants is living in his house, and he deduces that he has been away for seventy years. An old man in his eighties recognizes him, because Wei looks exactly the same as he did when he left. Finally, in an ending typical of a literary tale of this kind, we are told that "he returned to the mountains and no one knows what became of him." On the model of the Wang Zhi story, the Chinese version has been largely assimilated to a Daoist immortality story.

The four-part Chinese version of "A Voyage to Lilliput" is not as extreme a case of assimilation. Indeed, in certain episodes it stays fairly close to the original and even augments it, while eliminating other parts. In general, it focuses on the adventurous aspects of the story and ignores the political and institutional satire that is at its heart. This is scarcely surprising, because the satire, even if we ignore its veiled references to particular people and events, is distinctly European and could hardly have been translated into Chinese in any assimilative translation. How, for example, could the Chinese translator deal with the ideological dispute between those who open their boiled eggs at the big end and those who open them at the small end, which happens to be the main subject of contention between Lilliput and the neighboring country of Blefescu? He would have had to begin by explaining how eggs were eaten in England, which is something only a preservationist would attempt. The Chinese version does not entirely neglect the exotic customs of the Lilliputians, but it relegates them to a brief list at the end of the story, when Gulliver is telling of his experiences. And they are there for their curiosity value rather than for satirical effect.

The political intrigue is also omitted—not only the machinations of Gulliver's enemy at the Lilliputian court but also the rivalry between Lilliput and Blefescu. In the original, after Gulliver has towed away the Blefescu fleet, he finds himself in high favor with the emperor, but he quickly falls into disfavor when he declines to conquer Blefescu and turn it into a province of Lilliput. In protesting against the emperor's imperialistic ambitions, he declares that he "would never be an Instrument of bringing a free and brave people into Slavery." The Chinese omits the whole episode; in fact, it goes in the opposite direction and reports that "later the neighboring islands on all sides of Lilliput offered their allegiance to the emperor." Gulliver loses favor for other reasons, too, which are present in the original: he puts out a fire in the imperial palace by urinating on it, angering the empress, and he inadvertently tramples the crops, angering the peasants. However, instead of fleeing to Blefescu and repairing a boat as in the original, he stays in Lilliput and builds his own boat. This change has been prepared for earlier in the translation: when Gulliver is forced to accept a list of conditions, the translator adds an extra one to provide for it. The Chinese version was evidently designed from the beginning to focus on a few main adventures—the shipwreck, Gulliver's capture and eventual release, towing away the enemy fleet, extinguishing the palace fire, and building a boat and leaving the island.

The question of the narrative's provenance is raised twice in the translation: at the opening of the first installment and at the close of the last. The opening claims that the text was from an old manuscript provided by a friend. (Note the reference to a friend as source, as in the "Rip Van Winkle" translation; again, presumably a westerner is meant.) The story goes on to say that the Chinese version will excerpt and adapt the text, which it does. The close of the last installment returns to the same subject and adds a promise to publish more material from the same manuscript. The promise resembles one at the end of "A Strange Tale of the Country of Naisu," where the translator also plans to translate the next tale. In neither case did he do so.

In the translation the setting is transferred to China. The narrator, whose name is not given, is from Dinghai on Zhoushan island of Zhejiang province. His background is only very briefly told. His father, a merchant, has introduced him to the merchant's life. Whereas in the original Gulliver becomes a ship's surgeon—a profession that may not have been so common in China— his Chinese counterpart takes a post as a bookkeeper on a merchant ship. The last port of call, before the ship is blown off course, is in Hainan.

Of the content omitted in the Chinese version, I have already mentioned Gulliver's background, the satirical account of the politics and institutions of Lilliput, and Gulliver's departure for Blefescu. The translator also ignores those passages in which Gulliver worries about his situation or reflects on the past, as well as the occasions when he projects himself into the future and describes the present with the benefit of hindsight, as in: "It was three weeks before I realized . . .". In the all-important category of the added text, the most significant cases are the amplifications of visual description. Swift's spare style affords little help to the visual imagination. In fact, it is only when one compares the original with the translation that one realizes how little of such description Swift provides. For example, when Gulliver first sees the emperor of Lilliput, the English merely says, "The Emperor, and all his Court, came out to meet us." The Chinese version, in the second installment, finds it necessary to expand this as follows: "The emperor came out of the city with all the officials of his court in their carriages. Swarms of servants were in attendance, and the cries of the heralds sounded like the twittering of birds. The emperor wore a crown on his head with tassels dangling down, and his robe was of yellow embroidered silk. The attendants holding the parasols and hand-warmers were all eunuchs, as pretty as the little puppets that children play with." Again, the details of the storm appear far more vivid in the Chinese than in the English. Among many other specific touches, there is a scene in the second installment in which Gulliver strips naked, which causes all the women in the crowd to turn and flee. The situation is compared to that in a theater near the end of the performance, when some in the audience are still watching the stage while others are already making their way out. The palace fire in the fourth installment is compared to the fire that destroyed the Qin emperor's favorite palace, and Gulliver's urination is described as a waterfall cascading into the Yangzi river. One simile even has a foreign reference: the Lilliputian army is said to be arrayed "as in a western painting."

"Notes on Countries Overseas" focuses on only the adventures of "A Voyage to Lilliput," simplifying them but also livening up their details, but the third translation, "A Strange Tale of the Country of Naisu," gives a more balanced treatment of its English original. It is a translation of part of the introductory chapter and virtually the whole of chapter 2 of *The Pacha of Many Tales* by Frederick Marryat (1792–1848).[4] In all, the Chinese translation corresponds to about twenty pages of the English novel.

Marryat is best known for his novels of life at sea, and *The Pacha of Many Tales*, set in the Middle East, is unusual among his works. It consists of a collection of stories in a frame. The Pasha of Egypt—"pacha" is an alternative spelling of "pasha"—in the Ottoman Empire needs stories for his own amusement in the evenings, and his crafty assistant, the vizier Mustapha, does his best to supply them. Mustapha begins by having the *Thousand and One Nights* read aloud, but the pasha soon tires of this, and, in emulation of the book, tries to persuade his own favorite to "dishonor his harem" and then play Scheherezade's role as storyteller. This she wisely refuses to do. Mustapha then suggests to the pasha that they disguise themselves and roam the streets of Cairo to look for potential storytellers. The frame story is an obvious imitation, in fact a parody, of *Thousand and One Nights*, one that is likely to offend modern sensibilities with its gross ethnic comedy. In his imitation, Marryat even goes so far as to invent a rascal, Huckabuck, who imitates and parodies Sindbad's accounts of his seven voyages. However, the novel also goes beyond parody of the *Nights* and of travelers' tales in general. Some of the stories show the influence of the *Decameron*, while one of them, "The Wondrous Tale of Han," is actually an English version, narrated by "a Chinese poet" who has found his way to Cairo, of the famous Yuan dynasty play *Hangong qiu* (Autumn in the Han palace).[5]

The Pacha of Many Tales was originally published piecemeal in *The Metropolitan*, a London literary journal of which Marryat was for a time the editor. The first tales told to the pasha, including the sections translated into Chinese, appeared in 1831. The initial story, "The Camel-driver," was not chosen for translation, probably because of its specific setting and prominent religious content—it deals with a pilgrimage to Mecca. The story chosen was the second, "Story of the Greek Slave," which is linked to the third, "Story of the Monk." The pasha and the vizier are roaming the streets of Cairo when they overhear two men, a slave and a monk, arguing in highly suspicious terms about how to make the best wine. Both men are summoned to the pasha's court to tell their stories. After the slave has finished his, the pasha praises it and says to Mustapha: "We'll hear the other man tomorrow." The sixth and final installment of the Chinese translation of "Story of the Greek Slave" ends with a promise by the narrator that the monk's story will follow in the next issue, but in fact, as in the case of *Gulliver's Travels*, no more was ever published.

The slave's story is a series of comic horrors. As an expert wine maker employed in a winery, he happens to kill another worker in a fight, then hides the man's body temporarily in a wine cask. Before he can take the body out and dispose of it, however, the winery is visited by the aga, a local official, who suspects that the finest wine is being withheld from him and insists on tasting the contents of all the casks that are hidden from sight. He finds that the wine from the cask with the man's body in it has such a splendid flavor—so much "body," as the English puts it, in an obvious pun—that he takes the cask away with him. As soon as he discovers a man's body inside, he returns to the winery to exact vengeance. Naturally, his suspicions fall on the owner of the winery, and the slave does nothing to correct his mistake. As a result, the owner is sentenced to drown in a cask of his own wine. Several further developments of the same kind follow. Before the slave finally manages to escape to sea, the aga himself has ended up in a cask of wine.

The Chinese translation begins with material from the introductory chapter on the dangers of a pasha's life (he serves at the mercy of a bloodthirsty sultan) as well as on the dangers of a vizier's life (he serves at the mercy of a callous pasha). This particular pasha was originally a barber who became a soldier and obtained his present position by boldness and cunning. His vizier, Mustapha, obtained *his* position by outrageous flattery and cynical opportunism. The translation moves the setting from Cairo to a vague location somewhere in the far west of China, perhaps Xinjiang, where the Turkish sultan becomes the Great Khan of the imaginary country of Naisu. The pasha—the word is retained in the translation as "*basha*"—is the governor of a territory named Dapo. The word "vizier" is kept, as "*huxi*," and this particular vizier, Mustapha, even retains his name, Mofa. In the original the slave was Greek, but here he is said to be a native of Yiliguo, which is unlikely to refer to Hellas but might suggest Ili. (That territory, seized by Russia the year before, was in the news at the time.)

The translation sometimes amplifies the original text but more often condenses it. In general, it stays closer to the original than "Notes of Countries Overseas" does to "A Voyage to Lilliput." Of the six installments, the material taken from the introductory chapter occupies the first and part of the second. The fourth and fifth installments actually end on a note of suspense, but there is no language that points to it, as one would expect in a vernacular novel. At a few places changes have been made to strengthen the motivation of the original. For example, in the fourth installment, the aga gives an order that the cask with the owner's body in it be placed in a prominent position in the wine store, so that "I may have the pleasure occasionally to look at my revenge." The Chinese turns his order into a warning to the slave not to cheat.

The main difference comes at the end of the story. In the original, the narrator, the Greek slave, after killing the aga, escapes the country by boat, but is shipwrecked and then captured by pirates who sell him as a slave in Cairo. In the translation, he is also captured by pirates and set to work. He dreams of a god who tells him he is going to be taken to a paradise, and he makes his way to the coast, where he finds a raft waiting for him. A great wind springs up and blows him as far as the capital city of Naisu, where he sells himself as a slave. The story ends rather abruptly. As the pasha comments to Mustapha: "How very strange! This sort of person actually had the protection of Heaven in surviving a terrible ordeal. Truly remarkable!"

At a lower level of generality, the translation naturally tends to omit anything that might have required cross-cultural explanation. (This is the opposite practice from *Xinxi xiantan*, which often seizes the opportunity to explain

foreign customs to the reader.) True, the words for pasha and vizier are explained to the reader, as well as a few items of essential information, such as
that barbers could become the confidants of their rulers, or that wine casks
were made big enough to hold the body of a man.

As one might expect, the sardonic tone of the English narrator is either
omitted or drastically reduced in the Chinese translation. In chapter 1 of the
original the pasha is described as follows: "His qualifications for office were all
superlative: he was very short, very corpulent, very illiterate, very irascible,
and very stupid." The Chinese renders this description much more positively, as "he was short, vigorous and capable, sharp-witted but obstinate." Again,
in the original, when Mustapha joins the band of pirates, we are told that he
"very faithfully served his apprenticeship by cutting throats." The translation
puts the point far more generally, without any of the sarcasm implied by the
word "apprenticeship."

Nor does the Chinese even try to imitate Mustapha's obsequious tone (obsequious almost to the point of mockery) in addressing the pasha. However, it
does often contrive to replicate and even expand upon the humor of the original. It tries to keep the pun of the word "body" as applied to wine, by remarking that the wine "really had standing (*shenfen*)."[6] In fact, at times the
Chinese is more amusing than the English, for example, when Mustapha is explaining to the pasha the danger to an official of putting anything in writing,
or when the slave in the story is calculating the advantages that will accrue
from placing the aga's body in a wine cask.[7] In the latter case, the English gives
the slave's reasoning as follows: "Thus did I revenge my poor master, and re-
lieved myself of any further molestation on the part of the aga." The Chinese
expands this to: "There are four advantages that will flow from this plan. First,
I won't have to give my wine away for nothing; second, I'll be free from the
mortal danger I'm in; third, I'll have avenged the injustice done to my master;
and fourth—this is the best one of all—I'll have gotten myself another body
to make premium wine with."

Can we hope to identify the translator or translators of the three pieces of
fiction translated in the early *Shen bao*? Not with any degree of certainty. However, for the reasons I gave in the last chapter on the *Xinxi xiantan*, I believe
that two were involved. It is worth noting that all four works translated, these
three and *Night and Morning*, were by well-known, indeed famous, authors,
the kind of authors a westerner like Ernest Major might well choose to introduce to Chinese readers. If Major and Jiang Qizhang did indeed cooperate in
translating *Night and Morning* into Chinese, it is likely that they were also the
translators of these three works. The stories were rendered in literary, rather

than vernacular, Chinese for two reasons: their nature as fiction of the strange (*zhiguai*) and their publication in a newspaper printed in literary Chinese. The fact that they are far more assimilative than the *Xinxi xiantan* follows from the translators' decision to present them as original Chinese compositions, not as translated fiction.

After the *Shen bao* fiction was published in May and June 1872, six or seven months elapsed before the first installment of *Xinxi xiantan* in the journal *Yinghuan suoji*, during which, if my supposition is correct, the two translators were working on the first sections of *Night and Morning* as well as planning and operating their new journal. In the newspaper they published their foreign fiction in Chinese guise, but in the journal they presented it openly as translation. In that case, Major and Jiang's translations represent a three-year attempt to bring foreign fiction to a Chinese readership, the most sustained effort until that of Lin Shu at the turn of the century.

A Brief Comparison with Lin Shu's Method of Translation

A clearer perception of these translations—those in literary Chinese as well as the vernacular *Xinxi xiantan*—emerges from a comparison with the work of Lin Shu (1852–1924), whose first translation of a novel was published in 1899.

In considering Lin Shu's translations, we have to take at least three factors into account. First is the identity of his collaborator; over the course of his career, Lin Shu worked with many men, each of whom no doubt influenced the choice of which novels to translate as well as the manner of their translation. Second is the stage of Lin's own development as a translator; Qian Zhongshu, who has examined Lin Shu's treatment of the language of some of the original novels, notes that his choice of diction changed over time, and that from about 1913 the quality of his work actually declined.[8] Third is the nature of the original novel translated.

Here I look at three novels on which Wei Yi, perhaps the best (and certainly the most prolific) of Lin Shu's early collaborators, assisted him: *Ivanhoe*, by Walter Scott, translated in 1905; *David Copperfield*, by Charles Dickens, translated in 1908; and *Gulliver's Travels*, by Jonathan Swift, of which the first two parts, the voyages to Lilliput and Brobdingnag, were translated in 1906. All three translations were published by the Commercial Press in Shanghai.

In terms of their translating practice, Lin and Wei may be described as preservationists, emphasizing "adequacy" to a considerable degree. This judgment may seem surprising in view of the textual omissions and insertions for

which Lin Shu is notorious. However, in comparison with the previous translators, he has a strong tendency toward preservation, particularly in the case of
Gulliver's Travels.

In *Ivanhoe,* translated under the title of *Sakexun jiehou yingxiong zhuan* (A
tale of heroes after the Saxon debacle), Lin's chapters match those of the original novel; he has made no attempt to present them in the Chinese fashion.[9]
Scott's numerous historical explanations, some of which could easily have been
deleted, are rendered faithfully into Chinese. The internal comments on the
book and its progress are also translated. More important still, Lin and Wei
have followed Scott's gradual introduction of his characters—first the surrounding scene, then a glimpse of the character followed by minute external description, and finally the identification. *Ivanhoe* begins with a description of the
great forest that once flourished between Sheffield and Doncaster, goes on to
give a detailed social and historical background, and only then describes the particular scene in the forest in which two figures, still nameless, are to be observed.
In due course they turn out to be Gurth, a swineherd, and Wamba, a jester. The
translators faithfully reproduce the order in which information is conveyed as
well as the angle from which the narrator describes the scene, unfamiliar though
both must have been to the traditional Chinese novelist and his public.

Despite a piecemeal reduction of text, the language of the translation adheres to the original wherever possible. The names of people and places, no
matter how insignificant, are transliterated.[10] Sometimes the Chinese follows
English syntactical order so closely that, in Qian Zhongshu's opinion, the
translations deserve the pejorative term of *yingyi* (literal translation). Images are
also often translated directly, while jests, such as those of Wamba, are rendered
in transliteration, at the cost of having to add explanatory notes.[11] There is
only one instance of a distinctive cultural comparison with China, and it is giv-
en not in the text but in a note.[12]

What has been omitted or drastically changed? The poems that introduce
each chapter, like the songs and poems sung or quoted by characters, have been
deleted. (A few are summarized.) But the most important change is the steady
reduction in text that I have referred to. Lin Shu has replaced a complex, even
convoluted syntax with a simpler, more direct one. I shall argue later that this
is necessitated in part by the incompatibility between Scott's and Lin Shu's
prose styles.

The translation of *David Copperfield,* published under the title *Kuai rou
yusheng shu* (A posthumous son's story of his life), shares many of the features
of the *Ivanhoe* translation. Names are regularly transliterated, even to the extent of translating "Mrs. David Copperfield," for example, directly as "*Mixisi*

Dawei Kaobofei'er." Puns are also transliterated—and then explained in notes.[13] The English order of conveying information is adhered to, even when it conflicts with Chinese practice. A note in the translation of chapter 5 points out the difference between the English and Chinese order and assures the reader that the former has been preserved.[14] On the other hand, obvious digressions, such as that on the caul at David's birth in chapter 1, are eliminated, as are various whimsical images. Some implications in the English are brought out, as they are in the *Ivanhoe* translation. Specific cultural references are either omitted or generalized,[15] and there is no attempt to explain foreign customs and objects to the Chinese reader as in *Xinxi xiantan.*

Just as in the *Ivanhoe* translation, the text has undergone a piecemeal reduction. Dickens's elevated, periphrastic style, laden with humorous qualifications, has been replaced by a simpler syntax and a more direct narration. But Lin Shu was aware of what was lost in the process. He notes in his preface that Dickens always treats the "lowest level of society" (*xiadeng shehui*) with all of its "revolting and despicable" attributes in a "beautiful, marvelous style" (*jiamiao zhi bi*), which makes the reader hold his sides with laughter. Some of the ironic gap between the style and the object of description is apparent in the Chinese translation, but not enough, and in compensation Lin Shu has resorted to inserting his own language in the same humorous spirit. In my opinion, this is the reason behind the comic additions that Qian Zhongshu has noted in Lin's translations of Dickens.

Much of what I have said about *Ivanhoe* and *David Copperfield* applies also to *Gulliver's Travels*, which was translated under the title of *Haiwai xuanqulu* (A humorous tale of countries overseas). Swift listed the main contents of each chapter at its head, and the Chinese version dutifully translates his list. The copious political material is retained. Terms are freely transliterated.[16] Lin Shu's preface shows that he understood the nature of *Gulliver's Travels* as a satirical allegory (*yuyan xiaoshuo*) rather than simply as a tale of strange happenings. He includes the dispute between the Big-endians and Little-endians in chapter 4 that I referred to in discussing the *Shen bao* translation of the *Voyage to Lilliput*, but he also illustrates the dangers of dealing with exotic cultural material. (He assumes that, in eating their eggs, the English made a hole at one end of the egg and then sucked out its contents.) In at least one case, he falsifies the original text. When in chapter 6 Gulliver explains that in Lilliput children are regarded merely as the result of their parents' concupiscence and therefore owe their parents no affection, this was evidently too much for Lin Shu, who frequently in his prefaces stresses the importance of filial piety. He changes the passage to give it an entirely different meaning.

One peculiarity of the translation from Swift is that it has not been simplified and reduced. I think the reason has to be sought in the nature of Swift's style, which is economical, direct, and dedicated to conveying information in the most efficient way possible. In translating Swift, as distinct from Scott or Dickens, Lin Shu seems to have had had little trouble adjusting his literary Chinese style to that of the original work.

Compared to the translators of *Night and Morning*, Lin Shu and Wei Yi were indeed preservationists. The strongest evidence is the fact that, in contrast to the earlier translators, Lin Shu actually created a new form for the Chinese novel—a literary Chinese novel with a new structure and a new role for the narrator. This form was to a large extent adopted by Chinese novelists writing in the second decade of the twentieth century.

Finally, we may wonder why Lin Shu's translations, despite their preservationist bias, proved so much more popular than the assimilationist *Xinxi xiantan*. We can guess at several of the reasons, which include the attractiveness of Lin Shu's style (despite its frequent literalism) and the nature of the novels that he and Wei translated. But no doubt the most important reason was the time in which they worked, a time when a receptive readership existed for foreign fiction.

NOTES

1. In installments after the first, "Bashaguan xiaoshuo" (Tales of the pasha) was appended to the title.
2. See chapter 4.
3. See Li Jianguo, *Tangqian zhiguai xiaoshuo jishi* (Shanghai: Shanghai guji chubanshe, 1986), 553–57.
4. All references are to the edition by Routledge (London, 1862).
5. If the source was the minimal version by J. F. Davis, *A Chinese Tragedy* (London: Oriental Translation Fund, 1829), Marryat has greatly elaborated the language.
6. See both the second and third installments.
7. See the second installment.
8. "Lin Shu de fanyi," in Xue Suizhi and Zhang Juncai, eds., *Lin Shu yanjiu ziliao* (Fuzhou: Fujian renmin chubanshe, 1982), 292–323.
9. See the *Lin yi xiaoshuo congshu* (Beijing: Shangwu yinshuguan: 1981), vol. 3.
10. Sometimes just the first name is transliterated, as if it were the surname.
11. See, for example, the spider image at the beginning of chapter 15. For one of Wamba's jests, see the end of chapter 1.
12. See chapter 35. It likens the injunction to silence ("life and death are in the power of the tongue") of the Knights Templar to a saying of the Song dynasty Confucians.

13. See the pun on "baboo" (babu) in chapter 1.

14. See chapter 5. David Copperfield agrees to write to Peggotty with Barkis's proposal, then reveals that he has already written the letter that afternoon—before returning to the narrative present.

15. E.g., in chapter 1 the reference to his father's grave in the churchyard is reduced to the mere mention of a grave.

16. E.g., in book 2, chapter 2, "manikin" is transliterated—as are "*nanunculus*" and "*homuncelitino*"—and then explained in a note as *xiaoren* (midget). Few of the geographical terms that Lin Shu transliterates receive any annotation.

CHAPTER 6

The New Novel Before the New Novel—
John Fryer's Fiction Contest

T HE STORY OF the modern Chinese novel, as it is often told by literary historians, begins with Liang Qichao, more specifically with his founding of the journal *Xin xiaoshuo* (New fiction) in Yokohama in 1902. In his advertisement for the journal Liang set forth the categories of subject matter he recommended, ranging from the historical and the political to the detective, romantic, and supernatural. Liang's own *Xin Zhongguo weilai ji* (The future of new China), published in installments in *New Fiction* in 1902 and 1903, is generally considered the earliest of the "new novels," and most of the famous novels of the late-Qing period first appeared in serial publication from 1903, several of them in Liang's journal.

Told in this manner, however, the story ignores an earlier "new novel," one that deserves to be considered in its own right as well as in terms of its contribution to late-Qing fiction. The promoter of this earlier "new novel," which he labeled *shixin xiaoshuo*,[1] was, strangely enough, a foreigner working in Shanghai.

John Fryer (1839–1928) was an Englishman who lived and worked in China from 1861 until 1896, when he left to take up the Agassiz Professorship of Oriental Languages and Literature at the University of California. While in China he served for twenty-eight years, from 1868 to 1896, as head of the translation department of the Jiangnan Arsenal, where, working with Chinese colleagues,[2] he translated a prodigious number of works, mostly science and engineering textbooks. More than any other single person, he is credited with introducing nineteenth-century western science to the Chinese.[3] Fryer also showed himself a tireless and gifted entrepreneur in sponsoring other ventures in scientific education: he was honorary secretary of the Chinese Polytechnic Institution and Reading Room in Shanghai from its inception in 1874; in 1876 he founded a journal of popular science, *Gezhi huibian* (*The Chinese Scientific Magazine*, later renamed *The Chinese Scientific and Industrial Magazine*); from 1877 onward he served as general editor of the School and Textbook Series Committee, which sponsored the publication of teaching materials for use in schools; and in 1884 he established his own science bookstore and publishing house in Shanghai, the Chinese Scientific Book Depot. (Branches were later set up in other cities.) One has only to read the minutes of the Chinese Polytechnic Institution or the School and Textbook Series Committee to see the extent to which Fryer was the driving force behind both institutions.[4]

It was as owner of the bookstore that he briefly involved himself in the development of Chinese fiction. In May 1895, seven years before the publication of Liang Qichao's *Xin xiaoshuo*, he announced a public contest for new fiction and advertised it in the press.[5] The seven leading contestants were to receive prizes, and their work was to be considered for publication. Fryer also held out to prizewinners the possibility of long-term employment as writers. What he was seeking was fiction with a social purpose; it had to attack, as well as suggest remedies for, what he saw as the three great afflictions of Chinese society: opium, the examination essay, and foot-binding.

Let me wind up this particular story before going on to discuss the contest, its causes, background, and effects. In due course Fryer issued a report that listed the prizewinners and criticized various common faults in the other entries. Then in June 1896 he left his position at the arsenal and moved to California. So far as is known, none of the entries was ever published; presumably all 162 manuscripts have been lost. (Had they survived, they would, by their sheer numbers, have dominated the fiction of that decade.) But Fryer's contest was not without its aftereffects. First, two novels survive that it clearly inspired, even though they were apparently never entered in it. One of them, published at the end of 1895, ought, in my opinion, to be regarded as the earliest modern Chinese novel; the other, although written in June 1895, was published (in revised form) only in autumn 1897. Second, the kind of socially engaged or exposé fiction that Fryer was advocating may not have exerted a great influence on the thinking of Liang Qichao, who had very different ideals in fiction, but it had a significant effect on the purpose and practice of fiction during the following decade.

Fryer, who had headed for China straight after graduating from a London normal college, evidently picked up much of his scientific knowledge from textbooks and manuals while working in China. (One of his earliest tasks at the Jiangnan Arsenal was to order scientific books and apparatus from London.) From at least the late 1860s, his consuming idea was that China's salvation lay in education, particularly in science and engineering; hence he strenuously objected to the examination system on the grounds that it channeled all education above the elementary level in another direction. In a talk entitled "Why Japan Has Developed Differently from China,"[6] he singled out "three great evils," opium, the literary examination essay, and foot-binding, and described the essay, whose "highest ambition was to reproduce the past," as an "insidious waste of time, thought and energy" that "has kept the brainy people . . . busily and harmoniously engaged." In another context, he was quite capable of appreciating the essay for its own sake,[7] but in terms of its social effects he called it suicidal. He blamed it, and the educational system geared to it, for stifling inventive genius: the student "becomes a mere literary machine, with a prodigious memory, but with about as much original thought as a phonograph or a type-writer."[8] Fryer abominated opium use and foot-binding as much as anybody—he was involved in the formation of the Natural Feet Society (Tianzuhui) in Shanghai in April 1895[9]—but he saw the examination essay as the great institutional obstacle to progress. During the 1870s and 1880s he sought to extend the scope of the examinations to include "western learning," particularly science, but from 1895 on he began calling for outright abolition of the traditional essay. These and other ideas he shared with Chinese reformers, on whom his scientific translations exerted a considerable influence.[10] In a talk delivered in California in 1900 he expanded on what the examination system was suppressing:

> New opinions, new systems of philosophy, new forms of government, new theories to account for the existing state of things, new possibilities to which the nation ought to direct its energies. . . . In a nation almost always in fear of political agitation and jealous of innovation, any departure from the old paths and the well-known landmarks is at once deprecated and strongly opposed.[11]

The timing of his fiction contest was no accident. The terms of the Treaty of Shimonoseki, which concluded the disastrous war with Japan, provoked instant outrage, particularly among the examination candidates gathered in the capital. Before the treaty was even ratified, Kang Youwei (1858–1927) had tried to present a mass memorial signed by the candidates. Such a furor among the elite was unprecedented in the nineteenth century, and foreign educators like Fryer were frankly elated, convinced that the long wished-for awakening was at hand. (Fryer writes of "the great burst of true patriotism that the war produced in all ranks of society."[12]) His advertisement, published a bare three weeks after the attempted submission of the memorial, was designed to seize the mood of that particular moment; he meant, if possible, to turn the furor against the things he most abominated in Chinese society.

It is harder to explain why Fryer left China so soon after the contest (and before any of the fiction was published). Jonathan Spence, who has given us an unduly depressing portrait of him, believes that his departure for Berkeley was "an admission of defeat."[13] But at the time Fryer left, his ideas had triumphed, or seemed about to triumph. As an editor of the "Educational Department" of the *Chinese Recorder*, he had recently written an article entitled "The Educational Outlook for 1896" that displays a positive (and most uncharacteristic) euphoria:

> The educational prospect for the year on which we have just entered is by far the most encouraging and satisfactory that has appeared in the entire history of foreign intercourse with China.[14]
>
> The war with Japan, with all its disasters and suffering, has not been without its educational lessons of immense benefit alike to the government and to the people of the "Middle Kingdom."

He goes on to refer to "the literary and other societies that have recently been formed," including, presumably, the Qiangxuehui (Society for the Study of Self-Strengthening) formed by Kang Youwei and Liang Qichao, and asserts that "the national system of education, as well as the forms of religion and government, are already being weighed in the balance and found lamentably wanting." He looks forward, as joint editor of the "Educational Department," to having "a rapidly increasing series of advancements to announce in each monthly issue for 1896." The same euphoric note is echoed in his private correspondence of the time.

The sales of translated books, which had been sluggish ever since the establishment of the translation bureau of the Jiangnan Arsenal, had begun to pick up.[15] In fact, the press could not even keep pace with the demand for some of the more popular items, and it was not long before Fryer found his own translations being pirated by the lithographic publishers.[16] If he had concluded at this point that his educational mission was a success and that he could simply declare victory and leave China, it would be understandable. He must surely have realized that the pioneer stage of introducing western science was over, and that others were now available to carry on the task he had begun. But although he did eventually turn his attention to other causes, such as the education of the Chinese blind, I know of no evidence to support that supposition. What caused him to move to Berkeley was not a sense of defeat or victory, but something far more mundane—a domestic concern for his own family and finances.

Early in 1892 his second wife, Eliza Nelson, an American missionary whom he had met and married in Shanghai, moved to Oakland so that the children— Fryer had four surviving children by his deceased first wife—could complete their education. Unfortunately, the value of silver, which had been declining slowly for decades, took a sharp dip in 1892, followed by further dips in 1893 and 1894. Fryer, who was paid by the arsenal in silver, now had to meet most of his expenses in dollars at a steeply reduced rate of exchange. In an August 26, 1892 letter to his brother George he describes himself as "half bankrupt" because of "the ruinous fall in silver."[17] (With his brother, who worked in a bank, he was always candid about such matters.) "My salary and savings are worth about two thirds of what they were, and every cent I send to America for the family costs nearly twice what it did years ago. Alas that I am tied to a silver country!" In another letter to his brother, written on March 31, 1894, he says he can no longer afford to keep his family in California and must bring them back to China.[18] Just at this point, however, he was approached about the Berkeley professorship, which had first been mentioned to him in 1893, when he visited the United States to report on the Chicago Exposition.[19] The negotiations and appointment took a considerable time, and Fryer did not leave until the middle of 1896. Even then he did not sever all contact with China, but returned each summer to manage the affairs of his bookshop and to do more translations for the arsenal.[20]

The organizational model for Fryer's fiction contest was a series of prize essay contests that he had conducted for the Polytechnic Institution since 1886. "The general object," he wrote in his 1887 report,

> is to try and induce the Chinese literati to investigate the various departments of Western knowledge with the view to their application in the Middle Kingdom. . . . To popularize Western knowledge among the literati it is necessary to take advantage of all such existing national characteristics [as the institution of the examination essay]; and hence it was conceived that in essay writing there existed a most powerful means for inducing the better class of Chinese to read, think, and write on foreign subjects of practical utility.

The contest is but the "thin edge of the wedge."[21] Prize essay contests were nothing new in China—they had long been used by missionaries to stir up interest in their doctrines—but Fryer's contest was distinctive, not merely in its objective but also in the shrewd understanding it showed of politics and the press.[22] His practice was to ask some high official of relatively enlightened views to propose a topic; Fryer would then advertise the contest in the newspapers. The official would judge the entries and also put up most of the prize money; the newspapers were happy enough to print the winning entries. Contests were held each quarter, and then the best entries for the year were published in book form, edited by the scholar Wang Tao. One reason for Fryer's speed on this occasion was the fact that he was sponsoring the fiction contest not from the Polytechnic Institution but from his own bookstore, under his own name, and at his own expense.

But what explains his choice of *fiction* as an instrument for his purpose? Since it had a lowly standing in China, why go to the trouble of trying to elevate it? Fryer seldom refers to fiction in his writings.[23] His Berkeley lectures on Chinese literature mention only *Sanguo zhi tongsu yanyi*, *Honglou meng*, and *Liaozhai zhiyi*, plus two well-known romances of the "brilliant and beautiful" type. His bookstore carried no fiction written after the eighteenth century.[24] Most Chinese narratives, he held, "are merely records of marvels, many of which are outside the limits of credibility, or are allied to the magical." His opinion of contemporary Chinese fiction, flourishing mightily in an era of cheap lithographic publishing, was distinctly low: "The country is flooded with trashy novels and stories which of course are professedly ignored by the literati though often if not chiefly read by them."[25]

More significant of his attitude toward Chinese fiction is a statement in his 1900 talk: "The tendency of modern times is in the direction of a popular and easy Chinese style; and this has been necessitated by the demand for newspapers and general literature—which would have to be written in a manner easily understood by the majority of readers, so as to ensure an extensive and ready sale."[26] Fryer had long shown a desire to interest a broader public, as in the case of his science magazine and school texts. The move to fiction was a far bolder step, however, and it may well have been inspired in part by the growth of newspapers and the power of journalism. In a paper written in 1901 he mentioned the demand for new newspapers, magazines, and periodicals, and remarked on the "mighty power of the press."[27] His fiction contest was, in fact, an appeal to the elite; he hoped to enlist them in writing for a broad public that included women and children, and he was convinced that a certain kind of novel was the ideal medium.

In planning the contest, he must have been advised by Chinese friends, perhaps including Wang Tao, although by the spring of the following year the relations between Fryer and Wang seem to have become somewhat distant.[28] Zhan Xi, author of *Hualiu shenqing zhuan*, one of the two surviving novels inspired by the contest, says that he checked with Wang Tao before deciding to have it published, which may at least indicate a belief that Wang was involved in the contest.[29]

Fryer makes it clear that, as we might expect, his idea derived largely from foreign fiction. In the July 1895 number of *The Chinese Recorder*, in the "Educational Department," there is a lengthy note, presumably by Fryer, explaining and justifying the contest:

> The immense influence for good that a well written story can exert over the popular mind has often been exemplified, but perhaps never more fully than in the case of *Uncle Tom's Cabin* . . . in awakening people against slavery. . . .
>
> What China now wants, among many things, is a story or series of stories of the same thrilling description, true to the life, exposing the great evils that are everywhere rampant, and which the government is either unable or unwilling to counteract. Opium, foot-binding, and the literary examination system. . . .
>
> Nothing but the most thrilling sentiments, expressed through the most effective pictures that words can portray, will be likely with the Divine blessing to suffice for the purpose. There are doubtless well disposed Chinamen fully competent to write such books, if they can only be got hold of.[30]

He goes on to talk of this kind of fiction as affecting "the hearts and consciences of all classes of society in a way that has hardly yet been attempted," and declares his intention to "produce a series of books that may be of service in educational work." He was writing for a missionary audience, but it seems likely that such works as *Uncle Tom's Cabin* did indeed inspire Fryer's contest and, very indirectly, the first modern Chinese novels.

His advertisement, headed "Qiu zhu shixin xiaoshuo qi" (A call for the writing of new fiction) appeared five times in the *Shen bao*, as well as in the *Wanguo gongbao* (Review of the times).[31] The same one appeared in the June number of the *Chinese Recorder*, among the advertisements at the back of the journal, together with an account in English. The Chinese version reads:

> I believe that there is nothing to equal fiction for moving people's hearts and minds and causing them to change their ways. With its wide and rapid circulation, fiction can, within a short period of time, become known to one and all, making it possible without difficulty to reform current practices. At

present the most serious of China's age-old evil practices are three in number: opium, the examination essay, and foot-binding. Unless some means can be found of reforming these practices, there is no prospect of China's ever attaining wealth and power. I therefore invite all Chinese gentlemen who desire strength and prosperity for their country to write new and interesting fiction that will demonstrate the great harm done by these three practices and offer ingenious solutions for their elimination. The setting out of the case as well as its argument should be fully integrated into the work so as to form a coherent whole, with the result that readers' hearts and minds will be so moved that they will strive to eradicate the practices. It is vital that the language be clear and easily comprehensible, and essential that the import of the work be interesting and in good taste, so that even women and children will be able to read and understand. The events narrated must be current and near at hand. On no account should old formulas be followed. In terms of its conception, the work should not place any value on strangeness or peculiarity, and it should also avoid anything that would inspire shock or terror.

The deadline for submission is the end of the seventh month. The prizewinners will be selected after careful consideration. The first name on the list will receive 50 dollars, the second 30 dollars, the third 20 dollars, the fourth 16 dollars, the fifth 14 dollars, the sixth 12 dollars, and the seventh 8 dollars.

Any fine works capable of changing people's hearts and minds will be printed and published. It is also our intention to offer their authors regular employment to write similar works.

On completing your entry, wrap it up and seal it, taking care to write your name and address on the outside of the parcel, which should then be sent to the Chinese Scientific Book Depot on Third Avenue in Shanghai. An acknowledgement will be issued on receipt of your entry. The announcement of results and awards will be issued from the same address. Respectfully, John Fryer, British scholar

The fact that Fryer published the advertisement under his own name was no doubt to guarantee the validity of the contest in the mind of the public. The English account, under the heading of "Chinese Prize Stories," puts the matter a little differently, for a different audience:

The sum of $150, in seven prizes, is offered by the undersigned to Chinamen who produce the best moral stories, combining a graphic description of the evils of Opium, the Literary examinations, and Foot-binding, with practical methods by which they may be removed. It is hoped that students, teachers and pastors connected with the various missionary establishments in China will be shown the accompanying advertisement and encouraged to take part in the competition; so that some really interesting and valuable stories, in the easiest *Wen-li*, may be produced, of a Christian rather than of a merely ethical tone, which will supply a long felt want and serve as popular reading books all over the Empire.

A receipt will be given for all sealed manuscripts, sent or delivered before the end of the seventh Chinese month to the *Chinese Scientific Book Depot*, 407 Hankow Road, or to

JOHN FRYER,

May 25, 1895 *Shanghai*

The chief difference between the Chinese and the English is that the Chinese says nothing about a Christian or even an ethical tone, whereas the English makes no appeal to patriotism (the attainment of wealth and power by China) and lays down no prescriptions about subject matter. The Chinese emphasizes newness of approach and requires that the fiction deal with contemporary reality. It asks merely that the language be simple, not that it be in easy literary Chinese. In fact, most entries, following the example of the Chinese novel, would probably have been in the vernacular.

In the "Educational Department" of the July *Recorder* there appeared the piece quoted above, about the example of *Uncle Tom's Cabin*. The October number contains a preliminary report noting that, by the close of the competition, about 155 manuscripts had been received, ranging "from a few modest pages written by the college student or village pedagogue up to the four or six volume sensational tale, bristling with poetry, which is the production of the expert novelist." Some of the manuscripts are in beautiful handwriting, tastefully bound, and even accompanied by illustrations. Several are "unmoral," and two "are positively immoral, and have been returned to their authors, who appear to know no better than they have written."

In March 1896 came the final report.[32] The prize money had been increased by $50, and the number of prizes increased to twenty. The names of the winners had been announced in the *Shen bao*, and the complete list of 162 names, plus an explanatory notice, has been sent to the *Wanguo gongbao* and the *Zhong Xi jiaohui bao* (Missionary review).[33] At least half of the competitors were from mission schools and colleges. At the end of the report Fryer adopted the disdainful tone often affected by contributors to the *Recorder* and other foreign-language publications of the time:[34]

There is a great paucity of new ideas among the Chinese, and hence many of these attempts are merely old literary rubbish and poetry worked up in a new form under a new name with but little attempt at disguise. It is a common remark that the inventive powers of the Chinese are of a low order, and this fact is abundantly manifested in these stories. There is but little originality in them. . . . This experiment has, however, drawn out a few stories that really are worth publishing, and it is hoped that some of them will be issued before the end of the year, so as to supply the need that is felt for light reading of a healthful, moral tone and useful instructive character.

The tone of this report and the fact that he used the word "experiment" no doubt signal his disappointment with the results of the contest. Although from our vantage point the contest seems to be one of his more notable contributions to the cause of reform in China, Fryer himself, who was not one to minimize his achievements, evidently set little store by it. It is not referred to again in his surviving writings, except in routine correspondence about the payment of prizes and the return of manuscripts.

The *Wanguo gongbao* and the *Missionary Review* printed the list of prizewinners, together with the report. At least a third of the winners chose to use pseudonyms—like the authors of the traditional novel—instead of their real names. In his (Chinese-language) report, entitled "Results of the Call for New Fiction," Fryer took the opportunity to explain the principles behind the ranking—and incidentally to try to influence the direction of the new fiction. These opinions did not circulate as widely as the advertisement, but it seems worthwhile to give them in part:

This office issued a call for new fiction on the subject of the three evils of opium, the examination essay, and foot-binding. The exposition was to be integrated into the work in the manner of a novel (*zhanghui xiaoshuo*) that would cohere from start to finish. The intention was to publish the fiction in order to move people's hearts and minds so that they would understand the need for reform. Since even women and children should be able to read and be moved by this fiction, the writers' purpose must be to seek out matter that was interesting and in good taste. The events narrated should be plausible, and the description truthful and apt.

We received 162 manuscripts, all of them the product of study, from gentlemen near and far. It has taken us a hundred days to read through them all. They all had the right intentions, but some were biased in their approach, giving too much weight to opium and too little to the examination essay;

some contained strange arguments and implausible events; and others narrated fantastic things, often involving dreams. Still others used language that was coarse and shallow, including much local patois, and even went so far as to favor lewd expressions and to verge on the indecent; with their constant talk of brothels, concubines and maids they could be seen as belonging to the old category of the obscene novel, in direct violation of the requirement that the fiction be an encouragement to virtue. How can they possibly be read or listened to by women and children?

Fryer explained that two kinds of entry were disqualified as prose fiction: the ballad with its songs and verses (presumably he was referring to the *tanci* and *guci* as well as the *daoqing*) and the disquisition. As in his advertisement, he was concerned that the argument be fully dramatized.

The idea that fiction had a unique power to sway people's emotions did not originate with Fryer, although he may not have been aware of its history in China; it is found at least as early as the preface to Feng Menglong's *Gujin xiaoshuo* of about 1621. Nor did the principle that fiction should deal with the real rather than the fantastic originate with him; it is found as early as Ling Mengchu's preface to his first collection of stories, *Pai'an jingqi*, in 1628. But there is still a gulf between the way those ideas were applied in fiction and the way Fryer proposed to apply them. Fiction had often been enlisted to promote familiar virtues and to attack familiar vices, but Fryer had singled out three social practices, all well entrenched, one of which, the examination essay, was the capstone of the educational and civil service system. Furthermore, he had linked them, in a way that had not been done before, to patriotic concerns, to China's prospects of attaining wealth and power. Fryer was asking the novel to perform a function it had rarely had in China—to treat and solve intractable problems of national concern. It was a conception of fiction that he must have known from the nineteenth-century English and American novel, but one that was scarcely familiar to his Chinese audience.[35]

※

Let me now turn to the two extant novels that constitute the most obvious legacy of Fryer's contest. *Xichao kuaishi* (Delightful history of a glorious age) is the earliest modern Chinese novel in two important senses: it is concerned with the distinctively modern crisis of China's survival as a nation under the military, technological, and cultural onslaught of the West, and it adopts new methods of narration. It also includes traditional elements—karmic reincarnation, martial arts, court cases, and Daoistic withdrawal from public life. Although *Xichao kuaishi* is a well-written work that duly attacks the three evils, it is doubtful that it would have won a prize from Fryer; he would surely have objected to its use of prophetic dream and karmic rebirth.

All we know of the authorship and date comes from the surviving edition in the library of Dongbei Normal University.[36] It was published in Hong Kong with a preface by the Man of Leisure of Hangzhou (Xiling Sanren) dated the equivalent of December 23, 1895. Its editing is attributed to the Ambrosia-sipping Layman (Yinxia Jushi) and its revision to the same Man of Leisure who wrote the preface. Surprisingly for a programmatic novel, the preface speaks mainly of the difficulties of fictional narrative and only secondarily of the three evils. These, it maintains, are the warp of the book, and the two main figures, Kang Jishi and Lin Menghua, are the woof. The preface rebuts the suggestion that the author was afflicted with a sense of grievance and deliberately wrote in a jocular vein—that would be to ignore the great pains he took in writing the work. The fact that the preface says nothing more about him suggests that the Man of Leisure was the author.

The novel has a notable opening. A provincial graduate from Hangzhou, a man of wide learning and uninhibited nature, is discussing the state of the nation with a few close friends. "Treating a nation is like treating a disease—you have to prescribe a remedy for it," he declares. He goes on to diagnose China as suffering from a chronic wasting disease, the remedy for which is to foster its vital energy. To his friends' amusement, he claims that if *he* held power in China, he would cure the national disease.

Climbing up Mount Ge by the West Lake, he and his friends come upon a pavilion called Guanriting (Pavilion for observing the sunrise). When they learn that a spectacular eclipse will occur the following dawn, they decide to stay, spending the night in a nearby temple. There the graduate dreams of an old man who is dispensing medicine to crowds of ailing people. His name in religion is Jueshi (Awaken the World), and he explains that China's three great afflictions are opium, the examination essay, and foot-binding; 70 percent of the population suffer from one or more. A brief argument ensues over foot-binding, which the graduate thinks may be pointless but is scarcely harmful to the nation. Jueshi stresses the pain and enfeeblement that result, and notes that none of the three afflictions has the sanction of ancient precedent—all are latter-day aberrations.

When the graduate professes a strong desire to save the nation, he is told that the time is not yet ripe. He himself is fated to die before long, but he will be reborn into the Kang family in Guiji of Shaoxing prefecture, and in his next life he will be able to fulfill the desire he has expressed—he will hold power and be in a position to cure the three evils.

The prophetic dream and the reincarnation belong to the traditional stuff of fiction, but the sun emerging after an eclipse, with its symbolic overtones, is a new development, one that becomes common enough in the fiction of the next decade. The headings of chapter 1 are as follows:

> After discussing the ills of the time, he tours the hills and has a dream,
> While writing a new book, he embodies his ambitions in allegory.

The author is obviously identifying himself with the graduate whose ambitions are about to be fulfilled in the next generation.

Chapter 2 tells of the hero's father, Kang Fengji, who as a young man was about to compel a young girl to have sex with him when he looked up, "saw the red sun in the heavens," and promptly had a change of heart (2.459). Perhaps as a reward for his virtuous restraint, he fathers a son, Kang Jishi ("benefits the times"), a prodigy who reads widely in practical subjects as well as in the classics, but who loathes the examination essay.

Kang Jishi's story is interwoven with that of Lin Menghua, a highly intelligent but weak-willed creature who serves as a handy foil. (The author has in effect added two extra evils to the prescribed three, fiscal corruption and official injustice, both of them exemplified by Lin.) Kang Jishi's ideas on modernization are clarified in his arguments with Lin Menghua (see especially 5.481–82). Lin had written a piece called *Xinxue lun* (On the new learning), which Kang criticizes as glorifying western learning at the expense of the Chinese. He claims that much western learning is actually derived from the Chinese; hence the two cannot be considered separately. Even science and parliamentary government have their Chinese antecedents. He draws up a twelve-point document listing the reforms that he favors, including the abolition of the three evils, and arranges to have it presented as a memorial to the throne.

The second half of the novel deals mainly with Kang's suppression of a Muslim revolt in Gansu. A revolt did occur there in 1895, the first in over two decades, and the coincidence of dates is striking. The revolt broke out in August, and it was not until early December that the Chinese army gained its first victory. Since the preface of this novel is dated December 23, this seems to be an extreme case of the convergence of fiction and contemporary events that we find often in the next decade.

Kang's memorial is accepted, and the three evils are banned. He is appointed President of the Board of War and modernizes the army along western lines with the aid of some western advisers. Rather like a latter-day Judge Bao, he also solves the case of a general who has abused his power. At the very end of the novel, he meets a strange character who had earlier handed him a set of prophetic pictures. The man explains that Kang has already attained his life's ambition and that to continue in office would be superfluous. Kang departs to seek immortality.

We can only infer Fryer's influence on *Xichao kuaishi*, but in the case of the other novel, *Hualiu shenqing zhuan* (Love among the courtesans), the fact is stated unambiguously in both preface and prologue. The author was an ardent reformer named Zhan Xi (1850–1927) from Quxian in Zhejiang, whose parents were both published poets.[37] In the summer of 1895, he tells us in his prologue, referring to himself by his pen name, Lüyixuan Zhuren (Master of the Studio of the Green Impression), he was visiting Suzhou when he noticed Fryer's advertisement.[38] Impressed by the idea that fiction was the best means of changing the people's hearts and minds, he thought of a notable family, the Weis, neighbors of his in Quxian, who would serve as an admirable example.

The subject of the novel's composition is taken up again in the second-to-last chapter. After many vicissitudes, the Weis have formed a modern community and are growing rich. They now seek some way of publicizing their achievement, so that they may serve as an example to others. A friend of theirs, Zheng Zhixin, who appears to be an alter ego of the author's,[39] recommends the Master as a chronicler of the family's fall and eventual rise. The Master declines the commission, but six or seven years later, inspired by Fryer's advertisement, he recalls the case of the Weis. His employer (he is working as a tutor) encourages him to take his manuscript to Shanghai and call on Fryer. The employer also suggests a title, *Xing shi xinbian* (A new tale to awaken the world)—*Hualiu shenqing zhuan* (Love among the courtesans) is presumably a catchy title substituted by the publisher. The Master is about to travel to Shanghai when he has a nightmare in which he is confronted by representatives of the three special interests he has attacked in his book. The book ends abruptly, with the author awakening from his nightmare.

His preface repeats the information about the advertisement and adds detail. He wrote the novel in two weeks, he says, but instead of sending it to Fryer, he kept it with him as he traveled about the country. In the spring of 1897, when he was back in Shanghai making a living by his pen, he told Wang Tao about his manuscript and received his blessing to publish. But immediately afterward he had to go north again—he was in demand as an art connoisseur—

and had no time for revision. The seventh month found him back in Shanghai where, after adding new material at the beginning and end of the novel, he had it published. He feels compelled to comment on the changes that have occurred in China since he wrote the first draft in 1895. Natural Feet Societies have been established in Shanghai and Hubei, changes have been made in the examinations to include western learning, and local societies have been set up to prohibit opium. He passes on a friend's formula for suppressing the opium craving. He also apologizes for his occasional humorous tone, explaining it away as a characteristic feature of the novel genre. The preface is dated the ninth of the ninth month of 1897 in Shanghai.

His revisions must have covered more than just the beginning and ending. In chapter 14 (pp. 58–59), one character mentions reading a set of poems by the Master in that day's *Youxi bao* on the subject of *yeji* (low-level prostitutes). The poems appeared in the *Youxi bao* on the seventeenth of the eighth month, a scant three weeks before the date of the preface.[40] Other elements in the novel tie it closely to the author's life in Quxian as well as to the contemporary Shanghai scene.[41]

The novel conforms well enough to Fryer's prescriptions. The two eldest Wei sons are addicted to opium and obsessed with the examination essay, respectively, and the daughter suffers the pain and enfeeblement of foot-binding. The sons' pedantic tutor, Kong, illustrates the uselessness of the examination essay, and Zheng Zhixin speaks for the author. The novel is set anachronistically amid the chaos of the Taiping rebellion, mostly in Quxian and neighboring counties. The reforms it demonstrates stress practical learning, including technology. Books of modern science are mentioned, including some of those translated by Fryer. An engineer is brought in from Guangzhou to help open a silver mine and a Chinese-speaking westerner is hired to teach English, but little is said of either Chinese or western values beyond the importance of economic progress. The author's equation of himself with the narrator and his detailed account of the situation in which he came to write the work are characteristic of novels written after 1895.[42]

Beyond these two novels, Fryer's short-lived venture must have exerted an influence on modern Chinese fiction—even though its extent can only be guessed at. His was the first call for a specifically new kind of fiction, one that he defined as having two requirements: it had to engage social issues of immediate national concern, and it had to follow certain prescriptions that tended to distance it from traditional fiction. The engagement with social issues brought fiction close to journalism, but Fryer insisted that the dominant themes be fully dramatized, not merely expounded. His prescriptions for new forms and methods, simple as they were, preceded those of other critics by many years.

His ideas had a certain influence on Liang Qichao as Liang took his cautious first steps toward recommending fiction as a small part of a reformed primary school education.[43] Of the topics Liang recommends, the most important are the sages' teachings and the historical record, but he also suggests attacks on official corruption, the examinations, opium, and foot-binding, the last three presumably the legacy of John Fryer. After his escape to Japan at the end of 1898, Liang began to espouse the political novel, basing himself on Japanese examples[44]—the Japanese novelists had themselves been influenced by the political novels of Edward Bulwer Lytton and Benjamin Disraeli—and had nothing more to say about the novel of social criticism. Even in 1902, when listing the types of fiction his journal would publish, he ignored it. Only in the eighth issue was the omission rectified and the social novel (*shehui xiaoshuo*) included.[45]

Needless to say, Liang Qichao's influence on many aspects of late-Qing literature was infinitely greater than Fryer's. But Fryer's call for a new fiction came a good seven years before Liang's. And although Harriet Beecher Stowe (and perhaps also Charles Dickens and others) may seem remote from late-Qing fiction, Fryer's conception of a novel that exposes, and seeks remedies for, current social ills is closer to its characteristic temper, with its frequent excoriation of social evils, than Liang's notion of the political novel. It is likely that Fryer's contest did in some degree affect the general direction of late-Qing fiction. The story of the modern Chinese novel would not be complete without it.

NOTES

1. *Shixin*, "fresh, in season" or "fashionable," here evidently means "new."
2. The colleagues were true collaborators. According to Fryer's account, he would dictate an oral translation sentence by sentence, and the writer would put it into easy literary Chinese. After any problems had been discussed, the writer would then revise it, normally without any checking by the foreigner. See Fryer, "Science in China," *Nature* 24 (May 19, 1881): 5.
3. On the value of Fryer's scientific translations, see Xiong Yuezhi, *Xixue dongjian yu wan-Qing shehui* (Late-Qing society and the dissemination of western learning) (Shanghai: Shanghai renmin chubanshe, 1994), 567–85.
4. For the minutes of the former, see, e.g., *Celestial Empire* 3:3 (Jan. 21, 1875): 57–58. For the minutes of the latter, see the "Educational Department" section of the *Chinese Recorder* from 1893 to 1896.

5. The contest was noted briefly by Wang Shuhuai in his *Wairen yu wuxu bianfa* (Foreigners and the 1898 reforms) (Nankang: Academia Sinica, 1965), 40. The first person to set out the main facts about Fryer's contest in the context of late-Qing fiction was Huang Jinzhu in "Jiawu zhi yi yu wan-Qing xiaoshuojie" (The Sino-Japanese war and the late-Qing novelists), *Zhongguo wenxue yanjiu* (National Taiwan University, May 1991):3–7.

6. From an undated typescript in carton 1 of Fryer's "Correspondence and Papers," which are preserved in the Bancroft Library of the University of California at Berkeley. The Fryer material consists of one box of correspondence, including his bookshop correspondence from March 1896 to July 1901 ("Letter Journal"), plus six cartons of other papers, mostly in typescript. The contents of cartons 4–6 have not been classified and are unavailable to readers. There is also a collection of Fryer's published papers entitled "The John Fryer Miscellany."

7. See "The Normal Chinese Essay," of which there is a copy in carton 1. It was originally a talk delivered in California in 1902.

8. "Chinese Education—Past, Present and Future, Part I," *Chinese Recorder* (July 1897):334. The essay was originally a talk delivered in California in December 1896.

9. The subject of foot-binding reached a new level of prominence when Alicia (Mrs. Archibald) Little established the Natural Feet Society in Shanghai in April 1895, the month before Fryer's announcement of his contest. Fryer was evidently advising her. At the meeting of the society on April 16, she raised Fryer's suggestion that they should persuade the foreign ambassadors to appeal to the emperor to forbid any official to marry his son to a woman with bound feet. (See *Celestial Empire*, April 26, 1895, supp., 3.) It was characteristic of Fryer to think of an institutional solution. His suggestion was actually incorporated in a memorial the following year; see *Records of the Triennial Meeting of the Educational Association, 1896* (reprint, Taipei: Ch'eng Wen, 1970), 286. A letter in the "Letter Journal" of March 11, 1896 indicates that Fryer's bookshop had conducted an essay contest for the society. Fryer may actually have been the first to designate this particular combination of evils. Other writers used the terms *sanbi* or *sibi* (four evils) with a different content; see, e.g., an editorial in the *Zilin Hubao* of April 3, 1897 that designates geomancy and religious superstition together with the examination system and opium as the four evils. The *Shen bao* in January and February of 1896 carried seven editorials entitled "Western Friends on the Subject of China's Evils" that never use the term *sanbi*. In his advertisement Fryer did not imply that *sanbi* was an accepted term, but in his report on the contest, written over a year later, he did.

10. He first met Tan Sitong in 1893; see Wang Shuhuai, *Wairen yu wushu bianfa*, 103–104. Adrian Arthur Bennett notes that a high proportion of the titles in Liang Qichao's list of translations of important works of western learning, *Xixue shumubiao*, were works that Fryer had helped translate; see *John Fryer: The Introduction of Western Science and Technology Into Nineteenth-Century China* (Cambridge: Harvard University, East Asian Research Center, 1967), 103–104.

11. "The Literature of China," *The University Chronicle* 4 (1901): 167.

12. "The War between China and Japan," a typescript article in carton 2 of Fryer's papers; see 31. The article must have been written soon after the end of the war.
13. *To Change China: Western Advisers in China, 1620–1960* (Boston: Little, Brown, 1969), 156–57. Spence quotes a short passage by Fryer about the rigors of his job as translator and comments, "his summation of his life's work makes bleak reading." But the passage is from Fryer's "Science in China," published in 1881, fifteen years before he left China. Actually it was first published in the *North China Herald* of Jan. 29, 1880, only three months after his wife's death, which may account for the tone of weary resignation in this particular passage.
14. *The Chinese Recorder* (Jan. 1896):36–39.
15. See a letter of June 7, 1897 in the "Letter Journal."
16. See *Chinese Recorder* (Aug. 1897):383. Since the Japanese war, "it has been impossible to reprint some of the more popular of them fast enough." On pirating, see *Chinese Recorder* (Sept. 1897):444. A June 23, 1897 letter to W.A.P. Martin in the "Letter Journal" also refers to heavy pirating.
17. In "Correspondence and Papers," carton 1.
18. Ibid.
19. See Nellie Blessing Eyster, *A Beautiful Life, Memoir of Mrs. Eliza Nelson Fryer 1847–1910*, (Berkeley, Calif.: Privately published, 1912), 61.
20. Fryer did not regard the move to Berkeley as necessarily permanent. He left his colleagues in the Educational Association with the impression that he would be back before long. (See *Records of the Triennial Meeting, 1896*, 19.)
21. See his report, "Chinese Prize Essays," in *The John Fryer Miscellany*, vol. 1. The report was evidently written in 1887. The essay contest is described in Wu Jianren's novel *Ershinian mudu zhi guai xianzhuang*, chapter 15.
22. Before joining the arsenal, Fryer served for eighteen months as part-time editor of the *Shanghai xinbao* (Shanghai gazette). He even tried out briefly as subeditor of the *North China Daily News*, but the job was too hectic for him; see his letter to his brother of February 6, 1868 (misdated 1867).
23. There is an unfinished novel about the Jewish settlement in Kaifeng in carton 3 of "Correspondence and Papers."
24. See "Chinese Literature, Part Two," in carton 1, 42. On the bookshop's holdings, see Bennett, *John Fryer*, 112–15.
25. "Chinese Literature, Part Two," 43.
26. "The Literature of China," 165–66.
27. "The Chinese Problem," in carton 1, 34. This article, evidently written early in 1901, is Fryer's most forceful statement about the Chinese situation. The armies of "the chief nations of the world . . . have desolated and looted the Metropolis, and even the Imperial palace, committing atrocities equaling, if not surpassing, those of the Goths and Vandals at Rome *and at least vying with those perpetrated by the Chinese themselves.*" (The italicized passage was added to the typescript afterward by hand.) Fryer goes on to excoriate the missionaries for upsetting the existing religions, including ancestor worship, and then, "having sufficiently stirred up a hornets' nest,"

calling in the aid of their consuls" (10). Traders are equally to blame: "Bibles and opium have gone hand in hand all over the country" (13).

28. This much is suggested by a letter of March 23, 1896 in the "Letter Journal" from Fryer to Joseph Edkins. It refers to an article in the *Shen bao* on the prize essays that is "evidently from the hand of Mr. Wang Tao." That day's editorial argues that the sponsors of the essay contests should go beyond essays and promote scientific education in general. It seems strange that Wang Tao had not contacted Fryer before publishing it.

29. P. 1.

30. Pp. 330–31.

31. See *Shen bao*, May 25, 28, 30, June 4, and June 8; and *Wanguo gongbao* 77:31.

32. It was issued from the offices of his magazine, dated the middle of the tenth month of 1895. I don't know why it took so long to get published. The tone of the report reflects the rapid movement of opinion during 1895; it is much less tentative about reform than the advertisement is.

33. See the March 1896 numbers. Both journals, citing limitations of space, printed only the report and the prizewinners. The *Shen bao* printed neither.

34. However, this is the only place in Fryer's writings where I have noticed this tone.

35. Of course, some Chinese novels did satirize the examination system and even footbinding, but their satire cannot be compared to the condemnation and remedies called for by Fryer.

36. Reference is to the 1998 reprint.

37. On Zhan Xi and his family, see *Quxian zhi* (Gazetteer of Quxian) (Hangzhou: Zhejiang renmin chubanshe, 1992), 556–57.

38. He says it appeared in the *Hubao*, which is probably a mistake for *Shen bao*.

39. His age, examination status, and opinions tally with those of the author. Moreover, it is he who tells the author about the Wei family.

40. The poems appeared on September 13. He was certainly working in Shanghai at the time. His advertisements of paintings for sale appeared on September 20 and October 1 and 3, and his biography of a Shanghai courtesan on October 13. The editor of the *Youxi bao* at the time was Li Boyuan, soon to become one of the best known novelists of the late Qing.

41. For example, Zheng Zhixin's extravagant praise of Puyang Zeng and his family as benefactors in chapter 21 (89–90). Puyang Zeng was a fellow artist from Quxian. (See *Quxian zhi*, 472.) There is a reference to the aborted love affair between Zou Tao and the courtesan Su Yunlan in chapter 14 (57), an affair that was the basis of Zou's novel *Haishang chentian ying*; see chapter 2 of this book. At the very least, chapter 14 of *Hualiu shenqing zhuan* must have been heavily revised in 1897.

42. See chapter 1.

43. See chapter 3.

44. See his "Yiyin zhengzhi xiaoshuo xu" (The translation and printing of political novels), *Qingyi bao* 1 (eleventh month 1898): 53–54.

45. The listing appeared in a foldout advertisement entitled "Zhongguo weiyi zhi wenxuebao *Xin xiaoshuo*" (China's only literary journal *Xin xiaoshuo*) inserted in *Xinmin*

congbao 14 (seventh month 1902). Yan Tingliang has argued persuasively that the political novel was always central to Liang Qichao's thinking about fiction; see his *Wan-Qing xiaoshuo lilun* (Late-Qing fiction theory) (Beijing: Zhonghua, 1996), 63–70. On the origins of Liang's categories, see Ye Kaidi (Catherine V. Yeh), "Guanyu wan-Qing shidai de xiaoshuo leibie ji *Xin xiaoshuo* zazhi guanggao erze" (On the categories of late-Qing fiction and two advertisements for *New Fiction*), *Shinmatsu shōsetsu* 12 (1989): 112–21.

CHAPTER 7

The Second Stage of Vernacular Translation

OR MANY YEARS after the publication of the vernacular Chinese translation of Bulwer Lytton's *Night and Morning*[1] no other renderings of
fiction appeared in Chinese, except for the handful of religious stories
translated by missionaries and their assistants. Not until the 1890s did other
secular translations begin to appear, and then they were all in literary Chinese,
not the vernacular. The earliest was a summary account—it can scarcely be
called a translation—of Edward Bellamy's *Looking Backward*, done by Timothy Richard with the aid of a Chinese collaborator. It was followed by several
Sherlock Holmes stories translated by Zhang Kunde and published in the
journal *Shiwu bao*, which was edited at the time by Liang Qichao; *La dame
aux camélias* by Alexandre Dumas *fils*, translated by Lin Shu and Wang
Shouchang; and Shiba Shirō's *Kajin no kigō*, translated by Liang Qichao and
published in the first of the journals that he edited while a political refugee in
Japan.[2] To the best of my knowledge, it was not until February 1902 that a
second full-length novel was translated into the vernacular—Jules Verne's
Deux ans de vacances.[3] The translation appeared in Liang Qichao's second
journal, *Xinmin congbao* (Renovation of the people); Liang himself translated
the first half and his colleague and fellow exile Luo Pu[4] the second. It was soon
followed by other vernacular translations in Liang's third journal, *Xin xiaoshuo*
(New fiction), as well as in *Xinmin congbao*, which continued to appear. The
period beginning in 1902 was therefore a second stage in the translation of fiction into the vernacular.

I propose to examine Liang and Luo's translation of the Jules Verne novel as well as another work, Zhou Guisheng's (1863–1926) translation of a French detective novel. Zhou is often described as the earliest translator of fiction into the vernacular, although that distinction properly belongs to Jiang Qizhang or—among late-Qing writers—to Liang Qichao.[5] But if not actually the earliest, Zhou was certainly among the earliest vernacular translators and, more important, he specialized in translation as such, particularly of detective and science fiction, rather than in novel writing. In 1906 he founded in Shanghai the first Chinese organization of translators, the *Yishu jiaotong gonghui*. He was also a close friend and colleague of the novelist Wu Jianren, who wrote some of the commentaries on Zhou's translation of the detective novel I have referred to. A primary reason for choosing the two works translated by Liang Qichao and Zhou Guisheng is that both men discuss their translations in the light of Chinese and western models.

The traditional Chinese model constrained virtually all of the earliest vernacular translations. By contrast, translators into literary Chinese, with no strongly defined novel tradition to contend with, had a much freer hand. Lin Shu, the great exponent of the translation of fiction into literary Chinese, copied the narrative methods of foreign fiction with a surprising degree of fidelity. True, he was capable of adjusting his translations to suit his own ethical and other standards,[6] but, as I showed in chapter 5, he was essentially a preservationist in terms of narrative method, certainly in comparison with Jiang Qizhang. By his approach, Lin effectively created the literary Chinese novel that flourished in the first two decades of the twentieth century.[7]

I shall not attempt to give an extensive account of either the Liang or the Zhou translation. Instead I shall select a few salient features that proved significant in considering the translation of *Night and Morning* in chapter 4: formal features such as the nature and function of the narrator, the opening and the chapter transitions; and thematic shift as shown in both the translation and the commentaries.

Deux ans de vacances

Jules Verne's novel, first published in Paris in 1888, is an adventure story about fourteen New Zealand schoolboys whose parents have arranged for them to take a sea voyage around their country during the summer vacation. The night before the boys' scheduled departure, they find themselves adrift on the ocean and at the mercy of a gale that—in an incredibly short space of time—drives them right across the Pacific to an uninhabited island that turns out to be somewhere off the coast of Chile. (Much later, one of the boys admits to having cast off as a prank.) No adults were on board at the time—the captain and his men were all carousing on shore—and the only crew member present was a cabin boy. Predictably, the fifteen boys face a series of dangers from the elements as well as from various wild animals, not to mention a cutthroat band of mutineers that descend on the island. Less predictably, conflict develops among the boys; the natural leader, Briant, who is French, is repeatedly challenged by another boy named Doniphan, and the tension between the two becomes so acute that at one point Doniphan and his friends secede and set up their own camp. In Verne's preface, he says that he wrote the novel to show the bravery and intelligence of which boys are capable.

Deux ans de vacances was translated into English by an anonymous translator as *Two Years' Vacation*,[8] and then from English into Japanese by Morita Shiken as *Jūgo shōnen* (Fifteen boys).[9] Liang and Luo translated it from Morita's Japanese under the title of *Shiwu xiao haojie* (Fifteen young heroes). Of the eighteen chapters of the translated version, Liang was responsible for the first nine, which form a unit, covering the boys' first year as castaways. In the inaugural number of *Xin xiaoshuo*, that of February 8, 1902, Liang had published under the *xiaoshuo* rubric[10] the opening scene of a play (*chuanqi*) called *Jiehui meng* (A dream of holocaust) that he had written himself. It consists entirely of a single character holding forth on the tragic state of China, and it ends by invoking the precedent of Voltaire, who had used the media of fiction and drama to protest against the condition of France under Louis XIV. But Liang never published any more of his play. In the second number of the journal, the same section is filled instead with the first chapter of *Fifteen Young Heroes*. An accompanying note explains that the playwright, who is not identified in the journal, needed more time to consider his work.

Liang's purpose in translating the novel is obvious even from the title, in which "Young Heroes" replaces the "Boys" of the Japanese. Liang frequently refers to the youths as heroes in his text, and his commentaries emphasize heroic enterprise and a sense of adventure. This theme was also present in Jules Verne's novel, as well as in the English and Japanese translations, but Liang takes it further; the thematic change he makes is not so much a shift as an intensification of a theme that already existed. He had long taken an interest in the education of boys; the series of articles he wrote on institutional reform in 1897 give detailed instructions on class schedules and curricula, and even allow a modest role for certain kinds of fiction.[11] Moreover, while he was translating this novel, he was publishing in the same journal a series of articles on the various reasons for China's lack of progress. One reason was that the Chinese had shown no interest whatever in adventure and discovery.[12] Where, for example, was the Chinese Columbus or Livingstone? Liang's translation of the Jules Verne novel should be seen in the light of that concern.

His first four chapters are followed by pertinent commentaries that amount to directions to the reader—refining the notions of adventure and discovery. The fact that the boys' parents arrange a sea voyage for their sons is a sign of the value placed by western societies on adventure. The factionalism that develops among the boys is not really to be deplored, because competition is a condition of all progress.[13] However, freedom of action has to be accompanied by a sense of self-discipline—Liang goes so far as to praise the English type of public school, which he had observed in Australia and America.[14] Some of Briant's statements are enthusiastically endorsed by the commentator: "We must realize that there are things outside ourselves that are even greater than we are,"[15] and "This is a time of terrible danger for us all. If we stick together, perhaps we can help each other survive, but if we split up—that's the way to certain death."[16] Of this last statement, Liang adds, "My compatriots ought to recite this to themselves three times a day." In the text itself, as distinct from the commentary, this kind of reflection is comparatively rare, much rarer than in the next novel I shall consider. The most obvious case occurs in chapter 9, when one of the boys, who has caught and apparently tamed an ostrich, prepares to ride it. The ostrich rears up and bolts, throwing its rider off, and Liang cannot resist a political analogy: "Just as, when the people of a country have acquired the necessary knowledge and experience, they will no longer blindly tolerate their bondage under a barbaric government."[17]

The translation carries no preface, but the commentary at the end of the first chapter makes some of the same points that we might expect to find in one. Liang notes that the English preface—he implies that he has read it—explained that the translation was concerned with the sense of the text rather than its words, and that it substituted the "English form" of the novel while remaining true to the meaning of the French original.[18] Morita Shiken's preface likewise claimed that the "Japanese style" had been substituted for the English without any departure from the meaning. "And now this translation of mine," Liang continues, "will entirely replace the Japanese style with the form of Chinese vernacular fiction. However, I am confident that I have not been unfaithful to Morita and, that being the case, even if Jules Verne himself were to read my translation, he would hardly say that I have distorted his work."

Liang's claim to have converted the novel into the form of traditional fiction is perfectly true—with some interesting reservations. In fact, he has gone much further in accommodating the Chinese model than either the English or the Japanese translators did in accommodating their respective models. Liang frequently refers self-consciously to the Chinese model in his commentaries. For example, he describes the opening of the novel, despite his adaptation of it, as offering a shock to Chinese readers; he claims that the chapter endings he has fashioned are superior to those of his Japanese exemplar; and in the commentary to chapter 4, the most significant case, he defends his use of a mixed language somewhat less colloquial than that of the typical novel.

> This book began by imitating the form of *Shuihu zhuan, Story of the Stone,* and the like, in making exclusive use of the colloquial (*suhua*). But the time it took to translate presented me with a very difficult problem. By using a combination of literary and vernacular language, I found that I was able to cut the work in half. I calculate that in translating the first few chapters, I was able to write only 1,000 characters per hour, but on this occasion [chapter 4] I wrote 2,500. In my translating, I am intent on saving as much time as possible and am therefore compelled to use a mixture of literary and vernacular. I know perfectly well that this practice does not conform to the proper style of vernacular fiction, and when the whole work is revised for publication, I shall make the necessary adjustments. Nevertheless, this experience does demonstrate that the division between the spoken and the written languages is one of the greatest inconveniences affecting Chinese literature. However, the subject of literary revolution is not one that is easily addressed.[19]

Despite the formal changes, Liang's is, for its time, quite a responsible translation, fairly close to the Japanese in sense while remaining idiomatically Chinese. If it omits some of the technical information in which Verne delighted, there are other items that it adds. It often fills out the dialogue with a sharper rhetoric than the Japanese. Luo Pu, continuing the translation after Liang left off, makes the only substantial change in content. He turns Kate, a woman who has been cast away on the island, from a middle-aged lady's companion into a fifteen-year-old beauty. (This younger Kate nurses the injured Doniphan, which leads to the novel's only romance.)

The most culturally bound part of a Chinese novel—perhaps any novel— was its opening, which decided fundamental questions such as where and how the tale was to begin, and by whom and on what authority it was to be told. We have seen how Jiang Qizhang rearranged even Lytton's occasional "blind" chapter openings to make them conform to a Chinese order. Verne's *Deux ans de vacances*, after a brief listing of the first chapter's contents, begins almost as blindly as Lytton's chapters:

> Pendant la nuit du 9 mars 1860, les nuages se confondant avec la mer, limitaient à quelques brasses la portée de la vue.

It goes on to tell of a boat driven by the gale, but the reader still does not know where the boat is, who is on board, or where it is heading, let alone who is giving us this account of it and on what authority he is doing so. Although both the English and Japanese translations accepted this beginning and translated it faithfully enough, its abruptness was evidently too much for Liang Qichao. After a traditional pair of chapter headings that correspond after a fashion to the list of chapter contents given in the French novel, he inserts a long *ci* lyric, the last four lines of which run as follows:

> This isn't wild or careless talk.
> I urge my young compatriots:
> Bestir yourselves and boldly act,
> And see you don't waste your lives.[20]

He then introduces the narrative:

> Readers, what do you suppose this lyric is alluding to? Our story tells how, forty-two years ago, on the night of the ninth of March 1860 by the western calendar, black clouds filled the sky. . . .

The main theme of the novel, as Liang understands it, has been expressed in the lyric, while the narrative itself has been safely located within the traditional narrator-audience relationship. But in Liang's judgment that is still not enough to satisfy Chinese readers. The opening remains too abrupt, as he admits in his end-of-chapter commentary. Readers will be bewildered by its mystery, he concedes, but he does not attempt to justify the technique, beyond asserting that it demonstrates the "abundant vitality of western literature."

Verne preserves the mystery until chapter 3, which he devotes entirely to background explanation. This presented Liang Qichao with another huge problem, because he favored the traditional kind of chapter that closed on a note of doubt or suspense or anticipation. To provide such an ending, he plucked an episode from elsewhere and grafted it onto the end of his chapter 2. Briant is struggling ashore with a line from the stranded boat when he is caught in a whirlpool and disappears from sight. End of chapter. In an interesting variant of the usual formula, the reader is then advised to "wait for the next number of *Xinmin congbao* to come out."[21]

Chapter 3 in the next number of the journal begins:

> The previous chapter has told how Briant was caught in a whirlpool and disappeared from sight. But readers, there was no need to worry about him! He couldn't possibly die. He's the main figure of this book,[22] and without him we wouldn't have fifteen young heroes any more! However, these last two chapters have related a number of hair-raising events in a most haphazard way. After all, what country do these boys come from? What race do they belong to? Where is their boat, the *Sloughi*, heading? And why is there no captain on board, just this handful of young boys still wet behind the ears? I imagine that readers will have grown very impatient with all these puzzles, and so now I'm going to take the time to fill in the background for you.[23]

But if Briant is not to drown, he cannot be left there in his whirlpool. At the beginning of chapter 4, which appeared a month after chapter 2, Liang comes to the rescue, writing in the same humorous tone:

> Readers, chapter 2 told how Briant, struggling ashore alone in an effort to save his companions, was caught in a whirlpool and disappeared from sight. Your translator[24] promised that you would learn the rest of the story when the next number of *Xinmin congbao* came out. But by now a *second* number has come and gone, and a full month has elapsed. That must be considered a grave offense on the part of your translator. However, it is also an instance of deliberate delay at a moment of eager anticipation, which is a well-established practice among novelists, and in that case I cannot be held solely to blame. But enough of all this idle chatter! Readers, you will recall what I told you a month ago. Briant had just leaped into the sea with one end of the rope tied to the boat and the other end fastened around his chest, but it's now a month later. Gordon and the others pulled frantically on the rope until they dragged the unconscious Briant back on board, where eventually he regained consciousness.[25]

The narrator's voice addressing his readers was established at the beginning of the novel. There and elsewhere throughout the translation, it corresponds to nothing similar in the Japanese. When the Japanese translation switches from the narration of events to some general statement or to an explanation, the Chinese usually addresses a question explicitly to the readers (*kanguan*) and then supplies an answer introduced by *yuanlai* (The fact was) in the time-honored way. (For the most part, the answers do not invoke distinctively Chinese analogues, as occurs often in *Xinxi xiantan.*) There are numerous occasions, also, when the Chinese narrator intervenes with the same formulae to explain matters of time, order, or focus, as we saw at the opening of chapter 3.

But this merely testifies to Liang Qichao's thorough conversion of the Japanese translation to the model of the traditional Chinese novel. What is remarkable, compared with previous translations, is the voice of the narrator *as translator*. One instance occurs at the end of chapter 2, where the reader is told, in a variant of the traditional instruction, that if he wants to know what will happen next, he should wait for the next number of *Xinmin congbao*, rather than for the next chapter. Another occurs at the end of chapter 6, where the reader is instructed to "wait until the translator takes up his brush again and writes it down."[26] The long passage at the beginning of chapter 4, as translated above, is also directly attributed to the translator. "Your translator promised that you would learn the rest of the story when the next number of *Xinmin congbao* came out." He then excuses himself on the grounds that he has been merely employing the delaying tactics of the novelist. In the Chinese version the translator has, in effect, superimposed himself upon the narrator, and in the numerous cases of direct address to the reader it is sometimes not possible to separate the voice of the narrator from that of the translator.

The translator's playfulness, of which several examples have been given, is not to be attributed to mockery of the Verne novel. Nor was it intended to detract from the force of the work being translated, although it may sometimes have had that effect. It was in fact a common feature of the traditional novel, intended to amuse readers and hold their attention, particularly while the novel's plot was developing.

One of Liang's major structural adaptations was to change the division of chapters in order to conform to traditional Chinese practice. He draws attention to this in his commentary on chapter 1, claiming that his division will be "even better than that of the original text,"[27] by which he presumably means the Japanese version he is working from. What he has done is to end his chapters at moments of suspense or anticipation—the suspense is sometimes fabricated, as we have seen—and to provide the usual chapter-ending formulae, consisting of a couplet of verse, a question addressed to readers, and the advice to turn to the next chapter for an answer. Within the chapter itself, he does not use paragraphing to break up the text, as the Japanese does, but prefers narrative locutions instead. One of his innovations is a series of dots marking a switch from one mode to another, for example from speech or action to explanation and vice versa.

I have referred frequently to the commentaries Liang appended to his first four chapters. They should be seen as a set of explanations of the original work as well as of the major changes he was making by adapting to the tastes of his Chinese readership. But the commentaries are also a set of reading instructions, guiding readers and correcting their probable misconceptions, and sometimes alerting them to what will come next. Most important, of course, they give Liang an opportunity to express his main concerns. After four successive commentaries, he presumably felt that he had informed the reader sufficiently on these points.[28]

There are a number of omissions, all relatively small. For example, the distinction between a yacht and a schooner, the sort of point about which Verne loved to reveal his knowledge, is omitted, as is the fact that Briant speaks English with a French accent. (Both would have appeared in chapter 1.) On July 15, Briant remarks that it is St. Swithin's Day, and repeats the traditional belief that, if it rains, the sun will not be seen again in the sky for the next forty days.[29] The Japanese version copies this faithfully enough,[30] but Liang omits all reference to St. Swithin and merely mentions the popular belief. This is characteristic of him—not to burden his translation with unnecessary information.

His additions are of several kinds. As I have said, he often livens up the dialogue. Occasionally he adds a point that is not in the Japanese. Many of the additions are designed to make the description more vivid by the use of figurative language; for example, the boat in the grip of the waves was "a slave deprived of all right to freedom."[31] He also introduces a few distinctively Chinese references, mainly in his later chapters.[32]

Margot la balafrée

Novels of adventure, like *Deux ans de vacances*, were one of the most commonly translated types in the early twentieth century. In addition to those actually labeled "adventure fiction" (*maoxian xiaoshuo*), a number of those labeled "science fiction," particularly the novels of Jules Verne, could also be included under the same heading, as could many novels by Rider Haggard, the most translated foreign author of the time. However, there was another type that was even more commonly translated—the detective or crime novel (*zhentan xiaoshuo*). One scholar has estimated that these constituted as many as half of all the novels translated during the period.[33]

Of the detective novels that Liang Qichao published in his journals, the majority were French. Typically, they give a relatively minor role to the detective, who does not dominate as in the Sherlock Holmes stories. The earliest was *Li-hun bing*, from a novel by an unknown author, possibly American, which Luo Pu translated, presumably from the Japanese version, and published in *Xin xiaoshuo*, beginning with the first number (November 14, 1902). The following year, 1903, saw several detective novels serialized. *La main coupée* by Fortuné du Boisgobey (1821–91), the most popular French writer of detective stories of the 1870s and 1880s, was translated into Chinese under the title *Meiren shou* (The beauty's hand) by a writer purporting to be a woman and published in the *Xinmin congbian*.[34] The translator was working from the Japanese version by Kuroiwa Ruikō (*Bijin no te*) of the English *The Severed Hand* (1886). Another, more interesting French novel, still unidentified, was translated as *Yichun yuan* (Welcome Spring Park) by a translator based in Shanghai who is known only by his pseudonym.[35] It is labeled a "legal novel" (*falü xiaoshuo*), and it is largely concerned with French judicial procedure, but it could just as easily have been called a detective story. Finally, another novel by du Boisgobey, *Margot la balafrée* (Margot the scarred), was translated by Zhou Guisheng from the English version, *In the Serpent's Coils*,[36] under the title of *Dushe quan*. The translation ran from no. 8 (July 9, 1903) to no. 24 (January 1906), and was never completed, reaching only about halfway through the original. In 1905, a separate translation of *Margot la balafrée* from the Japanese version of a different English translation was also published in Shanghai.[37] Readers were left to puzzle over of the conundrum of two apparently different novels with identical plots.

Zhou's translation was accompanied by notes and copious commentaries, most of which were written by Wu Jianren. Zhou reciprocated by writing the commentaries and notes for *Dianshu qitan* (Strange tale of the electric art), a novel about death by electro-hypnosis that Wu was currently publishing in *Xin xiaoshuo*. (He was reworking an existing literary Chinese translation to fit the vernacular model.)[38] Although labeled a love story (*xieqing xiaoshuo*), *Dianshu qitan* could just as easily have been called a detective novel.

These translations employ a wide variety of different methods. The translator of *Meiren shou*, for example, follows the traditional Chinese model but adds a lengthy prologue on reformist ideas and the emancipation of the serfs in Russia,[39] while, at the other extreme, *Yichun yuan* employs an unobtrusive narrator, ignores the traditional chapter transitions, and contains no perceptible reference to the Chinese situation. It seems that by 1903 at least, narrative method had become a matter of choice; it was not forced upon the translator by the traditional model.

Margot la balafrée is a sensational novel in the du Boisgobey manner. It tells how Tiburce Gerfaut, a Paris sculptor, is stumbling home from a convivial gathering when he comes upon what turns out to be a murder. In trying to catch the culprit, he is blinded by vitriol flung in his face. The novel begins with a dialogue between a testy Gerfaut and his solicitous daughter Camille before he goes out to attend the gathering. In the course of the dialogue, Camille reveals that she is engaged to marry Philippe de Charny, news that is distinctly unwelcome to her father. Eventually, Margot, the actress who flings the vitriol in Gerfaut's face, is found to be in league with Charny in a plot to gain control of Gerfaut's considerable fortune.

The translation, which is in a more colloquial Chinese than any other I have mentioned, is reasonably close to the English—except for Zhou Guisheng's numerous insertions, a subject to which I shall return. Wherever possible, Zhou either omits or finds general equivalents for the novel's culture-specific terms: soirées, Hercules, the Tuileries, Bohemian life, toasting (with wine), etc. The word "swell" is translated in lively fashion as *youtou guanggun*, "foppish rogue," while "tyrant" is translated weakly as "harsh, mean-spirited father." In one case, Zhou elects to explain a difficult notion, but misleadingly. The novel's narrator has said that Michelangelo was Gerfaut's god, which Zhou interprets to mean that Michelangelo was the patron saint of sculptors, in much the same the way as Lu Ban was for Chinese carpenters or Bo Le for grooms and drivers.[40]

The opening is left blind, as in the original. The discussion between Gerfaut and his daughter, covering several pages, is set out on the page in both French and English versions without any indication of the speakers' identity, and without even any tags ("he said," "she said"). Astonishingly, Zhou Guisheng translates the text just as it is, without a shred of extra information. He does not set the dialogue off in separate lines as in the French and English, presumably because space was at too much of a premium, but he takes care to mark off each speech with right-angled brackets. Even so, such an opening must have seemed strange to the average reader, and Zhou prudently adds a statement just before the opening of the first chapter explaining and justifying it. He notes the traditional Chinese preference for setting out the hero's background first, as well as the Chinese insistence on prologues, introductions, poems, or disquisitions at the head of a novel. This work by "the great French writer Bao Fu" (Fortuné du Boisgobey) comes to the reader out of the blue. However, Zhou goes on, close examination shows that the opening has a rationale of its own, and he will not presume to change it. In any case, the use of such openings is common among European novelists, and he intends to translate this one directly, in order to introduce it to Chinese fiction writers, adding: "I sincerely hope that they will not deride it as an unsound practice."[41]

In fact, Zhou's introduction of the new practice soon bore fruit, as has often been pointed out. His friend Wu Jianren made spectacular use of a blind opening in his novel *Jiuming qiyuan* (The strange case of the nine murders), which began publication in *Xin xiaoshuo* a little over a year later.[42]

In contrast to his acceptance of the blind opening, however, Zhou adheres to most of the other features of the traditional Chinese model, in particular its chapter transitions. The English version, like the French original, is divided into a small number of long, untitled sections, which Zhou chops up at moments of suspense and shapes into Chinese-style chapters; in this respect, he is no different from Liang Qichao. But he makes far more insertions in the narrative than Liang does. At the beginning of chapter 3 of *Fifteen Heroes* and again at the beginning of chapter 4, Liang comments humorously in his capacity as translator, but he never tries to explain foreign culture or condemn the Chinese system. (He leaves that to his prologue poem and his end-of-chapter commentaries.) By contrast, Zhou's numerous insertions are for the most part clearly labeled as those of the translator, and many of them refer explicitly to China, almost always from a critical or mocking point of view.

A humorous insertion in chapter 3 is concerned with the hackneyed techniques of fictional description. Gerfaut is admiring the handsome appearance of Marcel Brunier, whom he has just met:

> What a pity Marcel was born in France! In France they'd never heard of any truly handsome men, and so as a result Gerfaut had no one to liken Marcel to. Now if Gerfaut had been Chinese and were engaged in writing a novel, he would surely have wanted to say that Marcel's face was like a cap jade, his lips seemed to be daubed with vermilion, his looks resembled those of Pan An, and his talent was the equal of Song Yu's.

When Marcel gives Gerfaut an opening to start expounding his aesthetic theories, an insertion explicitly mentions the translator:

> It occurs to the translator that Gerfaut, as a Frenchman, had never studied any Chinese books. If he had, he would surely have slipped in a quotation here, citing the following passage from Confucius: "It is fitting that we should hold the young in awe. How do we know that the generations to come will not be the equal of the present?"[43]

When in chapter 4 Gerfaut makes his ill-fated decision to walk home rather than take a cab, the narrator makes the point that this decision

> involved Bao Fu [Fortuné du Boisgobey] of France in writing the book *Dushe quan*, Zhixin zhuren [Zhou Guisheng] of China in translating it, Jianchan zhuren [Wu Jianren] of China in commenting on it, and the staff of the New Fiction Society in printing it. All of the above were kept frantically busy. Why *was* that? All because of Gerfaut's change of mind.[44]

In chapter 20, when a mysterious ring is found in a pawnshop, he comments:

> I expect that all of you readers, being the perceptive people you are, will already have guessed something of the real explanation. But since the author of the book has chosen to use this method, I, as his translator, can hardly give the game away.[45]

The fancy dress ball in chapter 19, attended by young women of good family as well as the demimonde, calls for an explanation:

> Having grown up in free countries amid great prosperity, such girls are not prepared to sit apathetically at home like Chinese girls and endure their loneliness. Instead, they go off to the theater with their parents and enjoy themselves.[46]

When Jean Carnac, the hero of the novel, invites a young woman to dance and she accepts, a further explanation is required:

> This is the custom in France, where no boundaries exist between acquaintance and stranger, male and female. In China such a thing would be inconceivable.[47]

The translation is equipped with commentaries at the end of most of its chapters and also with numerous upper-margin notes. Twelve of the commentaries, signed with Wu Jianren's pseudonym, are concentrated in a few blocks of chapters (3–5, 9–11, 18–23), which also happen to have more upper-margin notes than any of the others. It seems likely that the majority of the notes in those chapters were also by him, and that the other commentaries and notes were by Zhou Guisheng. This assumption is supported by an examination of their contents.

Both Wu and Zhou comment in the traditional manner on the significance of this or that item in foreshadowing or echoing other events. In only one case does Wu mention a western technique, praising the writer for omitting the speech tags.[48] More significantly, he frequently points out Zhou's insertions. In his commentary at the end of chapter 3, Wu insists that the jesting tone of the insertions is not superfluous; without it, readers would become bored. "This is the only solution open to novelists. The western original isn't like this at all."[49] He also directs a series of comic remarks at the translator. For example, in chapter 3, when Zhou is mocking Chinese social etiquette, he asks, "He *will* go and insert these idle criticisms of everyone. Isn't he afraid they'll all be angry with him?"[50] When in the same chapter, Zhou makes fun of descriptive clichés in fiction, Wu comments, "He's translating a novel himself. Why bother to make fun of novelists?"[51] In chapter 20, Zhou inserts the general remark that women all over the world are fascinated by jewelry. Wu's note runs: "Now he's abusing women all over the world. Doesn't the translator fear that the world's women will turn on him?"[52]

There is a clear distinction in tenor between the commentaries by Wu Jianren and the passages inserted by Zhou Guisheng. Zhou was using the French novel to denounce the Chinese political system and mock Chinese manners. Wu Jianren, on the other hand, although more open to technical experiment than any other novelist of the late Qing, was extremely conservative when it came to adopting western ideas and fashions; in fact, he can reasonably be called a cultural nationalist.[53] In his commentaries and notes he uses the French novel as a negative example of western attitudes and customs. Take the case of the fancy dress ball. Zhou's commentary describes the grand theaters of Europe, where the boxes are lined with women of noble family accompanied by men.[54] In the center of the hall large numbers of men and women mix together, dressed in such grotesque costumes that it is impossible to make out anybody's identity. They are not actors and actresses, however, as Zhou is careful to point out, but simply members of the audience who have deliberately dressed up to get a laugh. "There are also men who use this as a pretext for carrying on with women," he adds. "They mingle with the crowd, meet up with women, and are then able to lead them out and start enjoying themselves in wild dancing."

Wu Jianren pounces on this last statement, which he takes as an admission. "That last passage was written by the translator himself. It provides ample evidence of the customs of the so-called civilized or free countries. All those in our country who blindly worship freedom—can *this* be what they are looking for? One theory holds that if the old ways have not been completely eradicated from our minds, things will seem alien to us and we will disapprove of them. If so, I would not presume to deny it in my case." In an upper-margin note on the scene in the theater, someone, probably Wu, remarks: "Western countries delight in having fun, but China emphasizes decorum."

In one instance, he claims responsibility for persuading Zhou Guisheng to insert a particular long passage in the text. In his commentary on chapter 9, he explains that the passage in which Camille frets over her father's safety was not part of the original novel:

> I made a point of discussing it with the translator, and so he inserted this passage in the text. However, although it was lacking in the original, I know that that night Camille would certainly have been preoccupied with these concerns. Hence, although the passage has been fabricated, it is by no means superfluous.[55]

In a traditional father-daughter relationship, the father's concern for his daughter should be at least balanced by her concern for him, and although we have heard much of Gerfaut's thoughts, we have heard little of Camille's, hence Wu's insistence on the insertion. But he also had a particular reason— to refute the fashionable agitation for what was then known as "family revolution" (*jiating geming*). Wu was locked in a bitter dispute with the westernized younger generation, who were calling for the end of "family despotism" and even for the institution of "free marriage." At the end of chapter 11, which stresses the teacher-pupil relationship between Gerfaut and Carnac, he claims that the French novel is a "textbook for present-day society,"[56] even though, as he acknowledges, some will criticize his views as backward.

Thematic shift in the case of this novel resolves itself into a tug of war between translator and commentator, the former trying to use du Boisgobey's theme, which in its French and English versions had no obvious political subtext, to promote social change in China, the latter trying to portray it as a dreadful warning against the adoption of western ways. At the end of chapter 6, in a commentary presumably by Zhou Guisheng, he remarks on Gerfaut's being taken to the police station.[57] It's a lucky thing, he says, that Gerfaut was born in France, for had he been born in China, he'd have been subjected to torture. "Whenever I read books from civilized countries, either history or fiction, I cannot help feeling a boundless sympathy for my compatriots. This is just one example."[58] In his commentary at the end of chapter 8, he deplores the fact that Gerfaut, in volunteering to find the murderer, has aroused the suspicion of one of the policemen. "This is the sort of thing that drives honorable men to despair."[59] Wu Jianren, by contrast, much as he deplored the Chinese situation in his other works, is intent on condemning foreign influence.

These translations by Liang Qichao and Zhou Guisheng show the hesitation of the earliest translators when confronted with the unfamiliar forms of western fiction. They tentatively accept some new features, such as the blind opening, but for the most part they stick close to the Chinese model. Thematic shift in the direction of political reform is the general rule in translations from the West during this period, even in the case of entertainment novels like *Margot la balafrée*. It is accomplished mainly by insertions and end-of-chapter commentaries, as the translators take advantage of the license allowed them by the traditional Chinese fictional model.

The acceptance of foreign features was extremely rapid, in translated novels as well as in original fiction. Although the traditional model continued to hold the loyalty of some translators, the majority soon adopted, to some degree, the forms of western fiction.[60] By the end of 1905, a scant three years after Liang Qichao began his translation of Jules Verne, a vernacular novel owing nothing whatever to the traditional model was written entirely in the voice of the main character.[61]

NOTES

1. See chapter 4.
2. A Rider Haggard novel was translated by Zeng Guangquan in 1898 or 1899 and published in a Shanghai paper, *Changyan bao*, according to Guo Yanli, *Zhongguo jindai fanyi wenxue gailun* (Hankou: Hubei jiaoyu chubanshe, 1998), 29.
3. In single-chapter installments, it ran from no. 2 (Feb. 22, 1902) to no. 24 (Jan. 13, 1903). It was not the first Chinese translation of Jules Verne. Xue Shaohui and her husband Chen Shoupeng translated *Le tour du monde en quatre-vingt jours* together into literary Chinese in 1900, Chen providing the oral version, Xue the written. See Guo Yanli, *Zhongguo jindai fanyi wenxue gailun*, 168–70.
4. Author of the novel *Dong-Ou nü haojie* about the Russian nihilist Sofia Perovskaja. His novel began appearing in the first number of *Xin xiaoshuo*.
5. On Zhou Guisheng, see Yang Shiji, *Wenyuan tan wang* (Shanghai: Zhonghua shu-ju, 1945), 10–14. Other information can be found in Zhou Guiqing's anthology of Zhou's translations, *Dushe quan, wai shizhong* (Changsha: Yuelu shushe, 1991), and particularly in Guo Yanli, *Zhongguo jindai fanyi wenxue gailun*, 345–55.

6. For example, in his translation of *La dame aux camélias*, he omits most of Armant's intellectual speculations but dwells lovingly on the scene between Marguerite and Armant's father in which she promises to sacrifice her love for the good of Armant's family. Lin Shu also adapts and trims the ending to emphasize the reconciliation of Armant with his family.

7. See chapter 10 on this kind of novel. It is interesting that one of the most important features of the traditional novel, the narrator's dialogue with his readers, reappeared in the literary novel, albeit in a different guise.

8. New York: George Munro, 1889.

9. Tokyo: Ohashi Shintarō, 1896.

10. In this period, the word "*xiaoshuo*" could still encompass plays as well as fiction.

11. See chapter 6.

12. See "Xin min shuo" 5, *Xinmin congbao* 5 (third month 1902): 1–11.

13. See the commentary at the end of chapter 2. *Xinmin congbao* 4:96.

14. See the commentary at the end of chapter 3. *Xinmin congbao* 5:98.

15. See the commentary at the end of chapter 1. *Xinmin congbao* 2:100.

16. See the commentary at the end of chapter 2. *Xinmin congbao* 4:96.

17. See *Xinmin congbao* 13:86.

18. See *Xinmin congbao* 2:100.

19. *Xinmin congbao* 6:83.

20. *Xinmin congbao* 2:93.

21. *Xinmin congbao* 3:96.

22. This kind of gambit is also found in earlier fiction. See, for example, *Ernü yingxiong zhuan*, the beginning of chapter 6.

23. *Xinmin congbao* 4:91.

24. Note how the word "translator" has taken the place of narrator or author.

25. *Xinmin congbao* 6:77.

26. *Xinmin congbao* 10:96.

27. *Xinmin congbao* 2:100.

28. Note that the translator of *Xinxi xiantan* also commented only on the first few chapters, probably for the same reason.

29. Chapter 9. See *Xinmin congbao* 13:83.

30. See chapter 6, 106.

31. See chapter 1, *Xinmin congbao* 2:96.

32. In chapters 8 and 9 there are references to Qin Shi Huangdi, Yu the Great, etc.

33. See Aying, *Wan-Qing xiaoshuo shi* (reprint, Beijing: Renmin wenxue, 1980), 186.

34. From no. 36 (1903) to no. 85 (1906). It was first published by E. Plon in Paris in 1880.

35. Wuxinxianzhai. He translated several novels, mostly from English.

36. London: Vizetelly, 1885. The original French was published by E. Plon in Paris in 1884. Zhou Guisheng's forte was translating from the French, but in this case he was using the English version, as can be seen from a comparison of the texts.

37. See Tarumoto, *(Xinbian zengbu) Qingmo Minchu xiaoshuo mulu* (Jinan: Qilu shushe, 2002), 492. The second translation, *Mu yecha*, is said to be based on *Nyoyasha*, Kuroiwa Ruikō's translation of *The Sculptor's Daughter* (London, 1884).

38. The literary Chinese translation, by Fang Qingzhou, was based on a Japanese novel, *Shinbun uriko* by Kikuchi Yūhō, that claims to be a translation of an English original. Fang's translation is no longer extant.

39. In the Chinese manner, the translator also includes poems and lyrics reflecting on developments in the novel.

40. See chapter 3. *Xin xiaoshuo* 9:112–13.

41. *Xin xiaoshuo* 8:115.

42. It was first published in *Xin xiaoshuo* from no. 12 (eleventh month 1904). Speech in the opening section is also marked by square brackets. Wu developed this novel from an earlier Chinese work. It may perhaps be seen as his attempt to write a Chinese crime novel.

43. *Xin xiaoshuo* 9:112. For the quotation from Confucius, see D. C. Lau, trans., *The Analects* (London: Penguin, 1979), 99.

44. *Xin xiaoshuo* 9:117.

45. *Xin xiaoshuo* 19:45–46.

46. *Xin xiaoshuo* 18:122.

47. Ibid.

48. See chapter 3, *Xin xiaoshuo* 9:108.

49. *Xin xiaoshuo* 9:113–14.

50. *Xin xiaoshuo* 9:107.

51. *Xin xiaoshuo* 9:110.

52. *Xin xiaoshuo* 19:46.

53. The clearest contrast between the views of the two men is seen in Wu's comment on Zhou's "Ziyou jiehun," published in *Yueyue xiaoshuo* (second month 1908): 74. Wu writes: "The translator [Zhou] advocates the importation of new culture. I advocate the restoration of the old morality." See also chapter 9.

54. *Xin xiaoshuo* 18:126.

55. *Xin xiaoshuo* 12:144. An upper-margin note beside the passage describing Camille's concern runs, "Ought not a son or daughter to think along these lines? Those people nowadays who would destroy the social order and are constantly talking about family revolution ought to pay heed to this."

56. *Xin xiaoshuo* 13:151.

57. *Xin xiaoshuo* 11:129.

58. Chapter 6, commentary.

59. *Xin xiaoshuo* 12:133.

60. For example, the novelist Xu Zhuodai translated Heinrich Zschokke's *Das Abenteuer der Neujahresnacht* in 1905, probably from the Japanese, under the title of *Da chuxi*. It is a vernacular translation that owes no allegiance to the Chinese model. See the edition published in the Zhongguo jindai wenxue daxi series (Shanghai shudian, 1991), *Fanyi wenxueji*, vol. 1.

61. *Qin hai shi* (Stones in the sea); see chapter 9.

CHAPTER 8

Wu Jianren and the Narrator

If the novelists of China share my concern over social issues but disagree with
my opinions, why don't they come out with their own views and turn them
into novels, so that we can hold a debate on the condition of society?

—*Adventures in Shanghai*, author's note

W
U JIANREN is probably the best example of the change to the modern in Chinese literature, if we understand "modern" as requiring
two conditions: a concern on the part of the writer with the national and, more particularly, the cultural crisis that faced China; and an attempt to express that concern by nontraditional literary methods. He is the best
example, at least among fiction writers, for two reasons. Of the famous late-
Qing novelists, he is the only one whose fiction spans the last decade of the
nineteenth century—his first novel was published in 1898[1]—and the first
decade of the twentieth. His 1898 work may not have been the earliest modern
novel by the definition given above—that title would have to go to the anonymous *Xichao kuaishi* (Delightful history of a glorious age) published in December 1895,[2] a key year for modern Chinese fiction—but it was certainly among
the earliest. However, Wu was definitely the most innovative late-Qing writer
in terms of technique. He experimented boldly with temporal order, with closure, and above all with the position, nature, and identity of the narrator.

It is the narrator and the focalized character or center of consciousness that
I shall take up here. Wu Jianren experimented constantly with these two elements, at least as much as Lu Xun, who is sometimes given credit for experiments that Wu had made a decade or two earlier. Moreover, of all the changes
in technique during the late-Qing period, those regarding the narrator and
center of consciousness, concerned as they often are with the author's writing
persona, seem the most significant. I shall not try to catalogue all of Wu Jian-

ren's experiments. What I shall do is briefly illustrate their range and function before concentrating on the three novels that form his principal critique of Chinese society and culture.

※

Two short stories represent the extremes of his methods. "The Homework Inspection" (*Cha gongke*) and "The Wronged Spirit of the Opium Addict" (*Hei-ji yuanhun*) were both published in 1907 in *Yueyue xiaoshuo* (alternative title *All-Story Monthly*), the journal that Wu Jianren edited.[3] The former is as free of overt narratorial presence as a story can be. It begins with a telephone dialogue between someone at a police station and someone at a school. No speakers' names are given, and the speech is not even tagged; the mere arrangement of the dialogue on the page is all we have to go by.[4] The story continues with dialogue between the teachers and the inspectors, who are searching for copies of a forbidden revolutionary journal, and it ends with dialogue among the pupils, still without any attribution, which reveals that they have hidden their copies in their pants. It is a simple story made more effective by its extraordinary narratorial economy.

"The Wronged Spirit of the Opium Addict" shares contemporaneity with "The Homework Inspection" but is a far more complex story. At its heart lies the tragic history of an opium addict, whose death on the street the author-narrator has just witnessed. The history, which takes up fully half the text, is written on a sheet of paper that the addict thrusts into the author's hand. It is preceded by an introduction and a prologue story, and followed by a short epilogue. On its own it would make for unbearable reading, and I assume that the surrounding text is there to present it obliquely, lest it overwhelm the reader with its avalanche of misery.

In his introduction the author-narrator plays self-consciously with the conventions of fiction. He says that his story concerns a real incident that he himself witnessed, so he cannot adapt it to fit the usual formula, i.e., he cannot give it a conventional closure. Bowing to another convention, however, he will provide it with a prologue, although he fears that its supernatural elements will render it unsuitable for the modern scientific age. After a farcical prologue story about the origins of opium cultivation, the author-narrator returns in person to provide the narrative context for the addict's history. Steps have recently been taken in China to eliminate the cultivation and use of opium within the next decade. A British philanthropic organization is trying to persuade

London to ban the opium trade, and the secretary of that organization, who is visiting China, has just given a talk in the Zhang Gardens that the author attended. The date and hour of the talk are given, as are the names of the dignitaries present. (The details are accurate; a newspaper from the following day identifies the speaker as J. G. Alexander, secretary of the Society for the Suppression of the Opium Trade, and describes the occasion as a demonstration attended by 500 people.[5]) As the author-narrator emerges from the gardens, elated at the thought that China may soon be free of its appalling burden, he trips over the dying addict. A page of dialogue follows, and then the man's life story. It concludes with the author's hope that the addict will not have died in vain and also with a gesture of defiance toward his contemporaries: "When my opium-smoking friends read this, they're bound to attack me for being too harsh, but I really don't care. Let them say what they like."[6]

The story is notable for its blend of fiction and reportage, a mixture—usually an assimilation of fiction to reportage—that is one of the distinguishing marks of the late-Qing novel. (Note the story's topicality: the demonstration in the Zhang Gardens took place on December 13, 1906, and the story appeared in the following month's *Yueyue xiaoshuo*.) At different times the author-narrator is both fiction writer, in his introduction and prologue, and reporter, when describing the demonstration and his encounter with the addict. As fiction writer, he speaks with a lighthearted irony; as reporter, he plays it straight.

We should not imagine that Wu Jianren's experiments were directed toward finding some all-purpose narrative solution; they were always dictated by the kind of novel he was writing. When it suited him, he was quite capable of reverting to an outmoded method of narration and using it with a special twist, as he does in his novel *Qing bian* (Passion transformed).[7] In this last, unfinished work, he presents the narrator as a storyteller addressing a live audience, one who regularly intervenes with pointed comments on the action. The prologue begins jocularly with what I have called Wu Jianren's cultural nationalism. It is of particular importance in this novel, because he is writing about the White Lotus sect and its magical arts.

> If you gentlemen were to look at these arts with foreign eyes and listen to them with foreign ears, you'd shake your foreign heads, wave your foreign hands, spit your foreign spittle, open your foreign mouths, and say, "Tut, tut! Oh, dear! What rot! Such things just don't exist."[8]

The novel deals with things that belong to a Chinese fictional world, and must be seen as part of that world in order to be appreciated. This fact justifies the traditional use of a simulated oral narrator, since the martial arts were closely associated with oral fiction.

The narrator's comments amusingly reinforce the traditional thinking. At one point he remarks, "Oh, dear! Gentlemen, I'm surely in your bad books by now. In this civilized age of ours, all superstition has to be eradicated." He takes satirical shots, too, at familiar targets like the slogan "free marriage." A degree of self-mockery lies behind the narrator's pose; he is asserting the validity of traditional beliefs, but at the same time, by his exaggerated rhetoric, he is poking a little fun at himself. In his last novel, Wu Jianren deliberately turned to a quasi-traditional method, merging his own ironic authorial voice with that of a storyteller.

The three novels that embody Wu Jianren's principal critique of Chinese society and culture are *Ershinian mudu zhi guai xianzhuang* (Strange things observed over the past twenty years, 1903–10), *Xin shitouji* (The new story of the stone, 1905–8), and *Shanghai youcanlu* (Adventures in Shanghai, 1907). As David Der-wei Wang has observed, each novel has a naïve hero.[9] In terms of narrative method, the first is told by a first-person participant narrator, and the other two are for the most part restricted to a single third-person center of consciousness. I shall examine these narrators or centers of consciousness and show how they serve the particular purposes of Wu Jianren's social critique. In general, of course, naïveté has an obvious value for the satirist. A naïve hero has to be educated in the ways of the world, and in the process a great deal of satirical information can be conveyed quite naturally to the reader.

The use of a first-person participant narrator in Wu Jianren's *Strange Things Observed Over the Past Twenty Years* is considered the most striking technical innovation in modern Chinese fiction, and even now a reader accustomed to the traditional novel feels a certain amount of shock on finding the narrator's "I" scattered throughout its pages. However, the third-person restricted focus in the other two novels by Wu Jianren and also in *Lao Can youji* (The travels of Lao Can, published from 1903) may well be a greater innovation. As Chen Pingyuan has shown, numerous first-person narratives were written in the years following Wu Jianren's *Strange Things*, but hardly any restricted third-person narratives.[10] Furthermore, precedents existed for first-person narration in translated fiction and even in original fiction, the earliest case I know of dating from about 1839,[11] but there were no precedents for restricted third-person narration, at least in the vernacular novel.

Even so, Wu's use of the first-person participant narrator raises a number of questions. What is the precise nature of his narrator? What is the virtue of the method, and is it consistently applied? And why did Wu never use it again? *Strange Things Observed* was published (and evidently written) in sections over seven years, and before the last sections were written, he had completed a sequel entitled *Jin shinian zhi guai xianzhuang* (Strange things of the past ten years)[12]—the word "observed" is significantly missing from the title—that abandons the original method in favor of a traditional omniscient narrator. After Wu had taken the trouble to invent a first-person narrator, why did he cast him aside?

In fact, the original novel has two narrators and an editor. The principal narrator is the supposed author, who has kept a diary over a period of twenty years recording his own observations, adventures, and, particularly, the stories told to him by other people. Financially ruined, he entrusts the diary to a close friend and asks him to find some kindred spirit to publish it. This kindred spirit, who happens to share more than just the narrator's cynical view of Chinese society—he even has a similar pseudonym—turns the diary into a novel and provides it with notes. We are also told something of the manuscript's later history. The editor sends it to Liang Qichao's journal *Xin xiaoshuo* in Yokohama, where it is published in installments. Up to this point (2.6), the narrative is told not by the editor or by the author of the diary, but by an anonymous narrator.

At the end of the novel, the author explains his desire to have the diary published. The anonymous narrator then steps in to give the identity of the friend who has delivered the manuscript in chapter 1, and to tell about the publication of the complete work as a book. (Only the first 45 chapters had been published in *Xin xiaoshuo* before that journal closed down).

The idea of having some figure similar in experience and views to the author edit the work did not, of course, originate with this novel. We find it, for example, in *The Illusion of Romance* (*Fengyue meng*, preface dated 1848), in which both author and editor are reformed rakes and the editor writes the prologue chapter in the first person about his own experience.[13] And the idea of having a friend rework a diary into a novel is found in *Nanchao jinfenlu* (Fleshpots of Nanjing), published in 1897.[14] The friend turns the diary into a novel with himself as first-person narrator in the prologue and epilogue chapters but with omniscient narration in the rest of the work.

Wu's novel consists mainly of the diary author's observations and adventures, as well as the stories told to him by numerous characters, all of which he records in his diary. For the most part the characters are mere raconteurs, not involved themselves in the stories they tell. Behind the novel lie at least three literary Chinese forms, all associated with first-person narration: the diary, the notation book (*biji*, especially the kind of *biji* that consists of rather elaborate tales), and the travel record (*youji*). Both diary and notation book are kept constantly before the reader's eyes. In 17.124 the narrator describes himself as writing in his diary (*rijibu*). In 60.499 he hands the diary of his Guangzhou visit to his mentor Wu Jizhi, and Wu explains to Wen Shunong, one of his staff advisers, that the diary, in addition to "proper matters" (*zhengshi*), also contains things the narrator has seen and heard. In 79.670 the narrator badgers Guan Dequan, the manager of Wu Jizhi's Shanghai shop, to explain something to him, and Guan says that Wu has told him the explanation would be good material for the diary. At the end of the novel, in 108.938, the narrator refers to his text as "this notation book." From time to time he remarks that he has nothing to record in his diary, and his friends and colleagues frequently tease him about his habit of pestering them for items.

The stories he gets from his friends and acquaintances may or may not be news, but they do have to be "strange" in order to fit the title of the book. (The notes sometimes discuss whether stories actually qualify as strange.) But unlike the common Chinese conception of the word "strange," it does not refer here to supernatural events, freak occurrences, or odd instances of good and bad fortune. All the stories are about human deeds and misdeeds, particularly in the public realm but also within the family, and even the stories of family life usually turn out to be about men sacrificing their families for money or political advancement.

Wu Jianren was serving as editor of the Shanghai tabloid newspaper *Caifeng bao* when in 1898 he wrote his first known novel, *Haishang mingji si da jingang qishu* (The strange tale of the four guardian gods, courtesans of Shanghai).[15] Anecdotes formed a large part of the content of the tabloids, and his novel is also full of anecdotes, some scurrilous, about the four most notable courtesans of his day. Wu once showed the novelist Bao Tianxiao a scrapbook full of newspaper clippings and notes (on stories told to him by friends) that he used as material for his fiction.[16] The world of the newspaper, particularly the tabloid, was close to that of the late-Qing satirical novel.

Strange Things Observed simulates both a diary and a notation book. The stories are arranged in the order in which the narrator hears them, and the tellers and listeners are specified. There is usually some connection to a current topic of discussion. Several stories are so long as to cover several chapters and take several evenings to tell, and a few are interwoven with other events and even with other stories. But they rarely have the morally satisfying closure of the typical vernacular story; instead they represent a sardonic commentary on the current situation, leaving behind an aftertaste of cynicism mixed with robust humor. The occasional story that does have moral closure, such as that of the ex-prostitute and the porter in chapter 57, is paired with another lacking that closure—in this case, the story of a vicious brothel madam who is never brought to justice. One might argue that Gou Cai, the principal villain, suffers a just punishment in that he is murdered by his son, but the point is obscured by other events. The tale told in 103.883–104.896 is another excellent story, a cynical clash of human desires, but it, too, lacks moral closure.

The narrator, however, is far more than a mere recorder; he is a zealous seeker-out of strange stories. In 11.79 he says to a friend, "I want to hear only about strange things, I'm not interested in idle matters," and the friend responds, "Every time you see me, you ask me for a story." In 26.199 a staff adviser says, "I've heard Wu Jizhi and Wen Shunong say that you always like to pester them for news stories," and the narrator replies, "If you've got one for me, I'm willing stay up three whole nights, if necessary, in order to hear it." Sometimes we are told how he treats the stories; in 96.821, for example, he divides up the story told to him and copies it into his diary. In a couple of cases, he is himself the teller; he recounts one long story that runs from the end of chapter 97 to chapter 100 and takes three or four days to tell.

The significant fact about the narrator is that he steadily matures over the course of the novel. As it opens, he is only fifteen years (sixteen *sui*) old and is setting out into the world for the first time, traveling from his home near Guangzhou to see his fatally ill father in Hangzhou. His maturing is shown in his relations with others and also in the growing confidence and competence with which he handles himself, as well as in the cynical views he gradually forms about the world around him. He first shows his assertiveness in chapters 18 to 20, after returning to Guangzhou to rescue his mother from her bullying relatives. He soon begins to question other people's stories much more sharply (24.182) and to offer his own interesting arguments (39.309). At Wu Jizhi's suggestion, he covertly takes part in the marking of examination papers and does well despite his lack of qualifications (43.351). An upper-margin note to 77.653 remarks that his former naïveté has gradually been replaced by wisdom born of experience. By this time he is frequently taking the initiative in action as well as in discussion.

He carries on an ongoing dialogue with several characters who may be seen as his mentors—at least in the first half of the novel. The first is Wu Jizhi, ten years older but a fellow pupil at school, where he served as an informal mentor to the younger boy. By the time the novel opens, Wu Jizhi has passed the metropolitan examinations and is awaiting an appointment. In 4.26 the narrator says that Wu counsels him "like a father or elder brother." Their relationship gives the author a pretext for numerous exposés, explanations, and just plain lectures that would otherwise not have been plausible. Wu frequently ridicules the novice's remarks and questions, calling him naïve and childish, and even showing a little exasperation (4.36). The novice has an obvious, straightforward viewpoint, while Wu Jizhi provides the voice of experience, commenting cynically on society and politics. But we should not conclude that the narrator is really naïve, for he is no more so than the average reader. In fact he *is* the average reader, and the point of the book is that the obvious, straightforward viewpoint proves inadequate and the truth lies in his mentor's ironic interpretation of the facts. Wu Jizhi is quite conscious of his position as real-world mentor and refers to his efforts to wise the narrator up (6.40). He tells true stories, illustrative stories, even jokes, and his opinions generally fly in the face of conventional wisdom. For example, he criticizes the Shanghai philanthropists, whom everyone is praising, as interested chiefly in making a name for themselves (15.105–107).

As the single main vehicle for the novel's critique of society, Wu Jizhi is harshly critical of the decadence of some Manchus, especially the egregious Gou Cai (a pun on *goucai*, jackass), but he is equally harsh on the phony literati of Shanghai, whom he regularly divides into poetasters and "merchants" (*shikuai*). His views are summed up in the statement "There's nothing in this world that isn't a scam" (86.732), and the editor's note at the end of chapter 89 echoes that view: "It's the cynics of this world who are the perceptive ones."

An equally important mentor is the narrator's unnamed female cousin, the most attractive person in the book. She is a widow, a few years older than the narrator, and her sphere of advice is that of moral behavior, whereas Wu Jizhi's is the world of politics and business. She is practical, decisive, and efficient, and frequently makes decisions for the whole family. Her views, which are not cynical like Wu's, must have seemed quite advanced for the time.

She first intervenes in 20.146. The narrator has just routed the family's grasping relatives, and she reproves him for being too harsh. "It really matters how you express yourself, you know. I had several years of study before I was married, and ever since I've been a widow I've had no other means of amusing myself, so I've taken to reading books, all kinds of books, and now I'm a lot better informed than I used to be." As the narrator brings the family back to Nanjing by boat, he has ample time to talk with her, and in their talks she reveals surprising depths. "On this journey I feel as if I've engaged a teacher," he reflects. "When we get to Nanjing, I shall have Wu Jizhi to instruct me about the outside world and this cousin to instruct me about family matters. I'm sure I'll do well."

Within the limits of contemporary correctness, the cousin reveals herself to be an unusual young woman—even more unusual when compared with most of Wu Jianren's other female characters. As the family reaches Shanghai, she declares that she would like to see something of the city's excitement (21.149–152). She doesn't believe women should hide themselves from the public gaze. Only girls without self-respect would do such a thing; other girls would be quite unaffected by the presence of males. She also insists that girls ought to undertake a course of serious reading, not just *tanci* and novels, let alone risqué fiction. She doesn't hesitate to buy herself a copy of the illustrated satirical journal *Dianshizhai huabao* as well as a couple of newspapers (22.160). She offers the narrator a shrewd suggestion as to how he might handle his shifty uncle (22.161), and she rules on all matters of taste (see 22.164), frequently debating the narrator and sometimes mocking him. When an ugly fight breaks out at Wu Jizhi's house between Gou Cai's wife and concubine, it is the cousin who takes charge. Even the masterful Wu Jizhi defers to her judgment (44.354–359).

As the narrator matures, he is able to hold his own with her in debate, but she is still sharper than he; see, for example, her discussion of the nature of social obligation, in the course of which she persuades him that he is capable of altruism (42.341–342). After the narrator has assisted in the examination marking, he returns home grumbling about being cooped up for months, and she retorts, "Look, you've been cooped up for just one month, and you're complaining about feeling frazzled. Well, what about us women? We *never* get out!" (43.350). When the narrator shows her a lyric he has written, she ridicules it, because "men are *always* taking women as the subjects of their poetry" (40.320). She objects to his going to a high-class brothel, not because of the nature of brothels but because he may be contaminated by the phony literati he is likely to meet there (40.321). She also teaches him how to paint and to write lyrics (40.323–325). The editor's notes overflow with praise and even awe. "What a formidable woman!" he exclaims on one occasion. "I'm quite afraid of her!" (42:341).

A third mentor is the staff adviser Wen Shunong, who enlightens the narrator about practical matters and also occasionally mocks him. A fourth is Fang Yilu, who owns a small machine shop in Shanghai. He informs the narrator about the famous Jiangnan Arsenal and its defects, particularly those of the translation bureau. Other suppliers of stories include the shop manager Guan Dequan. In chapter 37 he accompanies the narrator on a visit to Suzhou, where they are entertained by a mediocre but bombastic artist, an incident that leads to scathing comments on contemporary art. The editor's end-of-chapter comment likens the satire to that of *The Scholars* (*Rulin waishi*), but claims that this work is more amusing.

But although the mentor-novice dialogue succeeds as a vehicle for satire, the method I have been describing is not maintained throughout the book; there is a perceptible shift away from it in the direction of older methods. Gradually the stories related by characters become less contextualized, with the result that it matters less and less who is telling them. There are also far fewer interruptions from listeners. Context, such as it is, seems often to be no more than a mere device for allowing a good story to be told. In chapter 57, for example, the narrator's visit to Guangzhou seems to have been created largely to accommodate the innkeeper's stories. In chapters 70 to 72 there are two good stories about a man and his family, but both are tied to the narrator by the thinnest of connections. A long story in chapters 80 to 84 is told by a man the narrator has met in a hotel; the only pretext for it is the narrator's expressed interest in going to Sichuan. But the most egregious case is that of Ye Bofen in chapters 90 to 93, where the whole elaborate story, together with a subplot or two, is supposedly included in the novel merely to explain why Gou Cai has been promoted to a new position.

There is also an increasing use of traditional expressions for the management of topic and time. Direct address to the reader becomes quite common, in expressions corresponding to "Who would ever have expected?", "Just imagine," "What do you think?", "Fate took a curious turn," and so forth. There are general comments, too, on the part of the various raconteurs, comments of the kind made by the traditional narrator of vernacular fiction. Sometimes speech is deliberately suppressed to tantalize the reader, and there is an increasing use of close description.

With these developments goes a partial retreat from the first-person narrator as established in the earlier part of the book. The fight between Gou Cai's wife and concubine in chapter 44 is described by an omniscient narrator under the heading of *yuanlai*, "The fact was." The reader has to assume that the narrator has somehow assembled the facts of this story and is telling it in this manner for the sake of convenience. In 49.399 the story is represented as told by someone, but it is still summarized after a *yuanlai*. The long episode in chapters 51 to 52 is omniscient narrative that no one could possibly have told to the narrator. The account of Gou Cai from chapter 87 through 95 (with the insertion of the story of Ye Bofen that I have mentioned) is represented as told by Wu Jizhi, but it is recounted in omniscient form, and the narrator himself does not reappear until chapter 95. These eight chapters, the most striking section of the novel, stand out because of the way they are told, which is at a considerable remove from the narrative method to which the novel has accustomed us. Presumably these changes resulted from the unbearable constraint that the first-person narrative imposed on a novelist trying to give a panoramic critique of his society.

The only direct acknowledgment of his revolutionary first-person narrative method comes in the editor's general comment at the end of the book, where the method is praised, but only as a structural device. After making a case for the symmetrical organization of the novel, the editor criticizes "recent fiction" for its tendency to ramify into many different story lines. This novel, by contrast, because of the single character dominating it, is well organized despite its complexity. (The editor likens the method to "ten thousand horses with a single driver at the reins.") Oddly enough, as I have explained, Wu Jianren's own sequel abandons the first-person method altogether—and incidentally serves as an excellent example of the very formlessness he is warning against.

Are we to conclude, then, that the first-person method as used in this novel has no value beyond the high degree of organization that it ensures, a value that becomes a liability in a novel of panoramic social satire? The characterization of the hero could certainly have been achieved in some other way, and his language register does not particularize him to any great degree. (I am referring to the narrative sections, not the dialogue.) However, given the number of stories that are recounted to the hero in this novel, the third-person method with its separate narrator and center of consciousness would surely have proved too cumbersome (as a narrative within a narrative within a narrative). And in general there is always a distinct value to the first-person method, in that the author-narrator is felt by the reader to be in charge of choosing the material he presents as well as the manner in which he presents it. The first-person and restricted third-person methods are not functionally equivalent, as is often claimed. The use of the first person, even if it is not maintained consistently, inevitably changes the nature of the material presented to the reader.

For the most part *The New Story of the Stone*[17] has a single third-person center of consciousness—that of Baoyu, hero of the original *Story of the Stone*, who gains a second life in which to achieve his goal of "repairing heaven." There are a few exceptions to the restricted narration, notably the narrator's introduction, highly self-conscious as to authorship and genre, and the close of the final chapter, when the narrative leaves Baoyu and tells how Youngman Old (Lao Shaonian, Baoyu's mentor in the latter half of the novel), finds the stone (Baoyu's jade) and reworks the inscription on it into this sequel.

The only other substantial section in which Baoyu is not present comes in chapters 12 to 14, when first the villainous Wang Wei'er and then the doltish Xue Pan (from *The Story of the Stone*) take his place. This is the section in which Wang joins the Boxers and lures Xue Pan into joining as well. It is a passage of savage satire without a single comment. Evidently none was thought necessary.

There are two major breaks in the novel, at the beginning of chapters 12 and 22, and in each case the narrator signals the break. Chapter 12 contains the sudden switch from Baoyu to Wang and then to Xue Pan. This change may have an extra significance, because the first eleven chapters were published in a journal, after which no more text appeared until the whole book came out three years later. The eleven chapters were labeled a social novel (*shehui xiaoshuo*), which indeed they are, but when the book was published, its label was changed to utopian novel (*lixiang xiaoshuo*), which it certainly is from chapter 22 on.[18] It seems as if the author changed his conception of the work in the course of writing it.

The second major break occurs when Baoyu enters the utopian world of the Civilized Zone (*Wenming jingjie*). At the beginning of chapter 22, the author-narrator refers to a secret about the novel that has been revealed to the public against his wishes. This may be a reference to a piece by his friend Tao Youzeng that refers to it as both a "scientific novel" and an "educational novel" in forty chapters.[19]

Why did Wu Jianren bother to write a sequel to a famous novel that uses only three characters from it and shifts the time frame by a couple of centuries? One explanation, of course, is the humor of the situation, especially when Baoyu comes upon the original novel and objects to its invasion of his privacy, and again when he hears with shocked amazement that the leading Shanghai courtesan is a woman named Lin Daiyu. There is also an advantage in taking a figure like Baoyu, who lived in everyone's imagination, a figure out of a settled past in which there was no national or cultural crisis, the very symbol of a stable culture, and pitching him into the modern predicament. Certainly his nature in the sequel bears little relationship to that of the old Baoyu, but his value for the author is that he is universally known and comes from a different time, when ideology was not so obviously out of joint with reality.

Most of the things that strike Baoyu as strange in the late-Qing world are products that have been developed or imported since his day. Oddly, the list does not include rickshaws, with which the original Baoyu could hardly have been familiar. Even more oddly, it does include foot-binding, with which he would surely have been familiar (even if it is not mentioned in *Story of the Stone*). In describing current efforts to end this practice, he minimizes the contribution of the foreign women who were the first to campaign against it.[20] Only superficially can this section be described as an attempt at historical reconstruction. To a far greater degree, it is designed to make a point about the West's industrial and cultural penetration of China.

If Baoyu is at first impressed by western products and practices—he goes so far as to start studying English—the feeling soon wears off, and he begins to question the imports on two counts: their effect on the Chinese economy and the fact that foreigners tend to discriminate against the Chinese. He is alarmed by the flood of imported products that are not paid for with Chinese exports and result in a huge outflow of Chinese silver. If goods are to be imported they must be useful. Usefulness is his great criterion, and he applies it rigorously. Many foreign products, for all their ingenuity, are frivolous—music boxes, phonographs, clocks, repeaters (watches that strike the hour when a button is pressed), and so forth. On the other hand, when he sets out on his travels, he is happy enough to take with him a foreign leather suitcase and a revolver.

Because he adopts such a sour attitude toward things that others rave about, Xue Pan calls him a puritan (6.183) and an old fogy (8.197) and declares, quite correctly, that he is a changed character. Baoyu's favorite term of disapproval for the imports is "pointless" or "boring." Champagne tastes like vinegar to him, and beer, brandy, and whisky are not much better. Foreign-style houses are inconvenient to live in. Under the influence of the reformist journals that are his staple reading, he becomes a scold and a drag in Xue Pan's eyes.

The second point is racial discrimination. This comes to Baoyu's notice in the case of the steamship companies, which employ only foreigners as pilots. Why is that, asks Baoyu (7.189). Because Chinese aren't reliable, he is told. He ridicules that answer and persists until he gets the right one, which is that the insurance companies, which are foreign owned, insist on foreign pilots; even the Chinese-owned shipping line conforms. For Baoyu this is the emblematic case of foreign privilege, and it sticks in his throat. What infuriates him even more is the deference that people pay to foreigners.

In the second half of the book Baoyu becomes a naïve visitor to the utopia of the Civilized Zone, where the marvels of science and social engineering evoke from him a rapturous response. The possibility that this work evolved from a social to a utopian novel in the course of its writing does not mean that it fails to make structural sense. It consists principally of Baoyu's two journeys of discovery: of the marvels of western modernity in the early chapters, culminating in his visit to the Jiangnan Arsenal, and, in the later chapters, of the superior marvels of the Civilized Zone. The two journeys balance each other; each is an exploration, but one set of marvels is western in derivation and disappointing, while the other is Chinese in derivation and inspiring.

But what of the other portions of the novel, such as the Boxer chapters (11–17) involving Wang Wei'er, Xue Pan, and eventually Baoyu himself? I believe that we can take the Boxer marvels as representing the false nostrums created from popular myth and designed to fool the credulous. We thus have a real but disappointing western modernity, a bogus unscientific utopia created out of myth, and finally a Chinese utopia built on a foundation of traditional Chinese morality combined with advanced science.

There is also another section, chapters 18 to 20, in which Baoyu is thrown into a Hankou jail on the evidence of a single absurd accusation. Without even the pretense of a trial, he is on the point of being murdered by the jailer when a compromise solution is worked out. This is a grim reminder of the current repression in China. A good parallel would be the incident at the beginning of *Adventures in Shanghai* in which the hero is arrested on trumped-up charges of being a revolutionary.

Finally, how do we explain Baoyu's dream in chapter 40 of successful reform in China? It is evidently a projection of Dongfang Wenming's aspiration to make the Civilized Zone so perfect that other countries will want to emulate it, leading eventually to a civilized world without warfare. The dream encompasses an international exposition in Shanghai showcasing Chinese and other products, tangible proof that China has caught up with the industrialized world; and also an international peace conference in Beijing presided over by the Chinese emperor, a symbolic indication of China's accession to the preeminent power of moral authority

Thus this novel, despite its piecemeal appearance, coheres in terms of several journeys of discovery: through the false civilization of the industrialized West, the corrupt chimera of Boxer beliefs, the Kafkaesque terror of current justice, and the true civilization of the Civilized Zone. In Baoyu's dream this true civilization is extended to China as a whole, enabling her to take a leading role in the world. All of this is encapsulated within two songs in the first and last chapters that express personal aspiration and despair.

Utopias are generally conceived in terms of what they are not, that is to say, in opposition to some known place with objectionable conditions. This is abundantly true of the Civilized Zone, and it is noteworthy that the opposition is not to traditional China but to the modern West. Wu Jianren's utopia is both anti-West and super-West, excelling at the applied science and industrialization by which the West has defined modernity, in fact beating it at its own game, while also claiming the heritage of Confucian morality. It claims, too, the heritage of other aspects of traditional learning, for example, Chinese medicine and the Daoist search for immortality, which the zone's scientists are about to put on a scientific footing. If there is a defining factor in the true civilization, it is the universal moral education that is taught within the family and at school and that the western nations conspicuously lack.[21]

The exuberant science fiction of chapters 22 to 40 is full of invidious comparisons with the West, of which I shall list only a few. The zone's clocks are better than the West's (22); they can speak the time, but when Baoyu likens the effect to that of a phonograph, his mentor Youngman Old points out that the sound is far clearer than that of a phonograph—there is no scratching. In the zone they don't use coal for heating—it is too dirty. (There are mines, but all the coal is exported to the West.) The zone's aerial cars are superior to those in the West (24); moreover, they aren't limited to a schedule, but are always on call (25). The zone wine affords all the pleasure of other wine but does not intoxicate (32). The zone has neither prostitutes nor actors (36). The occupants' way of waging war is superior, too; they don't kill enemy soldiers, merely anaesthetize them and revive them once the war is over. Their scientists have made discoveries, or are on the verge of making discoveries, that western scientists can only dream of: a kind of X-ray that gauges a person's moral quality; a powder that enhances the intelligence of intelligent people (unfortunately it also increases the stupidity of stupid people); and the technique of achieving immortality. Finally, they lack religious belief, and such a lack is a prerequisite for true civilization. Moral education of the Confucian variety is universal.

The zone is contrasted not only with the West but also with Freedom Village, in which mere anarchy prevails and Wu Jianren's *bête noire*, family revolution, is advocated. (Xue Pan lives in the village, and is presumably in his element.) Freedom Village enjoys the license of "barbaric freedom." "Civilized freedom," by contrast, is freedom under conditions of social order and established rules of conduct.

"Civilization" and "barbarism" are the key pair of words in the book. Wu refuses to concede true civilization to the West, and he understandably resents the suggestion that China is uncivilized. His utopia is the Civilized Zone, and "civilized" is defined as what is practiced there in terms of scientific progress, social organization, and personal and social morality. Another expression he uses with particular scorn in this novel as well as in *Adventures in Shanghai* is *mei wai*, "toadying to foreigners." The term is first used in chapter 7, when Baoyu meets a man named Bo Yaolian (a pun on *buyaolian*, "shameless") who explains that Chinese are discriminated against as ship's pilots because they are unreliable. Baoyu asks Bo Yaolian whether he regards himself as unreliable too, and Bo replies by claiming to possess "a certain amount of the foreign temperament" (189).

Scorn for the worship of foreigners is the final note struck in the book. The narrator tells us that the stone (Baoyu's jade) has the source of this novel as well as the author's valedictory poem inscribed on it, and that if his readers don't believe him, they are welcome to go and see for themselves. However, only patriots who strive to preserve the "national essence" (*guocui*) will actually be able to see the poem, which is a declaration of both faith and despair. Those who toady to foreigners will see something quite different, a derisory poem in English. Presumably this is a final satirical thrust—the toadies might not even understand the poem if it were written in Chinese.

Adventures in Shanghai[22] begins with a bang, in fact with three bangs, after which the narrator explains that the noises are shots fired by soldiers at rioting peasants and then goes on to offer three views of the causes of the riots. It is clear that author and narrator are one and the same person, who is also to be equated with the commentator. The equation can perhaps be extended even further, to include one of the characters, the wise but cynical Li Ruoyu, who counsels the hero and argues with the revolutionaries.[23]

The cynical stance of the author-narrator in the opening passage is constantly reinforced by the commentator's notes, which work like a refrain, usually taking the form of "In the light of this incident, how can one help being a cynic?" But the opening passage also claims that cynicism is actually a mark of strong feeling and expresses the hope that readers will take this book "not as cynical words, but as a handful of scalding tears."

At the end of the novel the author-commentator proposes a debate on the Chinese crisis through the medium of fiction: "No man's opinions can help being one-sided, but if the novelists of China are as concerned as I am about social issues, and if they happen to disagree with my views, why don't they come out with their own ideas and turn them into novels, so that we can hold a debate on the condition of society?" The statement illustrates, better than any other, Wu Jianren's main justification for his fiction.

With the exception of such general comments by the author-narrator, the novel sticks to a single center of consciousness throughout, that of Gu Wangyan (a pun on the expression *gu wang yan*, "For what it's worth, let me say"). Gu is a bookish youth living in a remote village who lacks all knowledge of current affairs—he doesn't even know what the word "revolutionary" means. He clings to a naïve faith in honesty and fairness in the judicial system and expects to be able to reason his way out of the absurd charge that he is a revolutionary. Of course he becomes disillusioned, but on managing to escape from the village, he can think of no better response than to become a real revolutionary, although he is still unaware what the word means.

He differs from the I-narrator of *Strange Things*, who is merely young and inexperienced, and also from the Baoyu of *The New Story of the Stone*, who is a kind of Rip Van Winkle. But like those novels, *Adventures in Shanghai* is essentially the story of a gradual acquisition of worldly wisdom. Gu Wangyan's education comes in several stages. He is enlightened first by his servant:

"Master, you've read a lot of books, but you've no practical experience whatsoever. You've got to realize that this isn't a reasonable world. If the governor were to listen to reason, his career would be in jeopardy. In fact, any reasonable man would have been fired before he ever got to that rank. For that matter, any genuinely reasonable man would refuse a governorship if it were offered to him. You'd be better off appealing to a wild beast for justice than to the governor." (1.492)

The hero begins to gain experience by listening to other people's conversation. He overhears his neighbors talking about the soldiers and discussing whether to hand him over to the authorities in order to avoid trouble for themselves. And on board a ship bound for Shanghai, he overhears two students talking about studying in Japan; the conversation is a devastating satire of overseas study. After arriving in Shanghai, he begins a course of reading in the new revolutionary literature, beginning with Zou Rong's fervently anti-Manchu tract *Gemingjun* (Revolutionary army).

It is in Shanghai that he meets Li Ruoyu, the author-narrator's alter ego, who proceeds to give him a personal education, ridiculing the anti-Manchu radicalism of *The Revolutionary Army* and even going so far as to stage debates with the self-styled revolutionaries for his edification. Other mentors include his cousin, who is a shopkeeper in Shanghai, and also a man on the cousin's staff. By the last chapter, Gu, who is forced to leave Shanghai for Japan, has become wiser and more cynical, but is still undecided about his future. "When he considered how unjust the officials were, he genuinely wanted to join the revolutionaries, but when his thoughts turned to the conduct of some of those who were advocating revolution, he felt he would be sullying himself if he joined them. Having rejected both alternatives, he thought he would wait until he got to Japan and saw the caliber of the Chinese there before making up his mind what to do" (10.544).

The main criticism leveled by Li Ruoyu is of the importation of foreign culture, which jeopardizes the survival of Chinese culture.[24] The danger, according to Li, is not that people won't be open to new ideas but that they will be too open, taking the ideas to extremes. In any case, the time is not ripe for revolution, because if China descends into civil war, the foreign nations will only make further encroachments, as both the government and the rebels vie for the foreigners' support. Other countries may have gained from opening themselves up to foreign trade, but in China's case, open trade has always led to territorial concessions (6.518). Foreign products, ranging from children's toys to governmental systems, are well enough in their countries of origin, but they should be carefully compared with their Chinese equivalents before being imported, not accepted holus-bolus (8.531). Li firmly denies the revolutionaries' claim that Chinese tradition is deficient, for example, that it lacks the supposedly modern concepts of public morality and patriotism (8.531).

The essential prerequisite for the importation of foreign culture is moral education. People must not abandon their origins by becoming too open-minded (8.527); the result is that one comes to worship foreigners (8.528, 9.536) and even "to rely on foreigners in oppressing one's own race" (8.528). For his views Li is castigated by the revolutionaries as an old fogy with a "slave mentality" and also as a loyal servant of the Manchus, accusations that he hotly denies (6.521). Far more impressive is his ridicule of the revolutionaries, especially the egregious Wang Jie, who defends his opium addiction as a political act—he smokes opium, he claims, because the government is trying to ban it! To show that their revolutionary enthusiasm is hypocritical, Li pretends that he has been asked to direct a new government educational press, and then watches as the revolutionaries jettison their principles in a mad scramble for editorial jobs. Some of the novel's satire is hilarious, as when Tu Youmin, who is proud of his modern "girlfriend," to whom he has behaved impeccably "in accordance with the practice of civilized countries," objects that she "is interfering with his freedom" (8.527).

⌗

The significant point about Wu Jianren's choice of restricted narration, whether first-person or third-person, in these three novels is that it excludes the authoritative narratorial voice, replacing it with the reflections and judgments of characters who, while not duplicitous, are unreliable because of their ignorance or naïveté. The author-narrator's voice that is heard briefly in the prologues of *The New Story of the Stone* and *Adventures in Shanghai* is ironic; instead of giving authoritative guidance, it invites the reader to experience the national and cultural crisis through the mind and experience of an individual subjectivity. Of course, each of the three naïve heroes is instructed by mentors possessing both wisdom and experience, but except for the mentors of the Civilized Zone in *The New Story of the Stone*, which is utopian fantasy, they are not infallible. In any case, they do not speak with the authority of the traditional narrator.

We may compare these novels with *The Travels of Lao Can*, the only other major late-Qing novel to use restrictive third-person narration, at least for long sections. It has neither naïve subjectivity nor mentor; Lao Can himself, supremely wise and possessing almost infallible judgment, is a sufficient arbiter of morality and taste. The novel is in fact largely about his sensibility, sympathy, and ingenuity in finding solutions to problems, and its method is admirably suited to that purpose. For the broad satire favored by Wu Jianren, however, satire that leaves behind a residue of cynicism and despair, the exploration of society by a naïve subjectivity has clear advantages.

Although he works through an individual subjectivity, Wu Jianren's concern, of course, is not with the individual but with the Chinese crisis as he saw it, particularly the cultural crisis; the individual's experiences and views are important only insofar as they illustrate it. The narration may be on a human scale, but it always involves the larger question of the fate of China. Taken together, his three novels represent a great project, a disciplined attempt to respond in fictional terms to the cultural crisis. *Strange Things* is a rich, indeed priceless, collection of narrative "cases"—no other word will do—that illustrate the hideous disjunction between ideology and reality in the late Qing. Absurdities and instances of chicanery abound, narrated with an often uproarious humor but leaving behind them a deep residue of cynicism.

Even in the few years between *Strange Things* (begun in 1903) and the two other novels, *The New Story of the Stone* (begun in 1905) and *Adventures in Shanghai* (written in 1907), Wu Jianren's conception of the Chinese crisis evidently underwent a change of emphasis. These were years of hectic development. In 1905 the Tongmenghui (Revolutionary alliance), with its anti-

Manchu stance, was established and drew widespread support from intellectuals. (Like Liang Qichao, however, Wu Jianren believed that the foreign powers, not the Manchus, represented the main threat.) About this time, too, there was a craze for adopting the ideas and customs of the West,[25] which Wu Jianren detested. Partly in reaction against this craze, a movement gathered strength to preserve the best of the traditional culture (the "national essence").[26] Moreover, in 1905 Wu himself became more involved in political activity. When the U.S. Congress passed an extension of the Exclusion Act barring the immigration of Chinese laborers, he resigned his editorship of a newspaper in Hankou and returned to Shanghai to help lead the boycott.[27] It is noteworthy that both the extension and the boycott are prominently listed among current events in *New Story of the Stone* (40.403).

Although there is some criticism of foreign influence in *Strange Things*, notably in the section on the Jiangnan Arsenal and its translation activities, the main emphasis is on the dysfunctional Chinese social and governmental system. In the two later novels, however, the emphasis shifts dramatically to the crisis of modernity forced upon China by the western powers.

Adventures in Shanghai reveals the self-styled revolutionaries of Shanghai as self-serving hypocrites, but it does not provide Gu Wangyan with a solution to his personal dilemma, and at the end he is still uncertain what to do. *The New Story of the Stone* is quite different. In the first half Baoyu reacts against western material (rather than ideological) products, but in the second half he finds in the Civilized Zone a superior material *and* ideological culture that is also, to some degree at least, the heir to traditional Chinese culture. Here at last the decades-long problem of how to reconcile Chinese substance (*ti*) with western application (*yong*) is not so much solved as transcended. The zone's science and industry prove more advanced than the West's, its governmental system is superior, and Chinese traditional morality is observed instead of religion. This may be a utopian fantasy, but it is a fantasy that only the true patriot of Wu Jianren's definition, one who wishes to preserve the national essence, is able to share.

NOTES

1. *Haishang mingji sida jingang qishu.* See chapter 1.
2. See chapter 6.
3. See the editions in the Zhongguo jindai xiaoshuo daxi series (Nanchang: Jiangxi renmin chubanshe, 1988), 596–602 and 557–67, respectively.
4. Cf. chapter 7 above.
5. See the *North China Herald*, December 14, 1906, 629.
6. P. 567.

7. See the edition in the Zhongguo jindai xiaoshuo daxi series (Nanchang: Jiangxi ren-min chubanshe, 1988).

8. P. 302. The novel has several set pieces of description, which are rare in Wu Jianren's fiction. Unlike his other novels, it also has poems introducing the chapters.

9. Wang, *Fin-de-Siècle Splendor*, 272. Baoyu is described as a Candide-like figure.

10. *Zhongguo xiaoshuo xushi mushi de zhuanbian* (Shanghai: Shanghai renmin chuban-she, 1988), 8–11.

11. *Hui zui zhi dalüe* (Treatise on repentance), a tract by the missionary Karl Gützlaff that takes the form of a Chinese novel told by an I-narrator. See chapter 3 above.

12. Published in installments from 1909, in book form in 1910. See the modern edition in the Zhongguo jindai xiaoshuo daxi series (Nanchang: Jiangxi renmin chubanshe, 1988), 1–144.

13. See chapter 2.

14. See chapter 1.

15. See note 1 above.

16. Quoted in Chen, *Zhongguo xiaoshuo xushi mushi de zhuanbian*, 182.

17. See the edition in the Zhongguo jindai xiaoshuo daxi series (Nanchang: Jianxi ren-min chubanshe, 1988).

18. See introduction, v, for publication details.

19. *Yueyue xiaoshuo* 1.7 (second month 1907): 228–30.

20. See 195. Wu Bohui, a trusted friend of Baoyu's, says a group of men formed the anti-foot-binding society Buchanzu-hui in Shanghai, but had to disperse when the reform movement was crushed in 1898. Sometime afterward "a foreign lady" established the Tianzuhui (Natural Feet Society). The foreign lady was Alicia Little, who founded the society in Shanghai in April 1895 amid great fanfare. The Buchanzu-hui was set up in June 1897. See Yan Changhong, *Zhongguo jindai shehui fengsu shi* (Hangzhou: Zhejiang renmin chubanshe, 1992), 154–56.

21. As noted in Ouyang Jian, *Wan-Qing xiaoshuo shi* (Hangzhou: Zhejiang guji chuban-she, 1997), 152–53.

22. See the edition in the Zhongguo jindai xiaoshuo daxi series (Nanchang: Jiangxi ren-min chubanshe, 1988).

23. His views are a somewhat exaggerated version of Wu's. As an indication of the con-nection, note that in 7.524 Li recommends the opium antidote of Wu's friend, the doctor Peng Banyu, who appears in *Sea of Regret*.

24. For a statement on this subject, see Wu's commentary appended to Zhou Guisheng's "Ziyou jiehun," 71–74. He declares himself in favor of restoring the old morality rather than importing the new culture (*wenming*).

25. See, for example, *The Cambridge History of China* vol. 11, ed. John K. Fairbank (Cambridge: Cambridge University Press, 1978), 494.

26. In February 1905 the Society for the Preservation of Chinese Classical Studies (*Guo-xue baocunhui*) was founded in Shanghai. One if its aims: to preserve the "national essence" (*guocui*).

27. See Wei Shaochang, *Wu Jianren yanjiu ziliao* (Shanghai: Shanghai guji chubanshe 1980), 6.

CHAPTER 9

Specific Literary Relations of Sea of Regret

J UST A FEW MONTHS after the publication of his novel *Hen hai* (Sea of regret) in October 1906, Wu Jianren tried to describe for the readers of his
journal *Yueyue xiaoshuo* the process of the book's composition:

> It took me just ten days to finish my *Sea of Regret*, and then, without check-
> ing it, I sent it straight off to the publisher, the Guangzhi shuju. After it was
> published, I did chance to take it up and read it, but although the sad parts
> reduced me to tears, I still couldn't fathom why I had written it.[1]

This is all we know from the author himself about the composition of the most
successful short novel of the late-Qing period. Wu claims to have forgotten the
novel's background and denigrates the novel itself as stale, hackneyed, and
lacking in interest. There is just one thing in its favor: "Fortunately, although
it is all about passion (*qing*), it does not transgress the bounds of morality."
    In this essay I shall try to recover certain parts of that missing background—
namely, the novel's specific literary relations. The term "literary relations" can
have a broad meaning—for example, it can refer to literary genres or themes—
or else a narrow meaning, such as a particular literary work that the author has
used in some manner in the course of composing his own novel. It is the second meaning that I have in mind here and that I designate by the word "specific." However, even "specific relations" has a range of meanings. At one extreme it may mean nothing more than what are commonly called "sources,"

that is to say, other works from which the author has drawn some of his material. What I mean by it here is a special kind of source, one to which the author has reacted while also using it creatively for his own purposes. Cases of such literary relations are, of course, very common. The most obvious are sequels and parodies, which by their very nature need to acknowledge their literary relationship in order to exploit it. But there are also cases of specific literary relations that are not acknowledged, in which the author has creatively used a text while not referring to it either explicitly or implicitly. The study of such works is an important part of a novel's literary history, and it may supply information that confirms our interpretation. I believe that *Sea of Regret* is such a case. I am not suggesting that Wu Jianren copied from other works, or even that he imitated them, but that he wrote his novel at least partly in response to them.

Two texts that, in my opinion, are specifically related to *Sea of Regret* in this way are *Beinan shimoji* (An account of my ordeal), a narrative in diary form attributed to the Shanghai courtesan Lin Daiyu, and, much more significantly, *Qin hai shi* (Stones in the sea), a short novel by an author using the pseudonym Fu Lin. The diary was written in 1901, just after the Boxer uprising; the novel, in 1905.

Sea of Regret *and* Account of My Ordeal

Account of My Ordeal is attributed to Lin Pin, i.e., Lin Daiyu, the famous turn-of-the-century Shanghai courtesan.[2] (The name, that of the heroine of *Story of the Stone*, was given to her by her mentor, the courtesan Hu Baoyu.) The work purports to have been written in 1901 and carries a preface dated the fifth month of that year. It takes the form of a diary recording the writer's adventures during the Boxer uprising of 1900, when she and several companions, all courtesans from Shanghai, were trapped in Tianjin by the fighting. As they escaped by boat down the Grand Canal, they faced serious danger from both the Boxers and the foreign troops. The diary, which begins early in 1900 and continues until the end of that year, contains graphic details about the sufferings of the populace. For this reason, it is one of the more remarkable documents of its time—and also because it apparently comes from the hand of one of the most notorious women of the day.

A glance at the preface, however, makes us wary about attributing the authorship to Lin Daiyu. It is signed by Maoyuan Xiqiusheng, the pseudonym of Ouyang Juyuan (1883–1907), a brilliant young man who began his career by assisting Li Boyuan (at this time a newspaper editor, later a famous novelist) about the year 1899 and quickly became his right-hand man.[3] In the course of his short life, Ouyang left only one (unfinished) novel, plus prefaces to others by Li Boyuan, Wu Jianren, and others, but he also claimed to have ghost-written Li Boyuan's novels, and there is some evidence that he did at least contribute to them.[4] He consorted in time-honored fashion with the Shanghai courtesans, including Lin Daiyu. He must have met her in 1898 or 1899, when she, along with other leading courtesans, undertook the charitable task of building a collective tomb for courtesans who died young.[5] Li Boyuan and Ouyang Juyuan were among the chief contributors, and Ouyang even coauthored a play on the subject featuring Lin Daiyu.[6] His preface to the diary, however, gives no hint of any relationship with her. Instead, it praises her in euphuistic style for inventing a new literary form.

Not surprisingly, Ouyang was at once suspected of being the real author—or at least of serving as scribe for Lin Daiyu's oral account. Wu Jianren himself, in his *Hu Baoyu*, a series of biographies of Shanghai courtesans that he published in 1906, describes Lin Daiyu's predicament in Tianjin, but goes on to say that a man surnamed Tan rescued her and brought her south by way of Shandong, i.e., along the Grand Canal.[7] Tan is mentioned in the diary, but it is another courtesan, Su Yunlan, whom he is credited with rescuing.[8] If Wu's version is correct, Lin Daiyu escaped at the very beginning of the crisis, and the rest of her story has been fabricated. Wu concludes by adding that someone else wrote the diary and attributed it to her. The diary describes Lin Daiyu as writing poems at various historic sites along the route, and Wu Jianren, who had as low an opinion of Lin Daiyu's education as he had of her morals, seized on this point as proof that someone else had written the diary.[9]

Wu Jianren must have known the true story of the work's authorship. He had written a rather scurrilous novel featuring Lin Daiyu and three other Shanghai courtesans as early as 1898,[10] and he also knew Ouyang Juyuan. In fact, early in 1906, the same year he published his *Hu Baoyu*, he invited Ouyang to write the preface for his novel *Hutu shijie*. We can assume that at the very least Ouyang served as scribe for some parts of the diary, and that he probably wrote other parts of it on his own.

Wu Jianren evidently made use of the diary, which was one of the most graphic descriptions available to him of the tense situation in the north in the year 1900. The account in *Sea of Regret* of Dihua and her mother trying to get past Tianjin and follow the Grand Canal south through Shandong is based on it to a large extent. Each work tells of women traveling by boat to escape the fighting, and one of the women is seriously ill (Lin Daiyu in the diary, Dihua's mother in *Sea of Regret*). The angle of vision of the two works is also remarkably similar. Both boats are stalled in Great West Bay outside Tianjin, their passage blocked by numerous other craft belonging to city residents who have taken to the water to escape the danger.[11] Even from that distance the gunfire from inside the city is still audible and the conflagration plainly visible.

So many other boats are clustered there that the women's boat cannot work its way through, and several days pass before it finally gets free. It comes next to a place along the canal called Jinghai, and then to one called Duli. But in giving these names the diary makes two small but significant mistakes: Jinghai should come *after* Duli, and in any case Duli should be written Duliu. Since Wu Jianren makes the identical mistakes, we can assume that he was following the diary.

Little other verbal similarity exists between the two texts, but each describes the glow of the blazing cathedral as it lights up the faces of the distant onlookers,[12] and each tells in much the same terms how, on arriving at Duli, the refugees found Boxers swarming along the banks of the canal.[13] There are connections also between the diary's description of conditions inside Tianjin and Bohe's adventures in that city. For example, Lin Daiyu and her companions hide out in a musty building, blocking off the main entrance and leaving only a side door as exit; in *Sea of Regret* Bohe takes refuge in a rice warehouse of which the main entrance has been blocked up with rubble and only a side door remains free.[14]

An examination of Wu Jianren's use of *Account of My Ordeal* reveals at least two aspects that distinguish *Sea of Regret* from other contemporary works and that are essential to our appreciation. The first is the nature and position of the narrator or narrators. The ostensible narrator of *Account of My Ordeal* is Lin Daiyu herself, writing her diary. But alongside the record of her experiences, there is other information of a more general nature that she could not possibly have known at the time. Her diary is a chronicle of events of which she is the center, but someone (possibly she herself) must have added facts to it later. It is far from an on-the-spot record of events filtered through a single mind at a given time.

By contrast, it is precisely the restriction of information to what is known by Dihua (or by Bohe or Zhongai) *at the time* that distinguishes the narrative method of *Sea of Regret*. We are told of Dihua's thoughts, feelings, and actions, but she is not explained to us from any outside point of view. (When occasionally, for narrative convenience, her situation is explained, the fact is made very clear.) This is the great strength of *Sea of Regret*—that we see events as they unfold almost entirely through the minds of the major characters. There are few previous novels of which the same can be said.

The second aspect is closely related to the first: the relative absence of actual horror and violence in *Sea of Regret* as compared with *Account of My Ordeal.* For example, the latter describes in gruesome detail the scene of people being crushed between the boats in Great West Bay,[15] but in *Sea of Regret,* although the view from the boats of the fighting in Tianjin is preserved, as well as the fact that the boats are jammed together, there is no mention of people leaping into the water and being crushed. The worst horror described in the novel, the slaughter of Chen Jilin and his family in Beijing, is not even shown to the reader. The only actual violence directly presented at the moment it occurs is the shooting of Bohe by a foreign soldier,[16] but the wound is far from serious and Bohe quickly recovers.

Sea of Regret has actually been criticized for this very feature. Hu Shi in a 1922 essay noted the double romantic tragedy, but described *Sea of Regret* as "a rather simple narrative without much power in its description," and contrasted it unfavorably with another novel by Wu Jianren, *Jiuming qiyuan* (The strange case of the nine murders).[17] But a comparison of *Sea of Regret* with *Account of My Ordeal* indicates that both the limitation of point of view and the restraint in terms of horror were quite deliberate on Wu's part. He was concerned to show the minds of several young people, especially Dihua, as they faced the greatest personal crisis of their lives. At the same time, he evidently wanted to show how the fear of violence rather than the violence itself preyed on Dihua's mind. There are numerous records in other works of horrors and atrocities like those of *Account of My Ordeal.* Wu Jianren chose not to repeat them, but to focus on the fears and apprehensions, as well as the determination and courage, of a single naïve young woman. Paradoxically, because of this restrained presentation, her fears seem all the more vivid.

Sea of Regret *and* Stones in the Sea

The relationship of *Sea of Regret* to *Qin hai shi* (Stones in the sea), a novel published only five months earlier, can be established by an accumulation of similar plot elements rather than by any single textual borrowing. Here are some of the common elements. Each novel is set in a large compound in Beijing in the 1890s, a compound rented to one newly appointed official who promptly sublets part of it to a second newly appointed official. Hero and heroine—or heroes and heroines, for there are two engaged couples in *Sea of Regret*—meet for the first time in the family school. Eventually, the children are betrothed to one another by their parents. They grow up, but before they can marry, they are forced by the Boxer uprising to flee the capital. Two of the three sets of parents remain behind, either because the fathers feel they cannot desert their posts or because they believe the Boxers will triumph, and each man pays for that decision with his life, at the hands of either the Boxers or the foreign troops. The engaged couples are separated as they flee south by mule cart and boat, and in each case the girl flees with her mother in a harrowing journey past Tianjin and down the Grand Canal to Shanghai. There is a deathbed scene near the end of each novel, and both deaths are due—in very different ways—to opium.

Although *Stones in the Sea* was not published until May 1906, its preface is dated the equivalent of December 1905. Like *Sea of Regret,* it is a short novel in ten chapters. It reprints a note from Xu Nianci, editor of the Xiaoshuolin publishing house, praising the manuscript for its literary merits, notably its structure, but rejecting it because it did not fit the purposes of his firm.[18] The author's name was given in the first edition, by the Qunxue she (Sociology house), as Fu Lin, a pseudonym. When the novel was reprinted, the author was given simply as the editorial department of the same publishing company.[19] Perhaps Fu Lin was the pseudonym of one of the editors.

The most striking literary feature of *Stones in the Sea* is the fact that the whole novel is told in the voice of the hero, Qin Ruyu, as he recounts the life and death of his beloved, Gu Aren. This is not the first Chinese novel to be told in the hero's voice—Wu Jianren's own *Strange Things Observed Over the Past Twenty Years,* published in installments beginning in 1903, makes use of a first-person participant narrator—but *Stones in the Sea* is the first vernacular novel to apply the method consistently. By contrast, Wu Jianren's novel had to resort to a variety of devices in order to sustain it.[20]

In *Sea of Regret,* Wu Jianren does not try to emulate the method of *Stones in the Sea,* but he does use a restricted viewpoint in much of the novel, confining the reader's knowledge of events to the thoughts and actions of a few principal characters, notably Dihua. The crucial difference between the two novels is not in matters such as this, but in terms of moral values, particularly the value assigned to *qing,* passion, in the case of love and marriage. According to the captions above their titles, both works are classified as romances, but their conceptions of love and marriage are diametrically opposed. It is hard to resist the conclusion that the reason for Wu Jianren's reliance on elements from *Stones in the Sea*—his reason for writing his novel, in fact—was to counter the other work's thesis about love and marriage.

Stones in the Sea shows no hesitation in expounding its thesis. Its narrator is a sixteen-year-old youth in love with a girl from whom he is separated by the Boxer uprising. His father foresees the disaster that will befall the capital and prudently leaves for Shanghai, taking his son with him. The girl's father, however, insists on staying behind in the capital, where he perishes soon after the foreign troops arrive. As the girl and her mother attempt to travel south, she is victimized by an unscrupulous family friend and attempts suicide. When the youth finds her, she is on her deathbed. His book is written in her memory— and also in the cause of what was known at the time as "free marriage," that is to say, free choice in marriage.

Here is the narrator's condemnation of the moral principle that, in his opinion, was responsible for the tragedy:

> Reader, who do you imagine was responsible for doing us such grievous harm? None other, I regret to say, than the philosopher Mencius of the Zhou dynasty. Now, Mencius lived well over two thousand years ago, so how could he possibly do us harm? Strangely enough, he once made a preposterous assertion that has been passed down to the present day. Marriage, he declared, should take place only by the parents' command and through the good offices of a go-between; otherwise the young couple would earn the contempt of both their parents and the general public. It never occurred to him that marriage might be a matter that the young couple had a right to decide for themselves, that it was not something for parents and go-betweens to meddle in. . . . From ancient times to the present day, how many men and women, millions upon millions, have been destroyed! Even my love and I are among those ruined by Mencius. Oh, if only we knew freedom of marriage as it is practiced in civilized countries, we would never have suffered from Mencius's stupidity and been so badly hurt![21]

At the end of the novel, after describing the girl's death, he again places the blame on traditional values, summing up his theme as follows: "From first to last this book has been concerned with just one thing—passion (*qing*)."[22]

There is a flaw in the narrator's argument. The traditional marriage system was not the cause of his particular tragedy. His father, although at first opposed to the idea of an engagement, was eventually persuaded to agree to it. Her father, on the other hand, despite his conservatism, was always amenable. The primary reason for the tragedy was that the Boxer uprising and the threat of foreign intervention caused one of the families to flee, and the lovers became separated. Had both families fled, the marriage would presumably have taken place as planned. The narrator can legitimately argue that the traditional system forced him to resort to deception and even blackmail in order to court his beloved and should be condemned on that account alone, but he cannot reasonably argue that he has been prevented from marrying Aren. However, despite the flaw in the argument as applied to his own case, the novel still stands as an impassioned attack on the traditional marriage system.

Differing Concepts of Qing

Qing (passion, most often love) is the basis of the social morality propounded by both *Stones in the Sea* and *Sea of Regret*, but they conceive of it in radically different ways. Before contrasting those ways, let me briefly survey the meanings and uses of the term in the fiction of the time.

By the end of the nineteenth century, the concept of *qing*, which had been the object of intense interest in romances such as *Pin hua baojian, Hua yue hen, Qinglou meng, Hui fang lu,* and *Haishang chentian ying*, to say nothing of the various sequels to *Story of the Stone*, began to be used to justify "free marriage," if necessary in opposition to the parents' wishes. Two of the first translated novels to make an impact on the public were tragic romances concerned with marriage. *Bali Chahuanü yishi,* Lin Shu's translation of *La Dame aux camélias* by Alexandre Dumas *fils*, appeared in 1899, and *Jiayin xiaozhuan*, an incomplete translation by Yang Zilin and Bao Tianxiao of Rider Haggard's *Joan Haste*, in 1901–1902. (A complete translation of the latter by Lin Shu was published in 1905.) In both novels the heroine yields to the pleas of her lover's parent (in the first case the father, in the second the mother) and breaks off the engagement. Thus both novels had a double appeal for readers: they appealed to their desire for romance as well as to their pleasure in the traditional, sacrificial morality. The heroines sacrificed their own love for the sake of family— not their own families, but their lovers'.

By 1903, if not before, the subject of "free marriage" was being explicitly discussed and advocated in journals, pamphlets, and novels.[23] A novel actually entitled *Ziyou jiehun* (Free marriage) was published in August of that year. The supposed author appears in the first chapter, which is a kind of prologue, and gives a lecture to an audience of young men and women. He maintains that, of the various freedoms people were talking about, freedom of marriage was the one that "everybody delights in, everybody is willing to die for."[24] However, despite its title, freedom of marriage is not his novel's main subject; the author merely hopes that the cause will inspire his readers to champion other kinds of freedom.

So far as I know, the earliest novel in which freedom of marriage *was* the main subject is a short work in literary Chinese entitled *Henhai hua* (Flowers in the sea of regret), published in the second month of 1905,[25] some months before the writing of *Stones in the Sea.* Told in the first person by the hero's confidant, it appears to owe something to the example of *Bali Chahuanü yishi.* It claims to be a true story written in the summer of 1904 about events that had occurred in the autumn of the year before. The narrative has one unusual feature: it is continually interrupted by comments from the author and a friend who differ widely in their opinions as to the morality of the hero's and heroine's actions; the friend's is the more conservative voice.

Henhai hua tells a tragic love story about a girl who boldly declares her love for her brother's school friend, someone she knows only from his letters to her brother. (She has fallen in love with their sentiments.) The friend is already married (an arranged marriage), but the girl is willing to marry him anyway, as his concubine if necessary. After the hero and heroine have met in Shanghai, she decides not to elope but to confront her father and straightforwardly ask for his approval. Her father refuses her request and keeps her confined at home, where she wastes away and dies. The narrator blames her tragedy on the lack of freedom to marry.

In *Stones in the Sea,* as we have seen, love is assumed to be the proper basis for marriage, and the traditional system is excoriated. In his preface, the author goes to cosmic lengths, claiming that *qing* is the primal stuff of the universe. In contradicting Tan Sitong, whose *Renxue* (Study of *ren*) had maintained that *ren* (human-heartedness) was the primal stuff, he remarks: "I maintain that it is this one thing, *qing,* that the Creator used in creating the world."[26]

For his part, Wu Jianren redefines the concept in orthodox terms right at the beginning of *Sea of Regret. Qing* means all the various emotions or passions. When properly applied, it functions as moral passion, the psychological stimulus for virtuous action in a Confucian sense:

> In the eyes of the world, you must understand, passion is confined to sex, whereas the passion I am speaking of, the kind we possess from birth, is an innate quality that, as we grow up, we can apply to any sphere of life, the only difference being in the *manner* of its application. When applied to a ruler, passion means loyalty; when applied to parents, it means filial piety; when applied to children, it means parental love; and when applied to friends, it means true fellowship. Clearly, the cardinal virtues all derive from passion. As for sexual passion, the only word for that is infatuation.[27]

He has not even included the husband-wife relationship among his approved applications of passion.

The introduction then turns to romantic fiction, the category in which Wu Jianren has provocatively placed his *Sea of Regret*. When he castigates Chinese romantic fiction for writing about lust rather than passion, one assumes that he is talking about the likes of *Henhai hua* and *Stones in the Sea*, but in a note to the first edition he identifies *Story of the Stone* and *The West Chamber* (*Xi-xiangji*), the most famous Chinese novel and the most famous Chinese play, respectively, as his targets.

In Wu Jianren's view, there is no conflict between the individual self and the accepted social morality, as there is in *Stones in the Sea*; for him, it is the individual's passion that generates the moral behavior. Tendentiously, he takes up the ultimate case, asserting that a widow's resolve not to remarry, the classic example of a willed abstention from sexual passion, actually represents the height of passion. Why is that? Because, as an exceptional act of virtue, her self-restraint can only have been generated by an equally exceptional moral passion.

> According to one view, the chaste widows lauded by our forefathers had hearts like dead trees or dry wells; they were utterly unmoved by passion. I categorically deny it. The occasions on which the widows remained unmoved were precisely those on which their passion was at its height. In its conviction that passion is confined to sexual love, the world inevitably takes the term too lightly. What is more, there is many a "story of passion" that in reality describes not passion, but lechery, which it then tries to portray as passion. A true crime of the writer's brush![28]

Although *Sea of Regret* makes no explicit comments on "free marriage," it is clear that it is written in opposition. True, each of the engagements it describes ends in loss or tragedy, but the blame is placed on a kind of cosmic irony, rather than on the marriage system itself. In the last lines of the final lyric we are told that "true passion" (*zhen qing*) is revealed only in tragic circumstances: "When upheaval's joined with tribulation/True passion is at last displayed."[29] From a pragmatic point of view, we would have to conclude that Wu Jianren is undermining his own case. But he is not thinking pragmatically. He is concerned to show how two people, Dihua and Zhongai, particularly Dihua, can uphold the highest principles of moral behavior under terrible conditions. Dihua and Zhongai may be martyrs to the ethical code, but that does not mean Wu is seeking to change that code. Conditions may condemn Dihua's engagement to failure, but, far more significantly, they display her true passion in fulfilling to the last syllable every self-denying duty that could conceivably be expected of a daughter or fiancée. This is the exact antithesis of the indi-

vidual's inalienable right to love and marry—in defiance of parents if necessary—that is stressed in *Hen hai hua* and *Stones in the Sea.*

Sea of Regret concerns an engagement as seen through the eyes of Dihua.
The progress of her thinking shows how love is supposed to develop within an
arranged marriage. To a lesser degree we also follow the thinking of Zhongai,
who maintains his chastity in preparation for marriage. They are a model heroine and hero, and the author has faced the novelist's usual problem in presenting model characters. He is particularly successful with Dihua; rarely in
any novel has the thinking of a moral paragon been presented so affectingly.
The notes constantly refer to her naïveté as she balances fears and joys, torn between concern for her ailing mother and concern for her absent fiancé.[30] (The
notes purport to be by someone other than the author, but they may well be
by Wu Jianren.)[31] In chapters 6 and 10, during the period of Dihua's greatest
trials, the commentator occasionally addresses her directly, in an affectionate,
admiring, yet also slightly mocking way.[32]

We see her struggling with the minutiae of prescribed ethical behavior. Her
scrupulous observance of the multifarious prohibitions restricting a girl's conduct—summed up in the term *bixian*—sometimes causes the reader to lose patience with her. In chapters 9 and 10 even the commentator is driven to ex-
postulate against her habit of blaming herself for mishaps that are clearly not
her fault. In chapter 10, he notes that "she is still blaming herself—the word
qing is simply not adequate to cover it."[33] Virtually all of her actions are ascribed to *qing* (in Wu Jianren's definition). When in chapter 5 she is afraid to
awaken her mother, a note says, "people of passion are always filial."[34] When
she shows her gratitude to the good-hearted village innkeeper and his wife, her
generosity is described as that of a person of passion. However, when, on the
boat, she is forced to use the bedding left behind by Bohe and feels the stir-
rings of sexual passion, the note says, "When passion reaches an extreme, it becomes infatuation."[35] (The note does, however, praise the author for his per-
spicacity.) In chapter 8, desperate to save her mother's life, Dihua resorts to
cutting off a small piece of her own flesh and making it into a broth to serve
to her mother, a kind of folk medicine that Wu Jianren would normally have
scorned. The note, however, insists that her action must be considered filial
piety because of the passion that has generated it.[36]

The filial actions of Zhongai are also praised in terms of *qing.* In chapter 7,
when he refuses to leave his parents behind in Beijing, the commentator remarks: "No one with passion is unfilial, while no filial person is without passion."[37] Romantic and sexual love are also the subject of Zhongai's arguments
with his colleagues in chapter 8. When the colleagues challenge him for lacking

passion because he has refused to accompany them to the pleasure quarter, he claims that it is he who is the passionate one, and proceeds to ridicule them as dupes of *The Story of the Stone*: "Nowadays people see themselves as Baoyu and go off to join the singsong girls and apply Baoyu's passion to them."[38] One of his colleagues retorts: "I gather you don't feel any passion yourself, then?" "Of course I do," replies Zhongai. "I just try to apply it in the right place." The others then join in: "If you have to emulate Baoyu in finding the right place, you'll have your work cut out for you!" "Ah, but you see Baoyu never *did* apply his passion in the right place," replies Zhongai.

References to free marriage can also be found in some of Wu's other writing. For example, in *Dushe quan*, the novel translated by Zhou Guisheng from 1903 and commented on by Wu Jianren, the subject recurs again and again in Wu's end-of-chapter comments and marginal notes.[39] In chapter 18, first published in *Xin xiaoshuo* in the fifth month of 1905, Wu Jianren reacts vehemently to the novel's portrayal of a disastrous marriage in which a brutal husband lets his wife and baby starve while he spends all his money drinking and carousing. He takes this as proof that "free marriage" as practiced in the West is not necessarily successful. With heavy sarcasm, he pretends to speak in the voice of "the young men of the new learning" (*xinxue shaonian*) who love to mouth such catchwords as "civilization" and "freedom."[40]

"Free marriage." On hearing the term, I am intoxicated by it, I bow down before it. I believe that the husband-and-wife relationship is the beginning of all human relationships, and if that relationship can only be made free, all quarreling will be banished forever and family harmony established. However, after reading this chapter, I am dumbfounded. I haven't finished the book yet, so I still don't know how matters will turn out, but Adrien and Moumoute certainly *seem* to be husband and wife. Let's assume they are. Surely people in civilized countries don't still abide by all those unnecessary conventions, exchanging horoscopes and gifts and only acting "by the command of their parents and through the good offices of a go-between," formalities that restrict their freedom? Surely they don't *still* get married without even knowing each other?

We see from this example that the distinction between civilization and barbarism can be used only to differentiate individuals; it cannot conceivably be used to generalize about a country. If you want to claim that it can be applied to a country, then where do people like this couple come from? I certainly don't mean to base a dogmatic argument on such a trivial matter, but I do detest those people who love to talk of European civilization and culture

while constantly pointing to the barbarism of our country, and I am directing this question to them.

At the end of chapter 22 he comments on the fact that the heroine Camille
has been deceived. (She has chosen to become engaged to a man who, it turns
out, keeps a mistress and also gambles heavily.)

> Europe has always ignored the segregation of the sexes, and so women can so-
> cialize with men. That is simply not comparable to the situation of girls who
> have no experience at all, particularly a girl like Camille. Moreover, the girls
> of our country are scrupulous about segregation and regard it as a virtue to
> remain secluded in the women's quarters. They are utterly ignorant of the
> ways of the world. Why don't those people who speak so lightly of free mar-
> riage ever think of these things?[41]

In chapter 10, his upper-margin notes praise the father for his loving kind-
ness, and the girl for her filial behavior. Each has acted selflessly, out of regard
for the other. At one point Camille even blames herself for her father's going
blind. Wu's comment runs, "What did this have to do with her? Yet in spite
of that she contrives to regard it as her fault. She cannot be considered anything less than perfectly filial."[42] In some respects, his attitude toward Camille
seems to prefigure his later attitude toward Dihua.

In these examples, however, he is arguing in practical terms, not on principle. Adrien and Moumoute's marriage shows that "free marriages" are sometimes unsuccessful in the West; hence China should not be condemned for its
tradition of arranged marriage. Camille's unwise engagement leads to the assertion that Chinese girls are not ready for free marriage.[43] (In any case, they
regard it as a virtue to live in seclusion.) This appeal to culture and practicali-
ty contrasts with the appeal to universal principle found in the introduction to
Sea of Regret.

Wu's most direct statement about free marriage comes in comments that he
appended to a 1908 article by Zhou Guisheng. Entitled "Free Marriage," the
article consists of news items that Zhou had culled from the foreign press to
show the ill effects of western marriage practices, particularly the ease of elopement and the frequency of divorce.[44]

Wu Jianren's comments, which are almost as long as Zhou's article, begin
by drawing a distinction between himself and his friend. Zhou Guisheng is
generally in favor of importing the "new civilization," i.e., western culture,
while he, Wu Jianren, is in favor of restoring the old morality. Wu Jianren

claims that at the present time, just as the old morality is collapsing, there has been a sudden influx of western practices. Young people, with no grounding in the ancient texts, assume that the strength of the western nations is due to their civilization, and when they see anything different from what they are used to, they tend to imitate it, entirely forgetting their own cultural background. On this one subject of "free marriage," however, Zhou Guisheng's opinion happens to coincide with his. Wu Jianren claims that those who promote "free marriage" are acting out of their own self-interest and neglecting the needs of society in general. "Moral education is closely linked to social practice, and if you insist on destroying all that we have in order to follow the example of others, you yourself may do well, but society as a whole will not." Again Wu's argument is based on cultural considerations rather than a universal principle. What is the reason, then, for the principled doctrine that he propounds in *Sea of Regret?*

A growing cultural conservatism can be traced in Wu's thinking. One of his biographers says that in the last decade of his life, i.e., in the first decade of the twentieth century, he became increasingly concerned about preserving the "national essence" (*guocui*).[45] From 1903, if not before, he inveighed against the catchwords from the West that proved so attractive to the young and well educated. He believed that the new ideas from the West did not suit Chinese culture, and feared that traditional Chinese ethical thought and practice might be lost. These facts might explain the treatment of free marriage in his other works, but they hardly explain the doctrine propounded in *Sea of Regret*. I suggest that, because of his opposition to *Stones in the Sea*, in *Sea of Regret* he resorted to a universal doctrine of *qing* (stressing the traditional social obligations) in order to counter *Stones in the Sea*'s equally universal doctrine of *qing* (stressing individual rights).

Account of My Ordeal and *Stones in the Sea* belong to the history of the composition of *Sea of Regret* and are therefore of some importance, but can we go further and claim that a comparison with them will help our understanding of Wu Jianren's novel? I contend that we can. Perhaps the same conclusions might have been reached in other ways, for example, by comparing *Sea of Regret* widely with other literature of the period, that is to say, by studying its general rather than its specific literary relations. But a comparison with specifically related texts such as these can lead to conclusions that are more precise.

NOTES

1. "Shuo xiaoshuo," *Yueyue xiaoshuo* 8 (fourth month 1907): 209–10. References to *The Sea of Regret (Hen hai)* are to the edition in the Zhongguo jindai xiaoshuo daxi series (Nanchang: Jiangxi renmin chubanshe, 1988), 5–88.

2. It is reprinted in Aying, *Gengzi shibian wenxueji* (Beijing: Zhonghua shuju, 1958), 2:1065–85.

3. See Wei Shaochang, *Li Boyuan yanjiu ziliao* (Shanghai guji chubanshe, 1980), 490–98.

4. See the works quoted in Wei Shaochang, *Li Boyuan yanjiu ziliao*, 493–98, especially that by Bao Tianxiao.

5. Ibid, 520.

6. See Wei Shaochang, *Li Boyuan yanjiu ziliao*, 513–18. The title of the play was "Yugou hen."

7. "Sida jingang xiaozhuan," *Wofo Shanren wenji* 7:318. There is also a third version of Lin Daiyu's escape to the south, by Qian Zheng (Xinbo), in a book published in 1919; see Wei Shaochang, *Li Boyuan yanjiu ziliao*, 520.

8. See Aying, *Gengzi shibian wenxueji*, 1069. Her name differs slightly from that of the woman Zou Tao fell in love with; see chapter 1.

9. *Wofo Shanren wenji* 7:321.

10. *Haishang mingji sida jingang qishu.* See chapter 1.

11. *Account of My Ordeal,* 1075, and *Hen hai,* chapter 6, 46–48, respectively.

12. P. 1069 and chapter 6, 47, respectively.

13. P. 1077 and chapter 6, 48, respectively.

14. P. 1073 and chapter 7, 53, respectively.

15. P. 1075.

16. Chapter 7, 55.

17. *Hu Shi wencun erji* (reprint, Hefei: Huangshan shushe, 1996), 2:224.

18. A copy of the first edition is preserved in the library of the Shanghai Branch of the Chinese Writers' Union.

19. See the 1909 and 1913 editions in the Capital Library in Beijing. Reference here is to the modern edition in the *Zhongguo jindai wenxue daxi* (Shanghai: Shanghai shudian, 1991), vol. 6. It is based on the second or third editions of the novel, which make minor changes in the text. For example, they use the heroine's formal name, Renfen, rather than her familiar name, Aren.

20. See chapter 8.

21. Pp. 861–62. See *The Sea of Regret,* trans. Patrick Hanan (Honolulu: University of Hawaii Press, 1995), 22–23.

22. P. 924.

23. Articles advocating free choice in marriage go back at least to 1898. See an article from the *Nüxuebao, Zhongguo jindai funü yundong lishi ziliao,* 1840–1918 (Beijing: Zhongguo funü chubanshe, 1991), 144. Free choice in marriage was later combined with campaigns for equality of the sexes and for "family revolution."

24. See the edition in the *Zhongguo jindai xiaoshuo daxi* series (Nanchang: Baihuazhou wenyi chubanshe, 1991), 114. The author was Zhang Zhaotong.

25. There is a copy of the third edition, published in 1907, in the Shanghai Library. The author's name is given only as Fei Ming. Another early novel advocating freedom of marriage was *Qingtian hen*, published by the Xinxueshe in the twelfth month of 1905. Under the influence of *Bali Chahuanü yishi* and perhaps also of *Henhai hua*, it is told in the first person by a friend of the hero.

26. P. 860.

27. P. 5. *The Sea of Regret*, 103.

28. *The Sea of Regret*, 103–104.

29. P. 88. *The Sea of Regret*, 205.

30. It is possible to read into the account of her predicament a certain ambivalence on Wu Jianren's part toward *qing* and free marriage, but one should also note the consistent denigration of free marriage in his other writing, including his last, unfinished novel, *Qing bian*, of 1910.

31. No one is named as commentator. A reference to the author in chapter 8, 66, suggests that the commentator is someone else, but the comment on 67 attacking the "worship of foreigners" sounds like Wu Jianren.

32. He addresses her as *qing*, a term that indicates familiarity.

33. P. 86.

34. Chapter 5, 40.

35. Chapter 5, 44.

36. Chapter 8, 67.

37. Chapter 7, 59.

38. P. 64.

39. See chapter 7.

40. *Xin xiaoshuo* 2.5 (1905): 118–19.

41. *Xin xiaoshuo* 2.11 (1905): 81.

42. *Xin xiaoshuo* 2.1 (1905): 134.

43. A similar argument is made by Lu Xun, at least as far as elopement is concerned. See chapter 11.

44. "Ziyou jiehun," *Yueyue xiaoshuo* (second month 1908):63–74.

45. Li Jiarong, "Wofo Shanren zhuan," in Wei Shaochang, *Wu Jianren yanjiu ziliao*, 11. Li's brief biography was published in 1910, shortly after Wu Jianren's death. Wu's cultural conservatism is at its most extreme in his praise of the morality of the traditional *muyushu* oral tales of his native Guangdong (see *Xin xiaoshuo* for the fifth month of 1905 under the heading "Xiaoshuo conghua"). Note also his preface to his collection of Chinese detective stories, *Zhongguo zhentan zhuan*, published in the third month of 1906, shortly before *Sea of Regret*; see Wei Shaochang, *Wu Jianren yanjiu ziliu*, 323–24 and 244–47.

CHAPTER 10

The Autobiographical Romance of Chen Diexian

D URING THE FIRST two decades of the twentieth century, Chen Die-xian (1879–1940), better known by his pen name Tian Xu Wo Sheng (Heaven Bore Me in Vain),[1] was one of the most celebrated Chinese writers. However, like all but a few of those who were active just before the May Fourth movement, he has long since fallen out of favor, so far out that I shall need to introduce him and his works before broaching my subject, which is his successive attempts to write his own romantic autobiography.

Chen Diexian has several claims upon our attention. He was a remarkably versatile man in an age of versatile men, proficient in all the currently practiced genres of Chinese literature as well as in music and art, and also—this truly sets him apart from other writers—adept at industrial enterprise and management. His writings run from the last decade of the nineteenth century through the second decade of the twentieth—something that can be said of few other novelists. Furthermore, in an age of social satire, he was predominantly a writer of romance. I shall argue that his main literary significance lies in his successive attempts to tell his own romantic history. These culminate in a 1913 novel in literary Chinese entitled *Huangjin sui* (The bedevilment of money or, as I prefer to call it, The money demon), a novel that presents itself as both romantic fiction and unabashed autobiography.

He was born into a wealthy Hangzhou family.[2] His father, Chen Fuyuan, a doctor, and his uncle, an official, lived with their families in a large compound in the city. By his concubine, Dai, Fuyuan had four sons; Diexian was the third. (His principal wife, Wang, was unable to have any children.) The uncle had a son and two daughters, and there were girl cousins from other branches of the family who made frequent long visits to the compound. All together, including servants, the household numbered more than sixty people. From his early childhood Diexian was drawn more to the gentle and generous Wang as a mother than to his birth mother, whom he considered overly strict and censorious.

His father died in 1885 and Wang in 1893, and in 1897, following his uncle's death, when Diexian was 18, the families split up and the compound was sold. In the same year Diexian was married to Zhu Shu (also known as Lanyun, Danxiang, and Suxian), a girl to whom Wang had betrothed him long before.

Early in 1898 his birth mother forced a reluctant Diexian out of the family to earn a living as assistant to the commissioner of customs at Wukang, a couple of days' journey by boat from Hangzhou. After leaving his post and making an unsuccessful attempt at business in the Wukang area, he returned to Hangzhou and for the next decade occupied himself with various business ventures there. He and two friends took over a defunct newspaper, renaming it *Daguan bao*, mainly in order to publish literature, mostly their own. When the newspaper was banned for its editorial opposition to the Boxers, they started another, which suffered the same fate. In 1901 Diexian set up a shop in the center of Hangzhou, the Cui Li Company (Gather profit company), selling imported technical appliances. He soon followed it with a lithographic press. In 1906 he founded a library for the public, the Baomu She (All-you-can-read society), and in the next year a literary journal, *Zhuzuolin* (Forest of writings), which went against the trend of the time and specialized in poetry, drama, and criticism rather than fiction. In 1908, for reasons that are not entirely clear, his businesses went bankrupt, and he fell back on service as a staff adviser.

In 1913 he was appointed joint editor of the Shanghai magazine *Youxi zazhi* (alternative title, The Pastime), and in 1914 he was appointed editor of a magazine for women, *Nüzi shijie*, for which he and his wife wrote most of the copy. He was later given the influential post of editor of the daily literary page ("Ziyou tan," Free talk) of the *Shen bao*, which he resigned at the end of September 1918 because of the increasing demands of his business.[3]

In the early years of the century Diexian had begun to take a keen amateur interest in chemistry. By 1904, according to his son, he had turned one of his studies into a private laboratory.[4] He had a genuine interest in applied science, but he was also driven by a particular concern, that foreign companies held a monopoly on the production and sale of tooth powder—a universally used product before the invention of toothpaste. On analyzing the brands available, he found that the basic ingredient of the Japanese powder was calcium carbonate, while the superior, but more expensive, Russian brand used magnesium carbonate.[5] The task Diexian set himself was to find a cheap enough local source of magnesium carbonate to be able to compete with the Japanese brands on price. Eventually he found such a source in the waste substance known as bittern. At the time, however, he gave little thought to marketing the formula himself. He even publicized it in *Nüzi shijie* for anyone to use.[6]

It was not long before he changed his mind. By 1917 he had improved the formula, secured local sources of supply for the ingredients so as to survive a boycott of foreign goods (a prescient move), and begun production. In May 1918 he took his company, Family Industries, public.[7] The powder, with its various ancillary uses, proved a huge success. From it Diexian branched out into the manufacture of dozens of household products and set up factories in different parts of China, making large profits on tooth powder and cosmetics but losing heavily on the manufacture of paper. By about 1917 his business interests were taking precedence over his literary activities. He published management treatises as well as a selection of his business correspondence and continued to write occasional poetry and essays, but he wrote no more novels.

Let me turn to his literary work, in which he was extraordinarily precocious. He had written a full-length *tanci* under the title of *Taohua ying* (Peach blossom shadows) by the age of 14.[8] By 1900, if the bibliography attached to his joint publication *Sanjia qu* (Art songs by three poets) is to be credited,[9] he had written a score of works, including a collection that does not survive, *Diexian conggao*, in 36 *juan*; several volumes of poetry and song; many works on prosody and music; an opera, *Taohua meng* (Peach blossom dream); a novel, *Leizhu yuan* (Romantic destiny of tears), in 120 *juan*; and a sequel to the famous courtesan novel, *Haishang hua liezhuan* (Flowers of Shanghai), in 36 *juan*. He remained prolific until 1917 or 1918. The 1923 official bibliography lists 7 operas (*chuanqi*), 9 plays, 2 *tanci*, 31 novels, and numerous other works.[10] It does not list the multitude of pieces that he wrote for newspapers and journals.

Diexian specialized in the romance rather than in the satirical, utopian, detective, or historical novels that predominated in the first decade of the century. His work can be seen as growing out of *The Story of the Stone*. He identified with Baoyu in terms of growing up in a large and wealthy household, but even more in terms of his love for several different girls and women at the same time. (In fact, of course, his concept of love also owed much to the contemporary romance with its stress on "free marriage.") His first piece of narrative, the *tanci Taohua ying,* actually takes up the story of some characters drawn from *Story of the Stone,* while his first opera, *Taohua meng,* is an imaginative projection of his own experience in the spirit of that novel. His first novel, *Leizhu yuan,* retells the material of the opera in far greater detail and with added complications. Of the novels that he wrote himself—i.e., excluding those on which he collaborated—well over half describe themselves as romances of one kind or another. In the first decade, they were relatively few in number and all in the vernacular; in the second decade, like most of the romances written at that time, they were in literary Chinese.

In poetry, too, he favored the romantic-erotic over other modes, notably in a series of 180 poems that he wrote about a single romantic episode in the sixth month of 1898.[11] In his best-known collection, *Xin Yiyuji,* published about 1906, he includes many poems of the same kind.[12] The choice of title is significant, because it echoes that of a collection of poems by the Ming poet Wang Yanhong, who has been called the Chinese Baudelaire.[13] Even Diexian's occasional paintings were mainly of the crises in his romantic life.[14]

It is hardly surprising that the best of Diexian's romances are those that portray his own life as a youth and the romantic crises he experienced. In my opinion, they are superior to his other novels, such as his better-known *Yutian henshi,* which shows a total lack of irony and labors under too heavy a burden of tragic emotion.

❈

One can trace this kind of personal romance chronologically through his work. The earliest example was evidently the opera *Taohua meng* in 16 acts. The Fudan University Library has a movable-type edition by Diexian's Daguanbao publishing house with a preface dated 1900. It is an elaborate work with appreciative poems by his closest friends, Hua Chishi and He Songhua, who had joined him in founding the *Daguan bao* and in publishing *Sanjia qu,* and also by his wife Zhu Shu, his cousin Gu Yinglian, and others. The hero, Baozhu, represents Diexian, while the heroine, Wanxiang, represents Yinglian. A commentator's note attached to act 12 (*juan* 3, 18a) states that Chen Diexian's *Leizhuji* (presumably his novel *Leizhu yuan*) tells how in 1896 Wanxiang drowned in the Grand Canal.

Chen Diexian later revised the opera and published the first part of it under the title *Luohua meng* (Dream of fallen flowers).[15] An author's note dated the sixth month of 1913 says that the original work was completed in 1896, when he was just seventeen. It goes on to say that this revision will give the true names of the participants. In the revised version the name of Wanxiang has been changed to that of Gu Yinglian, his cousin from Suzhou. Yinglian, who was known as a poet, grew up in the Yiyuan (Harmony Garden) in Suzhou built by Gu Wenbin, but as an orphan and also as a niece of Wang, Diexian's mother, she spent much of her time at the compound in Hangzhou. In Diexian's openly autobiographical *Huangjin sui* of 1913, she drowns on the way to Yangzhou, just as in the opera. But Diexian's wife Zhu Shu, in the course of some notes on contemporary women's poetry in *Nüzi shijie*, remarks that Yinglian "could not marry my husband because, although she was three years older than he was, she belonged to the following generation."[16] Instead of Yinglian's drowning—the mere report of which in *Huangjin sui* was enough to induce Diexian to attempt suicide—Zhu Shu goes on to say that "in the end she died of melancholia," suggesting that she died because she could not marry Diexian. Yinglian's volume of poetry, entitled *Xiaotaohuaguan shiciji*, was named after the place she stayed during her visits to the Chen compound in Hangzhou.

The second major work depicting Chen Diexian's romantic odyssey is the novel *Leizhu yuan*. The official bibliography of 1923 says it was written in 1896, that is to say, in the same year as Chen wrote *Taohua meng*. His own colophon to the 64-chapter edition of 1907 says that he wrote the novel in 1898, while the chronological account of Chen's life by his son Chen Qu gives 1897. The last date is probably the correct one. As we saw, the 1900 bibliography in *Sanjia qu* says it was already in 120 *juan* by that time. Other references say 64 chapters (*hui*). In any event, only 32 chapters were published in 1900, by the Daguanbao publishing company. The book was expanded to 64 chapters in 1907 and to 96 chapters in 1916.

The 1907 edition includes a battery of appreciative poems, including one by the author previously published in the 1900 edition. In it he says that the book is "half imaginary, half true," and the events recounted are "from five years ago, but still painful."[17] His preface, like his wife's (under the name of Danxiang), stresses the connection to *Story of the Stone*. The prologue of the novel echoes the same theme, describing the work as "a dream world that the author has experienced."

The material is essentially that of *Taohua meng*, but with many additions, most of them playful. Diexian himself is represented as not one but two romantic heroes, Qin Baozhu and Sheng Quxian. (Note that Qu was the name he gave his son, and that Sheng is the surname of his rival in his later, thoroughly autobiographical novel, *Huangjin sui.*) His friends Hua and Yuan also appear as romantic heroes, in transparent disguise. Gu Yinglian, his cousin and first love, appears under her own name. In chapter 27 some of her poems are given. In addition, the 16 poems that Diexian wrote on a visit to the Harmony Garden are ascribed to her.[18] Her tragic drowning in the Grand Canal is recounted (in the novel she is miraculously rescued). Wanxiang, who formerly represented Yinglian, remains as heroine. She now represents, I think, both Yinglian and Zhenglou, Diexian's great love, a girl whom he had known since childhood. Diexian's wife also appears, under the somewhat chilling name of Leng Suxin. The novel is a *Story of the Stone*–inspired romance with an ideal ending, in which the author has shaped his experience to please himself. In the later novel, *Huangjin sui*, he describes the writing of *Leizhu yuan* as follows:

I derived a great deal of pleasure from writing that novel. If I wanted something done, that book was ready to oblige. Did I want a garden created? Done in a flash. Did I want a marriage arranged? Done to order. The people I loved I kept alive; those I hated I killed off. Not even the Lord of Heaven wielded the sort of power that I held in my hand.[19]

He notes that, as soon as he finished a section, his wife and Zhenglou, Hua Chishi, and He Songhua would compete to be the first to read it.

In the summer of 1898, on the seventeenth of the sixth month, Diexian slept with Zhenglou for the first time. He was seriously ill, and had just returned from Wukang. (In fact, unbeknownst to his family, Zhenglou, after receiving what purported to be a deathbed letter from him, had sent a servant to bring him back.) On the eighteenth, she and Diexian unwisely joined the rest of her family on an outing to the West Lake, where Diexian had a relapse and had to be rushed back to the house. Zhenglou was distraught, believing that their lovemaking had caused the relapse, whereas he, once he recovered, was overcome with guilt for ruining her reputation. The whole episode, which I have fleshed out with details from two sources I shall discuss below, was a key one in Diexian's life and in his writing. Not long afterward, he wrote the set of 180 poems that I have mentioned, poems that refer to these events.

Later, in his *Xin Yiyuji* collection, he included two more sets of eight poems each that give further details of the lovemaking and its aftermath.[20] They set the events out clearly, as told in later accounts. From their position in the volume, it would appear that the supplementary poems were probably written in

1904, after Zhenglou had fled Hangzhou and Diexian was in despair over losing her. He painted the farewell scene, entitled *Zhenglou qi bie tu* (Parting from Zhenglou in tears), and characteristically encouraged his friends and acquaintances to write poems on the subject. Zhenglou left in the tenth month of 1903, and then, after he had tried and failed to contact her, suddenly reappeared in the fourth month of 1905 and summoned him. He painted a picture of their reunion[21] and again encouraged people to respond in verse. He then made a selection of the verse and published it with his own critical commentary in his journal *Zhuzuolin*.[22] He also attached to his own poems on the subject a detailed account of his affair with Zhenglou, "Zhenglouji" (Story of Zhenglou).[23]

Zhenglou and her affair with Diexian recur many times in his poetry, beginning with some of his earliest childhood verses. It was a tortuous relationship, as a poem of 1901 makes clear:

> Long have I likened my heart to ashes,
> Flaring up and dying a thousand times.[24]

Naturally the affair was the subject of much discussion among Diexian's friends. About 1910, in answer to a question from a friend, he wrote a poem that said his love for her had not changed in twenty-five years, but that he could not give up his wife in order to marry her.[25] They lived apart, he wrote, their love having no need of physical intimacy. As late as May 1913, the month before *Huangjin sui* began serialization, we hear of Zhenglou again, paying a visit to Shanghai.[26]

Obviously "Zhenglouji" has to be used with caution, but it provides the most reliable account of the affair, and where it can be checked with other references in Chen Diexian's poetry and prose, proves to be correct. It is also a poignant narrative in its own right. It begins in 1886 with his first meeting with Zhenglou. He was seven at the time and she three years older. She lived next door and attended classes with the Chen family's tutor, studying alongside one of Diexian's cousins. His mother (Wang) rather favored her as a wife for him, but she never took up the matter, and in 1888 Zhenglou's family suddenly moved away and did not return until 1894, when she was seventeen "and had a small measure of personal freedom." Although they recognized each other at a distance, they were both too embarrassed to speak. Finally, Diexian persuaded her younger sister to convey a letter to her. Gifts were exchanged and a romance began.

In 1896 her family moved again, to another part of Hangzhou, and Diexian was invited to a party for Zhenglou's nineteenth birthday. He gave the house, which up to that point had no name, the title Jiuxianglou, playing on her and her sister's names. He also began visiting Zhenglou every day, but she was reserved and he "was never able to treat her as anything more than a sister."[27]

The following year, 1897, his marriage to Zhu Shu took place. It had been arranged long before, when he was eight or nine.

> Zhenglou had nothing to say, she simply took to her bed with some ailment or other. I did not presume to try to console her. She never could articulate the things that concerned her most deeply.

However, early in 1898, when he was pressed by his mother into serving in Wukang, Zhenglou saw him to his boat, and from then on, whenever he came or went, she would meet him and they would visit places around Hangzhou. That summer, however, Zhu Shu, Diexian's wife, came upon a dozen photographs of Zhenglou among his poetry manuscripts and realized that he was in love with her. As a good wife by the standards of that time, she set about persuading Diexian's birth mother—Wang was long since dead—to let him take Zhenglou as his concubine. When the question was put to Zhenglou, however, she made no response.

Later that summer in Wukang, in despair over his future, Diexian became so ill that he fully expected to die. He wrote the long letter of farewell to Zhenglou that prompted her to send a boat for him. Their lovemaking and his relapse followed. When his mother heard that he was recuperating at Zhenglou's house, she sent for him and forbade him to leave home. Various solutions were then proposed for the lovers, but Zhenglou had heard gossip about his mother's severity and would not agree to become his concubine. Nor would his mother allow him to set her up as his mistress. Diexian thought of suicide, but could not bear to desert his wife. "Moreover, Zhenglou believed that so long as we remained alive we would eventually be united, and since suicide would do no good, why even consider it?"

In 1901, in an effort to liberate himself from his mother, he set up his shop, the Cui Li Company, in the center of the city, where Zhenglou would often visit him in the evening. She even sold some of her jewelry and lent him money to expand his business. In 1902, presumably with her money, he established the lithographic press. Although he was swindled and lost heavily, he managed to beg the amount of the loan from his mother and repaid Zhenglou in full. "She was more than ever impressed with my integrity, and our friendship grew even deeper. When I wanted to give up the business and return to my studies, she alone opposed the idea."

In 1903, when it seemed once more that Zhenglou might become his con-cubine, she got into some kind of trouble and had to flee the city. "Before leav-ing, she called me to her in the middle of the night, and we sat there crying until dawn. I have no memory of what was said. Then at dawn she and her whole family departed. I painted the picture *Parting from Zhenglou in Tears* to record the incident." In 1905 she returned and once more summoned him to her at night. The misunderstanding was cleared up, and he proceeded to paint the picture of their reunion.

Not until 1912[28] did Chen Diexian treat his amorous history again in nar-rative, but this time he did so in the form of a full-length novel, *Huangjin sui,* which answers the various questions that "Zhenglouji" had left open. Why did Diexian's mother (Wang) not act on her intention to arrange a marriage? Why did Zhenglou's family suddenly decamp? Why did Zhenglou never marry? And where did her money come from? Her father was presumably dead, and her mother, it soon appears, managed to maintain her high position in socie-ty by serving as mistress to a succession of rich men and by holding gambling parties in her house. The family's sudden move was to avoid the law. Later, her mother forces Zhenglou to sleep with a rich man, after first getting her drunk. Zhenglou resigns herself to her mother's profession, but treats her patrons with an imperious contempt. Her declared aim is to win her independence in a world dominated by money.

Of course, the novel also brings to imagined life the scenes and events mere-ly hinted at in the shorter works—the family compound, the petty jealousies and rivalries, the boat journeys, the economy of Wukang, the business of run-ning a newspaper, and so forth. More important, it shows the other girls and women in Diexian's life, the objects of his "extensive love."[29] They include his cousin Gu Yinglian, his wife Zhu Shu, Zhenglou, another cousin, a beautiful nanny or maid, a Wukang peasant girl to whom he never even spoke in life but with whom he communed after her death, and a Suzhou courtesan.

But the greatest distinction of his novel is the amount of the narrator's thought and feeling expressed in it. This is one of the great characteristics, per-haps the greatest, of the novels of the second decade of the twentieth century, that brief flowering of the literary Chinese novel. Nothing of this degree had ever been seen before in the novel, despite occasional attempts, usually through poetry, song, or letters, to express emotional thought. *Huangjin sui* represents the literature of indecision, perplexity, torment, despair, ecstasy, and humilia-tion, particularly in regard to love and affection. Its first-person narration is exploited to the full as we follow Diexian through his childhood and youth, from the age of seven to his early twenties. The Chinese literature of childhood had always been sparse, the great exception being Diexian's inspiration, *Story of the Stone. Huangjin sui* portrays all the stresses and strains on a youth growing up in a large and complex household during rapidly changing times. In this society the family was still powerful, but weakening, challenged by such new notions as free choice in marriage and also by the business world with its new opportunities for independence. The novel reveals a sensitive, talented, spoiled but frustrated boy trying with little success to reconcile his own amorous feelings with the social codes of the time.

It also presents itself as straight autobiography, opening with Diexian, under his pseudonym of Heaven Bore Me in Vain, justifying his intention to write about a pair of apparently incongruous subjects—money and love. "Here I shall speak, not of the money-grubbers of this world, but of my own life, in which money has bedeviled me at every turn. I propose to describe my experience in my own words in this book, so as to reveal the nature of the bedevilment."[30] The novel ends, as it began, with the act of writing. The author's creative flow is blocked following an imagined rejection by Zhenglou, and he cannot continue. Twelve years have passed, but still he cannot give his book an ending. His experience has not provided anything that can be called a conclusion, and he cannot bring himself to fabricate one.

> For to this day Zhenglou and Shan [Diexian's personal name in this novel] are together one moment and apart the next, without ever finding a definite resolution. Money will continue to bedevil them the rest of their days, and since my book is not some wish-fulfilling fantasy, I cannot bring their story to a premature close; it *has* to be left up in the air. Should my readers fail to understand this, they will just have to wait for a sequel.[31]

As we shall see, the "ending without an ending" is a common characteristic of Diexian's romances.[32]

The colophon by Zhou Zhisheng, Diexian's longtime friend and the editor of his collected prose and verse, asserts that this novel is straightforward autobiography, unlike *Leizhu yuan*, which was "half true and half false." Zhou even claims that this book can serve as a "reference tool" for the earlier one. It will surprise no one to learn that these claims are exaggerated. It *is* a novel, after all, and at certain points experience has been adapted to suit the novel form or to accomplish some private purpose. If we accept "Zhenglouji" as Diexian's most accurate account of his romantic history, we cannot help noticing things that have been altered. First is the death by drowning of Gu Yinglian, already mentioned. If she did indeed die of melancholia, as Diexian's wife asserts, his continued use of the drowning story may indicate his reluctance to face the fact that she evidently died because she was unable to marry him. That would help explain his violent reaction in the novel to the news of her death.

Second, the events of the climactic year 1898 have been jumbled, perhaps to avoid embarrassment. In the novel, it is only after Diexian has returned to Wukang that he notices the absence of the photographs and concludes that his wife has taken them. The confrontation between husband and wife is then carried on by letter. In "Zhenglouji," his wife comes upon the photographs while he is still at home, and the confrontation, which is not described, takes place in person. In fictional terms, the former situation has certain advantages—it leaves Diexian prey to a world of doubt and suspicion that would have been quickly resolved had he been at home.

The third point is the date of birth of his first child. We know that his son was born in 1897, before Diexian went to Wukang or slept with Zhenglou. In *Huangjin sui,* however, the birth is placed at the end of 1898, after his affair with Zhenglou has cooled. I am not sure of the reasons for this change, unless it was to simplify a cluttered story line. But it is hard to believe that the discovery of the photographs did not cause strains in his relationship with his wife, strains that would surely have been exacerbated had she had a baby in her arms. Diexian's desire to avoid any criticism of his wife is natural enough—she was his first reader, after all—and he presents her throughout as a woman of exemplary, indeed excruciating, nobility. His only apparent criticisms, uttered half in jest—of her excessive love for her baby or of her comparative prudishness—could easily be construed as praise. Perhaps Diexian transferred the confrontation of that summer to the more formal medium of the letter to spare himself the re-creation of a painful scene.

Two other novels by Chen Diexian deal less directly with the Zhenglou affair. In each case the narrator is a woman representing Diexian's wife. *Jiao Ying ji* (The story of Jiao and Ying) is a short novel in literary Chinese that was first published in installments in the *Shen bao* in February 1913.[33] The narrator is a wife in a triangular relationship with her husband, Ying, and his protégée, Jiao. Jiao is a modern woman who believes in free choice and has run away from the threat of an arranged marriage. The novel is presented as an account given by the wife, in the course of which she addresses her readers and even asks them for advice. It tells of a series of perplexing events—perplexing to her, anyway—

involving her husband and Jiao. The key element of the plot is her husband's concern over his indebtedness, which, so she is told, he intends to resolve by taking out a life insurance policy and then, after making the minimum number of payments, killing himself. In the end, when all other measures have failed, his debts are paid for him by his protégée, who claims to have saved up the money while performing as an actress on the London stage.

What impresses the reader is the fact that the focus is not on these events, but on the wife's gradual (yet always imperfect) understanding of what is going on. This is a psychological novel about her doubts and suspicions as she receives item after item of information, each more improbable than the last. She cannot find anything out for herself, because she is pregnant and in poor health, and so she gets the news, true or false, in other ways—by letter, from informants, from a Shanghai newspaper—all the while fretting over what construction to put upon it. Even at the end of the novel, she is still unsure whether the whole series of events—the debts, the insurance scheme, Ying's rescue by his protégée—may not be a gigantic hoax perpetrated by her husband, Jiao, and a few others enlisted for the purpose. She addresses her readers as follows:

> Didn't you see those two walking hand in hand in the garden by moonlight? Who could they have been, if not Ying and Jiao? That is why I simply cannot rid myself of my suspicions. Is the story I have told you the truth? Or did Ying and Jiao deliberately concoct it in order to deceive me? That is a question I am still not able to resolve, and I am hoping that you, my readers, will be able to enlighten me.[34]

The novel is attributed to a woman writer with the pseudonym Shuxin nüshi and also to Chen Diexian (under his pen name Heaven Bore Me in Vain). She is described as writing it down and he as polishing her draft. This is the same combination of authors as in the next novel I shall discuss, *Ta zhi xiao shi*,[35] in which it is quite clear that the narrator represents Chen Diexian's own wife. So the narrator in *Jiao Ying ji* must also be meant to represent her, and indeed, the story roughly parallels the triangular relationship of which that wifely narrator formed part. But let me put aside the question of her actual contribution until I have discussed the other novel.

The title *Ta zhi xiao shi* might be translated as *A Short Account of "Him"*; the point is that the first-person narrator is the new wife of a man one year her junior, and in her modesty she cannot bring herself to address him or refer to him in any way that would indicate her seniority. So she evades the issue by addressing him as "you" and referring to him as "he" or "him."

The work is a close account of a tense passage in the narrator's life. She is engaged to be married to someone whom she has never met but whose poems she has read in the local paper. She is delighted with the poems, but soon realizes from their contents that the subject is no literary construct, but a flesh-and-blood person with whom her fiancé has been in love since childhood. Despite all of her forebodings, however, she decides that it is too late to back out of the marriage.

The bulk of the novel describes in excruciating detail the four days of the wedding celebrations. I doubt if there is any other Chinese novel that describes a wedding in such detail—at least from the bride's point of view. Her natural apprehension about marrying someone she does not know is multiplied by her fears of a loveless marriage, and she tries to guess which of the women at the reception could be the subject of the poems.

Like *The Story of Jiao and Ying*, this is a psychological novel that exploits its narratorial point of view. It produces in the reader a peculiar claustrophobia, as the wife pathetically pieces together her husband's past history. Decorum prevents her from simply asking anyone, and when she tries asking her husband, he proves evasive, if not downright deceptive. So the greater part of the story consists of her guesswork—speculations, fears, suspicions, doubts, false leads, and, finally, discoveries. Only in the last of its six sections does the work take on a wider aspect. She decides that she will have to trace her husband's mistress, and so she turns detective, not in person, but by employing others to act for her.

Why does she try to trace the mistress? She analyzes the question at length. Her husband, solicitous though he is, shows her no emotional warmth, which is a situation she cannot bear. Her only recourse is to welcome the mistress into the household as a concubine.

The mistress is identified, and the wife takes the first opportunity, while her husband is out of town, to meet her. The two women strike up a sort of friendship, but the mistress is loath to give up her hard-won freedom—she is now economically self-sufficient—for a confining, hierarchical existence under a mother-in-law known for her strictness. When the husband returns, the two women combine to confront him and thoroughly shame him. An amicable triangular relationship is clearly going to develop, even though the mistress declines to join the household. At this point the wife at last feels able to call her husband by his name.

As I have said, the heart of the story is the wedding and the bride's emotional reaction to it. Here are the bride's thoughts as she prepares for the groom's arrival:

I simply shut my eyes and tried to meditate, sitting there quietly while the maids dressed me and made me up. To my way of thinking my body was just a puppet on a stage, acting out some tragic drama. Of all the unpleasant experiences in life, there is none to equal this. I imagined that his sorrow would be similar to mine, but I was still ashamed to face him. Were it not for me, that other girl would be the one he was marrying, and how happy they would be! If I felt as depressed as this, their depression must be truly unbearable! Compared to them, I had nothing to gain or lose, so why did I have to feel so sad? But then the thought struck me that from now on my person would belong to him, and if his heart did not belong to me, everything I did would seem detestable in his eyes. And if *he* found me detestable, his whole family would follow suit and find me detestable, too, in which case my life would be intolerable. I wasn't about to grovel in order to win his favor, and if I tried to take a hard line and gain the upper hand, he might not stand for it. How *should* I behave, then? I thought and thought, but couldn't come up with an answer. All this time the others around me were interrupting my train of thought with meaningless pleasantries designed to distract me.

Then some loud music struck up, and an excited hubbub arose among the women, as each tried to be first with the news that the bridegroom had arrived to escort me to his house. I was expecting him to arrive with tear-stained cheeks, as some indication of the misery he was feeling, but from what the maid said, he looked entirely different—the picture of joy, in fact.[36]

This novel is attributed to the same woman author, Shuxin nüshi, as *Jiao Ying ji.* Here she is described as giving an oral rendering that Heaven Bore Me in Vain (Chen Diexian) "lightheartedly recorded." Diexian's own personal romance is obvious enough, and in advertisements for the book it is referred to explicitly.[37] These could only have been issued with his approval; they appeared in the journal *Libailiu* (Saturday), which was published by the same house as virtually all of his novels. They not only claim that the novel is about the marriage of Chen Diexian and his wife but also assert that she was the author, and describe that fact as unprecedented in romantic fiction.

It is certainly not implausible that Zhu Shu might have written the novel herself. She had published a volume of poetry,[38] and she was responsible for some of the regular features in *Nüzi shijie*, the journal in which *Ta zhi xiao shi* first appeared. Her husband had already enlisted his eldest son in writing fiction, and he would soon recruit his daughter; presumably he would also have encouraged his wife to write. But the official bibliography, which seems quite scrupulous about giving credit to collaborators, ascribes this novel to Diexian alone. We must conclude that he wrote it himself, borrowing his wife's voice as narrator. However, even if she did not write the novel, she probably had some input into it.

The connections of *Ta zhi xiao shi* to Diexian's own history are even clearer than in the case of *Jiao Ying ji*. For example, the girl who lives next door represents Zhenglou; the girl Suyan represents Gu Yinglian; the maid Xiao Cai represents Xiao Tan; and so forth. Most telling of all, the husband shows his wife a novel he has written, and she does her best to identify the people behind the characters. The novel is clearly Diexian's *Leizhu yuan.*[39]

<hr>

Where do these novels of Chen Diexian's stand in relation to the romantic tradition of fiction? A broad distinction has to be drawn between the romance, as in novels such as *Shitouji* and *Huayue hen*, and the romantic comedy, as in the "brilliant and beautiful" (*caizi jiaren*) novels and many operas. The translation of *La dame aux camélias* in 1899 and the translations of Rider Haggard's *Joan Haste* in 1901–2 and 1905 appealed to the same sensibility as the romance. *Henhai hua* (Flowers in the sea of regret), published in 1905, and the vernacular *Qin hai shi* (Stones in the sea), completed in late 1905 and published the following year, were the earliest Chinese romances of the period.[40]

The novels with which Diexian's later romances are usually associated are the tragic romances in literary Chinese of the second decade of the century, sometimes labeled "mandarin duck and butterfly fiction." These works represent the short-lived vogue of the literary Chinese novel as well as the equally short-lived vogue of the tragic-romantic theme. The earliest is usually said to be He Zou's *Suiqin lou* (House of the broken zither), serialized in the journal *Dongfang zazhi* (Eastern miscellany) in 1911, but the most popular was Xu Zhenya's *Yu li hun* (Jade Pear spirit), serialized in the newspaper *Minquan bao* in 1912.[41] Diexian's romances, which, though distinctive, share some of the features of these novels, were written at about the same time, if not earlier. *Huangjin sui* was written in 1912, while *Yuanyang xue*, *Jiao Ying ji*, and *Lixiao ji* were, according to him, written as early as 1908.[42] (So far as we know, they were not published until 1912 or after.) If Diexian's statement is correct, he anticipated by several years the trend of tragic—or at least problem—romances in literary Chinese.

But Diexian's romances also differ from those of his contemporaries in crucial respects. First, the other works may contain a strong autobiographical element, flaunting before the public a version of the author as romantic subject, but none goes as far as some of Diexian's works. *Huangjin sui*, in particular, qualifies as plain autobiography as well as romantic fiction; in fact, it deserves a place in the literature of Chinese autobiography, especially that of childhood and youth. Second, although some of Diexian's novels, notably *Yutian henshi*, carry the same burden of tragedy as other works of the time, most of his romances have a wry and cynical tone rather than a tragic tone. And finally, as befits his autobiographical concerns, he dispenses altogether with the conventional kind of closure, and even with the conventional kind of shape. As the author-narrator of *Huangjin sui* puts it, these novels end without an ending.

NOTES

1. His personal name was Shousong. Other names were Xu, Xuyuan, and Xihongsheng. He generally reserved the name Tian Xu Wo Sheng for his fiction.
2. The most important source for Chen Diexian's early life is his collected verse and prose, *Xuyuan conggao*, published by his Family Industries (Jiating gongyeshe) in Shanghai with an author's preface of 1924 and a postface evidently written after 1927. It is in 10 fascicles, including two fascicles of his daughter's poetry. It contains a bibliography of the works not included, "Jiwai shumu," which was compiled by Chen Diexian himself in 1923. (In the preliminary edition of his collected works, *Xuyuan conggao chubian*, it is specifically attributed to him.) Within the collection itself, the most important biographical sources are Chen Diexian's memoirs of his father and his father's wives as well as autobiographical poems such as "Wo sheng pian" (My life) in fascicle 3. The narrative "Zhenglouji," also in fascicle 3, is even more important; it will be discussed later in this essay. A series of essays, "Wo zhi xinnian" (My New Years), in the *Shen bao* of March 7–10, 1916 contain material on his childhood. His eldest son, Chen Qu (styled Xiaodie, later known as Chen Dingshan) compiled a chronological biography that formed part of the *Tian Xu Wo Sheng jiniankan*, a special commemorative number published by the *Zixiu zhoukan* paper shortly after his father's death on March 24, 1940. (There is a copy in the Shanghai Library.) The son also wrote a memoir of his father as an industrialist, "Wode fuqin Tian Xu Wo Sheng—guohuo zhi yinzhe." It was published in his *Chun Shen jiuwen xuji* (Taipei: Chenguang yuekanshe, 1955), 179–204, and has been frequently reprinted.
3. See *Shen bao*, September 30, 1918.
4. See "Wode fuqin Tian Xu Wo Sheng," 181.
5. See his lectures on the *Great Learning*, *Daxue xinjiang*, 5th ed. (Shanghai: Sanyou shiyeshe, 1934), 4–6.
6. See vol. 3 (March 1915).
7. See *Shen bao*, May 12, 1918.

8. See his preface to his *tanci, Ziyou hua* (Flowers of freedom), published by Zhonghua tushuguan (China library) in 1916. (There is a copy in the Shanghai Library.) He wrote *Taohua ying* for his mother (Wang), who died in 1893.

9. It contains the songs of Chen Diexian and his close friends, He Songhua and Hua Chishi. The preface is dated the seventh month of 1900. (There is a copy in the Fu-dan University Library.)

10. See note 2 above. The bibliography says he wrote 50 novels but gives only 31 titles. It gives another 74 titles of novels that he translated or on which he collaborated with others.

11. "Jiuxianglou jishi shi," *Xuyuan conggao*, fascicle 2.

12. The edition is by the Cui Li Company of Hangzhou. (It describes itself as No. 25 of Chen Diexian's *Yisuyuan congshu*.) There is a copy in the Harvard-Yenching Library.

13. Wang Yanhong's works were republished by Ye Dehui in 1905 and made a great impact on later writers of romances.

14. His paintings were listed by Zheng Yimei; see *Zheng Yimei xuanji* (Harbin: Heilongjiang renmin chubanshe, 1991), 299.

15. In *Nüzi shijie*, beginning with no. 1 (Dec. 1914).

16. *Nüzi shijie* 1 (Dec. 1914), "Guixiu shihua," 2.

17. References are to the edition in the Zhongguo jindai xiaoshuo daxi series (Nanchang: Baihuazhou wenyi chubanshe, 1991).

18. "You Yiyuan you huai Gu-shi Zhongjie," *Xuyuan conggao*, 2, 19b–20a. The poems are also found in *Huangjin sui*, part 3, properly ascribed to Diexian.

19. Part 3, 37. Reference is to the edition reproduced in *Zhongguo jindai xiaoshuo shiliao huibian* (Taipei: Guangwen shuju, 1980). It is in three parts, undated, but with a postface by Zhou Zhisheng dated summer 1914. It is evidently a facsimile reprint of the 1914 edition published by Zhonghua tushuguan. Regrettably, no independent modern edition of the novel has been published. There is a translation by Patrick Hanan, *The Money Demon* (Honolulu: University of Hawaii Press, 1999).

20. The first is entitled "Bulu wuxu liuyue shiqi jishi" and the second "You liuyue shiba shi." *Xin Yiyuji*, 14ab. They are reprinted with the rest of the collection in *Xuyuan conggao*, fascicle 3.

21. Entitled "Zhenglou ju ying tu."

22. See *Zhenglou ping shi ji*, *Zhuzuolin* 1–4 (third through sixth months, 1907).

23. See *Xin Yiyuji*, 15b–18a. The narrative is reprinted in *Xuyuan conggao*, fascicle 3, but without the title.

24. "Xinchou chongjiuhou wuri Jiuxiang jishi," *Xuyuan conggao* 2, 42b–43a.

25. "Da Xu Heseng jianwen Zhenglou ying shi," *Xuyuan conggao* 3, 49b.

26. The poet Lian Quan published four poems in the *Shen bao* of May 7, 1913 on Diexian's *Zhenglou qi bie tu* and added a note mentioning that the former owner of the Zhenglou had come to Shanghai to see Wang Yongxia, but had failed to meet her so far because of the bad weather. Wang Yongxia, a poet, was the wife of Chen Rongxian, Diexian's younger brother. I have not been able to find Zhenglou's original name.

27. An English translation of "Zhenglouji" is appended to *The Money Demon*.

28. It was finished by October 1912. See his note added to two poems in the *Shen bao* of October 29, 1912,which refers to his "newly written *Zhenglouji* novel." We know from Zhou Zhisheng's 1914 postface to *Huangjin sui* that *Zhenglouji* was the title Diexian favored before changing his mind and settling on *Huangjin sui.*

29. See part 1, 99.

30. When *Huangjin sui,* which first appeared in 100 installments in the *Shen bao,* was published in book form in 1914, a change was made in the opening: the narration was attributed to Diexian's interlocutor instead of to him. See part 1, 1–2. In my opinion, the original opening, as found in the *Shen bao* of June 27, 1913, is superior.

31. *The Money Demon,* 278. The passage is from part 3, 77.

32. In her commentary at the end of Diexian's *Taohua ying,* published in 1900, Gu Yinglian praises it for precisely this reason. See the revised version of *Taohua ying, Xiaoxiang ying tanci* (Shanghai: Zhonghua tushuguan, 1918). There is a copy in the Fudan University Library.

33. Like a number of Diexian's novels, it was issued in book form by Zhonghua tushuguan in 1917. There is a copy in the Wason Collection of Cornell University Library.

34. Pp. 58–59.

35. It was published in six installments in *Nüzi shijie* (Dec. 1914 to July 1915) and then advertised as a book in 1917 by Zhonghua tushuguan.

36. 1 (Dec. 1914): 3–4.

37. See, for example, *Libailiu* 112 (June 4, 1921). Note that when the book was first advertised in 1917, it was attributed to Chen Diexian; see *Shen bao,* June 18, 1917.

38. *Lanyunlou yinchao.* So far as I know, it is not extant.

39. Other novels by Diexian contain elements also found in the autobiographical novels, notably the vernacular novel *Liu Feiyan,* published in *Yueyue xiaoshuo* in 1907–8, and *Lixiao ji,* serialized in *Shen bao* in 1913. *Manyuan hua,* serialized in *Shen bao* in 1914, is told in the first person and is about the narrator's boyhood.

40. See chapter 9 above.

41. See particularly C. T. Hsia, "Hsü Chen-ya's *Yu-li Hun:* An Essay in Literary History and Criticism," *Renditions* 17–18 (1982): 199–240. The essay includes an account of the sentimental-erotic tradition in Chinese fiction, especially in *Hua yue hen.* See also Leo Ou-fan Lee, *The Romantic Generation of Modern Chinese Writers* (Cambridge: Harvard University Press, 1973), 68–78, on the writer Su Manshu.

42. In his "Jiwai shumu," he says that *Yuanyang xue, Jiao Ying ji,* and *Lixiao ji* were written in the last year of the Guangxu reign. They were the first of Diexian's novels to be published in *Shen bao.*

CHAPTER II

The Technique of Lu Xun's Fiction

F OR A MAN driven by ideas of the social purpose and efficacy of literature, Lu Xun (1881–1936) was uncommonly concerned with technique.
The concern appears hardly at all in his essays; he never cared for analyzing his own work, and he passed off all questions on the subject with self-
deprecating humor. It is his fiction that forces the conclusion upon us. More
than with other writers, each story is a venture in technique, a fresh try at the
perfect matching of subject and form. The high demands Lu Xun placed on
technique may account for some of the difficulty he found in writing fiction—
his stories had to be squeezed out of him, he said—but at the same time, it is
the obsession with technique, combined with the quality of the emotions and
judgments we sense behind his work, that makes his handful of stories the
most powerfully expressive art in modern Chinese literature.

"Technique" is intended here in its most extravagant meaning: everything
outside the "lump of experience."[1] Within this meaning, it is the larger, governing elements, such as rhetoric, narrative method, and fictional mode, "gross
technique" as they might be called, that are the subject of this essay, not Lu
Xun's maze of subtle, restricted, most verbal effects.

By something a little less than a coincidence, at the very time Lu Xun's first
vernacular story appeared, his brother, Zhou Zuoren, was completing a frankly
envious survey of modern Japanese fiction:

In China we have been talking about the New Fiction now for almost
twenty years, but we have practically nothing to show for it. Why *is* this?

In my opinion, the reason lies in the Chinese writer's unwillingness or inability to imitate.[2]

Although Lu Xun's first vernacular story, "Kuangren riji" (Diary of a madman, 1918), is no imitation but a fully independent work, it is steeped in the themes and conventions of Russian literature.[3] Lu Xun himself indicated the traditions within which his early stories had been written, and touched on the relations of his fiction with that of other writers. The obvious starting point, then, in any discussion of technique is with these literary relations as Lu Xun saw them.

He made two references to the subject, both suggestive rather than specific. In his 1933 essay "How I First Came to Write Fiction," he confessed to having no preparation, at the time he wrote "Diary of a Madman," other than the hundred or more foreign novels and stories he had read plus a little medical knowledge.[4] He did most of the reading during the years in Tokyo, from 1906 through 1909, when he and Zhou Zuoren threw themselves into the translation of foreign literature, especially Russian and Eastern European literature, with the avowed aim of altering Chinese ways of thought. To find out which authors were worth translating for his purpose, Lu Xun also read some literary history and criticism. His favorite writers at the time, he tells us, were Gogol, Sienkiewicz, Natsume Sōseki, and Mori Ogai. The activity came to a virtual halt after 1909, when he returned to China; he had no time to read fiction for the next five or six years. In 1935, in his introduction to a volume of the comprehensive anthology of the new literature, *Zhongguo xinwenxue daxi*, Lu Xun dealt with the question more directly.[5] The technique (specifically, the presentation and style) of his early stories created a stir in China, he wrote, simply because his readers were unfamiliar with European literature. He described the relationship of Gogol's "Diary of a Madman" to his own story, and the influence of Nietzsche's *Also Sprach Zarathustra*. And the close of his third story, "Yao" (Medicine), "clearly retains the somber chill one associates with Andreyev." From that point on, he "escaped from the influence of foreign writers," but although his skill matured, his later stories showed a lessening of emotional force.

Zhou Zuoren is far more informative. He was a born memoirist who felt none of Lu Xun's inhibitions about discussing himself or his writing directly, and one gains the impression, reading him, that the years of translation and discovery in Tokyo were the great years of his life. He was a literary collaborator of Lu Xun's at this period, indeed almost an alter ego, and his views are therefore of great value. Not only did the brothers work closely together, they even shared literary tastes. Gogol, Sienkiewicz, and Garshin were Zhou Zuoren's passions,[6] as they were Lu Xun's, and both men admired Vasilii Sologub, the Russian decadent.[7] Andreyev and Nietzsche, on the other hand, were inexplicable tastes to Zhou, who wondered whether his brother's passions for Andreyev and the Tang poet Li He could be related, thinking, no doubt, of the morbid imagination possessed by each. In Tokyo, the brothers planned the journal *Xin sheng* (*Vita Nuova* was to have been its alternative title), and, when that aborted, turned their energies to the translation series *Yuwai xiaoshuoji* (Anthology of foreign fiction), of which two volumes appeared in 1909.[8] The work was shared between them, with Zhou Zuoren translating from English and Lu Xun from German. On translations outside of the *Anthology*, they often worked in tandem, in time-honored fashion, with Zhou Zuoren translating orally and Lu Xun putting what he said into literary Chinese. After the brothers returned to China, they remained in close touch, even though Lu Xun was in Beijing and Zhou in Shaoxing. We can see from Lu Xun's diary that they exchanged letters every few days, and that there was a constant flow of books and manuscripts back and forth. After Zhou joined him in Beijing in April 1917, they were closely associated until the family quarrel of 1923. By talent and opportunity, Zhou Zuoren was uniquely able to record and evaluate Lu Xun's use of foreign literature.

He discussed the question in two places. One was a short article in the supplement of the *Chen bao*, just after the newspaper's serial publication of "A Q zhengzhuan."[9] It is the first contribution to the debate over the interpretation of that story that raged during the 1920s, but it is also a perceptive piece of literary criticism. The story's technique is described as that of irony (*fan yu*), a rare feature of Chinese fiction. The only two significant earlier examples are the Qing novels *Rulin waishi* (The scholars) and *Jing hua yuan* (Flowers in the mirror); the late-Qing satirical novel is considered too strident to qualify. Zhou goes on to assert that "the origin of the technique of 'The True Story of Ah Q,' to my knowledge, lay in foreign short stories, most notably those of the Russian Gogol and the Pole Sienkiewicz, while the Japanese writers Mori Ogai and Natsume Sōseki also asserted considerable influence." A few works are mentioned: Gogol's "Overcoat" and "Madman's Diary," Sienkiewicz's "Charcoal Sketches" and "Sachem," Ogai's "Chinmoku no tō" (Tower of silence), and Sōseki's *Wagahai wa neko de aru* (I am a cat), and it is worth noting that Zhou Zuoren and Lu Xun had translated "Charcoal Sketches" together in 1908–9,[10] that Zhou translated "Sachem" in 1912,[11] and that Lu Xun later translated the Ogai story.[12] By the technique of irony, Zhou means the humorous treatment of tragic, pathetic, or outrageous themes. But the irony of

"Ah Q," for all its foreign influence, is still distinctive; it is "long on the intellectual side and short on passion, long on hatred and short on love," rather like the satire of Jonathan Swift. (Zhou translated two of Swift's essays, "Directions to Servants" and the famous " A Modest Proposal," and it was perhaps to this mode of Swiftian irony that he was referring.)[13] In late 1936, after Lu Xun's death, in the first of two articles on his brother's literary education, Zhou reports that, in 1922, he showed the draft of his article on "Ah Q" to Lu Xun, who accepted his arguments.[14]

The second of the 1936 articles is Zhou Zuoren's most sustained attempt to treat this subject. It records in absorbing detail the halcyon period of discovery and translation in Tokyo: the bookshops; the foreign literary journals, especially the Berlin journal of translated literature, *Aus Fremden Zungen*; and the cheap series, such as the Universal-Bibliothek published by Reclam. With the first money they earned from a joint translation they rushed out and bought the whole set of Constance Garnett's translations of Turgenev, fifteen volumes in all. Lu Xun bought and pored over the massive, systematic histories of world literature by Gustav Karpeles and Johannes Scherr, with their handsome portraits of literary heroes like Mankiewicz and Petöfi.[15] His principal literary guide, however, was the radical thinker and critic Georg Brandes, a man of protean interests. Zhou Zuoren goes on to list the writers, and sometimes the particular works, that Lu Xun favored. (In the following summary of his list, I have also inserted other relevant information.) Among the Russian writers, Andreyev was Lu Xun's chief passion, a taste that Zhou did not share, except for three works, "Ben Tobit," "The Seven That Were Hanged,"[16] and *The Confessions of a Little Man During Great Days*.[17] Lu Xun translated two of Andreyev's short stories for the 1909 *Anthology of Foreign Fiction*, and began, but never completed, a translation of the long symbolist piece, *The Red Laugh*.[18] He translated two more stories for another anthology published in 1922.[19] There was also the brilliant writer of short stories, V. M. Garshin; Lu Xun translated his antiwar story, "Four Days," for the 1909 *Anthology of Foreign Fiction*,[20] and later, his "A Very Short Romance."[21] Other writers include Lermontov, Chekhov, Korolenko , and, of course, Gogol, not so much for *Dead Souls* as for "Diary of a Madman," "The Tale of how Ivan Ivanovich Quarreled with Ivan Nikiforovich," which Lu Xun planned to translate,[22] and the comedy *The Inspector General*. At this stage, Lu Xun was not impressed with Gorky. Among Polish writers, Sienkiewicz was his chief liking, not for the historical novels that made him internationally famous but for the short and medium-length stories of Polish and American life—Sienkiewicz lived in the United States from 1876 to 1878—that he wrote at the beginning of his career. Zhou

Zuoren and Lu Xun translated "Charcoal Sketches" together in 1908–9, but it was not published until 1914.[23] Zhou also mentions another long Sienkiewicz story, "Bartek the Victor," which bears a general similarity to "Charcoal Sketches"; to Zhou's regret, it had never been translated.[24] Among Czech writers, Lu Xun liked Neruda and Vrchlický, whose short pieces, humorous, wistful, and lyrical, were available in Reclam translations. Two works that Lu Xun greatly admired and intended to translate were *A Hóhér Kötele* (The hangman's rope), Petöfi's only novel, a highly macabre and melodramatic affair, and a volume of rural stories by the Finnish writer Päivärinta.[25] He had no interest in the French realists or naturalists, or the Japanese naturalists. His favorite Japanese writer was Sōseki; Zhou mentions *Wagahai wa neko de aru*, and notes that Lu Xun snapped up the installments of *Gubijinsō* as they appeared in the *Asahi Shimbun*.[26] He repeats his notion of influence, chiefly with regard to "Ah Q," but does not use the word "irony" on this occasion. Gogol and Sienkiewicz were the main models, with their use of a "humorous style to write about harrowing events," but, in a less obvious way, Lu Xun was also influenced by the delicate, felicitous touches of Sōseki's satire.

Although the years from 1906 to 1909 were the period in which Lu Xun's art germinated, his interest in fiction did not lie entirely dormant during the following years, as he seems to say; his statement has to be taken relatively. His first real short story,[27] "Huai jiu" (Looking back to the past), was written in 1911,[28] and his diary, which begins only in 1912, shows him receiving fiction intermittently from the Tokyo bookshops, especially Maruzen, as well as from his brother in Shaoxing, although most of the foreign books he read at this time were treatises on art. For example, in 1914, he received Japanese translations of novels by Turgenev, Dostoevsky, and Sienkiewicz, as well as three unnamed works.[29] He sent various English translations on to his brother, and also arranged for the publication of their translation of "Charcoal Sketches."[30]

At first sight, the attitudes that run through this account of his literary tastes seem to conform to contemporary standards circa 1910. His embrace of Andreyev, for example, and his dismissal of Gorky are exact reflections of common contemporary opinion and exact contradictions of their current reputations.[31] But his attitudes actually obey a much deeper logic. Lu Xun rejected the European realists and naturalists, as well as the Japanese naturalists, not because of Flaubert's objectivity or Zola's social determinism—later Chinese writers had no trouble using realistic techniques for social and political ends—but because he was simply not interested in the techniques of realism. His taste for Andreyev, who flirted with symbolism, and for Gogol, Sienkiewicz, and Sōseki, who specialized in satire and even irony, are indications of a search for

222 The Technique of Lu Xun's Fiction

a basically different method. But let me defer my discussion of this point until I have examined the specific relations between Lu Xun's stories and the work of some of these writers.

When Lu Xun says that the ending of his story "Yao" (Medicine, written in 1919) has the "somber chill" of Andreyev, is the remark to be taken generally or with regard to a particular Andreyev story? It is perfectly possible to take it generally. One of Andreyev's preoccupations was with what he called "metaphysical horror," a development of the purely physical horror of Edgar Allan Poe's tales. "The Abyss," for example, concerns the extinction of a person's belief in himself, the crushing of his moral identity, while "Lazarus" is full of cosmic horror.[32] The bleak and terrible scene in "Medicine" in which the revolutionary's mother, at his graveside, asks for a sign from the crow's flight (a potent symbol) and receives none, can be likened to the general effect that Andreyev sought to achieve. But this last scene in "Medicine" is so similar to the ending of Andreyev's "Silence" that I believe Lu Xun had that particular story in mind. "Silence" is Andreyev's most famous short story and part of his legend. It was the story that Gorky read to a weekly literary gathering in Moscow in 1900 and that made the author's name overnight.[33] And it was one of two Andreyev stories that Lu Xun translated for the 1909 *Anthology of Foreign Fiction*.[34]

"Silence" is the story of a proud, unbending man, Father Ignaty, whose daughter, having run away to St. Petersburg without his blessing, has now returned home broken in spirit and unable to articulate her despair. She takes her life by throwing herself under a train, and the shock leaves her mother paralyzed, unable to speak. The story is about Father Ignaty's battle with the silence that threatens to engulf him as he calls upon his dead daughter, in her old bedroom and again at her graveside, and upon his dumb, stricken wife, to speak to him. This is how the third of the four sections ends, as retranslated from Lu Xun's version in the *Anthology*:

> "Speak!" he repeated. His eyes, glaring, swept around the room, and he stretched out his arms. But the little attic room was silent. The whistle of a train could be heard in the distance. Ignaty glared more wildly than ever, and looking over his shoulder seemed to see the ghost of a horribly disfigured corpse. He picked himself up from the bed, slowly raised his gaunt hand, and pressed it against his forehead. At the door, he again whispered "Speak!" but all he received for an answer was—silence.[35]

This is the end of the story:

"My dear!" he stretched up toward his wife and gazed into her eyes. But neither forgiveness nor anger was to be found in them. Perhaps she had forgiven him, perhaps she even pitied him, but her eyes showed nothing at all; they were still and silent. And silence reigned over that lonely, desolate house.[36]

There is thus a slight but distinct thematic similarity between the main movement of "Silence" and the concluding movement of "Medicine." In addition, there are other, probable indications that "Silence" was in Lu Xun's mind, perhaps unconsciously, as he completed his story. Several times in Andreyev, silence is imagined as something tremulous and vibrating, on one occasion as a taut wire or string, which may have suggested the mysterious sound near the end of "Medicine":

The wind had dropped long before, and the dry grass stood stiff like wire. A tremulous sound vibrated and then grew fainter and fainter until it finally ceased to exist altogether, and the whole place became as still as death.[37]

The translation actually obscures the parallel contained in the dead metaphor of the Chinese, which runs "stiff like iron thread. A thread of sound. . . ." In "Silence," the lych-gate of the graveyard seems to open "a huge mouth surrounded by white, gleaming teeth," and in "Medicine," in a brilliant—perhaps too brilliant—simile, the grave mounds look like "*mantou* set for a rich man's birthday feast." Both stories contain images of immobility, the crow in "Medicine" "as if cast in metal" and the coachman in "Silence" who waits "as if made of stone" for some passenger who never comes. And the freed canary of "Silence" represents, at least to the servant's and Ignaty's minds, the dead girl's soul, while the crow in "Medicine" is associated by the mourner, in some degree, with her dead son's spirit.

The story of Andreyev's that is closest in theme to "Medicine" is "The Seven That Were Hanged," written in 1908 and known to Lu Xun. Although it is the most famous of the many Russian stories that describe the execution of revolutionaries in the aftermath of the 1905 revolution, it contains no hint of the technique Lu Xun was to use in "Medicine," not even the slight, local similarity that can be claimed for "Silence." The story that presaged, and perhaps suggested, the technique of "Medicine" was "Ben Tobit," on an entirely different theme. Ben Tobit is the man who had the toothache on the day Jesus was crucified. The story is told through his petty, irritated consciousness, as he plays the domestic martyr (deadly irony!) and is cosseted and fussed over by wife and friends. Sun Fuyuan, a close friend and onetime editor, says that Lu Xun gave

"Ben Tobit" as an example of a foreign work similar to "Medicine."[38] He must have been referring to the oblique presentation of the martyr's death through the mundane concerns of the teahouse owner and the callous conversation of the teahouse habitués, which does, of course, resemble the central technique of "Ben Tobit." Lu Xun's comment is noteworthy as a rare example of his serious interpretation of his own work. He does not say that "Ben Tobit" influenced the technique of "Medicine," but the conclusion seems inescapable. Oddly, the technique of "Ben Tobit" is exceptional in Andreyev, who favored the direct method of "Silence" and "The Seven That Were Hanged," whereas the technique of "Medicine" is, I shall argue, related to one of Lu Xun's main modes. Sun Fuyuan goes on to give another example from Russian literature, Turgenev's prose poem "The Worker and the Man with the White Hands,"[39] which, from the context, we must take as another parallel offered him by Lu Xun. Thematically, it is very close to "Medicine" and may have played some part in the story's composition.

Lu Xun acknowledged the debt of his "Diary of a Madman" to Gogol's story of similar name, while at the same time sharply distinguishing the two.[40] The relationship is important in terms of form, and there is a certain similarity of tone, but that is all. Gogol's story lacks the systematic symbolism that is the main point of Lu Xun's "Diary," and any comparison of the two stories is likely to dwell on the differences rather than the similarities. There is no known model for the complex method Lu Xun used, but the closest parallel appears to be *The Red Laugh*, Andreyev's symbolist novel on the horrors of war, which Lu Xun once began to translate.[41]

The Red Laugh is in the form of fragments of a diary kept by two brothers, one succeeding the other. The first brother, after service in the war, goes mad and dies, and the second fights off the encroaching madness until the final apocalyptic scene in which the earth gives up its dead. It appears that the red laugh issues from the earth when the earth itself goes mad, infecting people who participate in war or are contaminated by it in any way, even by reading of it in the newspaper. The second brother is struggling to preserve his values in a world that has come to accept war and killing as natural. It is an opposite vision to that of Lu Xun's madman. In the following passage, he explains his desperation to his crazed brother (the narrator), a war veteran whose legs have been amputated, as the latter takes a bath:

> "Judge for yourself: one cannot teach people mercy, sense, logic—teach them
> to act consciously for tens and hundreds of years running with impunity.
> And, in particular, to act consciously. One can become merciless, lose all sen-

sitiveness, get accustomed to blood and tears and pain—for instance, butchers, and some doctors and officers do, but how can one renounce truth after one has known it? In my opinion, it is impossible. . . . But time passes, and I'm beginning to get accustomed to all those deaths, sufferings and all this blood; I feel that I'm getting less sensitive, less responsive in my everyday life and respond only to great stimulants, but I cannot get accustomed to *war*, my brain refuses to understand and explain a thing that's senseless in its basis. Millions of people gather at one place, giving their actions order and regularity, kill each other, and it hurts everybody equally, and all are unhappy— what is it if not madness?" My brother turned round and looked at me enquiringly with his short-sighted, artless eyes.

"The red laugh," said I merrily, splashing about.[42]

Some of the animal imagery is reminiscent of Lu Xun's stories:

. . . prisoners, a group of trembling, terrified men. When they were led out of the train, the crowd gave a roar—the roar of an enormous, savage dog, whose chain is too short and not strong enough.

For men are always murderers, and their calmness and generosity is the calmness of a well-fed animal, that knows itself out of danger.

"You pretend that you are men, but I see claws under your gloves and the flat skull of an animal under your hat."[43]

And the antiwar speaker sounds a note heard in Lu Xun's "Diary of a Madman":

"You, who are young, you, whose lives are only just beginning, save yourselves and the future generations from this horror, from this madness."

"Suppose I'm mad, but I am speaking the truth."[44]

The conception of *The Red Laugh*, though similar to that of Lu Xun's story, also has pronounced differences. The mass of men, including the first brother, has gone mad; only a few have remained sane, particularly the antiwar speaker and the second brother. In the "Diary," the madman's insight is a discovery, he thinks, in the history of evolution, whereas the second brother in *The Red Laugh* is fighting to keep his sane vision when everyone around him has gone mad. But the great technical difference is in the obliqueness of the "Diary's" method: a madman's insight is to be taken, symbolically, as the truth. *The Red Laugh*'s method is direct; a sane man's perceptions are simply to be accepted as sane. Furthermore, its symbols are of the numinous kind, like a poetic metaphor, without clear reference, whereas the symbolism of the "Diary," for all its force, is rational and referential, in a word, allegorical.

According to Zhou Zuoren's claim, which Lu Xun apparently accepted, the technique of "A Q zhengzhuan" (True Story of Ah Q, 1921) was modeled on that of Gogol and Sienkiewicz, and also, to a smaller degree, on that of Sōseki. This was the technique of irony, defined as the treatment of tragic or outrageous matters in a comic spirit, and Zhou even notes that actual traces of the influence of Gogol and the others may be seen in "Ah Q." The claim seems incontrovertible. None of Lu Xun's stories is derivative in any important sense of that word, but the links to other literatures are both interesting and important, and nowhere are they stronger than in "Ah Q." The strongest is to Sienkiewicz.

In his early short stories, Sienkiewicz specialized in a sardonic irony. In "Sachem," a story about the fate of a tribe of American Indians, this is how the new town where the settlers have wiped out the Black Snake Indians is described:

> On the square where they had hanged the last Black Snakes, the citizens had erected a philanthropic institution. Every Sunday the pastors taught in the churches love of one's neighbor, respect for the property of others, and similar virtues essential to a civilized society; a certain traveling lecturer read a dissertation "On the rights of nations."[45]

Two longer works mentioned by Zhou in his 1936 article, "Charcoal Sketches" and "Bartek the Victor," show the feature he referred to. "Charcoal Sketches," despite its title, is a single long story, in eleven sections and an epilogue, that Sienkiewicz wrote in 1876 and published in installments in the Warsaw daily *Gazeta Polska*.[46] Each section has an ironic heading, like the sections of "Ah Q." It tells of the intrigue of the village secretary, Zolzik, a reptilian figure, to obtain the wife of the peasant Repa, and of Repa's murder of his own wife. Zhou Zuoren translated it, and Lu Xun revised his draft, in Tokyo in 1908–9, and Lu Xun had it published in Beijing in 1914. "Bartek the Victor" is in ten sections, without titles.[47] It was published in installments during 1882 in the Warsaw daily *Slowo*, at a time when Sienkiewicz was its editor. Unlike the case of "Charcoal Sketches," there is no certainty that Lu Xun read it, only a strong probability. It is mentioned in the notes on Sienkiewicz that accompany the revised *Anthology* of 1920, but it is not clear who wrote the notes; Lu Xun wrote the preface, Zhou tells us, even though his own name is attached to it. It is also mentioned in the notes to Zhou's translation of "Sachem," which appeared in *Xin qingnian* on October 15, 1918,[48] and again in Zhou's 1936 article on Lu Xun's literary education in a brief list of Sienkiewicz's stories; he must mean us to conclude that Lu Xun knew the story.

Bartek is a peasant living in a remote village in Poland, a man of great strength and even greater stupidity, who is drafted by the occupying Prussians to fight against the French in the war of 1870. His strength and his fierce temper serve him well in the war, and he returns to the village covered in medals— and with a head full of illusions. The illusions are quickly dispelled as he gets into a quarrel with a German settler, loses his property, and ends up with a jail sentence. In the election that occurs at the end of the story, he is intimidated into voting for the Prussian candidate, and when that fact becomes known, he loses whatever sympathy from his compatriots he had once enjoyed.

In both stories, the narrator adopts a tone of lofty irony in describing the pathetic or sordid events that take place in the village. The success of Zolnik's squalid scheme is labeled "The Victory of Genius";[49] earlier we have been nudged with the remark "Here I hope that the reader has understood sufficiently and estimated the genial plan of my sympathetic hero."[50] When Zolzik lusts after Repa's wife, the narrator explains that "the greatest men have committed follies under the influence of passion," and when Zolzik, chased by a dog, slips down in the pigsty, "his position . . . was so dreadful, indeed, that one would need the style of Victor Hugo to describe it."[51] To explain some trivial matter facing the village council, the policy of nonintervention of John Bright, the proponent of laissez-faire, is invoked.[52] In "Bartek the Victor," Bartek's part in the battle of Gravelotte is introduced as follows: "O Muse! Sing now of my Bartek, that posterity may know what he did!"[53] And afterward, in all his pathetic collisions with reality, he is referred to as "the victor of Gravelotte and Sedan."

The connections with Ah Q extend beyond narrative technique and general theme to certain broad features that may be the traces of influence that Zhou Zuoren observed. The disquisition on Ah Q's name is foreshadowed by a passage at the beginning of "Bartek the Victor." We are also told about Zolzik that "if he had proper biographies of all our celebrated people, we should read in the life of this uncommon man, that . . . ,"[54] and the term "proper biographies" may, just conceivably, have set Lu Xun thinking of his own ironical discussion of biography, and even of his title (*zhengzhuan*), although the story itself gives a different explanation. Zolzik's romantic longings are treated with the same high irony as Ah Q's, replete with classical analogies, although the Chinese analogies characteristically refer to woman in a different conception, as *femme fatale*. Bartek returns to the village in glory, as does Ah Q, and then finds himself on the wrong side in the election, as Ah Q does in the revolution. Zolzik is feted by the well-to-do families, distasteful as he is to them. And the crowd, in the end, turns against Zolzik's victims, Repa and his wife, and lauds Zolzik himself, simply because his scheme has been successful.

We may say that Ah Q is in the *tradition* of the two Sienkiewicz stories. The governing technique is, in a general sense, the same: the use of high irony on the narrator's part to treat the meanest figures of village life. But at the same time, the distinctive qualities of "Ah Q" are among its most significant. It makes less use of pathos than the Sienkiewicz stories; indeed, the sole object of pathos is Ah Q himself, and then only in the concluding stages. And the character of Ah Q, though superficially similar to aspects of Sienkiewicz's characters, is really of a different order, submitting to a far wider range of symbolic interpretation. Bartek may stand for the Polish peasantry, but he cannot be made to transcend his class, like Ah Q, and represent some part of the national character.

Gogol must have been one source of the Sienkiewicz technique, but his irony is not so pronounced, his works do not seem to touch "Ah Q" at so many thematic points, and he does not mix the comic and pathetic modes as Sienkiewicz and Lu Xun do. Irony is the central device of Natsume Sōseki's *Wagahai wa neko de aru*, but it is a very different kind of irony, and even in Zhou Zuoren's claim, Sōseki influenced Lu Xun only in terms of the individual phrase or figure.

I believe that the influence of Sienkiewicz's and Gogol's technique extends to other stories written at about the same time as "Ah Q." "Mingtian" (Tomorrow, 1919) enlists the narrator's lofty irony in the cause of pathos—"she was only a simple woman, and . . ."—and is presumably related to that side of Sienkiewicz's art. Indeed, the incident in "Tomorrow" in which the widow takes her sick child to the doctor, waits her turn, is treated condescendingly, and then struggles to carry the child home, meeting the bibulous peasant on the way, is strikingly similar in its outline, and even in some of its details, to the journey Repa's wife, in "Charcoal Sketches," makes to town, carrying her child.[55] It appears that in writing "Tomorrow," Lu Xun was affected, in his imaginative conception of the story, by vestiges of both the technique and the theme of "Charcoal Sketches," just as in "Ah Q." "Fengbo" (Storm in a teacup, 1920) is one of only two other Lu Xun stories to use this kind of narratorial irony, though it is far less pronounced than in "Ah Q." The story is a little reminiscent of Gogol in its benign cynicism without pathos or tragedy. It is a comic study in various shades of ignorance and self-deception, and the eulogy of the village by the boatload of passing literati has the same effect as Gogol's ironic apostrophe to his Mirgorod.

In a different context, Zhou Zuoren also points out the similarity between Garshin's "Scarlet Blossom" and Lu Xun's "Changming deng" (The lamp that was kept alight, 1925).[56] Garshin's madman thinks that the scarlet flowers in the asylum embody all the world's evil and must be uprooted. Lu Xun's madman has the same conviction about the lamp that is kept eternally alight in the village temple—it must be put out. But the similarity is confined to theme, in fact, to a single thematic device, and does not extend to technique; Garshin's madman is the center of consciousness, while Lu Xun's is described obliquely, through the perceptions of others. Lu Xun may have learned much from Garshin's formal technique, but the influence is not apparent in this particular story.

Lu Xun notes that his story "Xingfu de jiating" (Happy family, 1924) is in "imitation" of Xu Qinwen.[57] Xu, a young writer from the same part of Zhejiang as Lu Xun, audited his course in Chinese fiction at Beijing University, and his stories for the *Chen bao* supplement caught Lu Xun's eye. He became a protégé of Lu Xun and later a prolific writer of fiction, and in the 1950s he drew on his knowledge to write several volumes of studies of Lu Xun and his work. The story that Lu Xun claimed to have imitated was Xu's "Lixiangde banlü" (The ideal companion), a farcical piece written with a good deal of irony. It was written in 1923 and then collected in Xu's first volume of short stories, *Guxiang* (Hometown), which was published in 1926 with Lu Xun's aid.[58] The resemblance between the two stories is actually very slight, a point of theme only, and Lu Xun himself says that, although he meant to write something close to Xu's story, he strayed from his intention.[59] Xu felt that his stories had introduced Lu Xun to a fictional treatment of a younger generation of people than he had previously written about, and this impression seems to be borne out by the comment of Lu Xun's reported in the preface to *Guxiang*. On the other hand, Xu also notes the comment of Xu Guangping, Lu Xun's wife, that, in talking of imitation, Lu Xun had been mainly concerned to endorse the work of an obscure young writer.

The general relationship between Lu Xun's stories and Xu Qinwen's is more important than the connection between these two particular works. Actually, Lu Xun's "Happy Family" has more in common with Xu's "Yishou xiaoshi de xiejiu" (Composing a little poem) than with "The Ideal Companion"; it is the story of a poetaster writing a piece of doggerel amid all the vicissitudes of domestic life, and it is told through the man's consciousness. The relation between Lu Xun and his protégé seems to have been a reciprocal one. Certainly, Xu Qinwen made his own position as literary disciple abundantly clear. Some of his pieces, for example "Mao de beiju" (The tragedy of the cats),[60] appear to have been stimulated by Lu Xun's stories, and his studies of village life are even set in Lu Xun's imaginary Luzhen. On the other hand, the stories of Lu Xun's second collection, *Panghuang* (published in 1926), show some features not fully present in the first collection, *Nahan* (1923), but that had already appeared in a simpler, more rudimentary form in the stories Xu Qinwen had written in 1922 and 1923, between the two collections. I am not referring to Xu's treatment of the younger generation or of relations between the sexes, although this is of some importance in *Panghuang*, especially in "Happy Family" and "Shang shi" (Regret for the past, 1925), but to his use of that most restrained kind of irony, not present in the narrator's tone, that arises from the action itself.[61] Lu Xun used this technique in stories of character irony such as "Happy Family" and "Feizao" (Soap, 1924), in comparison with which Xu's stories, for example "Yi can" (A meal), seem like sketches or exercises. It is impossible to say to what extent Lu Xun observed and was stimulated by this technique in Xu's writing, and to what extent he himself fostered it. It seems clear, however, that one source of the technique was the *Rulin waishi* (The scholars), the masterpiece of this kind of irony, which Xu Qinwen heard discussed in Lu Xun's lectures.[62]

This brief investigation has shown that Lu Xun, in choosing an artistic tradition within which to work, was drawn primarily to Gogol, Sienkiewicz, and Sōseki, with their range of ironic techniques, and only secondarily to Andreyev and literary modernism. ("Ben Tobit," it must be remembered, was the exception in Andreyev.) The concept of irony, so far left undefined, is thus an appropriate point from which to begin the analysis of Lu Xun's technique.

The term "irony" escaped long ago from the fold of critical definition and has since led critics on a wild and exhilarating chase; its recapture does not appear to be imminent. There is thus no advantage in trying to find the highest common factor in its current uses; any meaning obtained will be so bland as to suit many different types of writing. We shall have to choose an appropriate basic or core definition of irony and limit our use of the term to it.

Basic or hard-core irony, then, is *the technique of raising something in the audience's estimation while appearing to lower it, or of lowering something in the audience's estimation while appearing to raise it.* Though not the most common definition, this is an old one, expressed in Quintilian's *laudis adsimulatione detrahere et vituperationis laudare*.[63] The most common definition refers to truth and falsehood rather than to praise and blame (raising and lowering), but that is too restrictive, confining irony to the cognitive truth of statements rather than to a total effect that may be as much emotional as cognitive; it is unsuitable for the definition of a rhetorical figure. In comparison with our notion of irony, "satire" will be taken as indicating both a technique and a purpose. As Ronald Paulson notes, "contemporary definitions of satire usually join two terms: 'wit or humor founded on fantasy or a sense of the grotesque or absurd' for one, and 'an object of attack' for the other; or fantasy and a moral standard; or indirection and judgment."[64] The purpose of satire is ridicule, which it achieves by various methods of reduction or belittling. The "lowering" techniques of irony may serve this function—in Lu Xun's fiction they are the primary methods—although they are not the only techniques that satire can use. The "raising" techniques of irony, of course, do not contribute to satire.

In this definition, irony is a rhetorical figure, not merely in verbal art but in all representational art. It may appear in different forms and functions within the same art; in fiction, for example, it may appear as a purely verbal statement by or about one of the characters, or it may constitute part of the whole structure or conception of the work if the narrator adopts an ironic attitude toward his characters or his story. It consists merely of producing an effect contrary to the artist's ostensible endeavor. The working of irony, in whatever form it appears, may be analyzed, for the sake of convenience, into three components: an object, a factor, and an effect. The factor is the irony-producing element; it works in the opposite direction to the way it appears to work. Instead of raising the object, as it purports to do, it makes the object comic or absurd or contemptible; or instead of lowering the object, as it purports to do, it makes the object noble or pathetic or tragic. In literature, as in our daily lives, understatement or overstatement for contrary ends is the commonest case of irony, and the irony of personal understatement is the only socially acceptable form of self-aggrandizement, or at least of self-assertion. Antony's funeral speech in *Julius Caesar* contains both kinds, overstatement about Brutus and understatement about Caesar. Ironic overstatement, when applied to the narrator's attitude, may constitute the mock-heroic; this is the main technique, for example, of Fielding's *Jonathan Wild*. It is this kind of irony that Zhou Zuoren seems to have been referring to in Gogol, Sienkiewicz, and Lu Xun. Ironic understatement is not so common in literature, or perhaps it is merely less frequently remarked, but it is the staple technique of what might be called the pathetic mode.

It is useful to distinguish *situational irony*, in which both object and factor lie in the "dramatized" part of the fictional work, from *presentational irony*, in which the factor is the tone adopted by the narrator who stands outside the action he is recounting. There are different kinds of presentational irony, according to the degree to which the narrator is given an explicit persona. At the most explicit, for example, we have the narrator in "Ah Q," who even refers to himself in the first person. Much fiction contains both situational and presentational irony, and also that hybrid kind in which a character, for the moment, becomes a narrator himself and thus a possible vehicle for irony, wittingly or not. A third major kind, commoner in the graphic arts than in the verbal, is what we may call *juxtapositional irony*, in which one section or one element of the structure may act ironically upon another; by ironic contrast it may lower or raise our estimation of the object.

This analysis is simplistic to the point of seriously distorting the working of irony. To isolate its elements as if they were the terms of some topsy-turvy law of dynamics is to give the impression that the factor is independent of the object, when in fact they coexist in the work of art and affect each other. It may even, in some cases, be impossible to say which is which, since both are equally factor and object, acting upon and being acted upon by each other. If, for example, the ironic factor consists of presentation by a naïve narrator, such as the boy in Lu Xun's "Kong Yiji" (1919), our estimation of the boy will inevitably be affected by our knowledge of his naïveté. In "Kong Yiji" this is not an important matter, since the primary object is clearly the derelict after whom the story is named. But in "Medicine," where there is an ironic juxtaposition between the two boys who are about to die in such different ways, the reciprocal effect is significant. Although the mechanical model of the working of irony is useful for clarification and is always applicable to a degree, it is never the whole critical truth; the interaction of object and factor is always more complex, and sometimes far more complex.

In literature, the most important case of situational irony is what may be called the irony of character, in which the ironic contrast is between a person's actions and his pretensions, or between the reality and a person's misperception of it. The factor consists of the pretensions or misperceptions that, by their absurdity or incongruity, make the characters seem ridiculous or comical. Half the heroes of Molière are examples of the former; Partridge in *Tom Jones*, Candide, and Don Quixote himself are examples of the latter. The misadventures that befall Candide are comical precisely because such things do not happen in the best of all possible worlds. The grandiose pretension or the heroic misperception ostensibly raises our estimation, but in fact by inappropriateness lowers it; this is one of the prime techniques of the satiric mode.[65]

The mechanism of irony, the tiny signals by which the writer reverses his own ostensible meaning, is too large a subject to enter upon here.[66] Some of the recourses of ironic speech are denied to the writer—the tone of voice, the wry smile, the raised eyebrow—but he is left with stylistic devices in plenty, most notably repetition, exaggeration, and patent contradiction. Nor will I try to account for the reader's response to irony, a response that, in most contexts, finds the ironic statement more forceful than any direct statement.

A certain ironic conception is found in Lu Xun's first piece of fiction, "Huai jiu" (Looking back to the past), a story written in 1911 in the context of the current revolution and the Boxer uprising. The narrator is a man recollecting his childhood, when there were constant rumors of the impending arrival of the rebels. The story is told in part with a nine-year-old boy's understanding; the judgment of the mature man is brought only occasionally into play. His tutor's hypocrisy is given extra force by the artlessness of the narrator's account. For example, he reflects the conventional view that the tutor, as an educated man, must be superior to the kindly, ignorant servants, but in such a way as to bring the reader to precisely the opposite conclusion. On another occasion, the nature of the irony makes the assumption of naïveté barely plausible: "People used to say that, search as you might in the town of Wu, you would never find a wiser man than our Mr. Baldhead. This was a fair statement. He could have lived at any time whatever, and he would have seen to it that he came to no harm."[67] It is significant that in this rather shapeless story, which does not contain some of the other characteristic features of Lu Xun's writing, irony is already present. Irony is the first, and perhaps the most pronounced, element of Lu Xun's fiction.

The closest structural parallel is "Kong Yiji," one of Lu Xun's best stories, which he wrote in 1919. The object of irony is the derelict scholar and the ironic factor the twelve-year-old boy who works at the inn. The irony is the kind we have called presentational, through a dramatized narrator. Although the story is represented as a reminiscence some thirty years after the event, the mature man's judgment is not allowed to condition the boy's naïveté. To the boy's mind, Kong, who is the butt of jokes by all the regular patrons, is merely a source of amusement in the midst of a dull job, and it is through the boy's dim, uncomprehending mind that we see the casual cruelty in which the derelict lives his life. Unlike "Looking Back to the Past," this story works according to the irony of raising, not lowering. Precisely because he is the object of derision, the pathos and horror of the old man's end are more convincing than they might have been in any direct portrayal through his own conscious-ness. Yet that is without doubt the way Andreyev would have approached this material, and Sienkiewicz also, probably with the aid of an ironic narrator standing outside the action.

Lu Xun's first vernacular story, "Kuangren riji" (Diary of a madman, 1918), has a different, though still all-embracing, ironic conception. The madman's perception symbolizes a set of insights into the traditional social system, but the working of the symbols is ironic. To relegate the symbolic truth about Chinese society to the perception of a madman is, on the surface, to dismiss it as mere raving. In fact, by the working of irony, his perception is given a singular force such as no *direct* symbolic account would be likely to achieve.

Focusing on Lu Xun's ironic techniques inevitably gives the impression of a mechanical application. In fact, each story has its unique demands and its unique solution. The boy working at the inn is the appropriate narrator for "Kong Yiji"; he fits within the realistic assumptions of the story, and he is a suitable ironic reflector of the old man. Similarly, the madman's perception is an appropriate artistic solution for the "Diary," not merely because it fits within the mode of the ironic symbolism but also because the nightmarish situation of the man who thinks he has discovered the truth of all the ages but can get nobody to heed him is the perfect metaphor for the difficulty and danger of rethinking accepted values.

Though remote from the "Diary" in the quality of its irony, "Toufa de gushi" (Story of hair, 1920) shares this characteristic—a sustained view is cast into an ironic light. This is Lu Xun's amusing discourse, with serious implications, on hair as the maleficent factor in modern Chinese history. It is a satirical technique to take some point and extend it with rare logic into a preposterous thesis, and it is not different in kind from a method Lu Xun sometimes uses in his essays. But the story is also an ironic statement, and more effective than any direct statement could be. Some of the experiences were Lu Xun's own and some of the opinions were those he was currently urging upon his students, but the whole thesis, suitably exaggerated, is put into the mouth of an eccentric, and thus treated ironically. The listener is present solely in order to characterize the speaker.

The irony that Lu Xun found in Sienkiewicz and Gogol was presentational, conveyed by a more or less dramatized narrator standing outside the action. This is the principal method of "Ah Q," and part of the method of "Tomorrow," "Fengbo" (Storm in a teacup), and "Duanwujie" (Double fifth, 1922), in which it is combined with other kinds of irony. In "Ah Q," the narrator's lofty tone is in violent contrast to the squalid events described, and the contrast makes the latter ridiculous. There is no need to illustrate this ironic technique, which comes under the broad definition of the mock-heroic—the treatment of Ah Q as candidate for a biography, the historical parallels to his pursuit of the serving woman, and so forth. The main literary problem posed by Ah Q, as distinct from the political controversy, is the change from a comic or ridiculous character to a pathetic character. Sienkiewicz's example shows that the change need not be taken as a contradiction. Both "Charcoal Sketches" and "Bartek the Victor" contain the "lowering" effect of irony as well as the "raising" irony of pathos; in fact, both kinds are attached to the figure of Bartek himself. Ah Q is stupid and depraved, unlike Bartek, who is stupid but decent, or Zolzik, who is clever but depraved. If Ah Q is to fill the quota of captured looters and suffer execution, as seems entirely proper according to Lu Xun's scheme of ironies, he cannot help but appear pathetic. Fittingly, he is treated with a different tone in the last section or two of the story, while the narrator's sardonic comments are reserved for others. One may easily argue that the change is too sudden, that the pathos has not been prepared for, but not that mock-heroic treatment and pathos have no business as used of the same character.

"Double Fifth," written immediately after "Ah Q," has some interesting thematic parallels. It is about an intellectual's apathy or detachment, rationalized in the slogan *chabuduozhuyi*, the principle of "there's little to choose between them," an excuse for not taking sides in a controversy. Like Ah Q's rationalizations, it is both psychological balm and tactical device. However, the narrator is not dramatized to the same extent as in "Ah Q," and the irony is less overt. The story stands between "Ah Q" and those stories of character irony without any overt narrator's comment that Lu Xun developed in his second collection, *Panghuang*. Presentational irony, of the raising and lowering kinds, respectively, also plays a part in "Tomorrow" and "Storm in a Teacup." In the former story, the narrator continually deprecates the widow, saying "she was only a simple woman, and didn't understand," a chorus of ironic understatement. "Storm in a Teacup" contains subtle instances of descriptive irony, for example, the use of pretentious phrases suitable for high political ambition to describe the simple aims of the boatman.

The irony of the narrator who is himself involved in the story does not need to be all-encompassing; any character whose words or thoughts are represented may, for that moment, be an ironic narrator. In "Medicine," where this technique is put to outstanding use, the revolutionary never appears, and our only knowledge of him is through the conversation of the teahouse regulars. Their talk, though highly critical, works as unwitting irony. In "Storm in a Teacup," there is the opposite kind of irony, as the passing literati wax lyrical about the villagers' rustic bliss. In the same story, the villagers' comic incomprehension of the great world is also ironic. Unwitting irony, in particular, works both ways; it reflects on the object, inversely, but it also reflects on the person uttering it.

The main structure of both "Medicine" and "Tomorrow" is juxtapositional irony. In this case, the ironic factor does not convey information about the object; it affects our opinion of the object by mere association with it. In "Medicine," the stories of the two boys run parallel, and the symmetry is sustained at the end when their mothers meet in the graveyard. It is the juxtaposition of the consumptive with the revolutionary, the consumptive in the foreground, the whole pathetic scene of ignorance and superstition, that heightens the tragedy of the revolutionary. This is evidently what Lu Xun meant by likening the technique of this story to "Ben Tobit." The ironic structure of "Tomorrow" is even clearer. As frequently in Lu Xun, the inn or teahouse is a natural symbol of heedless frivolity, the disregard of human tragedy. Here the inn is juxtaposed, quite literally, with the widow's house; the two stand side by side, and their association is reinforced by the fact that they are the only two places in town to have lights burning all night long. (For this last point, Lu Xun paid a small price in verisimilitude, as Zhou Zuoren explains.)[68] Drunken song begins the story, punctuates it, and brings it to an end, and can be regarded as a commentary on the tragedy next door. The revelers have really very little connection with the widow and her sick child. They mention her once or twice, there is a certain subdued sexual feeling present, and they offer to help after the child's death, but that is all. The inn's function is to stand in ironic contrast to the private tragedy.

Lu Xun was constantly changing the governing techniques of his stories, even in his short career as a writer of fiction. He soon dropped ironic symbolism, except in the much later *Gushi xinbian* (Old stories retold). Indeed, symbolism itself, by which I mean arbitrary symbolism, not the natural kind that continued to mark Lu Xun's work, was no longer a distinctive feature after "Ah Q." Presentational irony by an uninvolved narrator was hardly used again after "Double Fifth," in which it was already attenuated. With it disappeared certain features to which the technique apparently lent sanction—for example, the passages of scenic description such as those in "Storm in a Teacup" and "Double Fifth." Lu Xun showed a far greater degree of psychological interest in his second collection, manifested particularly in the irony of character—the contrast between the pretension or misperception on the one hand, and the action or reality on the other. In this kind of irony, there is no ironic narrator, for both object and factor are located within the character. Such narrators as there are in Lu Xun's later stories are involved in the action, and their biases form part of the reader's judgment of the story. These techniques are accompanied by an increasing insistence on the purity of fictional means, in particular, on the restrained use of time.

Let us use "time frame" for the time during which the main or enveloping action is represented as occurring. If there is a fully dramatized narrator, the main time frame will be the time he takes to tell his story, and the secondary time frame will be the time of the action he is recounting. Memories, relations or accounts, and visions of the future may all fall outside the time frame. In these terms, Lu Xun's stories observe an extraordinary economy: the main time frame in the later stories generally keeps within the unities of place, time, and action of classical dramatic criticism, with the addition of the memories and accounts. In "Zhu fu" (New Year's sacrifice, 1924), despite the lifetime of travail to which the reader feels himself subjected, the main time frame is a single day, all the rest being memory and account. With this economy goes a scrupulous attention to point of view. There is no absolute insistence on a single point of view in his stories—in "Lihun" (Divorce, 1925) there are three points of view, the girl's, her father's, and the narrator's—but there is certainly great restraint. A third feature is symmetry, a conscious shaping of the story so that the end echoes the beginning. First noticeable in "Tomorrow," in the revelers' drunken singing, symmetry becomes more common in *Panghuang*, in "Dixiong" (Brothers, 1925), "The Lamp That Was Kept Alight," "New Year's Sacrifice," and "Shi zhong" (On public display, 1925).

The three stories of character irony are "Soap," "Happy Family," and "Gao Laofuzi" (Master Gao, 1925). In each, the ironic contrast between pretension and action is made clear without any obvious comment. These are the stories that best exemplify the rather vague definition of satire found in Lu Xun's essays.[69] In his view, expressed several times, it is not necessary to invent the material of satire, which lies all around us in everyday life; it is only necessary to perceive it. And it is simply necessary to present the material *as it is*, subject to artistic control, of course, and with a little exaggeration allowed. This is a description, less precisely of satire according to our definition than of the lowering kind of situational irony, in which an objective or detached treatment of fictional material, by revealing the contrast between pretension and action or reality, becomes an ironic treatment. I suggested that it was this kind of irony in some of the early stories of Xu Qinwen that may have brought him to Lu Xun's notice, and that one source of the technique was the eighteenth-century novel *Rulin waishi*, one of the greatest examples in any literature of character irony.[70] Xu's stories, of course, are not to be compared with Lu Xun's. Xu was a novice, unable or unwilling to dispense with the crutch of the first-person ob-server, and his stories are a simpler form of fictional life. But it is not improb-able that, protégé as he was, he helped precipitate a development in Lu Xun's technique.

"Soap" is an acute psychological study as well as an example of character irony.[71] As in "Happy Family" and "Master Gao," the center of consciousness through which the action is viewed is that of the person satirized. To obtain the subtle psychological revelation of "Soap" within a few pages, without any obvious ironical comment, is an extraordinary achievement. "Happy Family" can be compared to Xu Qinwen's "Composing a Little Poem" and to Chekhov's "Hush!,"[72] two stories on similar themes. Xu's story has a similar method, but it is too farcical and much less complex; it does not have the ex-tra level of contrast between the writer's family and the ideal family he is writ-ing about.[73] Chekhov only rarely writes stories of character irony, like "The Princess,"[74] and "Hush!" has an entirely different method; he goes so far as to call his hero a "fourth-rate journalist." "Master Gao" is much less successful than the other two stories, mainly, I think, because Lu Xun has not obeyed his own dictum that the material of satire should be, if not actually true, at least potentially true. "Master Gao" strains the reader's credulity. Although the au-thor preserves his pose of emotional detachment, it appears that anger or frus-tration must have caused Lu Xun to lose his customary restraint.

"Divorce" is the last story in *Panghuang*, and perhaps the best. It fuses a number of methods, including character irony and presentational irony by a naïve narrator. The main center of consciousness is Aigu, a vengeful, spurned wife, who is also a naïve reflector. Her naïveté sets off the pretensions and hypocrisy of the principals in the divorce settlement, but there is also a conflict between her misperception and her own nature. "Brothers" is another story with some claim to the irony of character. The man who prides himself on his relationship with his brother, who sets himself up as a model for others, is re-vealed to himself, by a trick of his subconscious, as prey to selfishness and cal-lousness, even brutality. But the irony is more apparent than real. The gap be-tween misperception and reality is revealed to the hero, and he is appalled, unlike the heroes of "Soap" or "Master Gao," who are impervious to self-enlightenment. Moreover, the reality is not the reality of waking life, the prop-er field of the moralist, but that of the subconscious, and if an author's moral-ity had to take account of all the subconscious fantasies that attach themselves to seemingly innocent emotions, it would be complicated beyond belief. We do better to note the patent Freudianism, and liken the story to those of con-science and guilt that appear to involve a persona of Lu Xun, to which I shall refer later. Its similarity to the stories of character irony is superficial; "Brothers" may well owe more to Sologub's "A Kiss for the Unborn," a story on a remotely similar theme that Zhou Zuoren translated for the 1920 edition of the *Anthology*.[75] It is based, of course, almost entirely on experience: Zhou Zuoren's illness, Lu Xun's concern over it, and his relief when the illness turned out to be measles. Even the subconscious fantasy apparently originated in experience, in the "evil thoughts" that entered Lu Xun's mind.[76] This is Lu Xun's most private story, the only one that is not in large measure concerned with social morality.

Two stories, "Regret for the Past" and "New Year's Sacrifice," combine presentational irony with character irony in a more complex way than Lu Xun attempted elsewhere. Both have narrators who are themselves involved in the action, and both narrators—this point is never overtly made—are slightly false, or at least inadequate, personalities. Like the narrator in "Kong Yiji," they show us pathetic figures, and the pathos is heightened by the obliqueness of their presentation. But this kind of irony, of course, works both ways; it reflects on the narrator as well as on the figure he is presenting. This occurs with the boy's naïveté in "Kong Yiji," and it occurs even more significantly with the self-deception of these two narrators. Neither is specifically untruthful, but neither reflects the facts adequately or—a near-obsession with Lu Xun—with the appropriate use of conscience. In "Regret for the Past," the narrator, for all his penitence, does not quite do moral or emotional justice to the lover he has rejected. Although the story contains a good deal of moral ambiguity, it must be remembered that the lover is a social victim, like Aigu in "Divorce" or the madman in "The Lamp That Was Kept Alight." The narrator incurs moral responsibility because he has encouraged her to leave home, like Ibsen's Nora, and has then, for reasons not primarily of his own making, been unable to sustain the relationship. The girl's fate, as she is sent home to die among her unfeeling relatives, emerges with particular poignancy from the narrator's account.

The narrator of "New Year's Sacrifice" has less moral responsibility for the action, but an equal degree of moral inadequacy. Once, when the desperate woman asks him the metaphysical question that haunts her, he prides himself on his ability to give a pat, noncommittal answer. His conceit is surely gratuitous, even though at the time he is unaware of her plight. At the end of the story, that same day, when he ought, by any appropriate use of conscience, to be unable to get her death out of his mind, he banishes all thought of her in a blaze of New Year's Eve euphoria. The fineness of the implied author's conscience has set a standard of moral sensitivity that the narrator has, unknowingly, failed to meet, and against this background the fate of Xianglin Sao takes on an even greater poignancy. It is another example of Lu Xun's use of an oblique method, as in "Medicine," to carry a deeply moving theme. If this story is compared with Chekhov's "At Home,"[77] to which it bears some thematic similarity, we see the vast difference it makes to treat the story's center of consciousness directly, without distance or irony. Chekhov mediates his heroine's thoughts, explaining them to us and, in effect, validating them. He uses this method because the heroine is at the heart of the story, and the serving woman, who occasions her outburst of anger and then her spasm of conscience, is not very important. The net result of the distance with which Lu Xun treats his narrator is to throw attention upon the servant; the story's power comes from the author's detachment. The best demonstration of this is a comparison of "New Year's Sacrifice" with the 1956 film based upon the story.[78] It was apparently impossible for the scriptwriter, the dramatist Xia Yan, to find an equivalent for this narrative technique, and he dismissed the narrator from his script. The woman is the center of consciousness, and the film is her biography. It is not a bad film, although the effect is sometimes maudlin, but it lacks the story's emotional detachment and moral complexity, its obliqueness; and with that obliqueness, it has lost the story's expressive power.

"Shi zhong" (On public display) illustrates a new kind of all-encompassing ironic conception. It is a brilliant work, on the boundary of prose fiction, an extreme instance of Lu Xun's interest in ironic structure and conception. A criminal is brought out on the street under guard as a deterrent to the public—this is the significance of the title—and a crowd of onlookers forms. They jostle for position, wait, and then, when they see nothing about to happen, break ranks to rush away and gape at a rickshaw accident. There is no overt irony beyond a slight touch or two, most notably the phrase *shoushan zhi qu,* meaning the nation's capital, the premier city, and we know the ironic power that expression had for Lu Xun,[79] especially in a case such as this, where a feature of Chinese life that he loathed and despised is being described. There is no comment, no center of consciousness, and nobody is even named. Even my précis errs, in ascribing motives. Lu Xun's narrative is like a camera, moving here and there, picking up this detail and that action, reflecting the surface of things. It is the camera's detachment that constitutes the irony. Lu Xun loathed people's capacity for treating tragic or pathetic scenes as occasions for diversion or curiosity, instead of as matter for conscience and sympathy. (It was a scene of a similar kind that traumatically moved Lu Xun and caused him to devote himself to literature.) All emotion is suppressed. A placid observation replaces the fury and contempt that are called for. The narrative itself treats the scene as a diversion. Like voyeurs, we watch the onlookers who, like voyeurs, watch the criminal, uncomprehending. By the working of an ironic technique, the very lack of the appropriate passion gives the story its power.

A certain degree of character irony is apparent in "The Lamp That Was Kept Alight." To the village madman, the lamp burning in the temple is emblem and cause of all the evil in the world, and in his periodic fits he attempts to put it out. It is not suggested that the lamp is a symbol of evil for anyone but him; no ironic symbolism, of the order of "The Diary of a Madman," is intended. There is an ironic gap between the madman's perception and the reality, but there is also a gap between the villagers' misperception and the reality, because for them the lamp is both emblem and cause of the village's good luck. Moved by an equal superstition, the villagers band together in a cynical scheme to foil him. A little like Aigu in "Divorce," the madman is driven by motives with which we cannot sympathize, but, as in her case, we recognize that he is manipulated by people in authority driven by an equal folly.

"Bai guang" (White light, 1922) is another of Lu Xun's stories of madmen, about a man who goes mad after failing the examinations for the umpteenth time. It is told through the man's consciousness, more strictly through his sensations, as indicated in the story's title. He is treated with authorial distance, with detachment, and the story has a measure of character irony. There is also an element of presentational irony in the dry, impersonal coroner's report describing the madman's naked corpse, stripped by scavengers.[80]

The stories I have not so far considered constitute something of a group by virtue of both form and material. They are: "Yijian xiaoshi" (An incident, 1919) and "Guxiang" (Old home, 1921) in *Nahan*, together with the three memoir-type pieces that close the collection, "Ya de xiju" (Comedy of the ducks, 1922), "Tu he mao" (The rabbits and the cat, 1922), and "Shexi" (Village opera, 1922); and "Zai jiuloushang" (In the wineshop, 1924) and "Guduzhe" (The misanthrope, 1925) in *Panghuang*. All of these stories are told by a first-person narrator who is involved in the action, all of them embody Lu Xun's personal experience (mixed with other experience, in some cases), and none of them makes any prominent use of ironic technique.

To speak of personal experience as a criterion gives the impression of confusing an author's life with his work, a danger against which all critics are inoculated at an early age. But some such criterion is forced upon us by what Zhou Zuoren tells us about Lu Xun's work,[81] and by what we can observe as analytical critics. We know to what an extraordinary degree Lu Xun's fiction depends on fact; his stories are peopled with characters from his childhood, his family history, and his mature experience, including the "Diary's" madman, Kong Yiji, Ah Q, Runtu in "Old Home," Master Gao, the madman of "White

Light," Xianglin Sao in "New Year's Sacrifice," and so forth, often with their names almost intact, even though they are undeniably composite characters. Stories that do not contain Lu Xun's own personal experiences *as actor* have already been discussed; all of them use one or more kinds of ironic technique. Stories that do contain large amounts of Lu Xun's personal experience as actor are of more than one variety: these seven I have just mentioned, and also "Story of Hair," "Double Fifth," "Brothers," and "Looking Back to the Past," a more disparate group.[82] If, broadly speaking, we say that Lu Xun's fiction has two principal modes, one using a distinctly ironic technique and the other using authorial distance but without such a prominent use of irony, then the decision of whether or not to employ a persona may have helped to determine the mode.

A great difference may be observed on this point between the Chinese critics of the 1920s and 1930s and modern critics. The early critics did not hesitate to describe Lu Xun's use of his own experience as "self-analysis," "self-dissection," and even "self-criticism,"[83] and a statement by Lu Xun himself was sometimes quoted in support of the assertion: "It is true that I dissect other people from time to time, but I dissect myself much more often and much more savagely."[84] More recent critics, however, have not linked Lu Xun himself with the weak, cynical, or ineffectual people that his experience was often used to create. This is understandable. With one or two exceptions, the stories are not autobiographical; Lu Xun is not the world-weary cynic of "An Incident," the curmudgeon of "Story of Hair," or the lapsed idealist of "In the Wineshop." But we should not ignore Lu Xun's use of personae simply because the personae are not admissible as autobiography. The elements of his personal experience, as used in his stories, are generally made to involve matters of personal conscience and even guilt. Clearly, these emotions and this aspect of his experience lay close to the source of Lu Xun's creative imagination.

Lu Xun used the persona with a large measure of authorial distance. Often a second character, a first-person narrator, is used to put the persona at an even greater distance, as in "Story of Hair," "In the Wineshop," and "The Misanthrope." When the distance is not so large, narrator and persona are one and the same. These are the stories in which one is tempted to equate Lu Xun with his persona, although, obviously, the temptation should be resisted: "Looking Back to the Past," "Old Home," and the three memoir-type stories. Note that some of these involve childhood experience, which is always viewed from a distance and which is free from the burden of conscience and guilt. When the distance is greater, a rather passive listener and recorder is introduced, as in "Story of Hair," "In the Wineshop," and "The Misanthrope." Note also that in all of these stories Lu Xun is using other people's experience, as well as his own, in creating the persona. When the distance is greater still, an uninvolved narrator is combined with an ironic technique, as in "Double Fifth" and "Brothers." This scale is crude and does not do justice to the particular demands of each story, but it does show a connection between Lu Xun's attitude toward his own experience and his choice of creative method.

Irony is not entirely absent even from stories like "Old Home." The brilliant contrast between the narrator's memory of the young Runtu and his meeting with the adult Runtu can be seen as an example of juxtapositional irony. "In the Wineshop" could perhaps be interpreted as character irony, but the interpretation seems forced, since the hero is more or less aware of his own lapse from his ideals. There is irony of a different kind in "The Rabbits and the Cat" and "Comedy of the Ducks," pleasant tales of inconsequential happenings treated with a comic high seriousness. There is a certain ironic disparagement of the persona, of the kind often met with in Lu Xun's essays.[85] The latter story is about Eroshenko, the blind Ukrainian who taught Esperanto at Beijing University and was a close friend of Lu Xun's.[86] The story gently mocks his unworldliness.

The four stories I have not discussed are "An Incident" and "Old Home" from *Nahan* and "In the Wineshop" and "The Misanthrope" from *Panghuang.* The first pair is concerned with a moral and social revelation. In "An Incident," the revelation remains inchoate, the germ of an idea that will not grow but that the memory refuses to expel, an idea of fellow-feeling, a kind of social morality. In "Old Home," the revelation is of social inequality, of class difference, and it is fully articulated in a moving hope for the future. (Note that this kind of plea is confined to the *Nahan* collection, to "Diary of a Madman," "Story of Hair," and "Old Home.") The theme of "In the Wineshop" and "The Misanthrope" is not moral revelation, but failure to live up to the ideals of social service and morality that Lu Xun's generation had espoused. Both men are crushed by circumstances, and each man accommodates; one makes a pathetic attempt to justify himself, the other acts in full knowledge of what he is doing and with a certain despairing panache. As used in these stories, the elements of Lu Xun's personal experience seem to show a conflict between social ideals, one's duty to the broader society, and the bonds of family love and obligation, a conflict that wracks the conscience. "In the Wineshop" conveys the subject's failure in his own words, in a simple, natural way. "The Misanthrope," potentially a great story, seems to me to be inarticulate. The narrator hides his emotions, affection, helpless guilt, or whatever they may be, and the cry of grief with which he greets his friend's death is inexplicable unless the reader brings his own interpretation to the story.

I have not so far discussed Lu Xun as a satirist. Satire, here defined as the product of a technique (wit, indirection, etc.) and a purpose (ridicule) is, of course, predominant in Lu Xun's fiction, and the lowering kind of irony is its main technique.

Lu Xun's satiric purpose is, naturally, the aspect of his work that has attracted the great mass of commentary and criticism. But even for the student of Lu Xun's ideas, the importance of his technique must be stressed. No ironist of Lu Xun's delicate touch, working in a more or less realistic mode within the scope of the short story, is easy to interpret. It is possible to misunderstand him simply by taking an inadequate narrator at face value, as has sometimes been done in the case of "Regret for the Past" and "New Year's Sacrifice." And in stories of little or no explicit authorial direction, such as "In the Wineshop," ridicule and pathos may be so mixed as to make any categorical judgment difficult.

The ideals implied in Lu Xun's satire are concerned, in the main, with personal relations in society. This is the area of traditional Confucian ethics, which is no doubt why Lu Xun seized upon it for his satiric purposes. His first stories, with their obtrusive ironic techniques, were perceived by the public as symbolizing the great schism in contemporary culture, and are consequently the more famous. The concerns of some of the later stories seem, in contrast, rather slight—Lu Xun's conscience was exceedingly fine-meshed, and these are mostly stories that embody some of his own experience—but they are equally about social morality: relations between husband and wife, father and child, social hypocrisy, social apathy.

Lu Xun's ironic varieties belong to an artistic perception, not a philosophical perception—they do not form part of any "ironic vision of life."[87] They have several kinds of importance in his work. In the first place, since they emphasize the aspect of judgment, they serve the needs of the moralist. Any oblique treatment, for example the filtering of an event through an unfeeling or uncomprehending mind, contrives to throw the story upon the reader's faculty of moral judgment. Other fictional values are sacrificed to it—empathy, the illusion of the senses, the minor peripeties on which readers of popular fiction browse, like fish on plankton. Secondly, irony may serve the end of artistic expressiveness, the same end that is served by Lu Xun's purity of fictional means, his deliberate stripping down of the short story to simple scene and reminiscence. Finally, irony and detachment are a psychological and artistic necessity for a writer as gripped by moral rage, didactic passion, and private conscience as Lu Xun evidently was. A comparison with the celebrated ironists of the past will show this much in common: a predominantly moral and didactic passion, and the use of irony and persona, or mask, to render that passion in a valid artistic form. Irony and the mask are the best means of coping with any strong emotion that threatens to overwhelm the artist, a point that Lu Xun was almost alone in grasping, among the writers of his generation.

NOTES

1. See Mark Schorer, "Technique as Discovery," *Hudson Review* 1.1 (Spring 1948): 69. See also 67: "The difference between content, or experience, and achieved content, or art, is technique."
2. "Riben jin sanshinian xiaoshuo zhi fada," *Xin qingnian* 5.1 (July 15, 1918): 41.
3. Unless otherwise indicated, all of Lu Xun's stories referred to are to be found in his collected works, *Lu Xun quanji*, 16 vols. (Beijing: Renmin wenxue chubanshe, 1981), in vol. 1 if published in the collection *Nahan* (1923), in vol. 2 if published in the collection *Panghuang* (1926).
4. "Wo zenme zuoqi xiaoshuo lai," *Lu Xun quanji* 4:511–12.
5. *Lu Xun quanji*, 6:238–39.
6. See *Zhitang huixianglu*, 2 vols. (Hong Kong: Tingtao chubanshe, 1970), 2:680.
7. Zhou Zuoren translated one story and ten fables for the expanded version of the *Yuwai xiaoshuoji* (Shanghai: Qunyi shushe, 1920), evidently from *The Sweet-scented Name and Other Fairy Tales, Fables and Stories*, ed. Stephen Graham (New York: G. P. Putnam's Sons, 1915). For Lu Xun's reaction to the news of Sologub's death in 1929, see *Lu Xun quanji*, 7:178–79.
8. See *Lu Xun yiwenji*, 10 vols. (Beijing: Renmin wenxue chubanshe, 1959), vol. 1.
9. Qiming (pseud. of Zhou Zuoren), "A Q zhengzhuan," *Chen bao fujuan*, March 19, 1922, reprinted in *Zhou Zuoren wenlei bian* (Changsha: Hunan wenyi chubanshe, 1998), vol. 10 (*Bashi xinqing*): 129–32.
10. It was not published until 1914. See note 23 below.
11. See the note appended to the retranslation ("Qiuzhang") in *Xin qingnian* 5.4 (October 15, 1918): 403–4.
12. Included in *Lu Xun yiwenji* 1:462–71. It was first published in 1923.
13. See *Zhongguo xinwenxue daxi*, 10 vols. (Shanghai: Liangyou tushu gongsi, 1935–36), 10:362. Zhou was interested in irony and often refers to Lucian's *True History*.
14. Entitled "Guanyu Lu Xun," the articles appeared in the journal *Yuzhou feng* on October 24 and November 7, 1936, respectively. They are reprinted in *Zhou Zuoren wenlei bian*, vol. 10 (*Bashi xinqing*): 108–17, 118–26.
15. *Allgemeine Geschichte der Literatur von ihren Anfängen bis auf die Gegenwart* (3 vols., Berlin, 1901), and *Allgemeine Geschichte der Literatur* (Stuttgart: Conradi, 1880), with many expanded and revised editions, respectively. See Zhou Zuoren, *Lu Xun de gujia* (Shanghai: Shanghai chuban gongsi, 1954), 390–91.

16. Zhou translated "Ben Tobit" under the title of "Chitong" (Toothache) in *Xin qingnian* 7.1 (Dec. 1919): 65–68. For English translations of both "Ben Tobit" and "The Seven That Were Hanged," see *The Seven That Were Hanged and Other Stories* (New York: Modern Library, 1958).

17. See the English translation by R. S. Townsend (New York: Knopf, 1917).

18. See *Lu Xun quanji*, 7:123.

19. The *Xiandai xiaoshuo yicong*, published in Shanghai; see *Lu Xun yiwenji*, 1:313–38.

20. See *Lu Xun yiwenji*, vol. 1.

21. *Lu Xun yiwenji*, 10:576. It was first published in 1922. For English translations of Garshin's stories, see Rowland Smith, trans., *The Signal and Other Stories* (New York: Knopf, 1916).

22. See Shen Pengnian, *Lu Xun yanjiu ziliao bianmu* (Shanghai wenyi chubanshe, 1958), 197.

23. *Lu Xun riji*, 1:95. The translation, *Tanhua*, was evidently from Jeremiah Curtin, trans., *Hania* (Boston: Little, Brown, 1897), 291–374. It was published in Beijing by the Wenming shuju in April 1914; see Zhang Juxiang and Zhang Tierong, *Zhou Zuoren nianpu* (Tianjin: Tianjin renmin chubanshe, 2000), 942.

24. For an English translation, see Jeremiah Curtin, trans., *Yanko the Musician and Other Stories* (Boston: Little, Brown, 1894).

25. *Lu Xun de gujia*, 309. Lu Xun prized a tattered German translation of *The Hangman's Rope*, in the Reclam series. Mervyn Jones, *Five Hungarian Writers* (Oxford, 1966), 258, describes the novel as a story of blood revenge that is "devoid of feeling for its literary form," "frenzied," and "absurd."

26. Natsume Sōseki, *Sōseki zenshū* (Tokyo: Iwanami, 1993), vols. 1 and 4, respectively.

27. Lu Xun's "Sibada zhi hun" (The spirit of Sparta), a retelling of Leonidas's stand at Thermopylae, written in 1903, is prose narrative. See *Lu Xun quanji*, 7:9–16. He also made free adaptations of Jules Verne's *De la terre à la lune* and *Voyage au centre de la terre*, working from Japanese versions of English translations. Using a hybrid mixture of the literary and the vernacular languages, he put them into the form of the traditional novel, complete with illustrative verse, including poems from classical Chinese poets. See *Lu Xun yiwenji*, vol. 1.

28. *Lu Xun quanji*, vol. 7:215–21.

29. *Lu Xun riji*, 1:67, 119, 71.

30. Ibid., 102, 121.

31. Compare the estimation of Russian writers at this time by William Lyon Phelps, *Essays on Russian Novelists* (New York: MacMillan, 1911), whose preface is dated 1910. Apart from the obvious figures, the novelists treated are Gorky, Chekhov, Artsybashev, Andreyev, and Kuprin. Garshin is mentioned as an influence on Andreyev, who is described as "the man best worth watching—he is the most gifted artist of them all," that is to say, of the contemporary writers (284). Gorky's reputation was in decline: "From 1900 to 1906 everybody was talking about him; since 1906 one scarcely hears mention of his name" (215).

32. For English translations, see *The Seven That Were Hanged and Other Stories*.

33. See Alexander Kaun, *Leonid Andreyev, A Critical Study* (New York: B. W. Huebsch, 1924), 68.

34. See *Lu Xun yiwenji*, vol. 1.

35. *Lu Xun yiwenji*, 1:167. For an English translation of "Silence," see *The Little Angel and Other Stories*, trans. W. H. Lowe (New York: Knopf, 1916), 104–25.

36. *Lu Xun yiwenji*, 1:169–70.

37. *Lu Xun quanji*, 1:34.

38. *Lu Xun xiansheng ersan shi* (Chongqing: Zuojia shuwu, 1942), 20–21.

39. For an English translation, see Evgenia Schimanskaya, trans., *Poems in Prose* (London: Lindsay Drummond, 1945), 26–27.

40. On literary and other influences, see J. D. Chinnery, "The Influence of Western Literature on Lu Xun's 'Diary of a Madman,'" *Bulletin of the School of Oriental and African Studies* 23.2 (1960): 309–22.

41. *Red Laugh* was written in 1904. For an English translation, see Alexandra Linden, trans., *The Red Laugh, Fragments of a Discovered Manuscript* (London: T. Fisher Unwin, 1905). The metaphorical use of cannibalism in "The Diary of a Madman" to stand for social exploitation was in part suggested by the remarks of Zhang Binglin during the informal lectures he gave in Tokyo, which Lu Xun attended; see Zhou Xiashou (pseud. of Zhou Zuoren), *Lu Xun xiaoshuoli de renwu* (Shanghai chuban gongsi, 1954), 12. But it is a common enough idea, as witness Vasily's speech in Garshin's famous story "The Signal"; see the translation by Rowland Smith in *The Signal and Other Stories*.

42. *The Red Laugh*, 99–101.

43. Ibid., 123, 140, 176.

44. Ibid., 177, 178.

45. Jeremiah Curtin, trans., *Lillian Morris and Other Stories* (Boston: Little, Brown, 1894), 160.

46. See Julian Kryzanowski, *Dziela Sienkiewicza, Bibliografia* (Warsaw: Panstwowoy Instytut Wydawniczy 1953), 47, 90. The Chinese translation of "Charcoal Sketches" was evidently based on Jeremiah Curtin's in *Hania*.

47. It was translated into English on four separate occasions before 1916, according to Jerzy J. Maciusko, *The Polish Short Story in English, A Guide and Critical Bibliography* (Detroit: Wayne State University Press, 1968), 235ff. The quotations given below are from Jeremiah Curtin, trans., *Yanko the Musician and Other Stories* (Boston: Little, Brown, 1897), 155–281.

48. It was translated as "Qiuzhang." The note appears in *Xin qingnian* 5.4 (1918): 403.

49. In section 10 of the story, p. 367 in the translation in *Hania* by Jeremiah Curtin.

50. P. 337.

51. Pp. 313, 310.

52. P. 322.

53. Sienkiewicz, *Yanko the Musician and Other Stories*, 199.

54. Sienkiewicz, *Hania*, 298. Zhou must have been translating from Jeremiah Curtin's translation. He was working only from English at this time, and the one other English

translation available bore an entirely different title; see Maciusko, *The Polish Short Story in English*, 260–61.

55. See Sienkiewicz, *Hania*, 352–65. A similar episode, in which Repa's wife seeks help from a priest but is told that "God tries His faithful" (344), was referred to by Lu Xun in a 1925 letter to Xu Guangping; see *Lu Xun quanji*, 11:14–15.

56. *Lu Xun xiaoshuoli de renwu*, 179. For an English translation, see Rowland Smith, *The Signal and Other Stories*.

57. *Lu Xun quanji*, 2:35.

58. Beijing: Beixin shuju, 107–13.

59. On the relationship between the two stories, see Xu Qinwen's *Panghuang fenxi* (Beijing: Zhongguo qingnian chubanshe, 1958), 36–39, and *Xuexi Lu Xun xiansheng* (Shanghai wenyi chubanshe, 1959), 57–60.

60. All the stories mentioned here were included in Xu Qinwen's *Guxiang*.

61. In his *Panghuang fenxi*, 39, Xu describes his method as irony (*fanhua*). In *Xuexi Lu Xun xiansheng*, 57–60, he tells how Lu Xun coached him in using objective (actually ironic) techniques.

62. On Lu Xun and the *Rulin waishi*, see *Xuexi Lu Xun xiansheng*, 57. Xu reports Lu Xun as saying that *Rulin waishi* had little influence on his work. The greatest influence was Sienkiewicz, whose technique was very close to that of *Panghuang*. If this last remark is represented as Lu Xun's—it is not clear from the context—I think it must have been garbled; the connections of the *Panghuang* stories with Sienkiewicz are slight as compared with those of the *Nahan* stories.

63. *The Institutio Oratoria of Quintilian*, Book VIII, 6:54–55 (Loeb Classical Library edition, 3:332–33): "in '*ironia*,' or, as our rhetoricians call it, '*illusio*' . . . it is permitted to censure with counterfeited praise and praise under a pretence of blame."

64. *The Fictions of Satire* (Baltimore: Johns Hopkins Press, 1967), 3. In Chinese, the term *fengci* means satire, which may include the lowering kind of irony. *Fanyu* and *fanhua* generally stand for that kind of irony.

65. For the sake of completeness, let us note that character irony may raise as well as lower. To take an example from film, the characters played by Humphrey Bogart often pretended to a callousness that their actions belied. Their "raising" effect was due to the working of this kind of irony.

66. See Quintilian, speaking of oratorical irony, "This [*ironia* or *illusio*] is made evident to the understanding either by the delivery, the character of the speaker, or the nature of the subject. For if any one of these three is out of keeping with the words, it at once becomes clear that the intention of the speaker is other than what he actually says."

67. *Lu Xun quanji*, 7:218.

68. *Lu Xun xiaoshuoli de renwu*, 28.

69. "Lun fenci" (On satire), *Lu Xun quanji*, 6:277–79, and "Shenme shi 'fengci'" (What is satire?), *Lu Xun quanji*, 6:328–30.

70. Cf. Lu Xun on the character irony of the character Fan Jin in *Rulin waishi*: "Without a single expression of censure, his hypocrisy is laid bare." *Zhongguo xiaoshuo shilüe*, *Lu Xun quanji*, 9:223.

71. On its interpretation, see C. T. Hsia, *A History of Modern Chinese Fiction, 1917–1957* (New Haven: Yale University Press, 1961), 42–44.

72. Translated by Constance Garnett in *The Schoolmaster and Other Stories* (London: Chatto and Windus, 1916).

73. Note the ironic use of the term "happy family" in Lu Xun's piece on Ibsen's Nora, "Nuola zouhou zenyang" (What happens to Nora after she leaves home?), *Lu Xun quanji*, 1:158–64. It originated as a talk given in December 1923.

74. Translated by Constance Garnett in *The Duel and Other Stories* (London: Chatto and Windus, 1916).

75. He apparently translated it from *The Sweet-scented Name and Other Fairy Tales, Fables and Stories.*

76. See Zhou Zuoren, *Lu Xun xiaoshuoli de renwu*, 195–97, and Xu Shouchang, *Wo suo renshi de Lu Xun* (Beijing: Renmin wenxue chubanshe, 1952), 61–65. On the "evil thought," see Zhou Zuoren, *Zhitang huixianglu*, 1:323.

77. Translated by Constance Garnett in *The Duel and Other Stories.*

78. *Zhu fu, cong xiaoshuo dao dianying* (Beijing: Zhongguo dianying chubanshe, 1959) contains a "literary" version of Xia Yan's film script. It also reprints Xia's "Remarks on Adaptation," 115–24.

79. See "'A Q zhengzhuan' de chengyin," *Lu Xun quanji*, 3:381, where the phrase is used ironically in talking of public executions in Beijing.

80. The story "Buzhou shan," written in 1922, was later removed from the *Nahan* collection and included in *Gushi xinbian*, under the title "Bu tian" (Repairing Heaven). The story is told through the goddess's sensations, and there is a sardonic ending. Eventually it slips into a kind of Swift-like denigration of mankind. Any attempt to treat myth in terms of diurnal realism involves a kind of irony, but this story does not belong with the others discussed here.

81. Especially in *Lu Xun de gujia, Lu Xun xiaoshuoli de renwu,* and *Zhitang huixianglu.*

82. Zhou Zuoren maintains, in *Zhitang huixianglu*, 2:424–27, that "Regret for the Past" is an allegorical treatment of his breakup with Lu Xun, but even if this claim were true, it would still put this story at one remove from those discussed here.

83. For example, Zhou Zuoren in *Lu Xun xiaoshuoli de renwu*, 30 ("Story of Hair"), 114–15 ("Double Fifth"), 163 ("The Misanthrope"), and 185 ("In the Wineshop"). Fang Bi (pseud. of Mao Dun) in "Lu Xun lun," *Xiaoshuo yuebao* 18.11 (November 10, 1927): 39, refers to Lu Xun's self-analysis and self-criticism. He is speaking of "An Incident" and "Double Fifth."

84. "Xie zai *Fen* houmian," *Lu Xun quanji*, 1:283–84. This was written in November 1926.

85. Many of his essays present Lu Xun obliquely, in a relaxed persona that is obviously at a considerable remove from his real state of mind. Some of them follow the rambling, associative order of the memoir until they reach their subject, an indirect approach that again reminds one of his fictional techniques. For an author who uses the first-person pronoun incessantly, Lu Xun rarely wrote directly, in a seemingly straightforward persona. His brother, Zhou Zuoren, makes the obvious contrast.

86. "Comedy of the Ducks" recalls Eroshenko's fairy tale, "The Chicken's Tragedy," which Lu Xun translated; see *Lu Xun yiwenji,* 2:324–27. His preface is dated January 1922.

87. Visual art appears to have meant almost as much to Lu Xun as literature. It would be surprising if no connection could be drawn between his tastes in the two fields. His stories' deliberate simplification and obliqueness of approach can perhaps be compared with the simplification of line and expressive distortion of forms such as the caricature, cartoon, and woodcut, which also speak for the moralist and call for a moral judgment from their public.

Works Cited

Aesop. *Fables*. *Yishi yuyan* 意拾寓言. Trans. "Mun Mooy" and Sloth (Robert Thom). Canton: Canton press office, 1840. (Houghton Library, Harvard University)

Analects of Confucius. Trans. D. C. Lau. London: Penguin, 1979.

Andreyev, Leonid. "The Abyss." In *The Seven That Were Hanged and Other Stories* (New York: Modern Library, 1958).

——. "Ben Tobit." In *The Seven That Were Hanged and Other Stories*. "Chitong" 齒痛. Trans. Zhou Zuoren. *Xin qingnian* 7.1 (Dec. 1919): 65–68.

——. *The Confessions of a Little Man During Great Days*. Trans. R. S. Townsend. New York: Knopf, 1917.

——. "In Fog." "Andande yanaili" 黯澹的煙靄裡. Trans. Lu Xun. In *Xiandai xiaoshuo yicong*, 1922. *Lu Xun yiwenji*, vol. 1.

——. "Lazarus." In *The Seven That Were Hanged and Other Stories*.

——. "The Lie." Trans. W. H. Lowe. In *The Little Angel and Other Stories*, trans. W. H. Lowe (New York: Knopf, 1916). "Man" 謾. Trans. Lu Xun. *Yuwai xiaoshuoji*, 1909. *Lu Xun yiwenji*, vol. 1.

——. *The Red Laugh, Fragments of a Discovered Manuscript*. Trans. Alexandra Linden. London: T. Fisher Unwin, 1905.

——. "Silence." In *The Little Angel and Other Stories*, trans. W. H. Lowe. "Mo" 默, trans. Lu Xun. In *Yuwai xiaoshuoji*, 1909. Reprint, *Lu Xun yiwenji*, vol. 1.

Aying 阿英. *Gengzi shibian wenxueji* 庚子事變文學集 (Beijing: Zhonghua shuju, 1958).

——. *Wan-Qing xiaoshuo shi* 晚清小説史. Reprint, Beijing: Renmin wenxue, 1980.

——. *Wan-Qing xiqu xiaoshuo mu* 晚清戲曲小説目. Shanghai: Gudian wenxue chubanshe, 1957.

Ball, Hermann. *Thirza, oder die Anziehungskraft des Kreuzes*. Trans. Elizabeth Maria Lloyd, *Thirza: or, The Attractive Power of the Cross*. London: B. Wertheim, 1842. (British

Library) Trans. Ferdinand Genähr, *Jinwu xingyi* 金屋型儀 (A model of a golden house). Hong Kong, 1852. (British Library)

Barnett, Susan Wilson and John King Fairbank, eds. *Christianity in China: Early Protestant Missionary Writings*. Cambridge: Harvard University Press, 1985.

Barnett, Susan Wilson. "Practical Evangelism: Protestant Missions and the Introduction of Western Civilization into China, 1820–1850." Ph.D. diss., Harvard University, 1973.

Bays, Daniel H. "Christian Tracts: The Two Friends." In Susan Wilson Barnett and John King Fairbank, *Christianity in China*, 19–34.

Bellamy, Edward. *Looking Backward, 2000–1887* (1888). *Hui tou kan jilüe* 回頭看紀略. Trans. Timothy Richard. *Wanguo gongbao* (Dec. 1891–April 1892). Retitled *Bainian yijiao* 百年一覺. Shanghai: Guangxuehui, 1894.

Bennett, Adrian Arthur. *John Fryer: The Introduction of Western Science and Technology into Nineteenth-Century China*. Cambridge: Harvard University, East Asian Research Center, 1967.

Beschi, Joseph. *Strange Surpassing Adventures of the Venerable Gooroo Simple, and His Five Disciples Noodle, Doodle, Wiseacre, Zany and Foozle*. Trans. B. G. Babington. Boston: Ticknor and Fields, 1861.

Boisgobey, Fortuné du. *La main coupée*. Paris: E. Plon, 1880. *Meiren Shou* 美人手. Trans. Hongyege Fengxian nüshi 紅葉閣鳳仙女史. *Xinmin congbian*, from no. 36 (Aug. 3, 1903).

———. *Margot la balafrée*. Paris: E. Plon, 1884. *In the Serpent's Coils*. London: Vizetelly, 1885. *Dushe quan* 毒蛇圈. Trans. Zhou Guisheng 周桂笙. *Xin xiaoshuo* 1903–1905. *Dushe quan, wai shizhong* 毒蛇圈, 外十種. Ed. Zhou Guoqing 周國慶. Changsha: Yuelu shushe, 1991.

Bunyan, John. *Pilgrim's Progress*. *Tianlu licheng* 天路歷程. Trans. William Burns, 1853, 1865–66. *Shenglü jingcheng* 聖旅景程. Trans. Thomas Hall Hudson. Ningbo, 1870. (British Library)

Burns, Islay. *Memoir of the Rev. Wm. C. Burns, M.A.* New York: Robert Carter and Brothers, 1870.

Caiyu Daoren 蔡遇道人 (pseud.). *Jigua canzhui* 寄蝸殘贅. 1872 preface by author.

Cambridge History of China. Vol. 11, ed. John K. Fairbank. Cambridge: Cambridge University Press, 1978.

Cao Xueqin 曹學芹. *Shitouji* 石頭記 (i.e., *Honglou meng* 紅樓夢). 3 vols. Taipei: Lianjing chuban shiye gongsi, 1991.

Catalogue of the Chinese Imperial Maritime Customs Collection at the International Exhibition, Philadelphia, 1876. Shanghai: Inspectorate General of Customs, 1876.

Chang, Hsin-pao. *Commissioner Lin and the Opium War*. Cambridge: Harvard University Press, 1964.

Chekhov, Anton. "At Home." In *The Duel and Other Stories*.

———. *The Duel and Other Stories*. Trans. Constance Garnett. London: Chatto and Windus, 1916.

———. "Hush!" In *The Schoolmaster and Other Stories*, trans. Constance Garnett (London: Chatto and Windus, 1921).

———. "The Princess." In *The Duel and Other Stories*.

Chen Bohai 陳伯海 and Yuan Jin 袁進. *Shanghai jindai wenxueshi* 上海近代文學史. Shanghai: Shanghai renmin chubanshe, 1993.

Chen, Chi-yun. "Liang Ch'i-ch'ao's 'Missionary Education': A Case Study of Missionary Influence on the Reformers." *Papers on China* (East Asian Research Center, Harvard University) 16 (1962): 66–125.

Chen Diexian 陳蝶仙 (Chen Xu 陳栩). "Bulu wuxu liuyue shiqi jishi" 補錄戊戌六月十七紀事. *Xin Yiyuji.* Reprinted in *Xuyuan conggao, ce* 3, 14a.

——. *Daxue xinjiang* 大學新講. 5th ed. Shanghai: Sanyou shiyeshe, 1934.

——. "Da Xu Heseng jianwen Zhenglou ying shi" 答許荷僧見問箏樓影事. *Xuyuan conggao, ce* 3, 49b.

——. *Huangjin sui* 黃金祟. 3 parts. Reprint of the 1914 Zhonghua tushuguan edition. *Zhongguo jindai xiaoshuo shiliao huibian.* Taipei: Guangwen shuju, 1980. *The Money Demon.* Trans. Patrick Hanan. Honolulu: University of Hawaii Press, 1999.

——. *Jiao Yingji* 嬌櫻記. *Shen bao,* from Feb. 12, 1913. Shanghai: Zhonghua tushuguan, 1917. (Wason Collection, Cornell University)

——. "Jiwai shumu" 集外書目. *Xuyuan conggao, ce* 1.

——. "*Jiuxianglou jishi shi*" 九香樓紀事詩. *Xuyuan conggao, ce* 2, 33a–41a.

——. *Leizhu yuan* 淚珠緣. Zhongguo jindai xiaoshuo daxi series. Nanchang: Baihuazhou wenyi chubanshe, 1991.

——. *Lixiao ji* 麗綃記. *Shen bao,* from May 3, 1913.

——. *Liu Feiyan* 柳非煙. From *Yueyue xiaoshuo* 1.10 (Nov. 1907).

——. *Luohua meng* 落花夢. (Revision of *Taohua meng.*) *Nüzi shijie,* from Dec. 1914.

——. *Manyuan hua* 滿園花. *Shen bao,* from May 14, 1914.

——. *Sanjia qu* 三家曲. Co-authors, He Songhua 何頌花 and Hua Chishi 華癡石. Hangzhou, 1900. (Fudan University Library)

——. *Ta zhi xiao shi* 他之小史. *Nüzi shijie* (Dec. 1914–July 1915).

——. *Taohua meng* 桃花夢. Hangzhou: Daguanbao, c. 1900. (Fudan University Library)

——. *Taohua ying tanci* 桃花影彈詞, 1900. (Fudan University Library)

——. "Wo sheng pian" 我生篇. *Xuyuan conggao, ce* 3, 33b.

——. "Wo zhi xinnian" 我之新年 (My New Years). *Shen bao,* March 7–10, 1916.

——. *Xiaoxiang ying tanci* 瀟湘影彈詞. (Reprint of *Taohua ying.*) Shanghai: Zhonghua tushuguan, 1918.

——. *Xin Yiyuji* 新疑雨集. *Yisuyuan congshu* 一粟園叢書 series. Hangzhou: Cui Li Company, n.d. (Harvard-Yenching Library). Reprint in *Xuyuan conggao, ce* 3.

——. "Xinchou chongjiuhou wuri Jiuxiang jishi" 辛丑重九後五日九香紀事. *Xuyuan conggao, ce* 2, 42b.

——. *Xuyuan conggao* 栩園叢稿. 10 fascicles. Ed. Zhou Zhisheng 周之盛. Shanghai: Jiating gongyeshe, after 1927.

——. *Xuyuan conggao chubian* 栩園叢稿初編. 5 fascicles. Shanghai: Zhuyitang yinshuju, after 1927.

——. "You liuyue shiba shi" 又六月十八事. *Xin Yiyuji.* Reprint in *Xuyuan conggao, ce* 3, 14ab.

——. "You Yiyuan you huai Gu-shi Zhongjie" 游怡園有懷顧氏仲姊. *Xin Yiyuji.* Reprint in *Xuyuan conggao, ce* 2, 14b.

——. *Yuanyang xue* 鴛鴦雪. *Shen bao*, from Nov. 22, 1912. Shanghai: Zhonghua tushu-guan, 1917.

——. *Zhenglou ping shi ji* 箏樓評詩記. *Zhuzuolin* 1–4 (third through sixth months, 1907).

——. "Zhenglouji" 箏樓記. *Xin Yiyuji*. Reprint in *Xuyuan conggao, ce* 3, 15a–17b. Trans. Patrick Hanan, *Money Demon*, 279–84.

——. *Ziyou hua tanci* 自由花彈詞. *Shen bao*, 1912–13. Shanghai: Zhonghua tushuguan, 1916. (Shanghai Library)

Chen Pingyuan 陳平原. *Zhongguo xiaoshuo xushi mushi de zhuanbian* 中國小說敘事模式的轉變. Shanghai: Shanghai renmin chubanshe, 1988.

Chen Qu 陳蘧 (Xiaodie 小蝶, Dingshan 定山). *Chun Shen jiuwen xuji* 春申舊聞續集. Taipei: Chenguang yuekanshe, 1955.

——. *Tian Xu Wo Sheng jiniankan* 天虛我生紀年刊. Ed. Chen Qu. *Zixiu zhoukan* 自修週刊 (April 1940). (Shanghai Library)

——. "Wode fuqin Tian Xu Wo Sheng—guohuo zhi yinzhe" 我的父親天虛我生——國貨之隱者. *Chun Shen jiuwen xuji*, 179–204.

Chen Ruheng 陳汝衡. *Shuoyuan zhenwen* 說苑珍聞. Shanghai: Shanghai guji chubanshe, 1981.

Chen Sen 陳森. *Pin hua baojian* 品花寶鑑, ed. Xu Deming 徐德明. 2 vols. Taipei: San-min shuju, 1998.

China Directory for 1874. 1874; reprint, Taipei: Ch'eng Wen Publishing Company, 1971.

Chinese Recorder and Missionary Journal. 43 vols. Shanghai: American Presbyterian Mission Press, 1868–1912.

Chinese Repository. From 1832. 20 vols. Reprint, Tokyo: Maruzen, n.d.

Chinnery, J. D. "The Influence of Western Literature on Lu Xun's 'Diary of a Madman.'" *Bulletin of the School of Oriental and African Studies* 23.2 (1960): 309–22.

Clayton, George A. *Jidu shengjiao chuban geshu shumu huizuan* 基督聖教出版各書書目彙纂. Hankou: Shengjiao shuju, 1918.

Cottage on the Shore, or Little Gwen's Story. New York: T. Whittaker, n.d. (New York Public Library). *Guinuo zhuan* 閨娜傳. Trans. Mary Harriet Porter. Chinese Religious Tract Society, 1882. (British Library)

Couling, Samuel. *Encyclopedia Sinica.* London: Oxford University Press, 1917.

Crawford, Martha. *Sange guinü* 三個閨女. Shanghai, 1872. (Bodleian Library)

Cui Xiangchuan 崔象川. *Yuchanji* 玉蟾記. Guben xiaoshuo jicheng series. Shanghai guji chubanshe, 1990.

Davis, John Francis. *The Chinese: A General Description of the Empire and Its Inhabitants.* New York: Harper and Sons, 1836.

——. *A Chinese Tragedy.* London: Oriental Translation Fund, 1829.

Dean, William. *The China Mission.* New York: Sheldon, 1859.

Dickens, Charles. *David Copperfield. Kuai rou yusheng shu* 塊肉餘生述. Trans. Lin Shu 林紓 and Wei Yi 魏易. *Lin yi xiaoshuo congshu*, vol. 6.

Dolezelova-Velingerova, Milena, ed. *The Chinese Novel at the Turn of the Century.* Toronto: University of Toronto Press, 1980.

Dong Weiye 董偉業. *Yangzhou zhuzhici* 揚州竹枝詞. In *Yangzhou zhuzhici*, ed. Xia You-lan 夏友蘭 et al. (Yangzhou: Privately published, 1992).

Du Mu 杜牧. *Fanchuan shiji* 樊川詩集. Ed. Feng Jiwu 馮集梧. Beijing: Zhonghua shuju, 1962.

Dumas, Alexandre *fils*. *La dame aux camélias. Bali Chahuanü yishi* 巴黎茶花女遺事. Trans. Lin Shu and Wang Shouchang 王壽昌. *Lin yi xiaoshuo congshu*, vol. 7.

Eroshenko, Vasilii. "The Chicken's Tragedy." "Xiaoji de beiju" 小雞的悲劇. Trans. Lu Xun. *Lu Xun yiwenji*, 2:324–27.

Eyster, Nellie Blessing. *A Beautiful Life, Memoir of Mrs. Eliza Nelson Fryer 1847–1910.* Berkeley, Calif.: Privately published, 1912.

Fei Ming (pseud.). *Henhai hua* 恨海花 (Flowers in the sea of regret). 1905. 3rd ed. Shanghai: author, 1907. (Shanghai Library)

Feng Menglong 馮夢龍. *Gujin xiaoshuo* 古今小説. Ed. Li Tianyi 李田意. 2 vols. Hong Kong: Longmen shudian, 1982.

Fengyue meng 風月夢 (Illusion of romance; see also under *Mengyou Shanghai mingji zheng feng zhuan*). Shenbaoguan movable-type edition, 1883. Modern edition, Beijing: Beijing daxue chubanshe, 1990. Another modern edition by Wang Junnian 王俊年, *Xiaoshuo erjuan* 小説二卷. Zhongguo jindai wenxue zuopin xilie series. Fuzhou: Haixia wenyi chubanshe, 1990.

Fryer, John. "Chinese Education—Past, Present and Future, Part I." *Chinese Recorder* (July 1897):329–35.

——. "Chinese Literature, Part II." In "Correspondence and Papers."

——. "Chinese Prize Essays." In *The John Fryer Miscellany*.

——. "The Chinese Problem." In "Correspondence and Papers."

——. "Correspondence and Papers." (Bancroft Library, University of California at Berkeley)

——. *The John Fryer Miscellany*. (Bancroft Library)

——. "Letter Journal." In "Correspondence and Papers."

——. "The Literature of China." *The University Chronicle* 4 (1901): 165–75.

——. "The Normal Chinese Essay." In "Correspondence and Papers."

——. "Science in China Part II." *Nature* 24 (May 19, 1881): 54–57.

——. "The War between China and Japan." In "Correspondence and Papers."

——. "Why Japan Has Developed Differently from China." In "Correspondence and Papers."

Fu Lin 符霖 (pseud.). *Qin hai shi* 禽海石 (Stones in the sea). Shanghai: Qunxueshe 群學社, 1906; (Chinese Writers' Union, Shanghai Branch). 1909, 1913 editions (Capital Library, Beijing). Zhongguo jindai wenxue daxi series. Shanghai: Shanghai shudian, 1991, vol. 6. *The Sea of Regret*. Trans. Patrick Hanan. Honolulu: University of Hawaii Press, 1995.

Garshin, Vsevolod. "Four Days." In *The Signal and Other Stories*, trans. Rowland Smith (New York: Knopf, 1916). "Si ri." Trans. Lu Xun. *Yuwai xiaoshuoji*, 1909. *Lu Xun yiwenji*, vol. 1.

——. "An Incident." In *The Signal and Other Stories*.

——. "The Scarlet Blossom." In *The Signal and Other Stories*.

——. "A Very Short Romance." In *The Signal and Other Stories*. "Yijian hen duan de chuanqi" 一件很短的傳奇. Trans. Lu Xun. *Lu Xun yiwenji*, 10:568–82.

Ge Qilong 葛其龍. *Ji'an shichao* 寄庵詩鈔. 1878.

General Catalogue of Chinese Catholic Books. Hong Kong: Catholic Truth Society, 1941.

General Index of Subjects Contained in the Twenty Volumes of the Chinese Repository. 1851; reprint, Tokyo: Maruzen, n.d.

Genette, Gérard. *Fiction and Diction.* Trans. Catherine Porter. Ithaca: Cornell University Press, 1993.

——. *Narrative Discourse, An Essay in Method.* Trans. Jane E. Lewin. Ithaca: Cornell University Press, 1980.

——. *Narrative Discourse Revisited.* Trans. Janes E. Lewin. Ithaca: Cornell University Press, 1988.

Gogol, Nikolai. *Dead Souls.* Trans. Bernard Guilbert Guerney. New York: Rinehart, 1942. *Si hunling* 死魂靈. Trans. Lu Xun. First published 1935. *Lu Xun yiwenji*, 9:31–356.

——. "The Tale of how Ivan Ivanovich Quarreled with Ivan Nikiforovich." Trans. Ronald Wilks. In *Diary of a Madman and Other Stories.* London: Penguin, 1972.

——. "Diary of a Madman." In *Diary of a Madman and Other Stories.*

Guanglingqu zhi 廣陵區志. Comp. by Guanglingqu difangzhi bianzuan weiyuanhui. Zhongguo renmin gongheguo difangzhi congshu series. Beijing: Zhonghua shuju, 1993.

Guo Changhai 郭長海. "Lishao Jushi he Lichuang Wodusheng" 蠡勺居士和黎床臥讀生. *Ming-Qing xiaoshuo yanjiu* 明清小説研究 3–4 (1992): 457–61.

Guo Yanli 郭延禮. *Zhongguo jindai fanyi wenxue gailun* 中國近代翻譯文學概論. Hankou: Hubei jiaoyu chubanshe, 1998.

Gützlaff, Karl F. A. *Changhuo zhi dao zhuan* 常活之道傳. 1834. (British Library)

——. *Cheng chong bai lei han* 誠崇拜類函. Singapore, 1834. (British Library)

——. *China Opened.* London: Smith, Elder, 1838.

——. "Christian Missions in China." *Chinese Repository* 3.12 (1835): 559–68.

——. *Da Yingguo tongzhi* 大英國統志. 1834. (Harvard-Yenching Library)

——. *Dong xi yang kao meiyue tongji zhuan* 東西洋考每月統記傳. From 1833.

——. *Gujin wanguo gangjian* 古今萬國綱鑑. Singapore: Jianxia shuyuan, 1838.

——. *Hui zui zhi dalüe* 悔罪之大略. n.d. (British Library)

——. *Huimo xundao* 誨謨訓道. Singapore, 1838. (Harvard-Yenching Library)

——. "The Journal of a Residence in Siam and of a Voyage along the Coast of China to Mantchou Tartary." *Chinese Repository* 1.1 (May 1832): 16–25; 1.2 (June 1832): 45–64; 1.3 (July 1832): 81–99; 1.4 (Aug. 1832): 122–40; 1.5 (Sept. 1832): 180–96.

——. "Journal of a Voyage along the Coast of China from the Province of Canton to Leautung in Mantchou Tartary, 1832–33." *Chinese Repository* 2.1 (May 1833): 20–32; 2.2 (June 1833): 49–60.

——. "Pride and Humility." *Chinese Repository* 2.8 (1833).

——. "Remarks on Buddhism; together with brief notices of the island of Poo-to, and of the numerous priests who inhabit it." *Chinese Repository* 2.5 (Sept. 1833): 214–25.

——. *Sheng shu zhu shu* 聖書註疏. Singapore: Jianxia shuyuan, 1839. (Harvard-Yenching Library)

——. *Shifei lüelun* 是非略論. Malacca: Ying-Hua shuyuan, 1835. (American Philosophical Society Library)

——. *Shu zui zhi dao* 贖罪之道 (The doctrine of redemption). 21 chapters. 1834. (British Library)

——. *Shu zui zhi dao zhuan* 贖罪之道傳. 18 chapters. A rewriting and condensation of the above. 1836.

——. *Zheng xie bijiao* 正邪比較. Singapore: Jianxia shuyuan, 1838. (Harvard-Yenching Library)

Haggard, H. Rider. *Joan Haste. Ja'in xiaozhuan.* 迦茵小傳. Trans Lin Shu and Wei yi. *Lin yi xiaoshuo congshu*, vol. 9.

Haiyouji 海游記. Preface by Guanshuren. Reprint, Shenyang: Liaoshen shushe, 1990.

Han Bangqing 韓邦慶. *Haishang hua liezhuan* 海上花列傳. Zhongguo jindai xiaoshuo daxi series. Nanchang: Baihuazhou wenyi chubanshe, 1993.

Hanan, Patrick. "Chinese Christian Literature: The Writing Process." In *Treasures of the Yenching*, ed. Patrick Hanan (Cambridge: Harvard-Yenching Library, 2003), 260–83.

Hangzhou fuzhi 杭州府志. Ed. Wu Qingdi, Qi Yaoshan. 1922–26. Reprint, Zhongguo difangzhi jicheng series. Shanghai: Shanghai shudian, 1993.

He Mengmei 何夢梅. *Da Ming Zhengde Huang you Jiangnan zhuan* 大明正德皇遊江南傳. 1832. Reprint in *Guben xiaoshuo jicheng*, third series. Shanghai: Shanghai guji chubanshe, 1990. *The Rambles of the Emperor Ching Tih in Keäng Nan, a Chinese Tale.* Trans. He Jinshan 何進善 and James Legge. London, 1843.

He Zou 何諏. *Suiqin lou* 碎琴樓. First published 1911. Reprint, Zhongguo jindai xiaoshuo daxi series. Nanchang: Baihuazhou wenyi chubanshe, 1996.

Helliwell, David. "Two Collections of Nineteenth-Century Protestant Missionary Publications in Chinese." *Chinese Culture* 31.4 (1990): 21–38.

Hobson, Benjamin. *Quanti xinlun* 全體新論. Guangzhou: Hui'ai yiguan, 1851.

Hsia, C.T. *A History of Modern Chinese Fiction, 1917–1957.* New Haven: Yale University Press, 1961.

——. "Hsü Chen-ya's *Yu-li Hun*, An Essay in Literary History and Criticism." *Renditions* 17 and 18 (1982): 199–240.

Hu Congjing 胡從經. *Wan Qing ertong wenxue gouchen* 晚清兒童文學鉤沉. Shanghai: Shaonian ertong chubanshe, 1982.

Hu Daojing 胡道靜. "Shanghai de ribao" 上海的日報. *Shanghai tongzhiguan qikan* 2.1 (1934): 219–325.

Hu Shi 胡適, *Hu Shi wencun erji* 胡適文存二集 Reprint, Hefei: Huangshan shushe, 1996.

Huang Duo 黃鐸. *Quyuji* 胠餘集. Shanghai, 1911. (Shanghai Library)

Huang Jinzhu 黃錦珠. "Jiawu zhi yi yu wan-Qing xiaoshuojie" 甲午之役與晚清小説界. *Zhongguo wenxue yanjiu*. National Taiwan University (May 1991):1–18.

Hyatt, Irwin T., Jr. *Our Ordered Lives Confess.* Cambridge: Harvard University Press, 1976.

Illustrated Catalogue of the Chinese Collection of Exhibits for the International Health Exhibition, London, 1884. China Maritime Customs Miscellaneous Series No. 12. London: William Clowes and Sons, 1884.

Irving, Washington. "Rip Van Winkle." *The Sketchbook of Geoffrey Crayon, Gent.* Chicago: Belford, Clarke, 1886. "Yishui qishinian" 一睡七十年. *Shen bao*, May 28, 1872.

Jiang Qizhang 蔣其章. (See also under Xiao Jiluoan Zhu.) *Wenyuan jinghua* 文苑菁華. Shanghai: Shenbaoguan, 1873.

Jiang Ruizao 蔣瑞藻. *Xiaoshuo kaozheng xubian* 小說考證續編. Reprint, Shanghai: Gudian wenxue chubanshe, 1957.

John, Griffith and Shen Zixing 沈子星. *Hong zhuru* 紅侏儒. Hankou: Hankou Mission Press, 1882.

———. *Yin jia dang dao* 引家當道. Hankou: Christian Tract Society, 1882.

John, Juliet. *Cult Criminals: The Newgate Novels, 1830–1847*. London: Routledge, 1998.

Jones, Mervyn. *Five Hungarian Writers*. London: Oxford University Press, 1966.

Jones, William. *The Jubilee Memorial of the Religious Tract Society*. London: Religious Tract Society, 1850.

Karpeles, Gustav. *Allgemeine Geschichte der Literatur von ihren Anfangen bis auf die Gegenwart*. 3 vols. Berlin, 1901.

Kaun, Alexander. *Leonid Andreyev, A Critical Study*. New York: B. W. Huebsch, 1924.

Kikuchi Yūhō 菊池幽芳. *Shinbun uriko* 新聞賣子. First published in *Osaka Mainichi shinbun* in 1897. Osaka: Shinshindō, 1900. *Dianshu qitan* 電術奇談. Trans. Wu Jianren from a translation in literary Chinese by Fang Qingzhou 方慶周. From *Xin xiaoshuo* 1.8 (eighth month, 1903).

Kryzanowski, Julian. *Dziela Sienkiewicza, Bibliografia*. Warsaw: Panstwowoy Instytut Wydawniczy, 1953.

Lee, Leo Ou-fan. *The Romantic Generation of Modern Chinese Writers*. Cambridge: Harvard University Press, 1973.

Legge, James. (See also under He Mengmei.) *Yabolahan jilüe* 亞伯拉罕紀略. 1857 preface. Hong Kong: Ying-Hua shuyuan, 1862. (British Library)

———. *Yuese jilüe* 約色紀略. 1852 preface. Hong Kong: Ying-Hua shuyuan, 1870. (British Library)

Li Dou 李斗. *Yangzhou huafanglu* 揚州畫舫錄. Ed. Zhou Guangpei 周光培. Yangzhou: Jiangsu Guangling guji keyinshe, 1984.

Li Jianguo 李劍國. *Tangqian zhiguai xiaoshuo jishi* 唐前志怪小說輯釋. Shanghai: Shanghai guji chubanshe, 1986.

Li Jiarong 李葭榮. "Wofo Shanren zhuan" 我佛山人傳. In Wei Shaochang, *Wu Jianren yanjiu ziliao*, 10–15.

Li Longqian 李龍潛. *Ming Qing jingjishi* 明清經濟史. Guangzhou: Guangdong gaodeng jiaoyu chubanshe, 1988.

Li Ruzhen 李汝珍. *Jing hua yuan* 鏡花緣. Shanghai: Shanghai guji chubanshe, 1996.

Liang Qichao 梁啓超. (See also under Jules Verne.) *Jiehui meng chuanqi* 劫灰夢傳奇. *Xinmin congbao* 1 (first month, 1902): 105–8.

———. "Lun xiaoshuo yu qunzhi zhi guanxi" 論小說與群治之關系. *Xin xiaoshuo* 1 (tenth month, 1902): 1–8.

———. "Lun xuexiao, youxue" 論學校, 幼學. *Shiwu bao* 時務報 17 (twelfth month, 1896), 1a–4b; 18 (first month, 1897), 1a–3a; 19 (second month), 1a–3b.

———. *"Mengxue bao* yu *Yanyi bao* hexu" 蒙學報與演義報合敘. *Shiwu bao* 44 (Nov. 1897): 5ab.

———. "Xin min shuo" 新民説. *Xinmin congbao* 5 (third month, 1902): 1–11.

——. *Xin Zhongguo weilai ji* 新中國未來記. From *Xin xiaoshuo* 1 (tenth month, 1902).

——. "Xixue shumu biao" 西學書目表. In *Zhixue congshu chuji* 質學叢書初集 (Wuchang: Zhixuehui, 1897).

——. "Yiyin zhengzhi xiaoshuo xu" 譯印政治小説序. *Qingyi bao* 1 (eleventh month, 1898): 53–54.

——. "Zhongguo weiyi zhi wenxuebao *Xin xiaoshuo*" 中國唯一之文學報新小説. Foldout advertisement inside front cover of *Xinmin congbao* 14 (seventh month, 1902).

Lihun bing 離魂病, trans. Luo Pu from a Japanese translation by Kuroiwa Ruikō 黑岩泪香 entitled *Tantei* 探偵 (1890); see Tarumoto, *Qingmo Minchu xiaoshuo mulu*, 405. From *Xin xiaoshuo* 1 (tenth month, 1902).

Lin Daiyu 林黛玉 (attrib.). *Beinan shimoji* 被難始末記. Reprint, Aying 阿英, *Gengzi shibian wenxueji* 庚子事變文學集. Beijing: Zhonghua shuju, 1958, 2:1065–85.

Lin Shu 林紓, *Lin yi xiaoshuo congshu* 林譯小説叢書. Beijing: Shangwu yinshuguan, 1881.

Ling Mengchu 凌濛初. *Pai'an jingqi* 拍案驚奇. Ed. Li Tianyi 李田意. 2 vols. Hong Kong: Youlian chubanshe, 1966.

Liu E 劉鶚. *Lao Can youji* 老殘遊記. Zhongguo jindai xiaoshuo daxi series. Nanchang: Baihuazhou wenyi chubanshe, 1993.

Lu Xun 魯迅. "'A Q zhengzhuan' de chengyin" 阿 Q 正傳的成因. *Lu Xun quanji*, vol. 3.

——. "Buzhou shan" 不周山. First published in *Nahan*, then as "Bu tian" 補天 in *Gushi xinbian*.

——. *Gushi xinbian* 故事新編. First published in 1936. *Lu Xun quanji* 2:341–481.

——. "Huai jiu" 懷舊. First published in 1911. *Lu Xun quanji* 7:215–21.

——. *Lu Xun quanji* 魯迅全集. 16 vols. Beijing: Renmin wenxue chubanshe, 1981.

——. *Lu Xun riji* 魯迅日記. 2 vols. Beijing: Renmin wenxue chubanshe, 1959.

——. *Lu Xun yiwenji* 魯迅譯文集. 10 vols. Beijing: Renmin wenxue chubanshe, 1959.

——. "Lun fengci" 論諷刺. *Lu Xun quanji*, 6:277–79.

——. *Nahan* 吶喊. First published 1923. *Lu Xun quanji*, vol. 1.

——. "Nuola zouhou zenyang" 娜拉走後怎樣. *Lu Xun quanji*, 1:158–64.

——. *Panghuang* 彷徨. First published 1926. *Lu Xun quanji*, vol. 2.

——. "Shenme shi 'fengci'" 甚麼是 '諷刺'?. *Lu Xun quanji*, 6:328–30.

——. "Sibada zhi hun" 斯巴達之魂. *Lu Xun quanji*, 7:9–16.

——. "Wo zenme zuoqi xiaoshuo lai" 我怎麼做起小説來?. *Lu Xun quanji*, 4:511–14.

——. *Xiandai xiaoshuo yicong* 現代小説譯叢. First published in 1922. *Lu Xun yiwenji*, 1:313–434.

——. "Xie zai *Fen* houmian" 寫在墳後面. *Lu Xun quanji*, 1:282–87.

——. *Yuwai xiaoshuoji* 域外小説集. Trans. Lu Xun and Zhou Zuoren. Expanded edition, Shanghai: Qunyi shushe, 1920. Lu Xun's translations reprinted in *Lu Xun yiwenji*, vol. 1.

——. "Zhongguo xiaoshuo de lishi de bianqian" 中國小説的歷史的變遷 (1925), appended to Lu Xun, *Zhongguo xiaoshuo shilüe* 中國小説史略 (Beijing: Renmin wenxue chubanshe, 1979), 452–53.

Luo Pu 羅普. (See also under Jules Verne and *Lihun bing*.) *Dong-Ou nü haojie* 東歐女豪 傑. *Xin xiaoshuo* 1 (tenth month, 1902).

Lutz, Jessie G. "Karl F. A. Gützlaff: Missionary Entrepreneur." In Barnett and Fairbank, *Christianity in China*, 61–87.

Lytton, Victor Bulwer, Earl of Lytton. *The Life of Edward Bulwer, First Lord Lytton*. London: MacMillan, 1913.

Lytton, Edward Bulwer. *Alice* (1838). *Karyū shunwa* 花柳春話, translated together with *Ernest Maltravers* by Niwa (Oda) Jun'ichiro 丹羽純一郎 (1879). *Meiji hon'yaku bungaku shū* 明治翻譯文學集 (1972) in *Meiji bungaku zenshū* 明治文學全集 series.

——. *England and the English* (1833). Ed. Standish Meacham. Chicago: University of Chicago Press, 1970.

——. *Ernest Maltravers* (1837). 1840 edition, with new preface. *Karyū shunwa* 花柳春話, translated together with *Alice* by Niwa (Oda) Jun'ichiro 丹羽純一郎 (1879). *Meiji hon'yaku bungaku shū* 明治翻譯文學集 (1972) in *Meiji bungaku zenshū* 明治文學全 集 series.

——. *Night and Morning*. 1845 edition, with new preface. Philadelphia: Lippincott, 1865. *Xinxi xiantan* 昕夕聞談 (Idle talk morning to evening), trans. probably by Jiang Qizhang and Ernest Major. *Yinghuan suoji* 瀛寰瑣記, 1873–75. Separately published, Shanghai: Shenbaoguan, 1875.

——. *The Poems and Ballads of Schiller*. London: William Blackwood and Sons, 1844.

Lytton, Robert Bulwer. *The Life and Letters and Literary Remains of Edward Bulwer, Lord Lytton*. London: Kegan, Paul, Trench, 1883.

MacGillivray, Donald. *New Classified and Descriptive Catalogue of Current Christian Literature, 1901*. Shanghai: Society for the Diffusion of Christian and General Knowledge Among the Chinese, 1902. (British Library) Expanded edition, Shanghai: Christian Literature Society, 1907.

Maciusko, Jerzy J. *The Polish Short Story in English*. Detroit: Wayne State University Press, 1968.

Mackenzie, Robert. *The 19th Century, A History* (1880). *Taixi xinshi lanyao* 泰西新史覽要. Trans. Timothy Richard and Cai Erkang 蔡爾康. Shanghai: Guangxuehui, 1895.

Malan, César. *Le Pauvre Horloger de Genève. Zhongbiaojiang lun* 鐘表匠論. Revision by Justus Doolittle of the translation by Samuel Kidd, 1829. Fuzhou: American Tract Society, 1855. (Harvard-Yenching Library)

Mao Dun 茅盾 (Fang Bi 方璧 pseud). "Lu Xun lun" 魯迅論. *Xiaoshuo yuebao* 18.11 (Nov. 1927): 37–48.

Marryat, Frederick. *The Pacha of Many Tales*. London: Routledge, 1862. Partially translated as "Naisuguo qiwen" 乃蘇國奇聞. *Shen bao*, May–June 1872.

McMahon, Keith. *The Fall of the God of Money*. Lanham, Md.: Rowan and Littlefield, 2002.

Medhurst, Walter Henry. *China: Its State and Prospects*. London: J. Snow, 1838.

Mencius. Trans. D. C. Lau. London: Penguin, 1970.

Mengyou Shanghai mingji zheng feng zhuan 夢游上海名妓爭風傳, adapted from *Fengyue meng*. Reprint, *Shanghai mingji zhuan* 上海名妓傳, Zhongguo lidai jinshu xuancong series. Hefei: Huangshan chubanshe, 1993.

Milne, William. *A Retrospect of the First Ten Years of the Protestant Mission in China*. Malacca: Anglo-Chinese Press, 1820.

———. *Zhang Yuan liang you xiang lun* 張遠兩友相論. Malacca: Anglo-Chinese Press, 1819.

More, Hannah. *Parley the Porter. Liang ke yuyan* 兩可喻言. Trans. Mary Harriet Porter. Beijing: American Presbyterian Mission Press, 1875.

Mori Ogai 森鷗外. "Chinmoku no tō" 沈默の塔. In *Ogai zenshū* 鷗外全集 (Tokyo: Iwanami, 1971), 7:381–93.

Morrison, Robert. *Gushi Rudiyaguo lidai lüezhuan* 古時如地亞國歷代略傳. 1815. (Harvard-Yenching Library)

———. *Xiyou diqiu wenjian lüezhuan* 西游地球聞見略傳. Malacca, 1819. (British Library)

Murdoch, John. *Report on Christian Literature in China, with a Catalogue of Publications*. Shanghai: Hoi-Lee Press, 1882.

Natsume Sōseki 夏目漱石. *Gubijinsō* 虞美人草. In *Sōseki zenshū* 漱石全集 (Tokyo: Iwanami, 1993), 4:1–456.

———. *Wagahai wa neko de aru* 吾輩は貓でる. *Sōseki zenshū* 1:1–568.

Nüzi shijie 女子世界. Ed. Chen Diexian. Shanghai: Zhonghua tushuguan, from 1914. (Peking University Library)

Ouyang Jian 歐陽健. *Wan-Qing xiaoshuo shi* 晚清小説史. Hangzhou: Zhejiang guji chubanshe, 1997.

Paulson, Ronald. *The Fictions of Satire*. Baltimore: Johns Hopkins University Press, 1967.

Phelps, William Lyon. *Essays on Russian Novelists*. New York: MacMillan, 1911.

Ping Jinchuan quanzhuan 平金川全傳. Zhongguo shenguai xiaoshuo daxi series. Chengdu: Bashu shushe, 1989.

Qian Zheng 錢徵. *Xieyu congtan chuji* 屑玉叢談初集. Shanghai: Shenbaoguan, 1878.

Qian Zhongshu 錢鍾書. "Lin Shu de fanyi" 林紓的翻譯. In *Lin Shu yanjiu ziliao* 林紓研究資料, ed. Xue Suizhi 薛綏之 and Zhang Juncai 張俊才 (Fuzhou: Fujian renmin chubanshe, 1982), 292–323.

Qin Shou'ou 秦瘦鷗. "Wan-Qing xiaoshuo souyi—*Taiwan jinguo yingxiong zhuan* de faxian" 晚清小説搜遺——臺灣巾幗英雄傳的發現. *Shu lin* 書林 1 (1980): 48–49.

Qingfeng zha 清風閘. Ed. Li Daoying 李道英. Beijing: Beijing shifan daxue chubanshe, 1992.

Qingyi bao 清議報. Ed. Liang Qichao. 1898–1901. 12 vols. Reprint, Taipei: Cheng wen chubanshe, 1967.

Quintilian. *The Institutio Oratoria of Quintilian*. With English translation by H. E. Butler. Loeb Classical Library. Cambridge: Harvard University Press, 1958.

Quxian zhi 衢縣志. Ed. Quxian zhi bianzuan weiyuanhui. Hangzhou: Zhejiang renmin chubanshe, 1992.

Records of the Triennial Meeting of the Educational Association of China, Shanghai, May 2–4, 1893. Reprint, Taipei: Ch'eng Wen Publishing House, 1971.

Records of the Triennial Meeting of the Educational Association of China, Shanghai, May 6–9, 1896. Reprint, Taipei: Ch'eng Wen Publishing House, 1971.

Richard, Timothy. *Forty-five Years in China*. New York: Frederick A. Stokes, 1919.

———. "Scheme for the General Enlightenment of China." *Chinese Recorder* 23.3 (March 1892): 131–32.

Rolston, David. *Traditional Chinese Fiction and Fiction Commentary*. Stanford: Stanford University Press, 1997.

Scherr, Johannes. *Allgemeine Geschichte der Literatur*. Stuttgart: Conradi, 1880.

Schorer, Mark. "Technique as Discovery." *Hudson Review* 1.1 (Spring 1948): 67–87.

Scott, Walter. *Ivanhoe. Sakexun jiehou yingxiong zhuan* 撒克遜劫後英雄傳. Trans. Lin Shu. *Lin yi xiaoshuo congshu*, vol. 3.

Shen bao 申報. From 1872. Reprint, 400 vols. Shanghai: Shanghai shudian, 1982–1986.

Shen Pengnian 沈鵬年. *Lu Xun yanjiu ziliao bianmu*. Shanghai: Shanghai wenyi chubanshe, 1958.

Shiba Shirō 紫四郎. *Kajin no kigū* 佳人奇遇. *Jiaren qiyu*. Trans. Liang Qichao. From *Qingyi bao* 1 (eleventh month, 1898).

Shiwu bao 時務報. From 1896. 8 vols. Reprint, Taipei: Wen hai chubanshe, 1987.

Shuihu quan zhuan 水滸全傳. Taipei: Wannianqing shudian, 1971.

Sienkiewicz, Henryk. "Bartek the Victor." In *Yanko the Musician and Other Stories*, trans. Jeremiah Curtin (Boston: Little, Brown, 1894).

———. "Charcoal Sketches." In *Hania*, trans. Jeremiah Curtin (Boston: Little, Brown, 1897).

———. "Sachem." Trans. Jeremiah Curtin. In *Lillian Morris and Other Stories* (Boston: Little, Brown, 1894). "Qiuzhang" 酋長. Trans. Zhou Zuoren. *Xin qingnian* 5.4 (Oct. 15, 1918): 394–404.

Sologub, Fyodor. "A Kiss for the Unborn." In *The Sweet-scented Name and Other Fair Tales, Fables and Stories*, trans. Stephen Graham (New York: G. P. Putnam's Sons, 1915).

Spence, Jonathan. *To Change China: Western Advisers in China, 1620–1960*. Boston: Little, Brown, 1969.

Stretton, Hesba (pseud.) *Jessica's First Prayer* (1867). *Pin nü Leshijia* 貧女勒詩嘉. Trans. Adelia M. Payson. Fuzhou: American Presbyterian Press, 1878. (Harvard-Yenching Library)

Sun, Ching and Wong, Wan. *Catalogue of the London Missionary Society Collection Held by the National Library of Australia*. Canberra: National Library of Australia, Asian Collection, 2001.

Sun Fuyuan 孫伏園. *Lu Xun xiansheng ersan shi* 魯迅先生二三事. Chongqing: Zuojia shuwu, 1942.

Sun Jiazhen 孫家振. *Haishang fanhua meng* 海上繁華夢. Zhongguo jindai xiaoshuo daxi series. Nanchang: Baihuazhou wenyi chubanshe, 1991.

Swift, Jonathan. *Gulliver's Travels. Haiwai xuanqulu* 海外軒渠錄. Trans. Lin Shu and Wei Yi. Taipei: Wei Weiyi, 1990.

Tan Sitong 譚嗣同. *Renxue* 仁學. Beijing: Zhonghua shuju, 1958.

Tao Muning 陶慕寧. *Qinglou wenxue yu Zhongguo wenhua* 青樓文學與中國文化. Beijing: Dongfang chubanshe, 1993.

Tarumoto Teruo 樽本照雄. *(Xinbian zengbu) Qingmo Minchu xiaoshuo mulu*. (新編增補) 清末民初小説目錄. Jinan: Qilu shushe, 2002.

Tenney, William C. *The Conflict and the Victory of Life, Memoir of Mrs. Caroline P. Keith*. New York: D. Appleton, 1864.

Thompson, Robert Wardlaw. *Griffith John, The Story of Fifty Years in China*. New York: A. C. Armstrong, 1906.

Tomlin, Jacob. *Journal of a Nine Months' Residence in Siam*. London: Frederick Westley and A. H. Davis, 1831.

Toury, Gideon. *Descriptive Translation Studies and Beyond*. Amsterdam: John Benjamins, 1995.

Turgenev, Ivan Sergeyevich. "The Worker and the Man with White Hands." Trans. Evgenia Schimanskaya. In *Poems in Prose* (London: Lindsay Drummond, 1945), 26–27.

Vanderauwera, Ria. *Dutch Novels Translated into English*. Amsterdam: Rodopi, 1985.

Verne, Jules. *De la terre à la lune. Yuejie lüxing* 月界旅行. Trans. Lu Xun. First published 1903. *Lu Xun yiwenji*, vol. 1.

———. *Deux ans de vacances*. Paris, 1888. *Two Years' Vacation*. New York: George Munro, 1889. *Jūgo shōnen* 十五少年. Trans. Morita Shiken 森田思軒. Tokyo: Ohashi Shintarō, 1896. *Shiwu xiao haojie* 十五小豪傑. Trans. Liang Qichao (chapters 1–9) and Luo Pu 羅普 (chapters 10–18). *Xinmin congbao* 2–24 (Feb. 22, 1902–Jan. 13, 1903).

———. *Voyage au centre de la terre. Didi lüxing* 地底旅行. Trans. Lu Xun. First published 1906. *Lu Xun yiwenji*, vol. 1.

Waley, Arthur. *The Opium War Through Chinese Eyes*. London: George Allen and Unwin, 1958.

Walton, Catherine Augusta. *Christie's Old Organ, or "Home Sweet Home." Anle jia* 安樂家. Trans. Mary Harriet Porter. Zhongguo shengjiao shuhui, 1882. (British Library)

Wang, David Der-wei. *Fin-de-Siècle Splendor*. Stanford: Stanford University Press, 1997.

"Wang Jiaoluan bainian changhen" 王嬌鸞百年長恨. *Wang Keaou Lwan pih neen chang han*. Trans. Robert Thom. Canton: Canton press office, 1839. (Houghton Library, Harvard University)

Wang Jiquan 王繼權 and Xia Shengyuan 夏生元. *Zhongguo jindai xiaoshuo mulu* 中國近代小説目錄. Nanchang: Baihuazhou wenyi chubanshe, 1998.

Wang Junnian 王俊年. *Xiaoshuo erjuan* 小説二卷. Zhongguo jindai wenxue zuopin xilie series. Fuzhou: Haixia wenyi chubanshe, 1990.

———. *Xiaoshuo sanjuan* 小説三卷. Zhongguo jindai wenxue zuopin xilie series. Fuzhou: Haixia wenyi chubanshe, 1991.

Wang Shuhuai 王樹槐. *Wairen yu wuxu bianfa* 外人與戊戌變法. Nankang: Academia Sinica, 1965.

Wanshi (pseud.). *Qingtian hen* 情天恨. Shanghai: Xinxueshe, 1905. (Shanghai Library)

Wei Ren 韋人 and Wei Minghua 韋明鏵. *Yangzhou quyi shihua* 揚州曲藝史話. Beijing: Zhongguo quyi chubanshe, 1985.

Wei Shaochang 魏紹昌 "*Haishang mingji sida jingang qishu* shunei youguan zuozhe wenti de ziliao" 海上名妓四大金剛奇書書内有關作者問題的資料. In *Wan-Qing sida xiaoshuojia* 晚清四大小説家 (Taipei: Shangwu yinshuguan, 1993), 143–50.

———. *Li Boyuan yanjiu ziliao* 李伯元研究資料. Shanghai: Shanghai guji chubanshe, 1980.

———. *Wu Jianren yanjiu ziliao* 吳趼人研究資料. Shanghai: Shanghai guji chubanshe, 1980.

Wei Xiuren. *Hua yue hen* 花月痕. Beijing: Renmin wenxue chubanshe, 1982.

Wen Kang. *Ernü yingxiong zhuan* 兒女英雄傳. Beijing: Renmin wenxue chubanshe, 1983.

Wu Jianren 吳趼人. (See also under Kikuchi Yūhō.) "Cha gongke" 查功課. *Yueyue xiao-shuo*, 1907. Reprint, with *Hen hai* and other works, Zhongguo jindai xiaoshuo daxi series. Nanchang: Jiangxi renmin chubanshe, 1988, 596–99.

——. *Ershinian mudu zhi guai xianzhuang* 二十年目睹之怪現狀. 2 vols. Zhongguo jindai xiaoshuo daxi series. Nanchang: Jiangxi renmin chubanshe, 1988.

——. *Haishang mingji sida jingang qishu* 海上名妓四大金剛奇書. Zhongguo jindai xiaoshuo daxi series. Nanchang: Baihuazhou wenyi chubanshe, 1996.

——. "Heiji yuanhun" 黑籍冤魂. *Yueyue xiaoshuo*, 1907. Reprint, with *Hen hai* and other works, Zhongguo jindai xiaoshuo daxi series. Nanchang: Jiangxi renmin chubanshe, 1988, 557–67.

——. *Hen hai* 恨海 (Sea of regret). Zhongguo jindai xiaoshuo daxi series. Nanchang: Jiangxi renmin chubanshe, 1988, 5–88. *The Sea of Regret*. Trans. Patrick Hanan. Hono-lulu: University of Hawaii Pres, 1995.

——. *Hu Baoyu* 胡寶玉. (Alternative title, *Shanghai sanshinian yanji* 上海三十年豔跡). *Wofo Shanren wenji*, 7:309–56.

——. *Hutu shijie* 糊涂世界. Zhongguo jindai xiaoshuo daxi series. Nanchang: Jiangxi renmin chubanshe, 1988.

——. *Jin shinian zhi guai xianzhuang* 近十年之怪現狀. Zhongguo jindai xiaoshuo daxi series. Nanchang: Jiangxi renmin chubanshe, 1988.

——. *Jiuming qiyuan* 九命奇冤. *Xin xiaoshuo*, from no. 12 (Dec. 13, 1904). Zhongguo jindai xiaoshuo daxi series. Nanchang: Jiangxi renmin chubanshe, 1988.

——. *Qing bian* 情變. Zhongguo jindai xiaoshuo daxi series. Nanchang: Jiangxi renmin chubanshe, 1988.

——. *Shanghai youcanlu* 上海游驂錄 (Adventures in Shanghai). Zhongguo jindai xiaoshuo daxi series. Nanchang: Jiangxi renmin chubanshe, 1988.

——. "Shuo xiaoshuo" 說小說. *Yueyue xiaoshuo* 8 (1907, fourth month): 209–10.

——. "Sida jingang xiaozhuan" 四大金剛小傳. In *Hu Baoyu. Wofo Shanren wenji*, 7:317–23.

——. *Wofo Shanren wenji* 我佛山人文集. 8 vols. Guangzhou: Huacheng chubanshe, 1989.

——. "Xiaoshuo conghua" 小說叢話. *Xin xiaoshuo* 19 (fifth month, 1905): 151–52. Wei Shaochang, *Wu Jianren yanjiu ziliao*, 323–24.

——. *Xin shitouji* 新石頭記 (The new story of the stone). Reprint, Zhongguo jindai xiao-shuo daxi series. Nanchang: Jiangxi renmin chubanshe, 1988.

Wu Jingzi 吳敬梓. *Rulin waishi* 儒林外史, ed. Li Hanqiu 李漢秋. 2 vols. Shanghai: Shanghai guji chubanshe, 1984.

Wuxi xianzhi 無錫縣志. Shanghai: Shanghai shehui kexueyuan chubanshe, 1994.

Wylie, Alexander. *Memorials of Protestant Missionaries to the Chinese, Giving a List of Their Publications, and Obituary Notices of the Deceased, with Copious Indexes*. Shanghai: American Presbyterian Press, 1867. Reprint, Taipei: Ch'eng Wen Publishing Company, 1967.

——. *Notes on Chinese Literature*. Shanghai: American Presbyterian Press, 1867.

Xia Jingqu 夏敬渠. *Yesou puyan* 野叟曝言. Serialized in the *Hu bao* 滬報 and the (re-named) *Zilin Hubao* 字林滬報, 1882–83. Beijing: Renmin wenxue chubanshe, 1997.

Xia Yan 夏衍. *Zhu fu, cong xiaoshuo dao dianying* 祝福，從小説到電影. Beijing: Zhong-guo dianying chubanshe, 1959.

Xiao Jiluoan Zhu 小吉羅庵主 (pseud.) [probably Jiang Qizhang]. "Ji Yingguo 'Tatong' ju lunchuan dianmo" 記英國他咚巨輪船顛末. *Yinghuan suoji* 瀛寰瑣記 2 (eleventh month, 1872), 4b–5b.

——. "Renshen shengji lingji lun" 人身生機靈機論. *Yinghuan suoji* 2 (eleventh month, 1872), 3a–4a.

——. "Yuleguo ji" 魚樂國記. *Yinghuan suoji* 瀛寰瑣記 1 (tenth month, 1872), 12ab.

Xichao kuaishi 熙朝快史. Zhongguo jindai xiaoshuo jingpin daxi series. Hohhot: Nei Menggu renmin chubanshe, 1998.

Xin qingnian 新青年. From 1915. 14 vols. Reprint, Tokyo: Daian, 1962.

Xin xiaoshuo 新小説. From 1903. Reprint, 24 vols. Shanghai: Shanghai shudian, 1980.

Xinmin congbao 新民叢報. From 1902. Reprint, 17 vols. Taipei: Yiwen yinshuguan, 1966.

Xinxi xiantan. See under Edward Bulwer Lytton.

Xiong Yuezhi 熊月之. *Xixue dongjian yu wan-Qing shehui*, 西學東漸與晚清社會 (Late-Qing society and the dissemination of western learning). Shanghai: Shanghai renmin chubanshe, 1994.

Xiyi meng 希夷夢. Preface by Wang Ji (probable author). 1809; reprint, Shenyang: Liao-ning shushe, 1992.

Xu Qinwen 許欽文. *Guxiang* 故鄉. Shanghai: Beixin shuju, 1926.

——. *Panghuang fenxi* 彷徨分析. Beijing: Zhongguo qingnian chubanshe, 1958.

——. *Xuexi Lu Xun xiansheng.* 學習魯迅先生. Shanghai wenyi chubanshe, 1959.

Xu Shouchang 許壽裳. *Wo suo renshi de Lu Xun* 我所認識的魯迅. Beijing: Renmin wenxue chubanshe, 1952.

Xu Zhenya 徐枕亞. *Yu li hun* 玉梨魂. First published 1912. Zhongguo jindai xiaoshuo daxi series. Nanchang: Baihuazhou wenyi chubanshe, 1993.

Xuzuan Yangzhoufu zhi 續纂揚州府志. Ed. Yan Duanshu et al. Yangzhou, 1874.

Yaguanlou 雅觀樓. Reprint of 1867 manuscript. Guben xiaoshuo jicheng series. Shanghai: Shanghai guji chubanshe, 1990.

Yan Changhong 嚴昌洪. *Zhongguo jindai shehui fengsu shi* 中國近代社會風俗史. Hang-zhou: Zhejiang renmin chubanshe, 1992.

Yan Tingliang. "Guanyu Lishao jushi qiren de diandi yice" 關於蘯勺居士其人的點滴臆測. *Gansu shehui kexue* 5 (1992): 106–10.

——. *Wan-Qing xiaoshuo lilun* 晚清小説理論. Beijing: Zhonghua shuju, 1996.

Yang Shiji 楊世驥. *Wenyuan tan wang* 文苑談往. Shanghai: Zhonghua shuju, 1945.

Yangzhou zhuzhici 揚州竹枝詞. Ed. Xia Youlan 夏友蘭 et al. Yangzhou: Privately pub-lished, 1992.

Yanshan Yisou (pseud.). *Nanchao jinfenlu* 南朝金粉錄. Beijing: Zhongyang minzu xue-yuan chubanshe, 1994.

Ye Kaidi 葉凱蒂 (Catherine V. Yeh). "Guanyu wan-Qing shidai de xiaoshuo leibie ji *Xin xiaoshuo* zazhi guanggao erze" 關於晚清時代的小説類別及新小説雜誌廣告二則. *Shinmatsu shōsetsu* 清末小説 12 (1989): 112–21.

Yichun yuan 宜春苑. Trans. Wuxinxianzhai 無歆羨齋 (pseud.). From *Xin xiaoshuo* 6 (sixth month, 1903).

Yinghuan suoji 瀛寰瑣記. Ed. Lishao Jushi (probably Jiang Qizhang). From 1872. Shanghai Shenbaoguan. (Shanghai Library)

Yu Da 俞達. *Qinglou meng* 青樓夢. Xian: San Qin chubanshe, 1988.

Yueyue xiaoshuo 月月小説. Ed. Wu Yuanren. Shanghai: Qunxue she, 1906–9. 24 vols. Reprint, Shanghai: Shanghai shudian, 1980.

Zhan Xi 詹熙. *Hualiu shenqing zhuan* 花柳深情傳. Beijing: Beijing shifan daxue chubanshe, 1992.

Zhang Chunfan 張春帆. *Jiuwei gui* 九尾龜. Zhongguo jindai xiaoshuo daxi series. Nanchang: Baihuazhou wenyi chubanshe, 1991.

Zhang Juxiang 張菊香 and Zhang Tierong 張鐵榮. *Zhou Zuoren nianpu* 周作人年譜. Tianjin: Tianjin renmin chubanshe, 2000.

Zhang Zhaotong 張肇桐. *Ziyou jiehun* 自由結婚. Zhongguo jindai xiaoshuo daxi series. Nanchang: Baihuazhou wenyi chubanshe, 1991.

Zhejiang xiangshilu 浙江鄉試錄. (List of the successful candidates for the civil service examinations in Zhejiang province), 1870 examination.

Zheng Yimei 鄭逸梅. *Zheng Yimei xuanji* 鄭逸梅選集. Harbin: Heilongjiang renmin chubanshe, 1991.

Zhengyi Zi (pseud.). *Jinzhong zhuan* 金鐘傳. [city]: Leshantang, 1896.

Zhenliuzhai Zhuren (pseud). *Tai zhan shiji* 臺戰實紀. 1895; reprint, Taipei: Guangwen shuju, 1976.

Zhongguo congshu zonglu 中國叢書綜錄. 3 vols. Beijing: Zhonghua shuju, 1961.

Zhongguo jindai funü yundong lishi ziliao 中國近代婦女運動歷史資料 (1840–1918). Beijing: Zhongguo funü chubanshe, 1991.

Zhonguo jindai wenxue daxi 中國近代文學大系. Shanghai: Shanghai shudian, 1991.

Zhongguo jindai xiaoshuo shiliao huibian 中國近代小説史料彙編. Taipei: Guangwen shuju, 1980.

Zhongguo tongsu xiaoshuo zongmu tiyao 中國通俗小説總目提要. Beijing: Zhongguo wenlian chuban gongsi, 1990.

Zhongguo xinwenxue daxi 中國新文學大系. 10 vols. Shanghai: Liangyou tushu gongsi, 1935–36.

Zhou Guisheng 周桂笙. (See also under Boisgobey.) "Ziyou jiehun" 自由結婚. *Yueyue xiaoshuo* (second month, 1908): 63–74.

Zhou Yueran 周越然. *Yanyanyanzhai shuhua* 言言言齋書話. Shaanxi shifan daxue chubanshe, 1998.

Zhou Zuoren (Qiming 啓明, pseud.). "'A Q zhengzhuan.'" *Chen bao fujuan*, March 19, 1922. Reprinted in *Zhou Zuoren wenlei bian* 周作人文類編. Ed. 鍾叔. 10 vols. Changsha: Hunan wenyi chubanshe, 1998. *Bashi xinqing* 八十心情 10):129–32.

——. "Guanyu Lu Xun." *Yuzhou feng* 宇宙風, Oct. 24 and Nov. 7, 1936. Reprinted in *Zhou Zuoren wenlei bian*. *Bashi xinqing* 10: 108–17, 118–26.

—— (Zhou Xiashou 周遐壽, pseud.). *Lu Xun de gujia* 魯迅的故家. Shanghai chuban gongsi, 1953.

——. *Lu Xun xiaoshuoli de renwu* 魯迅小説裡的人物. Shanghai: Shanghai chuban gongsi, 1954.

——. "Riben jin sanshinian xiaoshuo zhi fada" 日本近三十年小説之發達. *Xin qingnian* 5.1 (July 15, 1918): 31–46.

——. *Yuwai xiaoshuoji*, trans. Lu Xun and Zhou Zuoren. See under Lu Xun.

——. *Zhitang huixianglu* 知堂回想錄. 2 vols. Hong Kong: Tingtao chubanshe, 1970.

Zhu Shu 朱恕. "Guixiu shihua" 閨秀詩話. *Nüzi shijie* 1 (Dec. 1914): 1–6.

Zhuxi chun she chao 竹西春社鈔. Reprint, *Zhonghua mishu jicheng* 中華謎書集成. Ed. Gao Boyu 高伯瑜 et al. Beijing: Renmin ribao chubanshe, 1991.

Zhuzuolin 著作林. Ed. Chen Diexian. Hangzhou: Yisuyuan, from 1906.

Zilin Hubao 字林滬報. Shanghai, from 1882.

Zou Rong 鄒容. *Gemingjun* 革命軍. Beijing: Zhonghua shuju, 1958.

Zou Tao 鄒弢. *Haishang chentianying* 海上塵天影. Zhongguo jindai xiaoshuo daxi series. Nanchang: Baihuazhou wenyi chubanshe, 1993.

Zou Zhenhuan 鄒振環. *Yingxiang Zhonguo jindai shehui de yibaizhong yizuo* 影響中國近代社會的一百種譯作. Shanghai: Zhongguo duiwai fanyi chuban gongsi, 1994.

Zschokke, Heinrich. *Das Abenteuer der Neujahrsnacht. Da chuxi* 大除夕. Trans. Xu Zhuodai 徐桌呆. Zhongguo jindai wenxue daxi series. Shanghai: Shanghai shudian, 1991. *Fanyi wenxueji*, vol. 1.

Glossary

A Q zhengzhuan	阿 Q 正傳	Bu tian	補天
Aige	愛格	Buchanzu-hui	不纏足會
An Ji	安驥	Buzhou shan	不周山
An Xuehai	安學海	*Caifeng bao*	采風報
Anle jia	安樂家	*caizi jiaren*	才子佳人
Bai guang	白光	Cai Erkang	蔡爾康
Baihua yanyibao	白話演義報	Cha gongke	查功課
Bainian yijiao	百年一覺	*Cha shisu meiyue tongji*	察世俗每月統
Bali Chahuanü yishi	巴黎茶花女遺	zhuan	記傳
	事	*chabuduozhuyi*	差不多主義
Bao Fu	鮑福	*Chang huo zhi dao zhuan*	常活之道傳
Bao Tianxiao	包天笑	Changming deng	長明燈
Baochaoguan	寶鈔關	*Changyan bao*	昌言報
Baomu She	飽目社	*Chen bao*	晨報
baoying	報應	Chen Chunsheng	陳春生
Baoyu	寶玉	Chen Diexian	陳蝶仙
Baozhu	寶珠	Chen Dingshan	陳定山
basha	把沙	Chen Fuyuan	陳福元
Bashaguan xiaoshuo	巴沙官小説	Chen Jilin	陳戢臨
bashi	把勢	Chen Jinghan	陳景韓
Beinan shimoji	被難始末記	Chen Pingyuan	陳平原
Bijin no te	美人の手	Chen Qu	陳蘧
bixian	避嫌	Chen Rongxian	陳蓉仙
Bo Le	伯樂	Chen Sen	陳森
Bo Yaolian	柏耀廉	Chen Shoupeng	陳壽彭
Bohe	伯和	Chen Tuan	陳搏

Cheng chong bai lei han	誠崇拜類函	*falü xiaoshuo*	法律小説
Chi xuan cuo yao	持選撮要	*fan yu*	反語
Chousi Zhuren	抽絲主人	*fang huozhai*	放火債
Chu ba zhuan	除霸傳	Fang Qingzhou	方慶周
chuancha	穿插	Fang Yilu	方佚廬
chuanqi	傳奇	*fanhua*	反話
ci	詞	Fei ming	飛鳴
Cui Li Company	萃利公司	Feizao	肥皂
Cui Xiangchuan	崔象川	Feng Menglong	馮夢龍
da cha	打岔	Fengbo	風波
Da Ming Zhengde	大明正德皇遊	*fengci*	諷刺
Huang you Jiangnan	江南傳	*Fengyue meng*	風月夢
zhuan		Fu Lin	符霖
Da Qing huangdi sheng	大清皇帝聖訓	Gao Laofuzi	高老夫子
xun		Ge Qilong	葛其龍
Da Yingguo tongzhi	大英國統志	Gemingjun	革命軍
Daguan bao	大觀報	*Gezhi huibian*	格致匯編
Danxiang	澹香	Gou Cai	苟才
daoqing	道情	*goucai*	狗材
Dapo	大坡	Gu Aren	顧阿紉
Dianshizhai huabao	點石齋畫報	Gu Jingxiu	顧敬修
Dianshu qitan	電術奇談	*gu wang yan*	姑妄言
Diexian conggao	蝶仙叢稿	Gu Wangyan	辜望延
Dihua	棣華	Gu Wenbin	顧文彬
Dixiong	弟兄	Gu Yinglian	顧影憐
Diyi qishu	第一奇書	Guan Dequan	關德泉
Dong-Ou nü haojie	東歐女豪傑	Guan Yu	關羽
Dong xi yang kao meiyue	東西洋考每月	Guan Zi	管子
tongji zhuan	統記傳	*guci*	鼓詞
Dongfang Wenming	東方文明	Guduzhe	孤獨者
Dongfang zazhi	東方雜志	*Guinuo zhuan*	閨娜傳
Du Caiqiu	杜采秋	*Gujin wanguo gangjian*	古今萬國綱鑑
Du Mu	杜牧	*Gujin xiaoshuo*	古今小説
Du Qinyan	杜琴言	Guo	郭
Du shi wen tian	讀史問天	Guo Lairen	過來仁
Duanchang bei	斷腸碑	*guocui*	國粹
Duanwujie	端午節	*guolairen*	過來人
Duli	獨立	Guoxue baocunhui	國學保存會
Duliu	獨流	*Gushi Rudiyaguo lidai*	古時如地亞國
Dushe quan	毒蛇圈	*lüezhuan*	歷代略傳
ernü	兒女	*Gushi xinbian*	故事新編
Ernü yingxiong zhuan	兒女英雄傳	Guxiang	故鄉
Ershinian mudu zhi guai	二十年目睹	*Haishang chentianying*	海上塵天影.
xianzhuang	之怪現狀	*Haishang hua liezhuan*	海上花列傳

Haishang mingji sida jingang qishu	海上名妓四大金剛奇書	Jiang Ruizao	蔣瑞藻
		Jiang Zhixiang	蔣芷湘
Haitong gushi	孩童故事	Jiang Zirang	蔣子讓
Haiwai xuanqulu	海外軒渠錄	*Jiao Ying ji*	嬌櫻記
Haiyouji	海游記	Jiaochang	教場
Han Bangqing	韓邦慶	*jiating geming*	家庭革命
Han Hesheng	韓荷生	*Jiayin xiaozhuan*	迦因小傳
Han Qiuhe	韓秋鶴	*Jidu shengjiao chuban geshu shumu huizuan*	基督聖教出版各書書目彙纂
Hangong qiu	漢宮秋		
Hanshang Mengren	邗上蒙人		
haohan	好漢	*Jiehui meng*	劫灰夢
haoliao	好了	*Jin Ping Mei*	金瓶梅
He Jinshan	何進善	Jin Shengtan	金聖歎
He Mengmei	何夢梅	*Jin shinian zhi guai xianzhuang*	近十年之怪現狀
He Songhua	何頌花		
He Zou	何諏	Jin Yixiang	金挹香
Hechashan Nong	鶴槎山農	*Jing hua yuan*	鏡花緣
Heiji yuanhun	黑籍冤魂	Jinghai	靜海
Hen hai	恨海	*Jinwu xingyi*	金屋型儀
Hengli shilu	亨利實錄	*Jinzhong zhuan*	金鐘傳
Hengmengan Zhu	蘅夢庵主	*Jiuming qiyuan*	九命奇冤
Henhai hua	恨海花	*Jiuwei gui*	九尾龜
hong yun tuo yue	烘雲托月	Jiuxianglou	九香樓
Hongmei guan	紅梅館	*Jiwai shumu*	集外書目
Hu bao	滬報	Jueshi	覺世
Hu Baoyu	胡寶玉	*Jūgo shōnen*	十五少年
Hu Shi	胡適	*Kajin no kigū*	佳人奇遇
Hua Chishi	華癡石	Kang Fengji	康逢吉
Hua yue hen	花月痕	Kang Jishi	康濟時
Huai jiu	懷舊	Kang Junmo	康君謨
Hualiu shenqing zhuan	花柳深情傳	Kang Youwei	康有為
Huang Shigong	黃石公	Kangji	康吉
Huangjin sui	黃金崇	*kanguan*	看官
hui	回	*Karyū shunwa*	花柳春話
Hui tou kan jilüe	回頭看紀略	Kong Yiji	孔乙己
Hui zui zhi dalüe	悔罪之大略	*Kuai rou yusheng shu*	塊肉餘生述
Huimo xundao	誨謨訓道	*Kuangren riji*	狂人日記
Humingshi daqiao	忽鳴士大橋	Kuroiwa Ruikō	黑岩泪香
huoqiang	火鎗	Lanyun	嬾雲
Hutu shijie	糊涂世界	*Lanyunlou yinchao*	嬾雲樓吟鈔
huxi	忽西	*Lao Can youji*	老殘遊記
jiamiao zhi bi	佳妙之筆	Lao Shaonian	老少年
Jianchan zhuren	趼廛主人	*Leizhu yuan*	淚珠緣
Jiang Mei	江湄	*Leizhuji*	淚珠記

Leng Suxin	冷素馨	*mingshi*	名士
Li Bai	李白	Mingtian	明天
Li Boyuan	李伯元	*Minquan bao*	民權報
Li Dou	李斗	*Mixisi Dawei Kaobofei'er*	密昔司大衛考伯菲而
Li Hongzhang	李鴻章		
Li Ruoyu	李若愚	Mofa	莫法
Li Yu	李漁	Morita Shiken	森田思軒
Lian Quan	廉泉	*Mu yecha*	母夜叉
Liang ke yu yan	兩可喻言	Muzhen Shanren	慕真山人
Liang Qichao	梁啓超	*Nahan*	吶喊
Liaozhai zhiyi	聊齋志異	Naisuguo qiwen	乃蘇國奇聞
Lihun	離婚	*Nan Song zhizhuan*	南宋志傳
Lihun bing	離魂病	*Nanchao jinfenlu*	南朝金粉錄
Lin Daiyu	林黛玉	Nian Gengyao	年羹堯
Lin Menghua	林夢花	Niwa Jun'ichiro	丹羽純一郎
Lin Pin	林礘	*Nüxuebao*	女學報
Lin Shu	林紓	*Nüzi shijie*	女子世界
Ling Mengchu	凌濛初	Nyoyasha	如夜叉
Lishao Jushi	蠡勺居士	Oda	小田
Liu caizi shu	六才子書	Ouyang Juyuan	歐陽鉅源
Liu E	劉鶚	*Pai'an jingqi*	拍案驚奇
Liu Qiuhen	劉秋痕	Pan An	潘安
lixiang xiaoshuo	理想小説	*Panghuang*	彷徨
Lixiangde banlü	理想的伴侶	Peng Banyu	彭伴漁
liyan	例言	*Pin hua baojian*	品花寶鑑
Lizhentang	立貞堂	*Pin nü Leshijia*	貧女勒詩嘉
Longqiu Jiuyin	龍湫舊隱	*Ping Jinchuan quanzhuan*	平金川全傳
Lu Ban	魯班	*Ping nan hou zhuan*	平南後傳
Lu Xun	魯迅	Pu Lin	浦林
Lun xiaoshuo yu qunzhi zhi guanxi	論小説與群治之關系	Puyang Zeng	濮陽增
		Qian huai	遣懷
Lun youxue	論幼學	Qian Qianyi	錢謙益
Luo Pu	羅普	Qian Xinbo	錢昕伯
Luohua meng	落花夢	Qian Zheng	錢徵
Lüyixuan Zhuren	綠意軒主人	Qian Zhongshu	錢鍾書
Luzhou Shiyu	鷺洲詩漁	Qiangxuehui	強學會
Mao de beiju	貓的悲劇	Qianliyan Shunfenger	千里眼順風耳
maoxian xiaoshuo	冒險小説	Qin Baozhu	秦寶珠
Maoyuan Xiqiusheng	茂苑惜秋生	*Qin hai shi*	禽海石
mei wai	媚外	Qin Ruyu	秦如玉
Mei Ziyu	梅子玉	*qing*	情
Meihua meng	梅花夢	*qing*	卿
Meiren shou	美人手	*Qing bian*	情變
Mengxue bao	蒙學報	*Qingfeng zha*	清風閘

Qinglou meng	青樓夢	*Shiwu xiao haojie*	十五小豪傑
Qingtian hen	情天恨	*shixin xiaoshuo*	時新小說
Qiu Wei'e	裘維鍔	Shouhe Ciren	瘦鶴詞人
Qiu zhu shixin xiaoshuo	求著時新小說	*shoushan zhi qu*	首善之區
qi	啓	Shousong	壽嵩
Qizhang	其章	*Shu jing*	書經
Quanti xinlun	全體新論	*Shu zui zhi dao*	贖罪之道
Qunxue she	群學社	*Shu zui zhi dao zhuan*	贖罪之道傳
Renfen	紉芬	*Shuihu zhuan*	水滸傳
Renjian wangliang zhuan	人間魍魎傳	Shuo xiaoshuo	說小說
Renxue	仁學	*shuobushu*	說部書
rijibu	日記簿	Shuxin nüshi	漱馨女士
Ruan Yuan	阮元	Sida jingang xiaozhuan	四大金剛小傳
Rulin waishi	儒林外史	*Siming suoji*	四溟瑣記
Sai Jinhua	賽金花	Song Yu	宋玉
Sakexun jiehou yingxiong	撒克遜劫後英	Su Huifang	蘇惠芳
zhuan	雄傳	Su Shi	蘇軾
sanbi	三弊	Su Yunlan	蘇雲蘭
Sange guinü	三個閨女	*suhua*	俗話
Sanguo zhi tongsu yanyi	三國志通俗演	*Suiqin lou*	碎琴樓
	義	Sun Fuyuan	孫伏園
Sanjia qu	三家曲	*suowei*	所謂
Shang shi	傷逝	Suxian	素仙
Shanghai youcanlu	上海游驂錄	Suyan	素妍
shehui xiaoshuo	社會小說	*Ta zhi xiao shi*	他之小史
Shen Zixing	沈子星	*Tai zhan shiji*	臺戰實紀
Shenbaoguan	申報館	*Taiwan jinguo yingxiong*	臺灣巾幗英雄
shenfen	身分	zhuan	傳
Sheng Quxian	盛蕖仙	*Taixi xinshi lanyao*	泰西新史覽要
Sheng shu zhu shu	聖書註疏	Tan Sitong	譚嗣同
Shengren yu daozei yu	聖人歟盜賊歟	Tan ying xiaolu	談瀛小錄
Shenxian tongjian	神仙通鑑	*tanci*	彈詞
Shexi	社戲	Tao Youzeng	陶祐曾
Shi bao	時報	*Taohua meng*	桃花夢
Shi caizi	十才子	*Taohua ying*	桃花影
Shi zhong	示眾	Tian Chunhang	田春航
Shiba Shirō	柴四郎	Tian Xu Wo Sheng	天虛我生
Shibian yu weixin	世變與維新	Tiandanren	恬澹人
Shi'eryuan Yuchanji	十二緣玉蟾記	Tianzuhui	天足會
Shifei lüelun	是非略論	*Tongshang yuanwei*	通商原委
shikuai	市儈	Tongyuanzi	通元子
Shisan Mei	十三妹	*Toufa de gushi*	頭髮的故事
Shiwu bao	時務報	Tu he mao	兔和貓
Shiwu congshu	時務叢書	Tu Youmin	屠牗民

Wang Jiaoluan bainian chang hen	王嬌鸞百年長恨	*Xichao kuaishi*	熙朝快史
Wang Jie	王傑	*xieqing xiaoshuo*	寫情小說
Wang Shouchang	王壽昌	*Xieyu congtan chuji*	屑玉叢談初集
Wang Tao	王韜	Xihongsheng	惜紅生
Wang Wei'er	王威兒	Xiling Sanren	西冷散人
Wang Yanhong	王彦泓	Xiling Xiashi	西冷下士
Wang Yongxia	汪詠霞	*Xin sheng*	新生
Wang Zhi	王質	*Xin shitouji*	新石頭記
Wanguo gongbao	萬國公報	*Xin xiaoshuo*	新小説
Wanxiang	婉香	*Xin Yiyuji*	新疑雨集
Wei	魏	*Xin Zhongguo weilai ji*	新中國未來記
Wei Chizhu	韋癡珠	*Xing shi xinbian*	醒世新編
Wei Shaochang	魏紹昌	*Xingfu de jiating*	幸福的家庭
Wei Xiuren	魏秀仁	*Xinmin congbao*	新民叢報
Wei Yi	魏易	*Xinxi xiantan*	昕夕閒談
wen	文	*Xinxin xiaoshuo*	新新小説
Wen Kang	文康	*Xinxue lun*	新學論
Wen Shunong	文述農	*xinxue shaonian*	新學少年
wendashu	問答書	Xinyin	心印
Wenming jingjie	文明境界	*Xiongdi xutan*	兄弟敍談
Wenyuan jinghua	文苑菁華	*Xixiangji*	西廂記
Wu Jianren	吳趼人	*Xixue shumubiao*	西學書目表
Wu Jizhi	吳繼之	*Xiyi meng*	希夷夢
Wu Zirang	吳子讓	*Xiyou diqiu wenjian lüezhuan*	西游地球聞見略傳
Wugeng zhuan	五更傳	Xu	栩
Wuxinxianzhai	無歆羨齋	Xu Guangping	許廣平
Xia Jingqu	夏敬渠	Xu Heng	許衡
Xia Yan	夏衍	Xu Nianci	徐念慈
xiadeng shehui	下等社會	Xu Qinwen	許欽文
xiang chuan	相傳	Xu Zhenya	徐枕亞
Xiangshan baojuan	香山寶卷	Xue Pan	薛蟠
Xiao Cai	小蔡	Xue Shaohui	薛紹徽
Xiao Jiluoan	小吉羅庵	*xutan*	敍談
xiao tuanyuan	小團圓	Xuyuan	栩園
Xiaodie	小蝶	Ya de xiju	鴨的喜劇
xiaoren	小人	*Yabolahan jilüe*	亞伯拉罕紀略
Xiaoshuo kaozheng xubian	小説考證續編	*Yaguanlou*	雅觀樓
Xiaoshuolin	小説林	*yan*	言
Xiaotaohuaguan shiciji	小桃花館詩詞集	Yan Fu	嚴復
		Yan Tingliang	顏廷亮
Xiaoxin xiaofu	小信小福	Yanbei Xianren	燕北閒人
xiaxie xiaoshuo	狹邪小説	Yangwen shuguan	洋文書館

Yangzhou huafanglu	揚州畫舫錄	*Yugou hen*	玉鉤痕
Yangzhou yanhua zhizhici	揚州煙花竹枝詞	*Yutian henshi*	玉田恨史
		Yuwai xiaoshuoji	域外小説集
Yang Zilin	楊紫麟	*yuyan xiaoshuo*	寓言小説
yanxinglu	言行錄	*Yuzhong hua*	獄中花
Yanyi bao	演義報	Zai jiuloushang	在酒樓上
Yao	藥	*zaixia*	在下
Ye Bofen	葉伯芬	Zeng Guangquan	曾廣銓
Ye Dehui	業德輝	Zhan Xi	詹熙
yeji	野雞	*zhang*	章
Yesou puyan	野叟曝言	Zhang Binglin	章炳麟
Yi can	一餐	Zhang Chunfan	張春帆
Yichun yuan	宜春苑	Zhang Jinfeng	張金鳳
Yijian xiaoshi	一件小事	Zhang Kunde	張坤德
Yiliguo	意里國	Zhang Xiaoshan	張小山
Yiliya jilüe	以利亞紀略	*Zhang Yuan liang you xiang lun*	張遠兩友相論
Yin jia dang dao	引家當道		
Yingguo xiaoshuo	英國小説	Zhang Zhaotong	張肇桐
Yinghuan suoji	瀛寰瑣記	Zhang Zhonghe	章仲和
yingxiong	英雄	*zhanghui xiaoshuo*	章回小説
yingxiong haojie	英雄豪傑	Zhao Erbao	趙二寶
yingyi	硬譯	Zhao Puzhai	趙樸齋
Yinxia Jushi	飲霞居士	Zhaoyangge	朝陽格
Yishengge Zhuren	漪生閣主人	*Zheng xie bijiao*	正邪比較
Yishou xiaoshi de xiejiu	一首小詩的寫就	Zheng Zhixin	鄭芝芯
		Zhenglou	箏樓
Yishu jiaotong gonghui	譯書交通公會	Zhenglouji	箏樓記
Yishui qishinian	一睡七十年	Zhenglou ju ying tu	箏樓聚影圖
yisu wuhua	一宿無話	Zhenglou qi bie tu	箏樓泣別圖
Yisuyuan congshu	一粟園叢書	*zhentan xiaoshuo*	偵探小説
Yiyuan	怡園	*zhiguai*	志怪
youtou guanggun	油頭光棍	*Zhinang bu*	智囊補
Youxi bao	遊戲報	Zhixin zhuren	知新主人
Youxi zazhi	游戲雜志	*Zhong Xi jiaohui bao*	中西教會報
Yu chanchu	玉蟾蜍	Zhongai	仲藹
Yu Da	俞達	*Zhongguo guanyin baihua bao*	中國官音白話報
Yu li hun	玉梨魂		
Yu Qian	于謙	*Zhongguo xinwenxue daxi*	中國新文學大系
yuanlai	原來		
Yuchanji	玉蟾記	*Zhongguo zhentan zhuàn*	中國偵探傳
Yue bao	月報	Zhou Guisheng	周桂笙
Yuese jilüe	約色紀略	Zhou Zhisheng	周之盛
Yueyue xiaoshuo	月月小説	Zhou Zuoren	周作人

Zhu	主	Zixiang	子湘
Zhu fu	祝福	*Ziyou jiehun*	自由結婚
Zhu Shu	朱恕	Ziyou tan	自由談
Zhuanxiang Laoren	篆香老人	Zou Bailin	鄒拜林
Zhuxi Chunshe	竹西春社	Zou Rong	鄒容
Zhuzuolin	著作林	Zou Tao	鄒弢
Zilin Hubao	字林滬報	Zunwenge Zhu	尊聞閣主
Zixiang	子相	Zuo Zongtang	左宗棠

Index